The Latina/o Midwest Reader

LATINOS IN CHICAGO AND THE MIDWEST

Series Editors
Frances R. Aparicio, Northwestern University
Juan Mora-Torres, DePaul University
María de los Angeles Torres, University of Illinois at Chicago

The Latina/o
Midwest Reader

Edited by
OMAR VALERIO-JIMÉNEZ,
SANTIAGO VAQUERA-VÁSQUEZ,
AND CLAIRE F. FOX

UNIVERSITY OF
ILLINOIS PRESS
Urbana, Chicago, and Springfield

Publication of this book was supported by funding from the College of Liberal Arts & Sciences at The University of Iowa and funding from the College of Liberal and Fine Arts at the University of Texas at San Antonio.

Library of Congress Cataloging-in-Publication Data
Names: Valerio-Jiménez, Omar S. (Omar Santiago), 1963– editor of compilation. | Vaquera-Vásquez, Santiago R., 1966– editor of compilation. | Fox, Claire F., editor of compilation.
Title: The Latina/o midwest reader / edited by Omar Valerio-Jiménez, Santiago Vaquera-Vásquez, and Claire F. Fox.
Other titles: The Latina Midwest reader | The Latino Midwest reader
Description: Urbana, IL : University of Illinois Press, [2017] | Series: Latinos in Chicago and the Midwest | Includes bibliographical references and index.
Identifiers: LCCN 2017000460 (print) | LCCN 2017003612 (ebook) | ISBN 9780252041211 (hardcover : alk. paper) | ISBN 9780252082771 (pbk. : alk. paper) | ISBN 9780252099809 ()
Subjects: LCSH: Hispanic Americans—Middle West—History. | Hispanic Americans—Middle West—Social conditions. | Middle West—Civilization—Hispanic influences. | Hispanic Americans—Cultural assimilation—Middle West.
Classification: LCC F358.2.S75 L375 2017 (print) | LCC F358.2.S75 (ebook) | DDC 973/.0468—dc23
LC record available at https://lccn.loc.gov/2017000460

Parts of Michael Innis-Jiménez's chapter appeared in his *Steel Barrio: The Great Mexican Migration to South Chicago, 1915–1940* (New York: New York University Press, 2013). © 2013 New York University Press. Reprinted with permission of New York University Press.

Parts of Marta María Maldonado's chapter appeared in her "Nuestro USA? Latino/as Making Home and Reimagining Nation in the Heartland," in *Crossing Boundaries: Ethnicity, Race, and National Belonging in a Transnational World*, ed. Brian Behnken and Simon Wendt (Lanham, Md.: Lexington Books, 2013), 83–102. Reprinted with permission of Lexington Books.

Excerpts from Felipe Hinojosa's chapter appeared in his *Latino Mennonites: Civil Rights, Faith, and Evangelical Culture*, 86, 127, 129, 149, 150, 153, and 154. © 2014 The Johns Hopkins University Press. Reprinted with permission of Johns Hopkins University Press.

Parts of Janet Weaver's contributions to her coauthored chapter appeared in her "Barrio Women: Community and Coalition in the Heartland," in *Breaking the Wave: Women, Their Organizations, and Feminism, 1945–1985*, edited by Kathleen A. Laughlin and Jacquline L. Castledine (New York: Routledge, 2010), 173–88. Reprinted with permission of Routledge.

We dedicate this volume to generations
of midwestern Latinas/os who have enriched
the region with their labor, culture, and politics.

Contents

Acknowledgments

The editors owe a debt of gratitude to the many wonderful colleagues who helped and encouraged us during the process of editing *The Latina/o Midwest Reader*. The idea for this anthology began to germinate at the Obermann-International Programs Humanities Symposium on the Latina/o Midwest held in fall 2012 at the University of Iowa. That symposium and the subsequent Latina/o Midwest Summer Seminar in 2013 were supported by various internal and external grants. Our initial funding for each project, however, was from the UI Obermann Center for Advanced Studies. We would like to thank its director, Teresa Mangum, for her encouragement, foresight in promoting Latina/o Studies, and perpetual good cheer. Our work was made much easier and more pleasant by the Obermann Center's staff, including Jennifer New and Neda Barrett. Teresa, Jennifer, and Neda helped us coordinate the logistics of planning and hosting the symposium and summer seminar, and also made the Obermann Center a welcoming work space in which to meet and discuss our projects. We also received valuable help from research assistants Adrienne Zimmer, Matthew McLaughlin, and Jeannette Gabriel.

We would like to express our appreciation for the scholars, students, and community members who participated in the Latina/o Midwest Symposium held at the University of Iowa. After such an exciting symposium that showcased the contributions of Latinas/os to the Midwest, we were thrilled to gather with colleagues who participated in the Teaching the Latina/o Midwest Summer Seminar at the Obermann Center for Advanced Studies the following year. This anthology is a direct product of many productive and energizing discussions at that summer seminar.

The editors would also like to thank the many colleagues, students, and community members who supported the Latina/o Midwest events. Although two of the editors, Omar and Santiago, have moved on to other universities, we have lasting memories of the collegial environment that fostered the Latina/o Midwest events. We are especially indebted to Claire for helping secure permissions for images and photographs, and for coordinating many logistical details related to this publication after our departures from the University of Iowa. In addition to this anthology, another legacy of the symposium and summer seminar was the establishment of a Latina/o studies minor at the University of Iowa.

Our editor, Dawn Durante of the University of Illinois Press, has been very supportive throughout this publication process. We would like to thank Dawn for advocating on behalf of this project and for believing in the need for this anthology. The text and arguments in *The Latina/o Midwest Reader* were strengthened through the constructive criticisms of the three external readers of the manuscript. We would also like to thank the Latinos in Chicago and the Midwest Series editors, Frances R. Aparicio, Juan Mora-Torres, and María de los Angeles Torres.

Finally, the editors would like to acknowledge the book subvention support from the Office of the Vice President for Research and Economic Development, the College of Liberal Arts and Sciences, and the Department of English at the University of Iowa, as well as the College of Liberal and Fine Arts at the University of Texas at San Antonio.

The Latina/o Midwest Reader

Introduction

History, Placemaking, and Cultural Contributions

OMAR VALERIO-JIMÉNEZ,

SANTIAGO VAQUERA-VÁSQUEZ,

AND CLAIRE F. FOX

The Latina/o Presence in the Midwest

In March 2013, María Sánchez was finally reunited with her six daughters and husband in Iowa City, Iowa, after being in Guatemala for twenty-one months. She had been deported months earlier after local officials turned Sánchez over to immigration authorities following a routine traffic stop. Through the diligent efforts of family and friends who provided emotional support, financial assistance, and legal aid, the Sánchez family, including a five-year-old, overcame the separation that the federal government's deportation policies created.[1]

Over the past ten years, the number of similar news stories about Latina/o immigrants in the Midwest has increased.[2] In 2006, immigrant rights activists staged massive demonstrations throughout the nation (including in major midwestern cities) to protest the proposed Sensenbrenner bill, which would have upgraded illegal entry into the United States into a felony. Two years later, Postville, Iowa, became the site of the largest workplace raid in the nation when approximately four hundred undocumented workers were detained in the Agriprocessors meat packing plant, and subsequently nearly three hundred were deported. At the same time, Chicago became a hub for student activists working on behalf of the DREAM (Development, Relief, and Education for Alien Minors) legislation as they spearheaded demonstrations, civil disobedience events, and teach-ins. This activism has been partially motivated by the Obama administration's aggressive immigration policies that led to record number of deportations.[3] The increasing number of mixed-status families has meant that the deportation of parents often leads to family separations, especially when young U.S.-born children are involved.[4] These types of high-profile cases have made Latina/o immigrants more visible throughout the Midwest. In turn, this increased visibility has led some observers to characterize Latinas/os as new immigrants to the region.

Frequent references to the Midwest as "the heartland" in U.S. popular and mass culture bring to mind archetypes associated with rural and small-town settings populated by the descendants of European pioneers and settlers, as well as core cultural values, including niceness and politeness as default modes of public interaction. Rather than reaffirm an image of the Midwest as a hegemonically white heartland, one of our motivations in compiling *The Latina/o Midwest Reader* is to challenge the notion that Latinas/os are newcomers to the Midwest. We emphasize that Latinas/os have resided in the region for over a century, and Latinas/os have contributed to the social, cultural, and economic dimensions of rural and urban midwestern communities. Since the late nineteenth century, Latinas/os have provided their labor to various midwestern industries and spread their culture throughout rural and urban areas. Mexican Americans and Mexicans were the first Latinas/os to arrive in large numbers to the Midwest, followed by Puerto Ricans, Cuban Americans, and eventually Central and South Americans. Knowing this immigration history will help us understand Latinas/os' long-standing ties to the Midwest, the region's appeal to new migrants, and the opportunities and tensions introduced by successive waves of Latina/o newcomers.[5]

Mexican Migration to the Midwest

Mexican Americans and Mexican immigrants were first attracted to the Midwest by jobs in railroads and agriculture. Ethnic Mexicans began arriving in the region to work in the sugar beet industry as early as the 1880s.[6] These agricultural migrants were not permanent settlers but sojourners who moved within the region according to seasonal harvests, and returned to Texas or Mexico after a period of work. Most were unaccompanied males who were either single or married men traveling without their families. Others were attracted to the region by seasonal work in the region's railroad yards. Local employers purposefully recruited unaccompanied males in order to depress wages by not paying enough to support families. This strategy also appeased local residents' fears that ethnic Mexicans (who were considered non-whites) might settle permanently in their communities. Recruited in Texas and in U.S.–Mexican border cities, these workers gradually established social networks that linked the Midwest with Texas and northern Mexico. Such networks would help continue the seasonal stream of ethnic Mexican migrants into the region for several generations.[7]

In the early twentieth century, developments in Mexico and Europe led to a change in the composition of the immigrant labor force in the Midwest. The flow of immigrants from Mexico into the U.S. Southwest that began during the nineteenth century accelerated with the outbreak of the Mexican Revolution in 1910. Immigrants had begun leaving Mexico in the middle of the nineteenth century to escape their debts, obtain higher wages in the United States, and flee the nation's political instability. This emigration stream increased during the last third of the nineteenth century as the economic policies of Mexico's dictator Porfirio Díaz expanded landlessness and unemployment.[8] In 1910, the beginning of the Mexican Revolution led to a surge in emigrants fleeing forced enlistments and military conflict. Approximately one tenth of Mexico's population emigrated, and most arrived in the United States attracted by social stability, political refuge, and economic opportunities. While the majority of Mexican immigrants arrived to work in the U.S. Southwest's burgeoning railroad development projects and expanding agricultural fields, some ventured into the Midwest to labor in agricultural and industrial occupations. Mexicans would fill a labor need created by the outbreak of World War I, which led to a decrease in the number of European immigrants who had supplied the Midwest's agricultural workforce. In response, agricultural interests successfully lobbied Congress to add a special clause in the Immigration Act of 1917 that would permit Mexican immigrants to enter the United States under a work contract (as braceros, or guest workers) and to exempt them from a literacy test and head tax.[9]

Agricultural employers in the Midwest gradually began replacing their European immigrant workers with ethnic Mexican laborers. This trend accelerated after the passage of the so-called quota laws in 1921 and 1924, which sharply reduced the number of legal immigrants from southern and eastern Europe. In order to address an unstable workforce, midwestern agricultural employers altered their recruiting strategies by targeting married men with families, who employers believed were more stable than single males who frequently switched jobs. This recruitment strategy also increased the available workforce because employers could now hire entire families for the harvests. The new strategy proved successful and led ethnic Mexicans to establish permanent residence throughout the Midwest. In addition to agricultural opportunities, urban industrial jobs also attracted ethnic Mexicans to cities like Detroit, Chicago, and Minneapolis. Railroad and industrial employers recruited some migrants directly to cities, while other Mexican workers moved from rural to urban areas during slowdowns in agricultural labor. For immigrants arriving from Mexico or after a brief stay in Texas, the Midwest was appealing because they experienced less overt racism there than in Texas.[10] Those migrating to midwestern rural areas also liked the slower pace of life, which was similar to the rural areas from which they came. A yearly pattern of circular migration between the Midwest and Texas or Mexico emerged for some agricultural workers and would eventually result in permanent settlement in the Midwest when some laborers left the migrant stream. Like Mexican immigrants to the U.S. Southwest, those who arrived in midwestern cities often believed their stays would be short because they would eventually return to Mexico. This planned returned migration explains the low levels of naturalization among Mexican immigrants as described by Michael Innis-Jiménez in his contribution to this book. However, as families grew with the addition of U.S.-born children, the mixed statuses of various family members placed additional pressure on heads of households to remain in the United States. As Innis-Jiménez shows, industrial employers actively recruited Mexican immigrants to Chicago, where they lived in polluted neighborhoods, labored in menial jobs, and faced discriminatory hiring practices. Mexican immigrants and Mexican Americans not only survived in such bleak conditions, but thrived by establishing businesses, creating social groups, and joining mutual aid societies that supported vibrant ethnic Mexican communities.

Essential Mexican and Puerto Rican Wartime Laborers

World War II created new employment opportunities for Latinas/os as Americans left civilian jobs to join the military. For the agricultural industry, the shortage of workers was acute because many rural laborers moved to urban areas for higher-paying and more stable jobs. As the war reduced agricultural production in Europe, U.S. harvests rose to meet worldwide demand, so the need for agricultural workers in the United States rose sharply. To address this increased need, the United States and Mexico established a guest-worker agreement, the Mexican Farm Labor Program, also called the Bracero Program, in 1942 that supplied contract male guest workers to the agricultural and railroad industries. While the majority of braceros were sent to work in the U.S. Southwest, some Mexican guest workers also worked in the agricultural fields of the Midwest.[11] In the aftermath of the war, Puerto Rican contract laborers joined Mexican braceros in the Midwest. As part of Operation Bootstrap / Manos a la Obra and as an effort to control the island's "overpopulation," the Puerto Rican government sent male seasonal contract agricultural laborers and female domestic servants to the mainland United States. Until the 1950s, mainland Puerto Rican communities were concentrated in the U.S. Northeast, primarily in New York City. The postwar migration of contract laborers, however, led to the establishment of Puerto Rican communities in various midwestern cities, including Chicago, Illinois; Milwaukee, Wisconsin; and Gary, Indiana.

These midwestern communities provided some of the first opportunities for interactions between ethnic Mexicans and Puerto Ricans in the nation. As Lilia Fernández discusses in her chapter, Mexican immigrants, Mexican Americans, and Puerto Ricans experienced a similar racialization process as nonwhites and nonblacks in housing, employment, and migration policies. Studies of the early and varied Latina/o communities of the Midwest are important because they demonstrate intra-group processes that are missed in scholarship that focuses only on one group of Latinas/os, and because they explore the similar challenges faced by ethnic Mexicans and Puerto Ricans despite differing migration statuses. The success of managed contract labor migration led Congress to continue the Bracero Program for the agricultural industry after the war. Mexico and the United States formalized a new agreement, Public Law 78, in 1951 to extend the guest worker program to meet the labor shortages caused by the Korean War. Congress renewed this law continuously until it expired in 1964. Although the Bracero Program was supposed to decrease undocumented immigration, the reverse occurred as former braceros often returned to the United States as undocumented laborers.[12] Ultimately, the midwestern agricultural industry's experience with the Bracero Program and Operation Bootstrap demonstrated its increasing dependence on an inexpensive and tractable labor force that continues today.

Immigration Reform and Changing Latina/o Populations

During the second half of the twentieth century, two immigration laws significantly transformed the Latina/o population in the Midwest and the nation. The first was the Immigration Act of 1965, which abolished the national-origins quota system established in the 1920s, and created preferences for immigrants who wanted to rejoin family members in the United States. This immigration reform law along with the Civil Rights Act of 1964 and the Voting Rights Act of 1965 represented a "high-water mark in a national consensus of egalitarianism, one from which much of the country has receded in subsequent years."[13] For a variety of complex reasons, the Immigration Act of 1965 radically reshaped the composition of subsequent immigrants. Under the Johnson-Reed Act (1924), most legal immigrants through the 1950s came from Europe and Canada. By the 1970s, however, half of the immigrants to the United States were from Latin America, a third from Asia, and the rest from Europe and Africa.[14] Concurrently, Operation Bootstrap's failure to increase employment in Puerto Rico led to more poverty, displacement, and migration to the U.S. mainland (which averaged 4,200 per year in the decade after World War II).[15] As they arrived in the Midwest, Puerto Ricans joined ethnic Mexicans and African Americans in acculturating to the region as nonwhite migrants. In addition to confronting struggles over discriminatory practices in employment and housing, they faced obstacles in education, which fueled their civil-rights activism. This activism led Puerto Ricans in Chicago to create the Young Lords Organization in the late 1960s, as Darrel Wanzer-Serrano's chapter explains, and inspired similar branches throughout the nation. The late 1960s, according to Janet Weaver's chapter, also witnessed Mexican Americans in Iowa lend support to California farmworkers' national grape boycott and campaign to improve the working conditions of local farmworkers. The struggle for civil rights was manifested in religious activism for Latina/o Mennonites, as Felipe Hinojosa explains in his chapter. Latinas/os had joined the Mennonite Church even before their arrival in the Midwest as a result of outreach efforts in Puerto Rico, Texas, and other parts of the Southwest. Influenced by antiwar activities, the farm workers' campaign, and the women's liberation movement, Latina/o Mennonites in the 1960s and 1970s pushed the predominantly white Mennonite denomination to adopt progressive positions and become more inclusive.

The second law that significantly transformed the Latina/o population was the Immigration Reform and Control Act (IRCA) of 1986, which legalized some 2.3 million undocumented immigrants who had been in the country continuously since 1982 and established employer sanctions. While the U.S. government's enforcement of employer sanctions was spotty, the passage of IRCA signaled a new era in which the United States increasingly relied on the militarization of the U.S.–Mexican border to decrease undocumented immigration. This strategy change had the unintended consequences of encouraging undocumented laborers to remain in the United States longer, establish permanent residency, and become more regionally dispersed beyond the Southwest. It also changed the immigrants' composition from a seasonal, rural, and predominantly male labor force to a permanent, urban, and increasingly female population.[16] Moreover, after the implementation of the North American Free Trade Agreement (NAFTA) in 1994, an increase in U.S. investments in and trade with Mexico led to the displacement and migration of workers and farmers as markets in Mexico were flooded with lower-priced U.S. imports.[17] Many of these displaced laborers ended up immigrating to the United States, where they joined Central Americans displaced by similar economic processes and by civil wars in the 1970s and 1980s. These immigrants have become essential community members and laborers throughout the nation. In addition to providing their labor to grow the U.S. economy, many immigrants contribute more in taxes than they receive in benefits from the U.S. government. For undocumented workers, this pattern is quite pronounced as they add an estimated $12 billion net annually to the Social Security fund in 2010, but will most likely not claim retirement benefits because of their undocumented status.[18] Ultimately, both immigration reform laws (1965 and 1986) have led to a surge in U.S.-based families with undocumented members and to the growth of the Latina/o population. NAFTA's enactment as well as the neoliberal policies adopted by Mexican and Central American governments spurred high levels of migration during the last third of the twentieth century. It is not surprising, therefore, that the Latina/o population grew mainly through immigration from 1980 to 2000, but since then has grown mainly as a result of native births as tougher border enforcement and hostile immigration laws have been implemented.[19]

Latina/o Demographic Growth

The growth of the Latina/o population has significantly changed the demographics and culture of the Midwest and the U.S. as Latinas/os have become the nation's largest minority group. The Latina/o population, some 50.5 million in 2010, was responsible for more than half (56%) of the nation's growth between 2000 and 2010. Latinas/os comprise 16.3 percent of the nation's population, and most live in one of nine states with long-standing Latina/o communities, including Illinois. Over the last three decades, the population has become more geographically dispersed as some regions have experienced phenomenal growth. For example, while the nation's Latina/o population grew by 43 percent from 2000 to 2010, it increased by more then 73 percent in eight of the twelve midwestern states. Latinas/os now make up 7 percent of the region's population, and are the "majority minority" in Iowa, Illinois, and several other states in the region. While many Latinas/os have moved to the region for urban jobs, others have filled a labor need in rural towns where the deunionization of the meatpacking industry has created economic opportunities for immigrants willing to work for nonunion wages. As Louis Mendoza argues in his chapter, this Latinoization of the nation has created specific challenges in the Midwest where the continuous out-migration of white youths to urban locales has left behind an aging low-growth population in small towns. Mendoza explains that immigrant workers, who provide the labor for industrial and service industries, increasingly maintain the way of life for older white midwesterners. The integration of Latina/o migrants is especially important in order to diffuse tensions and fears that the newcomers are changing the "traditional" characteristics of towns. The Latina/o population growth is particularly significant in the Midwest because Latinas/os accounted for all of Illinois's population growth, and their growth in Michigan helped stem the state's declining population.[20]

The demographic growth of Latinas/o has had a large impact on public schools and in higher education. Across the nation, Latina/o students make up almost one in four (24.7%) of K–12 students in public schools.[21] The trends also apply to the Midwest, where some of this growth has been even more pronounced. In Iowa, Latinas/os are the largest and fastest-growing ethnic minority population in the public schools. From 1985 to 2005, the number of Latina/o students in Iowa public K–12 education grew by nearly 600 percent.[22] Such rapid demographic changes have created unique challenges for school districts, which are trying to serve a growing immigrant population. As Carolyn Colvin and her coauthors explain in their chapter, one of the persistent myths that school administrators need to overcome is about "uncaring" immigrant parents. Colvin and coauthors found that immigrant parents were "caring, supportive, and concerned" of their children's education, but were frustrated with the typical communication models between schools and parents. The authors argue for new models in which parents and teachers collaborate in meaningful ways to eliminate cultural misunderstandings and address parental concerns. In higher education, the number of Latinas/os who are between the ages of eighteen and twenty-four and attending college surged to hit a high of 2.1 million students in 2011.[23] Because Latinas/os are now the largest minority enrolled at the nation's college campuses, university administrators have a great opportunity to address this growing population by adding Latina/o studies courses to the curriculum, hiring additional Latina/o studies faculty, and creating programs to improve Latina/o students' graduation rates. The increasing Latina/o population in the Midwest impacts regional politics, as is evident in ongoing debates about voter registration, immigration policy, and language acquisition. Latina/o history, acculturation, and political involvement are therefore relevant and timely topics for university students and faculty seeking to understand the changing profile of the Midwest and midwestern Latina/o studies.

Presence in Educational and Cultural Institutions

As the Latina/o population grows in the Midwest, it is important for regional universities to expand their services not simply to accommodate the demographic shifts, but also to raise awareness about the contributions of this community. An important step is to recognize the history of Latinas/os in the Midwest as not simply a recent migrant generation but as one that also has deeper roots in the region. Archives are important for this, as are Latina/o studies programs and cultural centers, for they can raise awareness about Latina/o presence but can also serve as sites of empowerment and community for students seeking a place for themselves.

A positive story about political action in the university setting comes out of the University of Nebraska–Lincoln. Contributor Amelia Montes offers a review of Latina/o studies and ethnic studies departments in the Midwest, and the problems they face. Blending a memoir with critical commentary, she traces the history of the programs she directs in Nebraska, speaking to the challenges these programs face. Her discussion focuses on a case where the administration at the University of Nebraska–Lincoln, without prior consultation with the program directors, tried to move the Institute for Ethnic Studies to a condemned building. Rather than acquiesce, Montes organized a protest with the help of various student organizations. The day before the protest was to begin, the senior vice chancellor, who had issued the directive to move the institute, agreed to a meeting where the program directors made their case for the importance of their center. In the end, the institute and its programs were allowed to keep their space. As Montes writes, "Swift action and mobilization helps to strengthen community ties. But it won't happen without first creating communities of understanding and making connections with differences among each other within the program and departments." Montes's call for communities of understanding is important for it also helps in the building of a sense of belonging. And, as she illustrates, an important element for this is the claiming of a place. Montes's example at the University of Nebraska–Lincoln is important for it offers a strategy for survival, and for creating a sense of belonging.

A way in which a power structure consolidates itself is through the creation of narratives that are imposed upon ethnic communities. These narratives of control then serve to justify policies of marginalization and disempowerment. In regard to the Latina/o community, one of these narratives of control is constructed around language. The assumption is that the Latina/o community only speaks Spanish and has no interest in acquiring English. Contributor Kim Potowski examines the issue of Spanish use and maintenance in the Midwest. One of the features of the language that she encounters is the variety of Spanish being spoken, from Mexican to Caribbean, and how this dialect contact creates new blends. Yet, when it comes to language maintenance, her research finds that "the more time spent learning in Spanish, the greater the *English*-language achievement of Spanish-speaking ELL [English Language Learners] students." In other words, research disproves the assumptions that the Latina/o community only speaks Spanish and that it is unwilling to assimilate.

The belief that Latinas/os only speak Spanish—despite the evidence—becomes a narrative of control that justifies policies of marginalization and exclusion. The logic of this narrative goes this way: as a community that only speaks Spanish, Latinas/os are unwilling to assimilate and since they do not belong (because of their unwillingness to assimilate), they are foreign and will always be so.

How, then to resist these narratives imposed from outside onto Latina/o communities? One way is through the telling of stories from within communities as a way to respond to statements or discourse imposed upon them. In this way, a more complete understanding of the Latina/o presence in the Midwest can be gained.

Theresa Delgadillo and Janet Weaver examine Latina lives in the Midwest through a perspective that blends both the historical Latina/o communities and the issues facing recent migrants. Drawing on personal interviews, and oral histories collected in the Mujeres Latinas collection of the Iowa Women's Archive at the University of Iowa, Delgadillo and Weaver illustrate the importance of an archive of oral histories as a strategy for countering hegemonic systems of control. In telling the stories by the women, and not stories about them, the authors also show how these women have also been the agents of change within their family structures. Also, by looking at a diversity of voices, they show how the Midwest, as a type of border space between the dominant Caribbean communities of the Eastern United States, and the Mexican communities of the Southwest, has been since at least the 1950s a site for Latinidad, where the different Latina/o communities meet, interact, and dialogue with one another. The use of oral history as a method is helpful for filling in "significant gaps in our knowledge about the history of Latina experiences, but they should also prompt us to collect and preserve important documents in publicly accessible archival repositories" (Delgadillo and Weaver).

Through the use of ethnographic accounts, personal narratives, sociolinguistic studies, and oral histories, Montes, Potowski, and Delgadillo and Weaver, in their respective chapters, demonstrate how the community counters hegemonic systems of control. By invoking cultural practice and ties to place, they are telling their own stories, responding to narratives of control that would see them simply as laborers or a foreign underclass meant to remain in the margins.

Rural and Urban Placemaking

The diverse urban and rural environments that comprise the midwestern United States reveal distinctive patterns of Latina/o community formation. In compiling this book, we are indebted to pathbreaking studies by scholars such as Dionisio Nodín Valdés, Zaragosa Vargas, David A. Badillo, Gabriela Arredondo, Nicholas De Genova, and Ana Y. Ramos-Zayas, who have produced meticulous and conceptually useful research on Latinas/os in the region's major cities, including Minneapolis, Detroit, and Chicago. As in the case of Lilia Fernández's and Michael Innis-Jiménez's contributions to this book, the former scholars emphasize the urban Midwest as a forge of interethnic and interracial contact and collaboration, activist movements, and thriving Latina/o neighborhoods, even in the face of widespread discrimination and criminalization of immigrants. Chicago in particular often appears on the map of U.S. Latina/o studies as an exceptional city, where for some residents, "Latina/o" has ceased to be an umbrella term and instead corresponds to a lived identity, as a multitude of different Latina/o groups interact in neighborhoods, schools, and workplaces. However, in exploring what Nicholas De Genova and Ana Y. Ramos-Zayas have identified in their study of Mexican and Puerto Rican Chicago as the potential for "counterhegemonic sociopolitical projects formulated in terms of Latinismo," we concur that

"Latina/o" does not refer to a shared set of cultural values or heritage.[24] Rather, it is a racialized and politicized concept, produced through everyday experiences and social interactions in specific historical and geographical settings. Frances Aparicio contributes to this line of research about the construction of Latinidad on the ground, observing in her study of mixed-Latina/o ethnic subjects, that while Chicago's reputation as the only truly "Latina/o" city in the United States and a laboratory for emerging Latina/o identities is "subjectively true" in the eyes of some of her informants, this reputation is "not historically accurate" (Aparicio, afterword), because in fact, Intralatinidad is also being forged in New York, Los Angeles, and other U.S. locations. Following Aparicio's balanced consideration, we want this book to distinguish those characteristics of the Midwest that are distinctive with respect to other regions of the United States, but we also hope that it will encourage further comparative work that integrates the Latina/o Midwest more fully into Latina/o studies scholarship and challenges the bicoastal dominance of the field.

Building on the existing scholarship about urban Latina/o populations, we also seek to underscore significant Latina/o presence in the region's rural and small-town communities, where often the stark inequalities of housing, education, and social services experienced by Latinas/os in large U.S. metropolitan areas are less pronounced, and instead experiments in dual-language immersion education are underway, and integrated housing, sports teams, and churches are the norm. In such locations, Latina/o businesses, institutions, and visual culture in the form of vernacular art, signage, monuments, and building construction often attest to the ways in which Latinas/os are making homes in the Midwest, and transforming midwestern landscapes in the process. Several contributors to this book variously refer to such practices as placemaking, worldmaking, or homemaking. They emphasize that placemaking is not necessarily the domain of architects and city planners, but rather refers to the collective, everyday forms of communication and community formation practiced by Latina/o midwesterners, who construct what María Cotera describes in her chapter as "narratives of belonging" through diverse self-representational strategies, including performance, storytelling, art and visual culture, bilingualism, and soundscapes, as well as through their physical presence in churches, workplaces, schools, nightclubs, community centers, and museums.

One example of Latina/o Midwest placemaking can be found on a farm near Clear Lake, Iowa, where a half-mile hike into a tilled field reveals a site dedicated to Richard Steven Valenzuela, better known as Ritchie Valens, who became a rock legend through his chart-topping and pathbreaking interpretation of the Mexican folk song "La Bamba." A modest memorial marks the location of the plane crash that claimed the lives of seventeen-year-old Valens, along with fellow musicians

Buddy Holly and the Big Bopper ("J. P." Richardson Jr.), and their pilot, Roger Peterson, on a snowy night in February 1959, shortly after the three musicians had performed at the nearby Surf Ballroom in Clear Lake.[25] The tender offerings that the farm owner and visitors have deposited along a barbed-wire fence include the names of the deceased engraved into steel replicas of vinyl records, a guitar, and an airplane, a whirligig made of aluminum gelatin molds, an antique microphone, love beads, flowers, stuffed animals, and fan letters. Although several pairs of thick-rimmed eyeglasses suggest that Buddy Holly draws a fair share of pilgrims to the site, the overall display of mourning is Latinized. Like the roadside memorials that increasingly dot midwestern highways, this vernacular tribute to "The Day the Music Died" links it to *descansos*, improvised memorials for fallen travelers dating from the Spanish colonization of the Americas, which still mark *parajes*, or stopping points along southwestern U.S. travel routes.[26] Although Valens's journey in February 1959 took him eastward rather than northward, his memorial partakes of a logic similar to that of descansos, which were intended to sacralize the ground where untimely or violent death has occurred. A native of Pacoima, California, Valens met death far from home, while on the Winter Dance Party tour. Yet in death, he has become a sort of honorary Iowan through the pilgrims who tend his memory in this out-of-the-way place.

In contrast to the Valens memorial, the Hero Street Memorial in Silvis, a medium-sized western Illinois city located 250 miles from Clear Lake, Iowa, is a weighty monument that forms the focal point of a public park and serves as a location for veterans' services. The sculpture's rectangular base features a series of eight bronze portraits of deceased Mexican American servicemen. Atop the portraits sits a Maya step pyramid structure that is in turn crowned by an enormous bronze eagle in flight, which clutches in its talons a rifle and the U.S. flag. This memorial was painstakingly designed by former junior high school teacher Sonny Soliz to commemorate deceased combatants in World War II and the Korean War, all of whom resided within a single block-and-a-half stretch of Second Street in Silvis, a neighborhood that has been dubbed Hero Street, USA.[27] Mexican immigrants who arrived to work in the Quad Cities railroad industry during the 1920s and 1930s established this neighborhood, and one hundred of their sons and daughters have gone on to serve in the U.S. armed forces, distinguishing Hero Street with a density of military service and loss that is unparalleled in other parts of the United States. In an interview for a documentary about Hero Street, Tanilo Sandoval, the surviving brother of two Hero Street servicemen killed in World War II, describes his brothers' sacrifice and the Hero Street memorial more broadly as an assertion of citizenship and attachment to *this* place: "We're of Mexican descent, but we're all Mexican Americans, and this is our country . . . this is *home*."[28] Sandoval's statement resonates in the very design elements of the

Hero Street memorial, the upper portion of which prominently features symbols identified with U.S. patriotism, while the foundation quite literally takes inspiration from indigenous Mexican architectural forms that circulated widely in the United States through the Chicano movement in the 1960s and 1970s.

The rock-and-roll prodigy whose plane happened to crash while touring in Iowa, the young servicemen who gave their lives in U.S. wars—these figures are regional heroes and have left visible traces of their presence in the Midwest. But, as José E. Limón underscores in his chapter, storytelling and performance also provide a means through which Latinas/os claim presence and assert their belonging to particular places, as in the case of the prolific South Texas writer and educator Tomás Rivera, whose stories about the Midwest are discussed in Limón's opening chapter to this book. As a child, Rivera and his family were migrant farm laborers in Iowa, Minnesota, Michigan, Ohio, Wisconsin, and the Dakotas. Limón argues that seasonal labor migration linking the Upper Midwest to South Texas over many decades led to the formation of trans-local communities that are crucial to understanding Rivera's narratives and his intellectual consciousness. A short distance from the Valens memorial in Clear Lake, Iowa, Rivera worked the beet fields in the small town of Crystal Lake, which provided the setting of "Las Salamandras" ("The Salamanders"), Rivera's famous story in which a young boy enacts his displaced rage against a prejudiced farmer and a brutal labor system by wantonly killing the hordes of salamanders that invade his family's tent during a nocturnal deluge.[29]

The Chicana writer Pat Mora commemorated Rivera's midwestern experiences in an illustrated children's book, *Tomás and the Library Lady*, which tells of the close relationship that a young Rivera developed with the public librarian in nearby Hampton, a north-central Iowa town of 4,500 people, during one of the author's periods of residence in the Upper Midwest in the 1940s. Today, local schoolchildren perform a play based on Mora's book at the Hampton Public Library, and residents are proud of their connection to the young man who went on to become the first Chicano university president. Pat Mora's account of Rivera's childhood experience foregrounds the midwestern setting as a significant location of inter-Latina/o and interethnic social interaction and community formation, rather than as a mere traumatic interlude or ellipsis within a larger South Texas–based narrative. In Hampton, stories by and about Rivera still circulate orally and through print culture and performance. They offer the community a means to imagine itself as a Latina/o midwestern town, and broadly speaking, to build a bridge between recent Latina/o arrivals and long-standing patterns of Latina/o residence in the area. For example, Joyce and Lee Blum, two retired Hampton residents who were friends of the late Bertha Gaulke, the librarian who befriended Rivera, recently repurposed Lee Blum's former office as a nonprofit Latina/o community center.[30] The suite of offices just off the town's main square is now known as La Luz Hispana and has been brightly transformed through Guatemalan and Mexican photos, posters, and art. There volunteers and other professionals offer free classes to Latina/o residents on topics ranging from art to nutrition, literacy, and workers' rights. The center is directed by Sister Carmen Hernández and assistant director Sister Maura McCarthy of the Dubuque-based Sisters of the Presentation.

Like many other rural communities in this region—such as Perry, Iowa, described by Marta Maldonado, and Lorraine, Illinois, described by Aidé Acosta in their respective chapters—Hampton, Iowa, is being reborn through the widespread recruitment of Latina/o laborers in the agricultural and meatpacking industries. Maldonado's chapter examines the demographic shifts of Perry since the 1990s. According to census data, in 1990 there were forty-seven Latina/o residents in the town. By the 2010 census, the data shows that the community was 35 percent Latina/o. One explanation for the rapid growth is the "restructuring of meatpacking and, more specifically, by the changes that such restructuring set forth in the local meatpacking plant." These changes have made the Latinas/os the main low wage labor force of the town. In the process, they have become instruments within the meatpacking economy, rendered invisible by the larger power structure. As Maldonado writes, "immigrants are at once wanted in particular contexts (as laborers), and unwanted and even rejected in other contexts, lacking realistic opportunities to live and work in the United States legally, being shrouded with a stigma of illegality and criminality by the media, and facing hostility in local contexts." While some Latinas/os whom she interviews recognize this position, there is also pushback by others, particularly the younger generations. Maldonado also notes how the Latina/o community pushes back against racial stereotypes by their show of presence in Perry.

In a similar vein, Aidé Acosta looks at how Latinas/os recast what it means to come from the rural heartland. As she writes, "In Lorraine, Mexicans have been present for over four decades since the recruitment of seven workers from Jiménez in northern Mexico. Yet they are not included or imagined as part of the social fabric of small-town Middle America. In the annual broomcorn festival, Mexicans—who are the primary labor force behind the local broom industry—partake in the festivities on the margins and as spectators." Through a focus on certain religious and cultural practices, she examines how the Latina/o community in Lorraine, Illinois, makes their presence felt despite being marginalized. She cites Latina/o practices such as *quinceañeras*, and religious celebrations as El Día de los Muertos, and La Fiesta de la Virgen de Guadalupe, as examples of the community making their presence known. These types of rituals are also forms of claiming home, of placemaking. By maintaining these celebrations, she argues that "cultural and religious rituals organized by migrants are not only channels that help them maintain connections to their backgrounds and histories, but are also political sites of culture in the current anti-immigrant context." Moreover, as sites of culture, they are also sites of belonging.

In Hampton, Perry, Lorraine, and other rural midwestern communities, emergent institutions and community interactions involving Latinas/os draw on complex networks of new and established Latinas/os, interfaith alliances, educators, labor organizers, activists, and community leaders. These make for small-town environments that are complex: on the one hand, they are often critically underserved by bilingual service providers and marked by exploitative labor practices and tensions between white European–descended residents and new immigrants. On the other hand, these often former "sundown towns"[31] are undergoing economic revitalization through immigration and Latina/o entrepreneurship, turning them into cosmopolitan, transnational, multiethnic, and multilingual communities, where members of different Latina/o and indigenous groups and generations not only interact with one another and with white midwesterners, but also with recent immigrants from Eastern Europe, Africa, and Southeast Asia.

As Jane Blocker and Ramón Rivera-Servera point out in their chapters, place-making also serves as a means for the transmission and enactment of collective memory and history. Just as José E. Limón notes that Tomás Rivera first perceived his own father as an "immigrant" while conversing with a Czech immigrant in Iowa, Blocker's chapter on Cuban-born midwestern artist Ana Mendieta observes that Mendieta's *Black Angel* film performance, enacted at the foot of a famous Czech funerary sculpture in Iowa City, references "Iowa as a site of immigration and cultural crossings, not only for Latinas/os . . . but also for displaced Europeans." Blocker goes on to note that Mendieta's site-specific work links the artist's personal history as a Cuban exile to that of the bereaved Czech mother and spouse who commissioned the *Black Angel*: "the film [Mendieta] produced on the [cemetery] site . . . is an effort to bear witness to the trauma of immigrant exile, of familial loss and separation, of having one's deepest sorrow spoken in a foreign language, and of the suddenness of death, traumas which she shared with other Iowans." Similarly, Ramón Rivera-Servera argues that the performances of Miss Ketty Teanga, the recently deceased Ecuadorian-Puerto Rican doyenne of the Chicago Latina/o drag scene, were a form of "queer homemaking." Miss Ketty performed history as she reanimated bygone Latina/o American drag repertoires, and her dance and musical forms instructed her younger fans about alternative patterns of cultural consumption as well, for her drawn-out boleros and melodramatic gestural style modeled slowness and demanded an attentiveness at odds with trends in mainstream drag and mass culture.

The counterpublics that coalesce at the intersections of sexuality, gender, and Latinidad, in turn have inspired the "coming out as undocumented" performance activism adopted by some immigrant rights groups in the Latina/o Midwest. About the Chicago-based activists affiliated with the Immigrant Youth Justice League, Rebecca Schreiber points out in her chapter that the activists' self-representational performance explicitly challenges dominant logics of Latina/o invisibility and hypervisibility, the former asserting that there are no Latinas/os in the Midwest or that Latinas/os are merely transient, and the latter marking Latinas/os as subject to surveillance through racialized U.S. immigration policies, the war on terror, and the war on drugs. The activist projects that Schreiber analyzes, such as the "No Papers, No Fear" campaign, demonstrate the potential for creative expression to articulate demands for social justice and present a rationale for citizenship based on presence rather than on documentation.[32] Decades ago Tómas Rivera also emphasized this through his stories, insisting that they were not to be read as nostalgic or melancholic, but rather as assertions of social equality. One of Rivera's most famous vignettes from his novel *Y no se lo tragó la tierra* (*And the Earth Did Not Devour Him*) is a litany of the unuttered desires and aspirations running through the minds of a group of migrants as they ride on a truck heading from Texas to the Midwest. In response to the migrants' future-oriented call for social justice, "Cuando lleguemos" (When we arrive), one might hearken the contemporary response of "¡Aquí estoy!" (Here I am!), shouted by MariCruz and María, two activists whose testimonies are discussed in depth by Schreiber. These women bravely asserted their presence as undocumented at a public hearing in which they decried the impact that Arizona SB1070 has had on their families and communities.[33]

These two phrases, "¡Aquí estamos!" and "Cuando lleguemos," capture the dual emphases of this book, that is, the long-term Latina/o presence in the region and the dynamism of communities that are continually in the process of formation and self-representation. Latinas/os have been in the Midwest for over a century, and evidence of Latina/o placemaking, expressive, and material culture is pervasive throughout this region. What is lacking, as Ramón Rivera-Servera so eloquently states in reference to Chicago's queer Latina/o communities, is "recognition, documentation, and celebration" of Latina/o Midwest populations and their histories, as well as the critical, analytical, and strategic concepts that help us to plot Latina/o Midwest narratives in relation to more established ones about Latinas/os in the United States, which tend to exhibit a bicoastal normativity or exclusivity. In this regard, María Cotera's account of her own role in helping to found Detroit's Museo del Norte is instructive. A Tejana academic migrant to the Midwest, Cotera did not set out to "discover" the Latina/o Midwest as much as she listened to the stories that Latina/o midwesterners told her and worked with them to develop a museum that would serve as "a catalyst for building new communities." through archives and storytelling. The Midwest is not only home to many famous Latinas/os, it also gave rise to many events that are important to the general history of Latinas/os in the United States, from the single largest workplace raid in U.S. history in Postville, Iowa, to the 2006 Chicago immigrant rights march, the founding of the Farm Labor Organizing Committee, the Young Lords, the *Revista Chicano-Riqueña*, Third Woman Press, and other pathbreaking interethnic collaborations. However, the documentation of these histories and their legacies is just getting underway. Contemporary projects aimed at assembling oral histories, founding archives, and creating partnerships between scholars and communities, such as those undertaken by the contributors to this book, represent our commitment toward integrating the Latina/o Midwest into the broader Latina/o studies field imaginary, and to extend this research to related scholarly projects as well, such as comparative race and ethnicity studies, critical mixed-race studies, and trans-American studies.

As in much Latina/o studies research emerging from the Nuevo New South, *The Latina/o Midwest Reader* seeks to identify the distinctiveness and neglected histories of Latina/o midwestern communities that fall outside of coastal field imaginaries.[34] We advance these perspectives not only to add to existing scholarship, but also, implicitly, to challenge prevailing ideas about Latina/o identifications. Several contributions to this volume highlight that mass recruitment of labor to the Midwest from South Texas, Mexico, Puerto Rico, and Central America, extending from the late nineteenth century into the present, provides the historical basis for contemporary patterns of rural, small-town, and urban Latina/o midwestern settlement. Likewise, scholars working on the Chicana/o-Mexicana/o midwesterners in particular point out that perspectives on the U.S. Southwest as an occupied ancestral homeland do not enter into Chicana/o-Mexicana/o narrative self-representations in the Midwest to the extent that diasporic and immigrant perspectives do, bringing Chicanas/os and Mexicanas/os into closer alignment with the diasporic imaginaries of other Latina/o groups, although the former continue to comprise the majority among Latinas/os.[35]

We concur with Frances Aparicio that Latinidad is better conceived as a material or symbolic space of interaction and emergent identifications on the part of people from distinct Latin American ethnic and national heritages, rather than as a preconceived ontological category. While her afterword to this book dispels the myth of Chicago as a "Latina/o melting pot" for Latina/o studies, at the same time it finds the city to be a significant location for charting emergent or hybrid Latinidades, stemming from decades of shared interactions around labor, activism, housing, schooling, and urbanization—interactions likewise described in Lilia Fernández's chapter focusing on the early twentieth century. It is not unreasonable to suppose that the subjects produced through such interactions are one reason why Chicago-based immigrant rights movements have played a central role in creating the type of virtual Latina/o communities described by Rebecca Schreiber, which once again reinsert themselves into national and transnational circulation, somewhat effacing regional identifications in the process of creating an activist media network. The Latina/o Midwest is thus a region of distinct but overlapping Latinidades, rural and urban, established and emergent, which have been forged over the past one and a half centuries through labor migration, urbanization, placemaking, and cultural production. Latina/o midwesterners play an important role in sustaining transnational, trans-regional, intra-regional, and virtual Latinidades and setting the agenda for future Latina/o studies scholarship.

Notes

1. Josh O'Leary, "Family Made Whole Again," *Iowa City Press-Citizen*, March 1, 2013.

2. According to the U.S. Census Bureau, the Midwest region consists of Ohio, Michigan, Indiana, Wisconsin, Illinois, Minnesota, Iowa, Missouri, North Dakota, South Dakota, Nebraska, and Kansas. http://www2.census.gov/geo/pdfs/maps-data/maps/reference/us_regdiv.pdf, accessed Dec. 10, 2016.

3. Between fiscal years 2009 through 2015, the Obama administration deported over 2.5 million immigrants. The increase in deportations is a long-term trend carried out by various presidential administrations and begun after the passage of the Illegal Immigration Reform and Immigrant Responsibility Act (1996). The deportation numbers have partly increased due to changes in who is counted in the U.S. Immigration and Customs Enforcement agency's deportation statistics. Unlike during previous administrations, the Obama administration began formally deporting undocumented immigrants apprehended at the border, who were previously called "voluntary returns." Brian Bennett, "High Deportation Figures Are Misleading," *Los Angeles Times*, April 1, 2014, www.latimes.com, accessed Dec. 13, 2016; Scott Horsley, "5 Things to Know about Obama's Enforcement of Immigration Laws," *National Public Radio*, Aug. 31, 2016, www.npr.org, accessed Dec. 13, 2016; Marc R. Rosenblum and Doris Meissner, "The Deportation Dilemma: Reconciling Tough and Humane Enforcement," *Migration Policy Institute*, April 2014, www.migrationpolicy.org/research/deportation-dilemma-reconciling-tough-humane-enforcement, accessed May 22, 2014; Julia Preston, "Report Finds Deportations Focus on Criminal Records," *New York Times*, April 29, 2014, www.nytimes.com, accessed May 22, 2014.

4. The term "mixed-status families" refers to families in which the members have different immigration statuses, for example, some might be U.S. citizens, others permanent residents, and still others undocumented workers.

5. We refer to "migrants" instead of "immigrants" because these workers included Mexican Americans and Mexican immigrants (and in some cases, Mexican immigrants migrating to the Midwest from California, Texas, or other states). The term "Mexican Americans" refer to U.S. citizens of Mexican ancestry, while "Mexican immigrants" refer to Mexican citizens living in the United States as immigrants (regardless of immigration status).

6. J. García, *Conóceme en Iowa*, cited in Teresa A. García, "Mexican Room: Public Schooling and the Children of Mexican Railroad Workers in Fort Madison, Iowa, 1923–1930" (Ph.D. diss., University of Iowa, 2008), 51.

7. Dennis Nodín Valdés, "Settlers, Sojourners, and Proletarians: Social Formation in the Great Plains Sugar Beet Industry, 1890–1940," *Great Plains Quarterly* 10 (spring 1990): 112–13; Zaragosa Vargas, *Proletarians of the North: A History of Mexican Industrial Workers in Detroit and the Midwest, 1917–1933* (Berkeley: University of California Press, 1993), 25–26.

8. Omar S. Valerio-Jiménez, *River of Hope: Forging Identity and Nation in the Rio Grande Borderlands* (Durham, N.C.: Duke University Press, 2013), 182–84.

9. Dennis Nodin Valdés, *Al Norte: Agricultural Workers in the Great Lakes Region, 1917–1970* (Austin: University of Texas Press, 1991), 8–9.

10. Zaragosa Vargas, "Armies in the Fields: The Mexican Working Classes in the Midwest in the 1920s," *Mexican Studies/Estudios Mexicanos* 7, no. 1 (winter 1999): 52; Dennis Nodín Valdés, "Settler, Sojourners, and Proletarians," 111–14.

11. The Bracero Program employed approximately 4.8 million Mexicans, often with workers who agreed to multiple contracts over the course of several years. Manuel García y Griego, "The Importation of Mexican Contract Laborers to the United States, 1942–1964," in *Between Two Worlds: Mexican Immigrants in the United States*, ed. David Gutiérrez (Wilmington, Del.: Scholarly Resources, 1996), 45–85; Manuel G. Gonzales, *Mexicanos: A History of Mexicans in the United States* (Bloomington: Indiana University Press, 1995), 170–75; Omar S. Valerio-Jiménez, "The United States–Mexico Border as Material and Cultural Barrier," in *Migrants and Migration in Modern North America: Cross-Border Lives, Labor Markets, and Politics in Canada, the Caribbean, Mexico, and the United States*, ed. Dirk Hoerder and Nora Faires (Durham, N.C.: Duke University Press, 2011), 228–50; Zaragosa Vargas, *Crucible of Struggle: A History of Mexican Americans from the Colonial Period to the Present Era* (New York: Oxford University Press, 2011), 263; Marc Simon Rodriguez, *The Tejano Diaspora: Mexican Americanism and Ethnic Politics in Texas and Wisconsin* (Chapel Hill: University of North Carolina Press, 2011), 24–36.

12. Between 1964 and 1986, the number of legal immigrants from Mexico rose from 38,000 to 67,000 per year, while the gross undocumented migration increased from 87,000 to 3.8 million per year. Jorge Durand, Douglas S. Massey, and Emilio A. Parrado, "The New Era of Mexican Migration to the United States," *Journal of American History* 86, no. 2 (September 1999): 518–36.

13. Rogers Daniels, *Coming to America: A History of Immigration and Ethnicity in American Life* (New York: HarperCollins, 1990), 338.

14. Paul Spickard, *Almost All Aliens: Immigration, Race, and Colonialism in American History and Identity* (New York: Routledge, 2007).

15. Virginia Sánchez-Korrol, "The Historical Narrative," part 1 of *The Story of U.S. Puerto Ricans*, Centro: Center for Puerto Rican Studies, https://centropr.hunter.cuny.edu/research-education, accessed Dec. 13, 2016.

16. Durand, Massey, and Parrado, "New Era of Mexican Migration," 518–36.

17. David Bacon, *Illegal People: How Globalization Creates Migration and Criminalizes Immigrants* (Boston: Beacon Press, 2008), 60–64; David Bacon, "How US Policies

Fueled Mexico's Great Migration," *Nation*, Jan. 4, 2012, www.thenation.com, accessed May 13, 2014.

18. Shaila Dewan, "Immigration and Social Security," *New York Times*, July 2, 2013, http://economix.blogs.nytimes.com, accessed May 14, 2014.

19. Jens Manuel Krogstad and Mark Hugo Lopez, "Hispanic Nativity Shift: U.S. Births Drive Population Growth as Immigration Stalls," Pew Research Center, Hispanic Trends, April 29, 2014, www.pewhispanic.org, accessed May 14, 2014.

20. Anna Brown and Mark Hugo Lopez, "Mapping the Latino Population, by State, County, and City," Pew Research Center, Hispanic Trends, Aug. 29, 2013, www.pewhispanic .org, accessed May 11, 2014. Jeffrey S. Passel, D'Vera Cohn, and Mark Hugo Lopez, "Hispanics Account for More than Half of Nation's Growth in Past Decade," Pew Research Center, Hispanic Trends, March 24, 2011, www.pewhispanic.org, accessed May 14, 2014.

21. Richard Fry and Mark Hugo Lopez, "Hispanic Student Enrollments Reach New Highs in 2011," Pew Research Center, Pew Hispanic Center, Aug. 20, 2012, www.pewhispanic .org, accessed May 13, 2014.

22. Iowa Department of Education, A Report on Prekindergarten, Elementary, and Secondary Education in Iowa, Des Moines, Iowa, 2006, 31.

23. Fry and Lopez, "Hispanic Student Enrollments."

24. Nicholas De Genova and Ana Yolanda Ramos-Zayas, *Latino Crossings: Mexicans, Puerto Ricans and the Politics of Race and Citizenship* (New York: Routledge, 2003), 215.

25. Clear Lake Chamber of Commerce, "Plane Crash Site—The Day the Music Died," http://members.clearlakeiowa.com/list/member/plane-crash-site-of-buddy-holly-ritchie -valens-jp-the-big-bopper-richard-7383, accessed June 5, 2014.

26. In his song "American Pie," songwriter-singer Don McLean coined the term "the day the music died" to refer to this tragic plane crash. For more on *descansos*, see Rodolfo Anaya, Denise Chávez, and Juan Estevan Arellano, *Descansos: An Interrupted Journey* (Albuquerque, N.M.: El Norte Publications, 1995); Erika Doss, *Memorial Mania: Public Feeling in America* (Chicago: University of Chicago Press, 2010); and James Griffith, *Beliefs and Holy Places: A Spiritual Geography of the Pimería Alta* (Tucson: University of Arizona Press, 1992).

27. Hero Street Memorial Monument, www.herostreetusa.org/, accessed June 5, 2014.

28. The interview with Sandoval is part of a documentary in production titled *Hero Street*, directed and produced by Kelly and Tammy Rundle of Fourth Wall Films. See www.youtube.com/watch?v=jtAYl7oLfD4.

29. Tomás Rivera, "Las salamandras"/"The Salamanders," in *Tomás Rivera: The Complete Works*, ed. Julián Olivares (Houston: Arte Público Press, 2008), 127–30, 159–61.

30. For more information about La Luz Hispana, see https://es-es.facebook.com/LaLuz Hispana.

31. Eileen Diaz McConnell and Faranak Miraftab, "Sundown Town to 'Little Mexico': Old-timers and Newcomers in an American Small Town," *Rural Sociology* 74, no. 4 (2009): 605–29.

32. See, for example, Rivera's captivating reading of "Las Salamandras," recorded in 1973, http://digitallibrary.usc.edu/cdm/ref/collection/p15799coll79/id/197.

33. Arizona State Bill 1070, passed in 2010, is one of the strictest examples of anti-immigration legislation in the United States, particularly in the latitude it gives to law enforcement officers to screen individuals for potential violations of immigration status. At the time of this writing, some provisions of the bill have been upheld in higher courts, while others are being challenged. (See glossary entry.)

34. Bernadette Marie Calafell, "Disrupting the Dichotomy: 'Yo Soy Chicana/o?' in the New Latina/o South," *Communication Review* 7, no. 2 (April 2004): 175–204.

35. Theresa Delgadillo, "Exiles, Migrants, Settlers, and Natives: Literary Representations of Chicano/as and Mexicans in the Midwest," Julian Samora Research Institute, Occasional Paper No. 64, Latino Studies Series, Michigan State University, August 1999.

PART 1

The Browning of the Midwest

Conversations across "Our America"

Latinoization and the New Geography of Latinas/os

LOUIS MENDOZA

From my perspective, if you live in places like Iowa, Nebraska, the heartland if you will, you better be welcoming immigrants, because they are the ones who will be paying for your social security. The population is aging, and they are taking care of your future. There has been research comparing the economy of Chicago with the econo-mies of Detroit and Cleveland, particularly during the '90s and why Detroit's and Cleveland's economies didn't prosper as well as Chicago. Number one reason: immigration. In Chicago, Latinos primarily but immigrants in general reversed the decline of the population.

—Raúl Reymundo, executive director of the Resurrection Project in Chicago, quoted in Mendoza, *Conversations across Our America*

I am happily surprised to see a truck parked to the side of the road with the name Taqueria Monterrey emblazoned on its side. . . . Seeing the entrepreneurial presence of Latinos in an unexpected place re-minds me why this approach to research works; numbers alone don't capture the creativity and drive of people pursuing a vision. I decide to stop for a taco and to see what I can learn from the proprietor. The young mexicano in the truck tells me he came from Chicago with the hopes of eventually opening a restaurant at this location. I tell him about my trip and he explains to me that despite the fact that it appears he is in the middle of nowhere, a motel down the road has been recently converted to a migrant camp, almost all of the workers are from el valle, that is to say, South Texas. (August 30, 2007)

—Mendoza, *A Journey around Our America*

This chapter is based on research conducted during 2007 as I circumnavigated the country on a bicycle mapping the changing spatial ontologies of Latinas/os in long-established as well as new locations throughout the United States. The epigraphs above, taken from books based on this project, *Conversations across Our America* and *A Journey around Our America*, illuminate numerous aspects about life for Latinas/os in the Midwest; the pervasive presence of Latinas/os, including their migration to small towns, the entrepreneurial spirit, the increasing reliance on Mexican farm and dairy workers in the nation's breadbasket states, and the many acts of generosity and kindness I experienced from white midwesterners (and others) throughout my trip.

Over the course of this study I conducted more than ninety formal interviews with a diverse array of people from different ethnic backgrounds ranging in age from sixteen to ninety-two.[1] This chapter highlights midwesterners, mostly Latinas/os and Whites, living in Nebraska, Minnesota, Iowa, Illinois, and Michigan, and focuses on the challenges to social, cultural, political, and economic integration faced by those who are part of the Latinoization of the United States.[2] I use the term *Latinoization* to refer to the ongoing process of cultural and social change occurring in the United States as a result of the profound demographic shifts of the last fifty years. As I note elsewhere here, these shifts are only partially a result of immigration, but the persistent view of Latinos as perpetual outsiders fuels the myth that we are all immigrants. The interviews and firsthand observations from ground zero of the new geography of Latino migrations complicate and often contradict the vitriolic discourse of anti-immigrant pundits, politicians, and voices that inundate popular media forums.

In the spring of 2006, the United States experienced a series of unprecedented immigrant rights marches involving hundreds of thousands of people across the country as they sought to counter the rising tide of anti-immigrant discourse in the media and in the public at large. These marches occurred in response to highly visible anti-immigrant, anti-Latino discourse that revolves around the core of who "we" are as an immigrant nation, the cultural, philosophical and political qualities that define who "belongs" in the United States. Between the calls for amnesty, guest worker programs, border walls, and the repeal of birthright citizenship, a rampant xenophobia tinged, and continues to inform, debates on immigration as people express their fears that Spanish will supplant English as the national language, that a vast conspiracy is at work in which Mexico was planning to retake the southwestern states, that new immigrants are "dumbing down" the nation or stealing jobs, social services, and education without paying taxes—to name but a few of the more salient issues.

The anxiety of the mainstream population and social conservatives regarding demographic change has been primarily projected onto the undocumented population of Latinas/os in the United States; this is true despite the fact that demographic trends would persist even if the rate of entry into this country by undocumented migrants were to cease immediately.[3] Inflammatory rhetoric notwithstanding, the facts of how undocumented immigrants contribute to the U.S. economy are often overlooked or misrepresented. In recent years, anti-immigrant sentiments have given rise to hundreds of local ordinances prohibiting access to housing, education, and jobs. And since Arizona passed statewide legislation in 2010, we have seen many states strive to follow a trend that previously had been mostly limited to small communities. Amidst this climate, efforts to reform outdated immigration policies continue to be stalled at the federal level as politicians remain polarized by competing perspectives on the benefits and liabilities of immigrant workers.

As chair of the Chicano Studies Department at the University of Minnesota during this time, I had unique opportunities and responsibilities to be a resource of information and a facilitator of people's understanding of this "emerging" population. In my alliances and friendships with new immigrants and engagement with a broader public concerned about the impact of immigration, I gained new insight and appreciation for the harsh realities that influence immigrants' decision to leave home and risk life in *el norte*. I also witnessed the impact of what it is like to be considered a problem, an unwelcomed presence, even though ample evidence is available to indicate that workers and industries that depend on immigrant labor thrive in a mutually beneficial relationship. Further, despite the pervasive media portrayal of a strong anti-immigrant movement and the intensification of rhetoric by politicians during this time period, it was also clear that immigrant families routinely forge very strong intercultural community relationships at work and in their personal lives.

As I began conceptualizing a project on immigration and the Latinoization of the United States in fall 2006, I asked myself a series of questions: What can possibly shed new light on the immigration question and the changing U.S. demography? These issues are both uniting the Latina/o community and making us individual and collective targets of bigots, nativists, and everyday folks who think of all of us as outsiders without regard for facts about when, how, or why we came to be here. What information and whose voices are missing from the increasingly hostile debates? These questions loomed large as I thought of how I might help reframe the immigration discussion. I reached the conclusion that the best way to really explore this problem was to travel across the country and *see* firsthand the impact of new (im)migrations, and to *listen* firsthand to folks within and outside the Latino community to learn from their experiences.

As I made plans, the role the media plays in shaping the public's perception of Latinas/os' place in the national imaginary loomed large in the background. All too often we are portrayed as a cultural and economic threat to be regulated and micromanaged by laws writ large and small. These distorted images of Latinas/os strike many of us as absurd when we consider that our existence in the

Americas predates the existence of the United States as people who have roots in the region or who came as colonial settlers, even as we also share status with most Americans as multigenerational immigrants. What is lost on many people is that the upsurge in immigration across the southern border throughout the twentieth century is a direct result of U.S. policies that have actively recruited immigrant workers into the labor force and intervened repeatedly in the economic and political self-determination of Latin American countries—policies and practices that continue to this day. In other words, Latinoization is not a phenomenon that occurs with the United States as a passive actor, rather it is a consequence of the interconnectedness of imperialism and globalization, processes in which the United States is a primary beneficiary.

The New Cultural Geography of Latinoization

Many of the people I interviewed shared experiences of Latina/o workers and their families being welcomed by local institutions, but many also shared stories of ongoing tensions and resistance to their presence despite clear evidence of the need for their labor to the local economy. I also witnessed many times over what Victor Zúñiga and Rubén Hernández-León identify as the utilization of social capital by new immigrants to become "agents of their own incorporation and integration" into their new communities.[4] These actions have included efforts to increase access to higher education among undocumented students through state-based versions of the DREAM Act, the passage of immigrant sanctuary ordinances by cities, and public polices declaring noncooperation with immigrant enforcement authorities by local police departments.

For many Latina/o migrants, finding gainful employment in the Midwest has literally been a lifesaver, whether they are economic or war refugees from Latin America, or fleeing underemployment or gang violence in urban centers of the United States. Yet transition to the Midwest has not come without cost as many struggle to adapt to regional mores, which can be inscrutable. Being from Texas, I understand the particular ways that geography, race, and ethnicity can shape regional social norms. For instance, being open, warm, and welcoming to strangers in southern states is labeled southern hospitality. It's considered basic good manners to be polite. In contrast, shortly after arriving in Minnesota I was introduced to the notion of Minnesota Nice. I often found myself trying to explain how these two regional stereotypes are both similar and distinct. Despite a deep history of racism, when a Latino in Texas experiences southern hospitality, the "kindness" exhibited is transparent and one can usually discern whether or not it is sincere or just a veneer of good manners thinly masking racial animus. There are many cues that enable one to know how they are perceived because southern hospitality and overt racism are not mutually exclusive. In contrast, Minnesota Nice—and its corollaries in Iowa, Nebraska, Ohio, and Wisconsin—is much more difficult to discern, which makes connecting and integrating into local culture difficult for outsiders. This is especially true for those who are perceived as culturally or racially different. Entire websites are devoted to this topic, enabling posters to share their experiences and strategize on how to survive the seemingly contradictory cultural and social behaviors associated with Minnesota Nice, such as polite friendliness, an aversion to confrontation, emotional restraint, passive aggressiveness, and resistance to change. The result is that there is broad perception that Minnesotans and other midwesterners are insular, only superficially friendly, and not very hospitable at all to newcomers. For instance, on a 2012 Minnesota Public Radio special featuring this topic, one interviewee joked about how difficult it was to make friends by asserting that "Minnesotans are so nice—they'll give you directions to anywhere except their own house!"[5] Cultural dynamics impact the sense of belonging of newcomers to the Midwest and their ability to socially, culturally, and economically integrate into local communities.

In this chapter I identify features of the new cultural geography produced by Latina/o migration based on insights I gleaned from the interviews and conversations with people I met on my trip. Many of these conversations exemplify what Zúñiga and Hernández-León identify as the "novel geography of diverse receiving contexts," where each context "has its own racial hierarchy, history of interethnic relations, and ways of incorporating immigrant workers and their families."[6] While one can discern the challenges with social and economic integration that result from cultural difference, it is important to note that there are also many examples of locals from the dominant community making an extraordinary effort to be inclusive.

To comprehend the recent high rates of immigration, one must connect transnational histories of contemporary migrants to understand *why* they left their homeland. In Minneapolis, I interviewed Mariano Espinoza, the executive director of the Minnesota Immigrant Freedom Network, a position that followed years of union organizing.[7] He shared with me the contrast between the image of life in the United States he was socialized to believe in Mexico and the harsh reality of trying to earn a livable wage that many Latinas/os confront upon arrival.

> I came here looking for a place to work and have a better life. It was not really a difficult decision to come because since I was very young I wanted to come to this country. You hear and hear everyday that you have to go to *el norte*. You have to go to the U.S. if you want better opportunities. So I was always in my mind thinking about the U.S., but I didn't know that the jobs that we have in this country are really, really hard. I was not expecting to be working as a dishwasher or a room cleaner. I didn't know the language even though I went for two or three years to

school to learn English. It was not the same. Once I got to Minnesota, I never in my life had pictured myself having two full-time jobs. It was really painful. I worked at the Radisson Hotel in Bloomington. It was a huge hotel where sometimes they had banquets for two, three thousand people. Sometimes two or three dishwashers had to clean all the stuff. After two, three months my back was killing me. Sometimes you have to weigh if this is really a better life because you're killing yourself.[8]

In East Lansing, I met with Juan Marinez of the Michigan State University Extension Service. Juan's expertise is on Hispanic farm owners and the relationship between non-Hispanic farm owners and Hispanic farm workers. His observations on the rapid emergence of Latino farm owners and this connection to their familial history was provocative. "There's an interesting phenomenon in Michigan where Latino immigrants are becoming small farm owners. The kids start school and all of a sudden it hits them that they're there permanently. They're great savers so they can accumulate between $40,000 [and] $80,000 and that's good enough to get them a downpayment on a farm in Southwest Michigan. They can buy 40, 20, or 10 acres. They stay with family members and go back and work in Chicago until they establish themselves or get a job on a farm. They move and then they bring others with them" (46).

Immigrants promote economic revitalization as workers, entrepreneurs, and community builders. Immigration has boosted economic prospects in parts of the Midwest. In a study of the impact of immigration on Minnesota, the authors note that

> many stakeholders . . . praised the "revitalizing effect" that immigrants are having on previously endangered towns and neighborhoods. Throughout Minnesota, from the Twin Cities to small towns like St. James and college towns like Moorhead, immigrants are changing the face of community life. One of the most obvious changes that immigrant populations have brought is a strong entrepreneurial spirit, resulting in new commercial enterprises. Global markets, ethnic restaurants, and specialty shops can be found in what were formerly depressed and decaying downtowns. School districts with dwindling student populations—both rural and urban—are revitalized when new immigrants repopulate their classrooms. Local industries stay rooted in their home communities when an immigrant workforce keeps them viable. While struggles presented by language and cultural barriers mean that these changes are not always easy, there is strong agreement across Minnesota's state and local leaders that immigrants have given new life to countless neighborhoods and small towns.[9]

Katherine Fennelly notes that Hispanic-owned firms in Minnesota have grown 350 percent since 1990.[10] This pattern of economic and community revitalization was particularly noticeable in small towns throughout the Midwest, including

Melrose, Rochester, and Worthington, Minnesota; West Liberty and Postville, Iowa; and Carpentersville, Illinois. Here one could see visible signs of how Latino immigrants are filling seats in schools and churches and adding to the town coffers even as their presence has brought on new challenges of accommodation.

In many small communities across the country, a profoundly interesting sea change is occurring that is rarely covered in the media because it is not driven by violence or anger. Whether it is the fields of Nebraska or Michigan, the slaughterhouses of Iowa, or the meatpacking plants or dairy farms of Minnesota, there is a quiet but dramatic transformation being played out that involves the out-migration of young whites who, in their pursuit of new opportunities in urban areas, leave behind an aging and low-growth population. The result is that local businesses and manufacturers are left with little recourse but to seek (im)migrant labor to maintain the local economy. Even if this active recruitment of "outsiders" brings with it a certain discomfort among longtime residents, there exists a strong acknowledgment of the role of new immigrants in maintaining the economy and vitality of small towns.[11] The result is a cultural paradox in which the way of life of elderly whites is often preserved by the labor of new immigrants, who also bring cultural change to their new communities in the form of Spanish-language newspapers and radio, Mexican restaurants and *tienditas*, and a robust presence of Spanish language in the schools and on soccer fields. No doubt some resistance, resentment, and suspicion exist, but I think many, if not most, see that the future is about change. Fennelly notes that "the most dramatic demographic shift in the United States today is the aging of the population—a development that increases the tax burden on young workers who make payroll contributions to cover the costs of Social Security and Medicare."[12] In many parts of the Midwest, the aging of the population has been heightened by the out-migration of young native-born workers, a phenomenon that Peter Rogerson and Daejong Kim aptly call "the emptying of the Bread Basket of its breadwinners." Bob Lefebvre, president of the Minnesota Milk Producers Association has stated that "'about half of the cows that are milked in Minnesota are milked by someone of Latino descent.' For Lefebvre and the Minnesota dairy operations he represents, immigration has become a surprisingly important issue in recent years. Citing out-migration of young people from Minnesota's rural areas to more urban settings, and the difficulty of dairy work, Lefebvre explains that one of the state's mainstay agricultural industries is having a harder time finding workers."[13]

There is growing awareness that our destinies and well-being are intertwined. Whether it was from politicians, law enforcement officers, school leaders, employers, civic leaders, churches, or grassroots organizations, in communities like Melrose and Worthington, Minnesota, I was struck by the perspectives offered by non-Latinos who shared with me that their communities would not continue to survive without an influx of new immigrants. In Melrose, where immigrants have helped meet the labor needs of the town's largest employer, the Jennie-O Turkey processing plant, I met with people working with immigrants to ensure that they felt part of the community.

The tactics utilized by people who function as mediators between the longtime and new residents of small towns in the Midwest were premised on the following: (1) The idea that difference is just difference—that they need not be placed in hierarchical relationship to one another nor serve as the basis for fear between communities. (2) Recognition that being a facilitator of change requires a willingness to place oneself in an uncomfortable position as they sought to find common ground and dispel unwarranted fears of the host community. (3) Awareness that people share core values—as workers, as human beings, as immigrants or descendants of immigrants, and as members of the same community, that can be tapped into to cultivate a sense of reciprocity.

As I spoke with white Americans about the changing nature of their communities, feelings were clearly mixed. Without a doubt, there is a persistence of pride in the United States' immigrant heritage—and this legacy enables many to identify with the struggles faced by new immigrants. There is also an enduring respect for the strong work ethic of immigrants, their family values, and the sacrifices they make in coming here to survive and seek opportunity. For many folks, the idea that we are and should continue to be a "nation of laws" determined whether or not they were open to accepting newcomers. These folks were clearly bothered by the notion that undocumented immigrants were "lawbreakers," and at times they expressed the idea that their own ancestors had come here "fair and square." When confronted with the fact that under the present system, labor needs would not be met, I was often told that "something had to be done to fix the system."

In Iowa City I spoke with Ángel Gónzalez, a labor organizer and educator, who spoke to this issue.

> The one big hurdle I have to overcome every time I do a presentation on immigration is the sanctity of the law, so to speak. I just remind them of slavery and these are the sacred laws that were passed and then you go into civics and how is the law passed and their hand in creating it. First thing you learn in law is that it has nothing to do with justice, nothing whatsoever. When they say, "My grandfather didn't break the law when he came from Italy." I usually say, "What if you were in a situation where people are hungry, there's no work, your family is starving, and all there is between you and a future is a little river, what would you do? If you can tell me you would sit there and watch your kids starve, then I don't have anything else to talk to you about." But usually they say "Well, I'd cross any line." Well then there you go. Are you going to let the employer exploit them? The solution as far as I'm concerned is having full labor rights in the work place so that people

can take their future into their own hands, organize through the Union and take exploitive business owners to task. (104–5)

Local leadership is crucial in establishing the dominant tone and attitudes on how new immigrants are received. Immigration can bring social stresses as well, as native-born residents learn to adjust to an influx of ethnically dissimilar individuals. Again, this is particularly pronounced in rural towns with a high percentage of older residents. Much depends on whether local leaders embrace or resist demographic change. Where there are leaders who articulate the advantages of diversity, tensions tend to dissipate over time. The process is uneven, of course, as generational differences between youths and elders often emerge, with the latter often being more rigid in their attitudes toward cultural difference. Many communities have been defined by how they choose to respond to new arrivals. Although accommodating difference and change is hard work, communities that embrace newcomers have found that they are made stronger. Finally, communities that strive to be inclusive by respecting and embracing diversity have adopted a moral and ethical framework that views others as whole human beings with distinct histories, values, and qualities that complement their own and enrich their lives—not threaten it.

In Melrose, Minnesota, I spoke with Police Chief John Jensen about his role as mediator of change and the evolution of public attitudes among longtime residents and newcomers.

LOUIS: How would you characterize the way in which people have accepted the change?

JOHN: You know (*pause*) I would like to think it went smoother here than other places simply because we did our homework and we talked to places like Willmar and Worthington. I hope that we learned from some of their mistakes. And I think that really helped us. Just under the surface there may be a little resentment, in some cases a lot of resentment.

LOUIS: What is that resentment about? Jobs? Cultural change?

JOHN: I don't think it is so much about the jobs. More about cultural change, because everyone does things a little different.

LOUIS: It seems like Melrose has done a very deliberate job of trying to do things right and be sensitive. Why do you think Melrose is different from these other places?

JOHN: (*sighs*) I don't know if we are that much different. We've got good people in place. Between Sister Adela, George O'Brien, John and Peggy Stokman, Ana Santana, the Carbajals, Salvador Cruz—a lot of people who have set higher expectations, higher standards, gone the extra yard to make it easier for people to assimilate. I think that handful of people right there are one of the biggest differences. Our Catholic church has done a lot. (91)

John and Peggy Stokman of Melrose shared with me their deliberate choice of being facilitators of change in their retirement.

> **J&P:** We used to live in Minnesota long ago. We chose Melrose to live because we wanted to be in the vicinity of St. John's, St. Cloud, St. Paul for university and culture and things. We liked the connection at St. John's and we went there and asked the priest who was director of Hispanic Studies which community he would recommend. He recommended Cold Spring and Melrose and we looked at homes in both communities. Each community was about 20 minutes drive to St. John's, but there literally were no Anglo advocates here. Basically, we knew that in retirement we wanted to serve and involve ourselves in this type of outreach. It's been a real rich and meaningful life for us.
>
> **LOUIS:** What do your children think of it?
>
> **J&P:** Oh, they are supportive. We have to watch that they don't feel jealous or slighted, because you know the needs are great and they are right here and our children are sort of spread all over. . . . But politically we are in different places and there are several of our children who do not share the same philosophy with us on immigration. They say things like: "They've done illegal things, they need to go back home. . . ." That is not a comfortable thing for us at all. But you know what, that's where they are. And for us this issue has such a face. Maybe we'd think differently but this is about people we love and you know their goodness. (94–95)

Efforts to establish and resist local ordinances have intensified the racialization of the entire Latina/o community and generated organized grassroots and legal response efforts. From Carpentersville, Illinois, and the communities surrounding it, I learned that word of mouth had spread about the anti-Latino reputation of this small town. By the time I went there in late August 2007, many Latinas/os had already moved away. The 2008 economic crisis only intensified anti-immigrant sentiment. During President Obama's first term, we witnessed an increase of incidents of hate crimes against Latinas/os, rampant enforcement of immigration laws, intensification of border security, and zero action on immigration reform. Only as he was preparing for his reelection did the president make a bold move by enacting the Deferred Action for Childhood Arrivals (DACA) Program.

For many Latinas/os, the tension resulting from balancing the distinctiveness of their community while enhancing others' awareness of their common ground is difficult. More than ever being aware of one's civil and human rights is important. In East Lansing, Michigan, I asked elder Efrain Marinez (fig. 1.1.1) about the change he has witnessed since moving to Michigan from Texas as a young man.

1.1.1   Efrain and Francisca Marinez in their house in East Lansing, Michigan. Photo by Louis Mendoza.

LOUIS: Do you think things have changed for the better?

EFRAIN: Yes, I think in the [Motor Wheel] plant I made a lot of change. They didn't do it when I was there, but when I got out of there they started making all these changes. They didn't want you to know they made the changes. I had a big fight in the church and they made a lot of changes too, but only after a long time. They didn't want to admit that they were wrong. I told the bishop one time, "You're not my bishop, I don't respect you." And he said, "Why?" "Because you don't do anything for the Mexicans." The church didn't support the mexicanos during the marches. They just closed their eyes. I got mad with a priest once. John used to have a girlfriend, and he go and he tell the family to watch their girl 'cause she was dating a Mexican. I gave it to him, and he said, "I am sorry, I don't know what I was thinking." (222)

In Minneapolis, I asked Alondra Kiawitl Espejel (fig. 1.1.2), a young immigrant leader for Comprehensive Immigration Reform who was elected as Minneapolis's first Latina City council member in November 2013, about what drives her commitment.

The reward in working for immigration reform is the hope that you're building a better world, and the idea that you're connected to a civil rights struggle that

1.1.2   Alondra Kiawitl Espejel of the Minnesota Immigrant Freedom Network. In 2012, Kiawitl Espejel was the first Latina/o ever elected to the Minneapolis city council. Photo by Louis Mendoza.

goes back 500 years. I didn't see this before, but now I see that I may dedicate my lifetime to this work, and I may not see needed changes. Before, I would get so frustrated because I'd be like, "God, I want to see the change now. Why aren't things changing?" My teachers would have to remind me that the struggle is long and it's going to be years. Now, I get it. So is this work challenging? Yes. Is it hard? Yes. Is it rewarding? Yeah, because at night, I can go to bed and feel okay about what I did today. I can feel good about not being just one cog in the machine but actually trying to change the machine. (80)[14]

Recommendations for Immigrant Integration

Immigrants must be integrated into midwestern communities if they are to realize their potential as fully contributing members of society. Achieving this objective requires eliminating barriers, such as school and residential segregation, xeno-phobia, and discrimination that limit educational and occupational opportunities. Above all, state governments should provide leadership by articulating goals designed to foster integration and encouraging local governments to follow suit.

The creation of diversity coalitions to bridge cultural divides is a common strategy that I witnessed in several midwestern communities. Such coalitions may involve many different types of organizations, and they may take many different forms, but they generally share the goal of working to promote improved relations between foreign-born and U.S. residents. The sponsorship of and involvement in these coalitions by religious leaders, law enforcement personnel, businesses, or a coalition of local political, education, or community leaders reinforces my arguments that leadership and vision for an integrated community are crucial. In 2007, immigration scholars Schwei and Fennelly conducted a census of diversity coalitions in rural Minnesota and found evidence of fifty programs and initiatives, including programs focused on recreational and educational agendas, community educational forums, community festivals, civic engagement campaigns, and human rights commissions.[15]

Conclusion

This essay provides only a glimpse into the dynamics associated with an enormously complex and contentious issue—one that, if it is to be resolved, will require a diligent and protracted effort to lead us to a place where we gain new insight into our common ground and our mutual destiny with the residents of not just the United States but also the Americas. People I met on this journey taught me that actual relationships with and information about immigrants consistently trumps media propagated ignorance. As I traveled through small towns in West Texas, where being brown (or being "meskin") was all the probable cause needed for someone to be stopped in the 1960s, I was impressed and surprised at how much things have changed and how relationships were more complex and layered than once was the case in these communities. In communities where Friday night high school football is king and civil rights movements were once sparked by the exclusion of Chicanas from the cheerleading squad, the local newspapers now report on teams where the majority of players are Latinos. This resonated with a story I heard about a basketball team in Melrose, Minnesota, that refused to continue a game before an apology was made when an opposing player spat out a racial slur against their Latino teammate.

Across the country I have seen the dramatic difference between embracing diversity and acknowledging that it has always been a part of our social fabric or resisting it and cultivating an illusion of cultural homogeneity. Though the immigration debate is ostensibly about immigrants and the law, anyone who has experienced social marginalization knows that it is about much more. Notions of the law, legal status, and belonging are intimately intertwined and often pitted against one another. Latinas/os' pursuit of social justice and equity do not start and stop at the border. Any honest assessment of why we have such difficulty expanding our sense of belonging has to begin with the identification of why so many fear demographic and cultural change. The new geography of Latino demographic change mandates different conversations about inclusion and exclusion, conversations that will reflect regional histories, cultures, and social relations.

Notes

This chapter is based partially on my previously published works; see the bibliography.

1. Though I began the trip without any interviews scheduled, I was able to make numerous initial contacts with potential interviewees through my network of coworkers and friends. Many people I spoke with referred me to other interviewee candidates. In some cases I made "cold calls" or unannounced visits to people in their offices who appeared likely to be good sources of information. While not all of them were able to take the time to speak with me during my short time in their area, many people dropped what they were doing and took time to visit with me. I approached each interview as a conversation rather than as a structured interview.

2. The book-length works include interaction with a broader array of ethnic groups beyond Latinos and White Americans, though interactions with other than white ethnic groups on this issue was still minimal. This was so partially due to my random process of meeting people and being limited to being introduced to others in their social networks, and also, I believe, because Anglo Americans see themselves are an integral part of the polarized climate around immigration, they were more willing to share their opinions on the topic.

3. Sáenz makes the compelling point that Latino fertility and life span rates are a major factor for this. For Whites there are 1.1 births for every 1 death, whereas for Latinos there are 8.9 births for every 1 death. See Rogelio Sáenz, "Engine of U.S. Population Growth: Latinos and the Changing of America," presented at the University of Minnesota, Jan. 27, 2012.

4. Víctor Zúñiga and Rubén Hernández-León, eds., *New Destinations: Mexican Immigration in the United States* (New York: Russell Sage, 2005), xxvi.

5. Laura Yuen, "Newcomers Say It's 'Nice,' but Not Warm," Minnesota Public Radio, March 12, 2012, http://minnesota.publicradio.org, accessed Dec. 18, 2016.

6. Zúñiga and Hernández-León, xxvi.

7. Since our interview, Mariano has become the City of Minneapolis liaison to the Latino community, and a prominent leader in statewide policy reform efforts impacting Latinos. He was a principal player in the 2013 passage of the Minnesota DREAM Act.

8. Louis Mendoza, *Conversations across Our America: Talking about Immigration and the Latinoization of the United States* (Austin: University of Texas Press, 2012), 80–81. Page numbers for later quotations are cited in parentheses in the text.

9. G. Owen, J. Meyerson, and C. Otteson, *A New Age of Immigrants: Making Immigration Work for Minnesota* (St. Paul, Minn.: Wilder Foundation, 2010), 32.

10. Katherine Fennelly, "Prejudice Towards Immigrants in the Midwest." In *New Faces in New Places: The Changing Geography of American Immigration*, ed. Douglas S. Massey (New York: Russell Sage Foundation, 2010), 20.

11. Ann Millard and Jorge Chapa note similar dynamics in their important collection of essays, *Apple Pie and Enchiladas: Latino Newcomers in the Rural Midwest* (Austin: University of Texas Press, 2004).

12. Katherine Fennelly, "Immigration in the Midwest," Scholars Strategy Network, Basic Facts, April 2012, www.scholarsstrategynetwork.org, accessed Dec. 8, 2016.

13. Bob Lefebvre quoted in Owen et al., *New Age of Immigrants*, 30.

14. At the time of our original interview, Alondra's surname was Espejel. She has since changed it to Cano.

15. Tamara Downs Schwei and Katherine Fennelly, "Diversity Coalitions in Rural Minnesota Communities," *Cura Reporter* 37, no. 4 (winter 2007): 14, www.cura.umn.edu.

Al Norte toward Home

Texas, the Midwest, and Mexican American Critical Regionalism

JOSÉ E. LIMÓN

I appropriated the chapter title from one of my heroes, the late Willie Morris—social democrat, southern cultural critic, and former editor of *Harper's* magazine. Morris's best-known work is his 1967 memoir, *North toward Home* (1967).[1] I render Morris's title partially in Spanish—*al norte* toward home—to begin to underscore my focus on working-class Americans of Mexican ancestry, or Mexican Americans, in their movement from Texas to the Midwest and back. But I also turn to Willie Morris for more than my title. Let me use Morris's own social experience in Texas to begin to develop my argument, an argument in two parts: first, that the trans-local experience of Mexican Americans between Texas and the U.S. Midwest in the twentieth century merits critical delineation and further exploration, particularly in its cultural aspects; and, second, that this trans-local experience may perhaps be interestingly conceptualized as a possible example of what has been called critical regionalism. But at the outset, and recognizing the special transnational emphasis of this volume, I wish to underscore that my focus is the internal migration of the Mexican-origin community in Texas to the Midwest and less so in the international migration of people from the Republic of Mexico directly to the Midwest, as important as the latter is. Nevertheless, as I suggest in a moment, there is some overlap between these two migratory circuits.

Southwestward toward Home

Willie Morris traveled north from his native Mississippi—the home of his title—to spend the better part of his adult life in New York, both during his editorship at *Harper's* and afterward, although he did spend his final years in Mississippi—indeed, as a professor of creative writing at Ole Miss—where he died in 1999.

However, he comes much closer to my own trans-local interests, because his first extended excursion out of Mississippi was not northward at all, but rather southwest to Texas, initially in 1953 to attend the University of Texas at Austin, my own alma mater, where he also served as editor of the award-winning student newspaper, the *Daily Texan*.

As I look at the right-wing-dominated state of Texas today, I have the eerie feeling that we have gone back to Willie Morris's time in Texas in the 1950s and '60s. For as an undergraduate student editor of the *Daily Texan*, he editorially attacked the right-wing business interests, principally the oil and agricultural conglomerates, that ruled Texas at that time, as they did under Governor Rick Perry and continue to do today. As is too often the case, such right-wing power extended to the universities, including UT-Austin through the governor-appointed board of regents, which continues to pursue conservative policies today. They tried and failed to censure Morris and remove him from his editorship. After graduating with a degree in English in 1957 and spending a few years abroad as a Rhodes Scholar, Morris returned to Austin in 1960 as the editor of the *Texas Observer*, a well-known left-liberal biweekly, where he continued his attacks on big business but also on the system of racial segregation that oppressed African Americans and Mexican Americans in the state as well. And, of course, such views also made it virtually impossible for him to return to the Mississippi of that time.

As it happened, the late '50s and early '60s were important for Mexican Americans in Texas in two other important respects. In 1956, State Senator Henry B. González, a UT-Austin graduate representing a heavily Mexican American district in San Antonio, took to the floor of the Texas State Senate to filibuster for twenty-two straight hours against a series of segregationist bills intended to circumvent the 1954 Supreme Court decision, *Brown v. Board of Education*. González was physically threatened on the Texas Senate floor. That same year, González also ran an unsuccessful but close campaign for governor.[2] But the second important event of 1958 was the publication of "*With His Pistol in His Hand*": *A Border Ballad and Its Hero* by Américo Paredes, one of only three Mexican American professors at the University of Texas.[3] Paredes had just joined the faculty after attending UT-Austin as an undergraduate and graduate student overlapping with Morris.

Over time, Américo Paredes has become the best known of all Mexican American intellectuals and Latina/o studies scholars, the subject of no less than four intellectual biographies, including my own.[4] This centrality in Latina/o studies is still based on his 1958 "*With His Pistol in His Hand*," although his fiction appears slowly to be taking over the predominant definition of his creative life. All of us who write on Paredes necessarily take note of his predominantly Texas-based work, but none of us has placed Paredes in explicit relationship to the Midwest. In this chapter I hope to correct that omission.

Texas, *Our* Texas

"With His Pistol in His Hand" is principally a study of the Mexican American *corrido*, or ballad, form that Mexicans Americans in Texas deployed artistically to celebrate folk heroes who had resisted the imposition of an Anglo-American racist and economically exploitative domination of Mexicans in Texas. Such domination began as early as the 1830s, continued through the U.S.-Mexican War (also known as the Mexican-American War) of 1846–48, and on through the twentieth century and into our own time, affecting Mexicans residing principally in southern Texas, including the city of San Antonio. As Paredes reminds us, such Texas Mexicans traced their ancestry to the Spanish colonial settlement of southern Texas and northern Mexico beginning in the 1740s and/or later settlement shortly after Mexico became a republic in 1821. Let me call this core group the matrix, or *matriz*, because the Spanish term has a much closer association to womb or birth canal. In south Texas but also in northern New Mexico and parts of California, we have these historical core populations, dating from the Spanish colonial period. In Texas, from their colonial beginnings, these people engaged primarily in a ranching economy.[5] In a very real sense then, they became the first U.S. Latino group in 1848. The U.S.-Mexican War of 1846–48 was initially fought over and through south Texas, although Mexico was also invaded by sea. However, the U.S. soldiers who fought in this imperialist war came from many parts of the United States and, for the most part, after the war, the veterans returned to those places. Yet, fresh back from the U.S.-Mexican War, many of them were soon leaving those places again as part of the westward movement of the mid-nineteenth century, "lighting out for the territories," as Mark Twain's Huck Finn famously said. No doubt it was through a movement of such veterans that, paradoxically enough, first brought a sense of Mexicanness to the Midwest by way of memory and place names. Evidence for this early and odd conjunction, for example, is the 1851 founding in Iowa of Cerro Gordo County, which was named after the famous battle of the U.S.-Mexican War, as was Cerro Gordo, Illinois. In 1847, General Winfield Scott broke through the Mexican defenses at Cerro Gordo, or Fat Hill, on his way to taking Mexico City.

After the war, the post-1848 Mexican-origin population in Texas first experienced and endured a long and largely adversarial relationship with the new Anglo-American racialized capitalist social order that came to dominate Texas but also other parts of the now U.S. Southwest. For the most part, the birth was painful, such that we can also exploit the metaphor of labor pain. But, in comparison to other regions, such birth and labor pain were most socially intense in southern Texas. Between 1848 and the 1930s, the Mexicans of south Texas were largely dispossessed of their lands. The region was transformed into a major agricultural zone, at first with new cattle ranches in the nineteenth century worked largely by displaced Mexican Americans. Such racialized dispossession also led to social resistance in a variety of ways that included forms of folklore, as we see later in this chapter, but also politics, journalism, fiction, and even armed violence. Moreover, this growing sense of resistive difference was, of course, based on language and phenotype but also geography, as the largely Spanish-Mexican-origin southern part of Texas became a kind of native soil for this besieged population. From 1848 through the 1960s, we must then think of southern Texas as a racially intense place and structured as a labor hierarchy with most Mexicans at the bottom—a birthing scene, as I have already suggested but also a kind of social incubator of festering resentment and resistance. Over time, such Texas-based repression and resistance would increasingly implicate the Midwest, although the conjunction was there at its beginning (re: Cerro Gordo), followed almost immediately by a more material connection. For this we return to Américo Paredes.

Texas Mexican resentment and resistance to Anglo domination included forms of folklore as noted earlier, especially folk ballads, or *corridos*, and arguably, the most famous of these is the subject of Paredes's *"With His Pistol in His Hand."* That work focuses on one such ballad and its folk hero protagonist, Gregorio Cortéz, an otherwise real-life ordinary man who in 1901 was transformed into a ballad hero in Texas. This transformation began when, as a young man, Cortéz ventured north from his native Mexican south Texas toward central Texas, an area dominated by Anglo-Texans. He was looking for sharecropping work, only to find himself falsely accused of horse thievery and thereby in a gun fight with oppressive Texas lawmen. Knowing that he would surely be lynched if captured, Cortéz fled on horseback south to friendlier territory in southern Texas, all of which forms the corpus of heroic balladry. The story is well known in Mexican American studies, but for this writing, I want to focus a bit less on the dramatic gunfight and flight and a bit more on what brought Cortéz to central Texas in the first place: he was simply looking for work as a sharecropper, although I must also underscore his horsemanship in eluding capture. He seemed to have every intention of eventually returning to southern Texas among his people, although events certainly hastened his temporary return, as he made it as far as Laredo before he was captured. In his sojourn going and returning, for me Cortéz thus already becomes emblematic of the journey many Mexicans from southern Texas have taken *al norte*—to the north—but also back to south Texas, *al norte* toward home.

As far as we know, he went only as far as central Texas, but it is not at all inconceivable that in 1901 Cortéz could have pushed even farther north, perhaps into the Midwest, and that possibility is not at all speculative. We know this because other Mexicans from Texas had gone there before him; had he ventured farther *al norte*, he would not have been the first Mexican from Texas to venture into the Midwest.

From South Texas to Kansas

Here again Américo Paredes is of the greatest assistance. He has said much about the *corrido* of Gregorio Cortéz and the events of 1901, but Paredes also collected and commented on what he calls "the oldest Texas-Mexican *corrido* that we have in complete form."[6] "El Corrido de Kiansis" (The ballad of Kansas) dates from the 1860s. Always the cultural historian, Paredes offers the illuminating context for understanding this much earlier ballad (see the appendix to this chapter for his original Spanish transcription and an English translation).

The end of the Civil War and the burgeoning industrialization of the midwestern and eastern United States brought an intensified demand for beef, which the emerging great cattle ranches of Texas (especially in southern Texas) were only too ready to supply. Thus, says Paredes, "they gathered huge herds of cattle and drove them north to the railheads in Kansas." But he then unpacks the "they" in this statement: "What is not so well known is that it was cattle owned by Mexicans and Texas-Mexicans (some legally obtained from them and some not) that formed the bulk of the herds driven north from the Nueces–Rio Grande area, the so-called cradle of the cattle industry in the United States."[7] Paredes is likely referring to the cattle drives that started in 1867 along the Chisholm Trail, which started near San Antonio, the gathering site for the cattle coming in over smaller feeder trails from what he calls "the Nueces–Rio Grande area," or south Texas. From there it was a straight drive north to Ellsworth and Abilene, Kansas.[8] However, if much of this cattle was of former Mexican ownership, "not all cattle that went north were driven by Anglo cowboys. Many of trail drivers were Mexicans, some taking their own herds, others working for Anglo outfits."[9]

Thus were born the great but decidedly bicultural cattle drives from deep and conflicted south Texas to midwestern beef processing sites that became part of the cowboy mythology, seen for example in Larry McMurtry's *Lonesome Dove* series. Like other writers before him, McMurtry conveniently ignores the historical fact that many of the cowboys on these drives were not "cowboys" as such but rather *vaqueros*, from the Spanish word for cow, *vaca*—they were Mexican cowboys from southern Texas who spoke mostly Spanish, although undoubtedly they learned some English from the Anglo-Texan cowboys who were also part of the cattle drive.

Spanish-dominant speakers often Hispanicize English names in their own phonetics, and this is what happens in this *corrido* as the title and the speaker-singer in this ballad render the state of Kansas as "Kiansis," the same way that my father who drove long-haul trucks from south Texas into this state and others often spoke of Iow*a* with the accent on the final *a* (it was not until high school that I learned to put the accent on the *i*). In this ballad, the speaker-singer speaks of *Kiansis*.

It would appear that there was some degree of racial separation on these cattle drives to Kansas, with each racial group having its own distinctive organizational identity. The first two stanzas announce the drive to Kansas in the first line, but then has a *caporal*, or foreman, who clearly is Mexican and in charge of Mexicans, speaking in Spanish to another foreman who appears to be staying behind on this particular drive. In an interesting articulation of gender, he asks him to look out for his beloved and is assured that he need not worry because, if a woman is virtuous, it does not matter that she lives among men.

But immediately in the next stanzas, the narrative tells us of racial tensions. Thirty Anglo cowboys are not able to get five hundred rowdy cows cattle into a pen; a task accomplished by only *five* Mexican vaqueros in *fifteen* minutes, much to the amazement of the Anglo cowboys, marking the superiority of *vaqueros* at their common trade. As Paredes notes, "the Texas-Mexican possessed something else that gave him a certain status—the tools and techniques of the vaquero trade, in which the Anglo was merely a beginner. The Mexican with some justice could feel superior to the Anglo when it came to handling horses and cattle. Or facing occupational hazards."[10]

The Kiansis *corrido* speaks to such hazards. Once in the pen, the cattle continue in their rowdiness and an "Americano" orders the *caporal* into the corral to control them. The *caporal* refuses, but another *vaquero* volunteers, only to be killed by a bull. The *corrido* form often compresses the time frame of the events being narrated, so it is more than likely that all of these actions are now transpiring at the *end* of the cattle drive, which is to say *in Kansas*, as the cows are now being delivered from the open range into a pen. And we have even more reason to think that this job-related death has occurred far from home, as the final stanzas speaks of the dead *vaquero*'s mother asking for her absent son when the men return to south Texas. We might easily imagine her son now buried in midwestern, Kansas soil. As he completes his verses about this tragic cattle drive, the singer then offers his farewell, telling us he is off to find his beloved. But even as we speak of the dead remaining behind in the Midwest, it is also very likely that at least a few of the living also remained behind, perhaps to work in the very beef stockyards to which they had herded the cattle.

The Midwest Comes to Texas

The racist labor hierarchy that the Kiansis *vaqueros* and Cortéz experienced was mostly created by white southerners who had come to Texas after 1848, but especially after the defeat of the Confederacy in 1865. However, by the early twentieth century, new sets of social actors were added to the developing social drama. The eminent historian David Montejano tells us that as more appropriated land became available, especially in deep south Texas along the Rio Grande, local land companies began to market this land all over the United States for large-scale farming. However, for a variety of reasons, the largest number of U.S. buyers, and therefore future citizens of south Texas, came from places like Ohio, Wisconsin, and Iowa.[11] I confess that I do not know my midwestern history well enough to know in complex detail why such predominantly white midwestern farmers found it in their interest at that time to move all the way to Texas. They certainly were attracted by the prospect of relatively cheap land, the plentiful availability of water from the Rio Grande for irrigation, railroads to carry out the harvest. But a very important part of the equation was likely the availability of cheap and mostly Mexican labor, in part, the now children and grandchildren of the Kiansis *vaqueros* and Gregorio Cortéz, if you will. Unfortunately, although from the Midwest and not the South, for the most part these white midwesterners not only participated in and maintained the racist labor hierarchy, and indeed they intensified it, particularly in creating for Mexicans segregated neighborhoods, public areas, and schools, especially after 1910.[12]

The large-scale cash-crop agriculture these Anglo midwesterners created required far more Mexican labor than the local dispossessed Mexicans could have provided, but, as if by some grand design, these newly arriving midwestern white farmers and their families were met by yet another new set of social actors who greatly expanded the Mexican labor pool.

Al Norte through Texas

The Kansas *vaqueros* and Gregorio Cortéz had belonged historically to the early Spanish Mexican settlement of Texas—the *matriz*, the birth population—but it is quite clear that the most substantial expansion of the Mexican-origin population in Texas and the rest of the United States occurred in the first half of the twentieth century and largely as a result of the social chaos created by the Mexican Revolution of 1910. That revolution and its aftermath sent thousands of national Mexicans into the United States, but for my purposes, it is quite important to once again take note of the role of Texas in this massive immigration flow. Texas used such labor for its own agricultural development, but the state also became a staging ground and conduit for the further dispersal of such labor to the rest of the United States, including the Midwest. What the Kiansis *vaqueros* had started in the 1860s now became massively intensified. In his groundbreaking *Proletarians of the North*, labor historian Zaragosa Vargas tells us that Texas became "the greatest contributor of Mexican labor to other states." Indeed, it was "the hub on which the wheel of the Mexican population in the United States . . . revolved."[13]

However, it is important to sort out certain distinctions within this population as it was initially situated in this hub called Texas. We can note three such temporal distinctions. First, many of these working-class sojourners were in Texas only in the most temporary and technical sense in that they came by railroad to Ciudad Juárez; then crossed the bridge to El Paso, Texas; and then fairly quickly moved on to California, as historian George Sánchez has shown us.[14] A second and similar group, however, also journeyed relatively quickly through Texas, again using the railroads from Mexico to arrive first, not in El Paso, but in Laredo, farther down along the Texas border, and then making their way to San Antonio, another important labor distribution point, and from there largely to the closer, midwestern part of the United States, particularly to the Gary-Chicago-Detroit industrial hub. Obviously for my purposes, we do not want to lose sight of this second group, but it is the third group that interests me more.

This third group also entered Texas at Laredo and other downriver towns, but unlike the other two groups, they chose to remain in Texas for varying periods of time, some for the rest of their lives. Vargas is again most helpful in describing this more Texas-centered group in terms of its labor and its entrance into varying periods of social incubation in the new white-dominated racial hierarchy in south Texas. These longer-term immigrants joined those already resident Mexicans like Gregorio Cortéz, and for all intents and purposes they became Texans or, more appropriately, Tejanos. Together with the native residents now displaced from their ancestral lands, these Tejanos worked first at clearing the brush and mesquite that were impeding development in south Texas; then, they laid out irrigation systems fed by the nearby Rio Grande; then they planted and harvested the crops, primarily cotton, on the large-scale farming enterprises being developed by the newly arriving midwestern farmers. As they did so, they endured not only labor exploitation but racial discrimination as well. But in joining native Tejanos for long periods of time, they also seemed to have inherited the idioms and prac- tices of social resistance passed on from the examples of the Kiansis *vaqueros* and Gregorio Cortéz. Vargas reports labor strikes and walkouts from repressive labor conditions but also the formation of a resistive cultural consciousness: "the brash nature of Texas social relations shaped the consciousness of Mexicans— men, women and children alike—and was largely responsible for the ways they responded." But he adds that "the repressive working conditions and low wages characteristic of this industry [agricultural labor] eventually motivated tens of thousands to seek alternative work in the Midwest. . . . Mexicans migrating from Texas to the Midwest therefore made conscious choices to leave behind working and living conditions made doubly oppressive by racism."[15] Such migrant work- ers began their journey from the cotton fields of south and central Texas first to San Antonio, the main labor distribution point, and then on to the sugar beets of Michigan, the packinghouses of Omaha and Chicago, but also to the foundries of Indiana and Ohio. It is quite clear that many such migrant workers from Texas established permanent and exclusive residence in various parts of the Midwest. Vargas is certainly correct that the Midwest was a more hospitable place than Texas, but he also clearly acknowledges that such racial and class animosities were also present in the Midwest.[16] What is not so clear is the short- or long-term effect of their Texas experience with race and class in their new milieus, although in a few moments we will turn to one extended example. But while some, possibly many, established permanent residence, many others also developed the practice of circular migration: working *al norte* for periods of time and then returning to Texas, often with residences in both places. In other words, while many Mexican workers came directly through Texas to settle permanently in the Midwest, many others became trans-local U.S. citizens, living part of the time in Texas and part of the time in the Midwest, whether working in agriculture or in the industrial economy, for example in steel or auto manufacture. Indeed, even those who became more permanent residents returned periodically to Texas for weddings and other rituals, or just to visit friends and families. Over time, still others returned from the Midwest to establish permanent residences back in Texas.

Culture on the Move

While Vargas and others have foregrounded the political economy of labor in this movement from Texas to the Midwest, the role of culture seems to me to be understudied. Elaine Peña, for example, has examined the role of the Virgin of Guadalupe in forging communities between Chicago and Mexico, but the internal movement of culture between Texas and the Midwest has received less attention, especially as it contributes to a critical consciousness.[17]

We have already seen the role of Texas-based balladry relative to movement toward the Midwest, but at least three other key examples of a trans-local Texan-midwestern expressive culture may be noted. As with other Mexican-origin groups throughout Greater Mexico, that of southern Texas developed folk healing practices, including the veneration of major folk healers, charismatic practioners such as Don Pedrito Jaramillo, who practiced his craft in south Texas from the 1890s to end of his life in 1907. These healers continue to play an active role in people's lives even after their deaths, as they become folk saints with important pilgrimage sites, such as that of Don Pedrito, still active today near Corpus Christi, Texas. According to anthropologist Octavio Romano, the pilgrimage site was linked to Mexican Americans in the Midwest in two significant ways.[18] As such laborers were leaving south Texas for the Midwest, it was a customary practice to stop at the pilgrimage site to ask for Don Pedrito's blessing for the long journey and good fortune finding work, not to mention crossing through Anglo-dominated central and northern Texas. Conversely, while in the Midwest and in times of crisis, such as protracted unemployment or a death in the family back in Texas, it would not have been unusual for these same Mexicans to make the journey back to south Texas to visit the site for help as well. Both practices continue in the present day.

Don Pedrito symbolically and religiously accompanied Tejanos on their north-ward movement and back, but so did the entertaining, profane reality of another expressive form—*conjunto* and Tejano music. Indebted somewhat to the *corridos* that we have already noted, this was and continues to be kind of Mexican working-class country-western music danced primarily as a polka in largely commercial dance halls in Texas and the Midwest. Given hard, tedious daytime and weekday labor, such weekend music and dancing provided much needed entertainment, but also a forum for romantic courtship, community solidarity, and ethnic-class consciousness as its foremost scholar, Manuel Peña, has shown in a series of im-portant studies.[19] Ethnomusicologist David Harnish has shown us the specific implantation of such music in Ohio by way of master *conjunto* artist Jesse Ponce from San Antonio, Texas. Of particular importance to my developing argument is Ponce's close participation with the Ohio Farm Labor Organizing Committee in support of "migrant workers' rights and the preservation of Latina/o identity in Ohio and nearby states." The majority of such workers are from Texas. We also take note of Ponce's ambivalence toward Texas for racial, among other, rea-sons and his affirmation of the Midwest, particularly Ohio.[20] And, today we also have the Midwest Tejano Music Association operating out of Toledo. But such Tejano-style musicians also explored other more contemporary musical idioms beginning in the 1960s. The famous rock ensemble for the early 1960s, Question Mark and the Mysterians, had clear Tejano geographical and musical roots but came to the Midwest with the migrant labor stream, subsequently playing out of Adrian, Michigan, including their signature song, "96 Tears."[21]

Folk healers and music were two important ways that a distinctive and perhaps resistive cultural consciousness was transported from Texas to the Midwest but also back. When I was in high school, hearing "96 Tears" for the first time and learning that the band was formed by Mexican Americans originally from Texas did something wonderful to my Mexican soul. But this dialectical transmission of culture also happened in literary form in two interrelated stages.

The simplest but yet the most pervasive such literary form is the personal anecdote. Growing up as a kid in Laredo, Texas, in forums such as backyard barbecues, I recall hearing grown men who had been *al norte* speaking in expres-sive terms of places like Toledo in Ohio (whose name pronounced in Spanish wonderfully coincided with that of the ancient Spanish city); in Indiana, Garrrry (pronounced in Spanish with a rolling *r*), and in Wisconsin, Agua Clara (Eau Claire). In these stories, the midwestern streets were not paved with gold, but I heard of good money to be made in *las llantas* (tires), el auto, el *esteel* (steel) and, for those not as fortunate, of strawberry fields forever in Michigan. I listened in awe to stories of adventures driving through snowstorms in Iowa to make a Texas Christmas, but also of tragic truck accidents on the icy highways where entire families died; of nasty racist farmers in downstate Illinois, but also of friendly *mujeres polacas*—Polish women—in Chicago who were narratively constructed to resemble Amazons. As a boy in south Texas, I certainly remember thinking that I could not wait for my time to come to go *al norte*. Life took me on other journeys, but I suppose I finally made it as a migrant academic worker to Notre Dame, Indiana.

It was on the basis of such personal anecdotes that a generation of Texan Mexican American writers—fiction writers like Tomás Rivera and Rolando Hinojosa—created their wonderful works based on such midwestern recollections. Hinojosa's series of short novels trace the growth and development of two male protagonists, Rafe Buenrostro and Jehú Malacara, in the Lower Rio Grande Valley of Texas from the 1920s through the 1970s. Indeed, the first of these novels is simply titled *The Valley*. However, though indeed set mostly in the valley, it is as if Hinojosa cannot fully develop his two characters from boyhood to manhood without including the Midwest, like some necessary rite of passage. Rafe recalls that

> In Monon, Indiana, on the left hand side of Route 421 going north, there's a roadside place called Myrtle's, about two and a half blocks from a Shell station; we always stopped there to get gas up on the way to Benton Harbor during the cherry picking season. When we stopped at the Shell station, Dad and I would walk from there to Myrtle's for some doughnuts. Once, while the woman waited on us, she told my Dad that I was getting to be a little man now. Back in the truck once again, Dad turned to me and said, "This makes the sixth time that you've made the trip to Michigan, son."[22]

But it is another also famous south Texan writer—Tomás Rivera—who even more fully engages the Midwest in his otherwise Texas-based fiction, poetry, and essays. I count at least twenty references to the Midwest in his works, some brief but several elaborated, reflecting Rivera's own boyhood experience. In one such essay, Rivera speaks explicitly of his trans-local identity. He tells us that, "as a child . . . I lived in Iowa, the Dakotas, Minnesota, Michigan, Wisconsin and Ohio. My earliest recollections are of waking up on a farm in northern Minnesota close to the North Dakota border, where my parents and other relatives worked in the beet fields, surrounded by sounds I hear even today. These sounds of the farm animals and the voices of working men continue to have a distinct and almost unique clarity and quality."[23]

His famous modernist novel, *Y no se lo tragó la tierra* (*And the Earth Did Not Devour Him*), (2008), and other of his works are fundamentally structured around such journeys *al norte* to the Midwest. Through the voice and sensibility of a young male protagonist, the novel deals with migrant farm workers who labor in a racist Texas even as they make the long journey to the Midwest. In one such instance one migrant laborer riding in a truck with others speaks the following as the truck comes to a rest stop for a badly needed bathroom break: "Good thing the truck stopped here . . . I'm getting off. See if I can find a field or a ditch. Must have been that chile I ate, it was so hot but I hated to let it go to waste. I hope my woman is alright . . . carrying the baby and all. This driver we have this year is a good one. He keeps on going. He doesn't stop for anything. Just gases up and let's go. We've been on the road for over twenty-four hours. We should be close to Des Moines." As they ride in their trucks, and toward the end of the novel, the workers—in a collective cantatory voice—imagine that moment "when we arrive, when we arrive."[24] The imagined arrival in the Midwest becomes a mobile metaphor for the arrival of these oppressed farmworkers at social justice.

This is not to say that social justice is unequivocally located in the Midwest. In his short sketch "The Salamanders," Rivera tells us of an unkind farmer near Crystal Lake, Iowa, who, during a rainstorm, will not let Rivera's people pitch their tents near his house, forcing them into the wetter areas of his beet fields where they will be set upon by salamanders in the middle of the night.[25]

And, yet, in "The Great Plains as Refuge in Chicano Literature," Rivera gives us some reason to think that the Midwest had at least a more benign social character than that of Texas. "As a child I became aware of various differences between the people we worked for in Texas and the people we worked with in *el norte*. Perhaps just here in these words—worked *for* and worked *with*—is the main difference." But Rivera also makes a paradoxical discovery: he discovers immigrants in the Midwest, although initially not the Mexican kind, as he tells us that he "first realized what an immigrant was in the late 1940s in Duncan, Iowa. . . . To me the first real immigrant was Peter Falada, a member of the Czech colony in Duncan, Iowa. Upon our arrival, he asked us one question: 'When did you come over from the Old Country?' I was born in Texas, . . . so although we were strangers to Iowa, I had never considered myself an immigrant. But my father said, 'I came from the Old Country in 1915.' 'We beat you by five years' was Falada's reply." Falada was a man perhaps something like Willa Cather's Anton Rosicky in neighboring Nebraska. "For the first time," says Rivera, "I saw my father as an immigrant."[26]

Tomás Rivera was originally from Crystal City, Texas, a small agricultural town in south Texas surrounded by spinach fields almost wholly owned by the Del Monte Corporation. From these humble and oppressed beginnings, he went on to a higher education and was chancellor of the University of California at

Riverside in the 1970s while he was writing *Y no se lo tragó la tierra*. But for a fleeting change of mind on the part of his parents, he well might have become a permanent midwesterner, perhaps graduating from a midwestern university, although he did receive his doctorate at the University of Oklahoma in Norman.

Critical Regionalism

But as is well-known in Mexican American studies, Crystal City had another major place in the Mexican American imaginary. In the 1960s Mexican Americans were successful in wresting political power from the dominant Anglo-American power structure in Crystal City, including Del Monte, an often-rehearsed triumphalist episode in Mexican American historiography of Texas. What was not very well-known until recently is the way in which this victory in south Texas had clear ramifications in the Midwest. In his aptly titled *The Tejano Diaspora*, historian Marc Rodriguez has shown in detail how the political triumph of Mexican Americans in Crystal City was then, through the migrant labor stream, transplanted into successful political action in the Midwest, especially in Wisconsin. The latter activity, by the way, also included Tejano participation in the founding of academic Chicana/o studies programs at the universities of Wisconsin, Michigan–Ann Arbor, Michigan State, and Minnesota. Rodriguez concludes, "As a result of the quiet victories that resulted from activism in Texas and Wisconsin, Tejano children stayed in school longer, found better jobs within the working class, and, as time went on, entered colleges and universities at both ends of the diaspora."[27] However, we might also wish to note the manner in which midwestern universities—but especially the University of Michigan—trained a cadre of Texas-based scholars, educators, attorneys, and social workers, who then returned to Texas to participate in struggle and social change, beginning in the early twentieth century with attorney J. T. Canales, and going through to the present day with Carlos Arce, Quintín Vargas, Arturo Nelson-Cisneros, Yolanda Padilla, and others.

The foregoing sketches out some major instances of the Mexican American interplay between the two regions of Texas and the Midwest, without privileging one or the other. That is, while Tejanos brought their cultural and political resources into social struggle in the Midwest, it is also clear that their experience in the Midwest, with its greater latitude of political and social opportunity but also the sheer experience of distancing from Texas, proved to be invaluable resources that those who returned to Texas then brought to bear upon the social struggle in that state. We cannot imagine, for example, the work of Tomás Rivera without his journeys to the Midwest, and his novel serves as a record but also a critical diagnostic instrument in both regional cases. The pilgrimage site of Don Pedrito Jaramillo may be in south Texas, but he serves as a resource of hope, lessening anxiety for a family picking strawberries in Ohio. Question Mark and the Mysterians may have started with traditional Texan Mexican musical forms, but they push the expressive envelope decisively in the more open musical culture of Michigan with their "96 Tears."

Cheryl Herr but also Douglas Powell have elaborated the concept of critical regionalism after Kenneth Frampton to argue that within dominance of an encompassing capitalist modernity and post-modernity, discrete regions may generate resistive native cultural practices.[28] Eschewing any autonomous "authenticity," Herr sees such practices as sometimes encompassing selected forms of modernity itself in creative and often unpredictable ways but in paradoxical counterpoint to the very dominance of modernity. After Deleuze, she terms these assemblages, "to designate [constructions] composed variously of elements from regions that history has twinned." The assemblage, she continues, occupies "a continuum that includes additive bricolage, inventive code-breaking, and other forms of amalgamation and reconstruction."[29] Her chosen regions for testing these formulations are Ireland and the Irish presence in Iowa sharing a more or less common migratory history. For his part, in his work on Appalachia, Powell argues that "critical regionalism can use the construction of region to interconnect more fully, rather than disconnect, local places to broader patterns of politics, history and culture."[30]

Within such formulations and still under reflection, I am led to wonder if the Mexican-U.S. and Texas-midwestern regional and twinned relationship is construable in these terms, given the operation of these mobile and creative regions under an encompassing capitalist modernity but one now also inflected by race in a way not as evident in Herr's Irish data. As she further notes, between discrete though not radically separate regional spaces, "viewers would attend particularly to the role of economic historical events in producing perceived symmetries and to the transplanting of seemingly local issues from one place to another through migrating populations. In many instances, they could discern and begin to compose together a unified history of socioeconomic exchange and of aesthetic production."[31] This observation seems to me quite apt for capturing without regionally essentializing what happened with Mexican Americans between Texas and the Midwest from "El Corrido de Kiansis," to Tomas Rivera's novel, to "96 Tears" and possibly through the present day.

I have offered but a preliminary sketch of this particular interregional relationship that remains to be much more fully fleshed out with additional data and experiences. For example, were there other and probably more contemporary *corridos* speaking to this experience? Other forms of popular culture such as foodways? Other literary creations? Other instances of political mobilization? Many individuals who made the initial and substantial journeys from Texas in the first half of the twentieth century are still living and available as oral history sources, but conversely, what is the current state of such interregional migration at the present moment and with social media now available? Is there here a useful model for understanding other dynamic Mexican-U.S. and Latina/o interregional migratory experiences? Even the traditional Texas-California circuit remains understudied in these terms, as certainly does the contemporary current influx of Mexicans into the U.S. South. Current intellectual trends correctly call on us to examine transnational relationships in American studies, but we must not forget the national American experience, but now understood in dynamic and theoretically conceptualized interregional terms. For many Mexican Americans, such specific, though fluid, U.S. trans-localities may turn out to be their central social definition rather than either discrete, fixed regionalisms (south Texas, northern New Mexico, East Los Angeles) or a generalized transnationalism between ancestral home countries and the United States. I am wholly convinced that Texas and the Midwest forged just such an identity for Mexican Americans from the cattle drives of the nineteenth century well into our own time.

Notes

1. Willie Morris, *North toward Home* (New York: Houghton-Mifflin, 1967).

2. "Henry B. Gonzalez, Early Life and Entry into Politics," Briscoe Center for American History, University of Texas at Austin, www.cah.utexas.edu/feature/0611/bio_three.php.

3. Américo Paredes, *"With His Pistol in His Hand": A Border Ballad and Its Hero* (Austin: University of Texas Press, 1958).

4. José R. López-Morín, *The Legacy of Américo Paredes* (College Station: Texas A&M University Press, 2006); Ramón Saldívar, *The Borderlands of Culture: Américo Paredes and the Transnational Imaginary* (Durham, N.C.: Duke University Press, 2006); Manuel F. Medrano, *Américo Paredes: In His Own Words, an Authorized Biography* (Denton: University of North Texas Press, 2010); José E. Limón, *Américo Paredes: Culture and Critique* (Austin: University of Texas Press, 2012).

5. Andrés Sáenz, *Early Tejano Ranching: Daily Life at Ranchos San José and El Fresnillo* (College Station: Texas A&M University Press, 1999).

6. Américo Paredes, *A Texas-Mexican Cancionero: Folksongs of the Lower Border* (Urbana: University of Illinois Press, 1976), 25.

7. Ibid.

8. Wayne Gard, *The Chisholm Trail* (Norman: University of Oklahoma Press, 1979).

9. Paredes, *Texas-Mexican Cancionero*, 25.

10. Ibid.

11. David Montejano, *Anglos and Mexicans in the Making of Texas, 1836–1986* (Austin: University of Texas Press, 1987).

12. Ibid.

13. Zaragosa Vargas, *Proletarians of the North: A History of Mexican Industrial Workers in Detroit and the Midwest, 1917–1933* (Berkeley: University of California Press, 1993), 14.

14. George J. Sánchez, *Becoming Mexican American: Ethnicity, Culture, and Identity in Chicano Los Angeles* (New York: Oxford University Press, 1995).

15. Vargas, *Proletarians of the North*, 18–19.

16. Ibid., 28–31.

17. Elaine A. Peña, *Performing Piety: Making Space Sacred with the Virgin of Guadalupe* (Berkeley: University of California Press, 2011).

18. Octavio V. Romano, "Charismatic Medicine, Folk-Healing, and Folk-Sainthood," *American Anthropologist* 67 (1965): 1151–73.

19. Manuel Peña, *Música Tejana: The Cultural Economy of Artistic Transformation* (College Station: Texas A&M University Press, 1999), and *The Texas-Mexican Conjunto: History of a Working-Class Music* (Austin: University of Texas Press, 1985).

20. David Harnish, "Tejano Music in the Urbanizing Midwest: The Musical Story of *Conjunto* Master Jesse Ponce," *Journal of the Society for American Music* 3 (2009): 195–219, 196, 197, 209.

21. "Question Mark and the Mysterians Biography," Sing365: More than Lyrics, updated Aug. 12, 2014, www.sing365.com. Question Mark and the Mysterians, "96 Tears," *YouTube*, uploaded Nov. 8, 2006, www.youtube.com/watch?v=XeolH-kzx4c.

22. Rolando Hinojosa, *The Valley* (Tempe: Bilingual Press, 1983), 47.

23. Tomás Rivera, "The Great Plains as Refuge in Chicano Literature," in *Tomás Rivera: The Complete Works*, ed. Julián Olivares (Houston: Arte Público Press, 2008 [1985]), 319.

24. Tomás Rivera, *Y no se lo tragó la tierra/And the Earth Did Not Devour Him*, in *Tomás Rivera*, 115, 118.

25. Tomás Rivera, "Las salamandras" / "The Salamanders," in *Tomás Rivera*, 127–30, 159–61.

26. Rivera, "Great Plains as Refuge," 319.

27. Marc Simon Rodriguez, *Tejano Diaspora: Mexican Americanism and Ethnic Politics in Texas and Wisconsin* (Chapel Hill: University of North Carolina Press, 2011), 158.

28. Cheryl Temple Herr, *Critical Regionalism and Cultural Studies: From Ireland to the American Midwest* (Gainesville: University Press of Florida, 1996); Douglas Reichert Powell, *Critical Regionalism: Connecting Politics and Culture in the American Landscape* (Chapel Hill: University of North Carolina Press, 2007).

29. Herr, *Critical Regionalism*, 11.

30. Powell, *Critical Regionalism*, 26.

31. Herr, *Critical Regionalism*, 7.

Appendix

El Corrido de Kiansis (The Ballad of Kansas)

Cuando salimos pa' Kiansis con una grande corrida, gritaba mi caporal: —Les encargo a mi querida.—	When we left for Kansas on a big cattle drive, My caporal shouted, "Take good care of my beloved."
Contesta otro caporal: —No tengas cuidado, es sola; que la mujer que es honrada aunque viva entre la bola.—	Another caporal replied, "Have no fear, she has no other loves; For if a woman is virtuous, no matter if she lives among men."

Quinientos novillos eran,
todos grandes y livianos,
y entre treinta americanos
no los podían embalar.

Five hundred steers there were,
all big and quick;
Thirty American boys
could not keep them bunched together.

Llegan cinco mexicanos,
todos bien enchivarrados,
y en menos de un cuarto de hora
los tenían encerrados.

Then five Mexicans arrive,
all of them wearing good chaps;
And in less than a quarter-hour,
they had the steers penned up.

Esos cinco mexicanos
al momento los echaron,
y los treinta americanos
se quedaron azorados.

Those five Mexicans
penned up the steers in a moment,
And the thirty Americans
were left staring in amazement.

Los novillos eran bravos,
no se podían soportar,
gritaba un Americano:
—Que se baje el caporal.—

The steers were vicious,
it was very hard to hold them;
An American shouted,
"Let the caporal go into the corral."

Pero el caporal no quiso
y un vaquero se arrojó;
a que lo matara el toro,
nomás a eso se bajó.

But the caporal refused,
and a vaquero took the dare;
He got himself killed by the bull,
that's all he managed to do.

La mujer de Alberto Flores
le pregunta al caporal:
—Déme usted razón de mi hijo,
que no lo he visto llegar.—

The wife of Alberto Flores
asks of the caporal,
"Give me word of my son,
I have not seen him arrive."

—Señora, yo le diría,
pero se pone a llorar;
lo mató un toro fortino
en las trances de un corral.—

"Lady, I would tell you,
but I know that you will cry;
he was killed by a bull with a blazed face
against the rails of a corral."

Ya con ésta me despido
por 'l amor de mi querida,
ya les canté a mis amigos
los versos de la corrida.

Now with this I say farewell,
by my sweetheart's love;
I have now sung for my friends
the stanzas about the cattle drive.

Reshaping the Rural Heartland

Immigration and Migrant Cultural Practice in Small-Town America

AIDÉ ACOSTA

Every September, residents in the town of Lorraine in rural east-central Illinois celebrate the town's heritage as "broomcorn capital."[1] During the three-day annual festival, residents along with regional visitors eat, drink, shop, and learn how to make old-fashioned corn brooms while bluegrass and country music plays in the background. The town's festival is also an ethnographic moment of the changing demographics and social life of small-town Middle America. Mexican residents partake with fellow residents in the festivities, also enjoying turkey legs and onion blossoms as the children ride in the temporary Ferris wheel. The presence of Mexican residents, however, is generally invisible to local residents, who do not imagine the settlement of Mexican "newcomers" as part and parcel of the migration and broomcorn heritage of Lorraine. Mexicans in Lorraine are part of the changing geography of Latino migration into local settings, and becoming present in unexpected spaces and places, including the rural heartland.

While broomcorn material is now mostly imported, chiefly from Mexico, the local broom industry is the primary labor recruiter of Mexican migrants from the town of Jiménez in northern Mexico, Lorraine's counterpart in broom production. Although nowadays brooms are primarily produced with synthetic materials, the legacy of broomcorn production and the broom industry in Lorraine continue to be central in the residents' quotidian lives and in the local heritage. Broomcorn is a type of sorghum with long, fibrous seed stalks used as the working end of brooms. When fully grown, the plant has long green stalks similar to that of corn plants. During the late nineteenth century, Lorraine became the epicenter of broomcorn production, hence the town's legacy as "broomcorn capital of the world." During this period, Illinois became the primary producer of broomcorn in the United States, giving rise to the industrial production of

1.3.1 "Haciendo las escobas / Making the brooms." Mexican workers show spectators how to make old-fashioned brooms at the annual broom-corn festival in Lorraine, Illinois. Photo courtesy of Aidé Acosta.

brooms. The local broom industries, now expansive producers of housewares cleaning supplies, rely on Mexican labor to sustain the economic viability of the local companies and consequently the town of Lorraine.

The Mexican population in Lorraine significantly expanded during the 1990s, mirroring the broader demographic patterns in the region and the Midwest more generally. The majority of Mexican migrants in Lorraine originated from Jiménez, a small city near Monterrey in the state of Nuevo León in northern Mexico. Jiménez is also a major producer of corn brooms and known as the broom capital in Mexico. Consequently, the Lorraine population forms part of the transnational capital of broom production through their labor, as well as in the legacy of broom production of these two transnational sites. Mexicans began settling in Lorraine following the labor recruitment of seven men in 1967. At this time, these workers were recruited directly from Jiménez by the broom factory in Illinois. Shortly afterward, their families accompanied them, and subsequently created an extensive social and kin network that runs through Nuevo León, Texas, and Illinois. The family-owned broom company in Lorraine is among the small-town manufacturing companies that have attracted migrants. Mexicans comprise 90 to 95 percent of the workforce.[2] Today, Lorraine and Jiménez constitute a transnational migrant circuit, in which people, items, ideas, and emotions circulate in a continuous basis along this migrant corridor.

During the 1980s, Latinos began another wave of permanently settling down in small and rural towns outside of gateway destinations such as Chicago and Los Angeles.[3] Rapid and widespread growth in income and employment in the region provided the economic incentives for Latinas/os to migrate to new settlement regions in growing numbers by the 1990s. While this population is frequently referenced as the newcomers, they are in fact actors of a larger historical journey into the Midwest. At the beginning of the twentieth century, Mexican workers were recruited for various industries, primarily to work in agricultural fields and in the railroad and steel industries.[4] Nonetheless, during the 1990s the Latino population significantly expanded in regions with no previous significant history of Latino settlement, including the rural heartland. Latino populations are permanently settling and now calling small-town America home. It is now no longer a surprise to celebrate *quinceañeras* (coming-of-age celebrations) in the local parishes, or *jaripeos* (Mexican rodeos) in the local fairgrounds.

Through settlement and migrant cultural practice, Latinos are reshaping the American heartland, a place they also call home. The U.S. Bureau of the Census identifies twelve states as the midwestern region: Illinois, Indiana, Iowa, Kansas, Michigan, Minnesota, Missouri, Nebraska, North Dakota, Ohio, South Dakota, and Wisconsin. The heartland encompasses these locations, but also references this spatial region as a construction that does not have stark boundaries and includes the cultural constructions of this space as the heart of American culture. Although contradictory, the heartland is often associated with the image of small-town and pastoral life considered to be at the heart of Americanness. In this chapter I discuss the various ways in which contemporary Latino migration and settlement destabilizes the static notion of the American heartland as a quaint and unchanging place. I argue that in engaging diasporic cultural practice, migrants are invoking practice as a way of telling their *own migrant stories* in response to being treated as marked cultural, classed, gendered, and racial actors throughout the United States.

New Cartographies of Latino Migration

Several factors have impacted the contemporary cartographies of Latino migration, including employment and economic opportunities along with industrial growth in the Midwest, and changes in immigration law and increased surveillance along border states. While external factors have significantly altered migration patterns, individuals also engage in rationalized decision making as they seek to broaden their individual and collective opportunities. In this way, the rural heartland has become a place of economic and employment opportunities for Latino migrants, but also for the myriad opportunities and calmer lifestyle in comparison to urban cities. For migrants, these rural communities also offer a quaintness that often mirrors the experiences of their homeland, along with lower costs of living, lower crime rates, and a slower pace of life. In short, while economic and employment opportunities have offset the changes in the contemporary cartographies of Latino migration, the rural heartland is also attractive for migrants seeking an alternative lifestyle to urban centers and away from border states, where the threat of deportability is exacerbated with the constant physical presence of immigration agencies.

The contemporary migration shifts in the United States are intimately linked with neoliberal economic restructuring.[5] In Mexico, the implementation of the North American Free Trade Agreement (NAFTA) has widened the gaps of inequality, facilitating an exodus of emigration. Simultaneously, with neoliberal practices of downsizing and outsourcing, cheap labor became a necessity for U.S. industries. The intensified growth of Mexican labor migrants in midwestern rural areas is linked to the restructuring of agriculture and food processing, which in turn has caused a widespread reliance on Latino labor. Rubén O. Martínez argues that despite deindustrialization in the Midwest, labor demands in the service sector have contributed to the geographic dispersion of Latinos.[6] Latinas/os have become overrepresented in nonunionized poorly paid jobs, which are often monotonous and dangerous.[7] In Lorraine, for example, shoulder injuries are frequent for employees in the broom industry. Workers are exposed to the repetitiveness of pulling fibers to mold brooms that frequently lead to injuries.

The growth in employment opportunities in the region provided the economic incentives for Latinas/os to migrate to new settlement regions during the 1990s. The expansion of the Latino population throughout the Midwest is linked to the expansion of regional industries, including the meatpacking and poultry industries.[8] In Lorraine, the broom company consolidated its production under one roof during the 1980s. The company invested heavily during this time period, and became one of the largest virtually integrated houseware facilities in the country. Moreover, since the 1980s, the company has expanded its product lines to become the leading manufacturer of high-quality brooms, mops, and brushes in the United States. The company is increasing its market goals by seeking to become a major transnational supplier, and is currently a major supplier for large enterprises, such as Walmart and Lowe's. In light of NAFTA, this company serves an important role in supplying these large corporations that are presently expanding throughout North America.

In addition to economic growth and employment opportunities, immigration legislation during the 1980s also served as a catalyst for the demographic growth of Latinas/os throughout the Midwest and into other nontraditional migrant settlements across the United States. The passing of the 1986 Immigration Reform and Control Act (IRCA) offset migration out of gateway destinations since labor competition tightened with newly authorized workers.[9] Additionally, the Special Agricultural Workers (SAW) provision under IRCA provided legal residency for workers working in agriculture, also encouraging agricultural workers into the fields of the Midwest. At the backdrop of legalization was also an increased anti-immigrant debate, particularly in border states, including Proposition 187 in

1994 in California that sought to deny social services to migrant populations.[10] It is under this context that during the decade of the 1990s, according to Jorge Durand and his colleagues, while the percentage of migrants into traditional gateway destinations dropped, the percentage migrating into non-gateway destinations significantly increased. Latinas/os left historical migrant enclaves in search of opportunities elsewhere, including the rural Midwest.[11]

The migration experience of the Zepeda family from Jiménez into Lorraine illustrates these changes. Alfredo began a circular migration to the United States in the 1980s via Texas. In 1988, he was able to legalize his status under SAW. Soon after, his wife, Irene, and two sons legalized through the Family Reunification clause under the Immigration and Nationality Act of 1965. Their daughter no longer qualified since she was married at the time of the legal proceedings. Upon Irene's residency approval in 1998, Irene, Alfredo, and their youngest son relocated from Jiménez, Nuevo León, to Texas. Entering through El Paso, they settled in Odessa and worked in the service industry. Earlier that year, their eldest son, Miguel, had migrated to Illinois on the encouragement of kin. Alfredo recalls how the move arose from of the knowledge that in the town of Lorraine there was abundant employment, "pues él se vino por medio de toda la gente de aquí que es del mismo pueblo" (through all the people here who are from the same town), he tells me. Following their eldest son, the Zepedas relocated from Odessa, Texas, to Lorraine, Illinois, in April 2000.

Irene and Alfredo worked in the local broom factory until 2004, when they opened their small food business, Tacos El Norte. The migration of the Zepedas into the Midwest was a choice they made in relationship to family reunification, their knowledge of the economic and employment opportunities in the Midwest, and embedded in immigration legislations that facilitated their mobility. In relocating from northern Mexico to Odessa and into Lorraine they have tapped into their own bodies of knowledge, what Carlos Vélez-Ibáñez calls "transborder funds of knowledge" in creating opportunities for themselves and their family.[12]

Latinas/os make decisions of settlement given various circumstances they face in their lives and in search of their own well-being. These decisions, while often tied to the effects of the global economy, are also tied to various structural disparities and quotidian experiences. Women's decisions to migrate into new arenas are also correlated with the ongoing effects of patriarchy and of social inequalities. This was the case for Estefanía García, who migrated to Lorraine from the state of Jalisco in 2007. She decided to leave Jalisco with her four children after being subjected to her husband's physical and sexual assaults. After seeking help in various agencies in Mexico without any success, she made the strategic decision to leave the country for her own physical and emotional well-being, and in search of opportunities for her children.

Migration for Estefania was literally her option for survival out of an abusive relationship and failed governmental system that maintains women like her in a marginal position. At the same time, she felt a lack of support due to her father's belief that marriage should be forever, "Porque él decía, tú te casaste, va a ser para el resto de tu vida" (because he would tell me, you married and it will be for the rest of your life), she tells me. Estefania had to leave her town to seek safety elsewhere. She learned about employment opportunities in Lorraine from extended family members, who also helped her reach Illinois along with her children. "Aquí estoy feliz" (here, I am happy), she responds after sharing with me the struggle of dealing with depression and overcoming the trauma of being psychologically, emotionally, and physically abused. Where people migrate is also tied to notions of well-being for the family in addition to established networks. Estefania decided to relocate in Lorraine rather than to Chicago, because she felt that the calmer small-life life was best for her and her children. Her decision to move to Lorraine was propelled by a desire for safety, which town life provides for her and her family.

The experiences of both the Zepedas and Estefania mirror the broader ways in which people engage in rationalized decision making to ensure their survival and success. In the process, migrants seek to create the spaces and structures that alleviate the sense of disconnection from their places of origin by creating strong social bonds with other residents and constructing the cultural spaces that remind them of home while being at home in the heartland. Although migration can represent a traumatic dislocation from a geographical place, as well as cultural familiarity, individuals create spaces to alleviate the sense of isolation. This adaptation is particularly manifested in migrant cultural practice. As Latinas/os settle and make themselves at home through diasporic cultural practice, they also transform the rural landscapes into welcoming spaces of cultural familiarity.

In east-central Illinois, Latinas/os occupy two major migration patterns: seasonal and permanent. As with the earlier seasonal migration cycles of the early 1900s, Tejanas/os continue to occupy a significant role in seasonal agricultural labor.[13] Every year, seasonal migrants travel from the Lower Rio Grande Valley of Texas, principally from McAllen, to east-central Illinois for corn detasseling.[14] The migrants work long days, seven days a week for approximately three weeks following the 4th of July. They are brought to these Midwest rural communities by Texas recruiters who are aligned with large companies of the Midwest as well as area landowners. The recruiters, of Mexican origin themselves, are responsible for organizing cohorts of migrants to this region.[15] The migrants arrive to the rural communities in their own vehicles, many in large SUVs, with minimal to no money at all.[16] Most travel in groups or families with minimal essentials: clothing, toiletries, pots and pans, and maybe some food. Not all of them are as fortunate, however. Arriving at the Midwest already in debt from the money required for the travel, many migrants are forced to seek food from family they have not seen since the previous season. They also look for assistance from social services agencies, the recruiters themselves, or from other migrants.

The town of Air City, located in northern Champaign County in east-central Illinois, is host to a number of seasonal migrants during the hot and humid summers. Migrants begin arriving in the last days of June and begin work after the July 4th holiday. While many seasonal agricultural workers follow the various harvests, such as planting melons in Indiana and harvesting cherries and asparagus in Michigan or the potatoes fields in Idaho, and eventually return to the Lower Rio Grande Valley of Texas, many have also opted out of the agricultural migrant circuit and permanently settle in east-central Illinois. They find employment as service employees and/or in the local industries, including Solo Cup and Plastipak.

Tejanas/os along with Mexican and Guatemalan migrants are creating various migrant communities throughout east-central Illinois and as such are transforming the region through their settlement and cultural practices. As migrants settle, they engage in cultural activities and establish businesses that enrich their own individual and collective lives in their new places of settlement, as well as the local community life.

Migrants are dramatically shifting the rural landscapes of east-central Illinois. The small town of Lorraine, at the heart of Amish settlements since the late 1800s, for example, is presently home to several hundred Mexicans who have migrated from the same town in northern Mexico. Mexicans in Lorraine, like the Zepedas, are part of a diasporic network that connects people in Nuevo León, Texas, and Illinois. The Mexican community in Lorraine has significantly expanded in the last three decades.

According to the 2010 Census, "Hispanics" constitute 20 percent of the Lorraine population of three thousand residents. Moreover, the school demographics demonstrate that it is a fairly young population. The interactive Illinois Report Card illustrates that in 2012, at the high school level (7–12), 55.5 percent of the student population was white, while 41.2 percent was "Hispanic." This represented nearly a two-fold increase since 2005, when 74 percent of the student population was white, and 25 percent was "Hispanic."[17] At the elementary level (K–6), 56.1 percent of the population was white and 39.4 percent was "Hispanic" in 2012. Moreover, by 2012 both schools were showing a multiracial student demographic for the first time. At the high school level, 1.2 percent of the student population was multiracial, and at the elementary level, 2.6 percent of the student population was multiracial. The "multiracial" category, which was still fairly new in 2012, signals the interracial dynamics of intimate relations in everyday lives of Lorraine.

These demographics herald the future of Lorraine, where almost half of the student population is Mexican and continuously changing. The intimate discomfort currently felt about the changing local demographics by "old-timers" will transform with future generations, and particularly as the second generation of migrants engage with their peers in the various activities and socialization practices at the heart of small-town life. Nonetheless, the present demographics of Lorraine are visually present throughout the small town, with Mexican businesses, including a *taquería*, a *carnicería*, and a *tortillería*, contributing economically to the town. Businesses also importantly act as venues for social and cultural exchanges. Such interactions and items for sale, along with the visuals and familiar smells, foster a sense of home for migrants residing thousands of miles away from their places of origin. These places also transform the social landscapes of the rural heartland.

The American Heartland as Home

The changes in these new arenas have caused widespread panic and fear of the "Latino threat," as Leo Chavez has argued.[18] While working-class Latinos creatively thrive under the harsh circumstances they often confront, their hosts frequently greet them with a racist—and in some instances violent—welcoming fueled by decades of animosity against Mexicans. Latinas/os are frequently settling in towns and villages that have been homogenously white over several generations given the particular histories and experiences of these places. For example, many have a history as sundown towns that until recently had the unwritten law that decreed that no person of color be caught in town after dusk.[19]

Contemporary debates continue to embody de-humanizing practices against working class migrants. Mexicans, irrespectively of citizenship, continue to be constructed within racializing discourses of "illegal" and "alien." They represent disembodied beings, as anthropologist Michael Kearney (1998) argued, whose labor is desired, but not their lives.[20] One example is the passing of HR4437 in 2005, the Border Protection, Antiterrorist, and Illegal Immigration Control Act proposed by midwestern congressman James Sensenbrenner, but which failed to pass the Senate; along with subsequent local ordinances, including in Hazleton, Pennsylvania, and Carpentersville, Illinois, and the passing of Arizona's SB1070 (in 2010) and copycat statewide policies across the United States, including in Alabama's HB56 (in 2011) and Indiana's HB590 (in 2011). Local ordinances have been challenged and deemed unconstitutional. Similarly, statewide policies continue to be challenged and central in the current anti-immigrant debates.

The expansions of these various legislations throughout the United States illustrate the ways in which demographic shifts in the heartland have implications in law and policy. It is no coincidence that HR4437 was proposed by James Sensen-brenner, a midwesterner. While the bill failed at the Senate level given its unequivo-cal draconian anti-immigrant nature, it nonetheless offset a virulent immigration debate. HR4437 represented the consolidation of an anti-immigrant debate in public opinion and policy following Proposition 187 in California.[21] At the same time, it signals the ways in which the personal discomfort that is taking place at the inti-mate level as the faces of "new" neighbors change is implicated in contemporary anti-immigrant ideologies that inform public policy, and that has real implications at the individual levels. Nonetheless, these policies and the attached discourses have served as a catalyst for a virulent immigration debate and for a transnational movement for immigrant and human rights of the twenty-first century. It is within a context of the margins and anti-immigrant politics that people create alternative ways of belonging to counter legal and sociopolitical constructions.

In the rural Midwest, Latinas/os engage in various cultural practices in the process of inventing a sense of home. It has become common to celebrate *quincea-ñeras* in local parishes and Mexican-style rodeos in the region's fairgrounds. Cultural celebrations and religious rituals such as Las Posadas, El Día de los Muertos, La Virgen de Guadalupe, and Santa Eulalia—the patron saint of Gua-temalan migrants in the area—have all been significant moments in the develop-ment of the migrant community in the region. As diasporic practices, cultural and religious rituals organized by migrants are not only channels that help them maintain connections to their backgrounds and histories, but are also politi-cal sites of culture in the current anti-immigrant context. Diaspora as practice is also counter-discourse given that migrants are invoking practice as a way of telling their *own migrant stories* in response to being treated as marked cultural, classed, gendered, and racial actors in a new geography. These events celebrate traditional cultural practices in the context of the denial of their existence, and visually demonstrate to the larger community their affirmation of belonging, and as cultural citizens.[22] Cultural citizenship refers to the various sociopolitical struggles and demands a distinct social space for Latinas/os in the United States.

Latinas/os have become visually present in the rural heartland in the formal and quotidian settings. In Lorraine, Mexicans have been present for over four decades since the recruitment of seven workers from Jiménez in northern Mexico. Yet they are not included or imagined as part of the social fabric of small-town Middle America. In the annual broomcorn festival, Mexicans—the primary labor force behind the local broom industry—partake in the festivities on the margins and as speculators. For example, in figure 1.3.1, "haciendo las escobas," two Mexi-can employees from Jiménez illustrate to the public how to make old-fashioned brooms, the annual activity at the festival sponsored by one of the local family-owned companies. The workers are not imagined as the viability of the town through their lives, labor, and economic contributions, but rather remain in the background, while broomcorn takes center stage of the town's past and present legacy.

The broom industry is the primary economic viability of the town, and subsequently it is the migrant Latino labor that sustains the town's vibrancy. As Latinas/os have settled in places with no significant history of Latino settlement, the changes in these "new" arenas create localized and intimate discomfort, which becomes implicated in policy and public discourse. Nonetheless, through cultural practices, migrants are partaking in the reshaping the American heartland, a place they also call home.

Notes

1. Pseudonyms are used for all places and people in this chapter.

2. Stephen J. Lyons, "Nuevos Americanos: Is the Current Influx of Latinos so Different from Past Immigrations?," *LAS News* (University of Illinois, Urbana-Champaign), fall/winter 2005–6, www.las.illinois.edu/alumni.

3. Ann Millard and Jorge Chapa, eds., *Apple Pie and Enchiladas: Latino Newcomers in the Rural Midwest* (Austin: University of Texas Press, 2004).

4. Paul S. Taylor, *Mexican Labor in the United States* (New York: Arno Press, 1975 [1932]); Dennis Nodín Valdés, *Al Norte: Agricultural Workers in the Great Lakes Region, 1917–1970* (Austin: University of Texas Press, 1991); Juan R. García, *Mexicans in the Midwest, 1900–1932* (Tucson: University of Arizona Press, 1996).

5. Gustavo Del Castillo, "NAFTA and the Struggle for Neoliberalism: Mexico's Elusive Quest for First World Status," in *Neoliberalism Revisited: Economic Restructuring and Mexico's Political Future*, ed. G. Otero (Boulder, Colo.: Westview Press, 1996); Lisa Duggan, *The Twilight of Equality? Neoliberalism, Cultural Politics, and the Attack on Democracy* (Boston: Beacon Press, 2003); David Harvey, *A Brief History of Neoliberalism* (New York: Oxford University Press, 2005); David Fitzgerald, "Inside the Sending State: The Politics of Mexican Emigration Control," *International Migration Review* 40 (2006): 259–93.

6. Rubén O. Martínez, *Latinos in the Midwest* (East Lansing: Michigan State University, 2011), 6.

7. Douglas S. Massey, *New Faces in New Places: The Changing Geography of American Immigration* (New York: Russell Sage Foundation, 2008).

8. Millard and Chapa, *Apple Pie and Enchiladas*.

9. Eileen Diaz McConnell, "Latinos in the Rural Midwest: The Twentieth-Century Historical Context Leading to Contemporary Challenges," in *Apple Pie and Enchiladas: Latino Newcomers to the Rural Midwest*, ed. Ann V. Millard and Jorge Chapa (Austin: University of Texas Press, 2004), 26–40; Jorge Durand, Douglas S. Massey, and Chiara Capoferro, "The New Geography of Mexican Immigration," in *New Destinations: Mexican Immigration in the United States*, ed. Victor Zúñiga and Rúben Hernández-León (New York: Russell Sage, 2005), 1–20.

10. Leo Chavez, *The Latino Threat: Constructing Immigrants, Citizens and the Nation* (Stanford, Calif.: Stanford University Press, 2008).

11. Durand, Massey, and Capoferro, "New Geography of Mexican Immigration."

12. Carlos Vélez-Ibáñez, "Regions of Refuge in the United States: Issues, Problems and Concerns for the Future of Mexican-Origin Populations in the United States," Malinowski Award Lectures, *Human Organization* 63, no. 1 (2004): 1–20.

13. Marc Simon Rodriguez, "Defining the Space of Participation in a Northern City: Tejanos and the War on Poverty in Milwaukee," in *The War on Poverty: A New Grassroots History, 1964–1980*, ed. Annelise Orleck and Lisa Gayle Hazirjian (Athens: University of Georgia Press, 2011), 110–30.

14. Detasseling entails removing the long tassel to prevent cross-pollination.

15. Recruiters have been central in facilitating arrangements, often informal, for migrant workers and the employers. Dennis Nodín Valdés states that the recruiters, or *enganchistas*, played a significant role in recruiting laborers during the early migration of the twentieth century: "the *enganchistas* were hired by the companies and were sent to the border and into Mexico with the promise of seasonal work in the beet fields, good working conditions and high pay." Dennis Nodín Valdés, *Al Norte*, 9.

16. Guillermina Gina Núñez discusses the importance of investing in vehicles for migrant families, whose lives are defined by mobility. Guillermina Gina Núñez, "The Political Ecology of Colonias in the Hatch Valley: Towards an Applied Social Science of the U.S.-Mexico Border" (PhD diss., University of California, Riverside, 2006). Rather than investing in homes, migrant workers invest in vehicles that will be reliable for the travels they must embark on throughout the year. This reflects Gloria Anzaldúa's concept of carrying home on the back. Gloria Anzaldúa, *Borderlands/La Frontera: The New Mestiza*, 3rd ed. (San Francisco: Aunt Lute Books, 2007).

17. Illinois Report Card, Oct. 31, 2012, www.IllinoisReportCard.com.

18. Chavez, *Latino Threat*.

19. James W. Loewen, *Sundown Towns: A Hidden Dimension of American Racism* (New York: New Press, 2005).

20. Michael Kearney, "Transnationalism in California and Mexico at the End of Empire," in *Border Identities: Nation and State at International Frontiers*, ed. Thomas M. Wilson and Hastings Donnan (Cambridge: Cambridge University Press, 1998), 117–41.

21. Alfonso Gonzales, "The 2006 Mega Marchas in Greater Los Angeles: Counter-Hegemonic Moment and the Future of El Migrante Struggle," *Latina/Latino Studies Journal* 7, no. 1 (2009): 30–59.

22. Renato Rosaldo, "Cultural Ethnicity and Educational Democracy." *Cultural Anthropology* 9, no. 3 (1994): 402–11; William V. Flores and Rina Benmayor, eds., *Latino Cultural Citizenship: Claiming Identity, Space, and Rights* (Boston: Beacon Press, 1997).

PART 2

Essential Laborers and Neighbors

Mexican Workers and Life
in South Chicago

MICHAEL INNIS-JIMÉNEZ

Mexicans entering South Chicago for the first time in the late 1910s and 1920s were met by massive buildings and towering smokestacks. For the people who came from the Mexican or U.S. countryside, the smokestacks spewing plumes of black smoke and ash framed by a gray, polluted sky, the large mill buildings, the stench, the rundown houses, the dirt alleyways littered with the refuse of everyday life, and the soot that covered everything had to have been daunting and disorienting. The sight of smoke rising from smokestacks through the illumination provided by the furnaces' glare welcomed those who entered the neighborhood after dark. They came to work despite the industrial pollution and miserable living conditions.

In 1911, only a few years before Mexican settlement, observers drew a vivid picture of South Chicago. Sophenisba Breckinridge and Edith Abbott, two leading Chicago academics and social workers, described South Chicago as an area with "great chimneys belching forth dense masses of smoke which hang over the neighborhood like clouds of darkness . . . so that no whiff of the air comes untainted." The neighborhood's air was tainted despite nearby Lake Michigan, the river, and the meadows surrounding South Chicago. So close to nature, yet so far from fresh air, the neighborhood was filled with "huge mills behind high paling fences" that blocked out most access to fresh air from the lake.[1] Changes to the neighborhood between this 1911 observation and the early stages of Mexican settlement were for the worse as the population grew, industry prospered, and modern sanitation requirements went largely unenforced in South Chicago. The steel mills expanded and the neighborhood became more crowded, as demand for steel during World War I kept steel mills running at or beyond official capacity.

Breckinridge and Abbott describe in fine detail the dismal conditions of wide "unkempt" streets with a "dreary succession of small frame dwellings, dull in color, frequently dilapidated, uninviting and monotonous." They paint a depressing and bland picture of a soot-covered existence. They go on to lament that with "magnificent enterprise" came a "hideous waste of human life" where "the men who feed the furnaces and send the products of their toilsome labor to a world market sleep in these miserable overcrowded houses" while having no decent places for relaxation and recreation other than the "low saloons and dives" of South Chicago.[2]

Why then did this neighborhood and this city become a destination for Mexican immigrants and Mexican Americans? Despite its somber, polluted landscape, South Chicago stood for economic opportunity and hope. Mexicanos came through the encouragement of friends, after being recruited in Mexico or along the border, or after years of working in other parts of the Midwest and West. For those who migrated here, this community was nothing less than social and economic opportunity. That being said, internal and external factors made positive change challenging. Much like new immigrant populations in the United States today, Mexicans in South Chicago dealt with economic hardship, ethnic prejudice, nativism, and intra-ethnic divisions. These factors reinforced their sense of difference and their propensity to see themselves as sojourners desiring eventually to return to Mexico. Individual Mexican and Mexican American South Chicagoans, including steel workers, shop owners, union organizers, and social workers, emerged as community leaders. They, along with others, formed communities that were able to change their physical and cultural environment to help their members and to create a degree of resistance that helped Mexicans persevere.

With few exceptions, historical studies of Mexicanos in the Midwest center around rural or small-town workers. While not minimizing the contributions of Mexicans outside of the city, understanding how and why Mexicans acted on the urban environment can help us better understand today's Mexican communities in cities like Chicago. Zaragosa Vargas's *Proletarians of the North* and Dionicio Nodín Valdés's *Barrios Norteños* focus on the Mexican communities of Detroit and St. Paul, respectively, as well as the Upper Midwest more generally. Additionally, several histories of Mexicans in Chicago have contributed to understanding the complexities and importance of these urban communities.[3]

Why did steel mill managers first start hiring Mexicans in 1919? They chose their employees based on shifting racial hierarchies of a city and a country in turmoil. Even as these hierarchies were based on mainstream ideologies of race, individual preferences for particular groups varied from individual to individual and also depended on the available labor pool. Managers who hired Mexicans did so out of a necessity created by their refusal to hire African Americans during labor strikes or worker shortages. A manager at East Chicago's Inland Steel said he started employing Mexicans in significant numbers in 1919. At that time, Inland Steel sent employment agents, or *enganchistas*, accompanied by Mexican employees to Texas in search of workers. Advancing them their transportation costs, Inland recruited around 150 single men plus some families in that first wave. Inland Steel initially housed the Mexican *solos* (unaccompanied men) in bunkhouses while the few men with families settled in available housing near the mill. A manager at Wisconsin Steel said he hired a few Mexicans for a short time in 1920, but complained that they went "south again at first touch of cold weather."[4] If those employees did leave Wisconsin Steel, it was unlikely that cold weather was the determining factor. Although blaming the weather was a convenient and common excuse that deflected any blame from the foremen and managers, Mexicans did not tend to leave in the winter. In fact, the Mexican population of Chicago usually grew in the winter, as seasonal agricultural workers from throughout the Midwest regularly wintered in the city.

For Mexican workers, the concept of using an *enganchista* to find work in Mexico or the United States was not new. Employers in the United States and within Mexico had used labor agents for decades to contract Mexican workers for the railroads, the agricultural fields, and the mines of the Southwest.[5] *Enganchistas* were particularly important for hiring Mexicans to work somewhere like Chicago during the early phases of Mexican migration. Chicago was a distant place in a strange environment with few Mexicans.[6] Those who signed on with a labor agent typically agreed to work for a minimum amount of time in exchange for guaranteed work and transportation to the worksite.

Mexicans who worked in South Chicago faced discrimination and limited opportunities in the city, within the steel mills, in housing, and within the labor movement. Despite year-round employment in the mills, Mexican steelworkers were limited to a few positions and continued to face ethnic harassment and discrimination. Mill managers and Mexican steel workers interviewed in the 1920s emphasized the limited opportunities for Mexicans. With only a few exceptions, mills employed Mexicans in the lowest-paying, most menial jobs. Mexican immigrants to Chicago in the 1920s and 1930s realized that economic prosperity was not as readily available to them as they had believed when deciding to travel to the area. Although many Mexicans continued to be hopeful about employment opportunities in the Chicago area, many of their aspirations remained unfulfilled.[7] These migrants were adversely affected by the biases of the prospective employers, as they could only enter the industrial workplace where, when, and in the capacity allowed by mill managers.

Chicago society quickly racialized the new Mexicanos, while elevating European immigrants into a "white" status. This meant that the same environmental racism perpetrated against African Americans became acceptable against Mexicans in these industrial neighborhoods. Although other-than-white workers populated many of the compromised neighborhoods adjacent to their industrial places of employment, the status of the residents made continued environmental racism acceptable. As Chicago historian Sylvia Washington describes in reference to the Back-of-the-Yards, a neighborhood adjacent to the Chicago stockyards, "although there were not explicit legal policies or practices equivalent to race-based restrictive covenants or racial zoning laws that forced the immigrants into these spaces, the segregated geographical spaces that immigrants voluntarily created were disproportionately used as the final sink of the city of Chicago's waste as well as that of the packers."[8] South Chicago's environmental degradation and racism might not have reached the infamous heights of that in the Back-of-the-Yards, nonetheless the conditions in South Chicago would not have been acceptable in nonimmigrant or non–African American neighborhoods. A member of the Chicago Bureau of Social Surveys found that by 1925 Mexicans and African Americans had "found shelter in the most used, most outworn and derelict housing which the city keeps." Mexicans lived in "the old tenement districts [that had] long been experiencing a steady encroachment by industry and commerce" and were residential sections "destined for extinction."[9] Although census records list buildings shared by both white and African American occupants, cooperation between both groups against environmental racism was uncommon.[10]

For some railroad workers near South Chicago, home was a boxcar. Employers created neighborhoods, more accurately described as boxcar camps, for Mexican workers and their families. The 1925 Chicago and Western Indiana Railway "boxcar colony" was located between Eighty-Second and Eighty-Third Streets adjacent to railroad tracks. Anthropologist Robert Redfield commented that the neighborhood consisted of around twenty "very dilapidated box cars" scattered around repair sheds and railroad-yard buildings. Many had iron-pipe chimneys, while some had porches, potted plants, and even small chicken yards. Workers and their families occupied thirteen of these boxcars.[11] Several other boxcar camps existed throughout the outskirts of South Chicago. A 1931 *Christian Science Monitor* article by Dorothea Kahn celebrates the large number of Mexicans in the Chicago area and described the sometimes long-term nature of the camps, claiming that some Mexicans stayed in their boxcars for "six, eight, and even ten years," because they were rent-free and provided an environment that was "better than those in the crowded city" and "more like that to which the peasants were accustomed." Kahn praises the personalization of the boxcars, emphasizing that "some have gardens of flowers and vegetables" with "the more prosperous of the workmen families have installed electrics lights, put up little porches and had tiny farmyards where chickens and perhaps a pig help out with the family's living."[12] Despite the implied temporary nature of these camps, those living in these boxcars created a sense of community within the camps by improving the exteriors of their homes.

By adding porches, maintaining potted plants, and decorating the outside of their boxcars, the residents created a sense of pride, agency, and belonging despite their difficult economic and living conditions.[13] At first glance, the creation of a strong community seems implausible because of the temporary nature of the structures, converted from the world of the railroad. However, these workers and their families transformed those boxcars from a symbol of how the railroad companies dominated the lives of their workers, controlling their total environment, to an example of personalizing their environment and changing the industrial landscape to make it more human and humane. These alterations of their environment were one means of expressing connections among people, making visual allusions to a shared history and culture, and creating that shared culture in the face of larger differences.

Solos working for South Chicago steel mills during the early years of the settlement, from 1919 through the early 1920s, had the option of living in bunkhouses on steel-mill property, as boarders in boardinghouses, or with families in the immediate community.[14] Some *solos* preferred remaining in mill housing because of the abundance of prepared meals. A Mexican resident of South Chicago interviewed in 1928 recalled that in the barracks "the rooms were very nice and the food we ate was good." He said that the food provided by the steel mill was good and plentiful, but always American: "There was a variety and we never had too much of one thing but we never had tortillas, or menudo, tostadas, and the other things we liked." Some *solos* "made it a practice of staying out for supper and going to the families of some of the men in the neighborhood to eat" or would occasionally eat out for lunch because of their desire for Mexican food.[15] The quality of meals, though, varied greatly for *solos* renting rooms in the community.

This unidentified resident pointed out that another reason *solos* moved off company property was in order to separate themselves from the workplace during their off time. "After the day's work was done they wanted to get away from their work and forget about it and enjoy their leisure time. I remember one said to me once, 'This is too much like a prison. We work all day, then we eat in a big place all together, and sleep together. We never leave these walls of the factory.' I guess also we seldom had music or our theatre plays like the other Mexicans in Chicago did."[16] Many of the steelworkers who lived in the bunkhouses wanted to be part of the expanding community of Mexicans. As more Mexican families moved into South Chicago, the number of *solos* moving out of the bunkhouses increased. By the early 1920s, mills started closing down their on-premises housing, forcing everyone to find lodging in the neighborhood.[17]

In 1929, seventeen-year-old Serafín García started working in the steel mills. Employed as a laborer by Interstate Iron and Steel—later Republic Steel—García earned 39 cents an hour working ten hours a day, seven days a week. First assigned to a labor gang that cleaned open hearths, he later moved to an outdoor labor position that provided steadier shift work, working from 5:30 p.m. to 7:00 a.m.[18] García took an outdoor labor position despite the terrible work conditions because it provided steadier hours than did working on a labor gang, whose hours varied with the mill's production cycle.

Alfredo de Avila's first steel-mill job was as a laborer building and moving the railroads tracks that were used to move slag from the foundry to the Lake Michigan shore on mill property. This position was one of the least sought-after jobs at the mill and frequently fell to Mexican or African American workers after white workers had taken their pick. The job subjected de Avila and others to the brutal lakefront cold and summer heat while putting down and picking up railroad tracks as slag was distributed along the lakefront. Although working at the mill earned the worker credibility and respect within the Mexican community, everyone recognized this job as the bottom rung of the limited opportunities at the mill. Unhappy with this job, de Avila quickly found an indoor job. He was assigned to a furnace room as a molder's helper.[19]

Benigno Castillo started at Illinois Steel—later U.S. Steel—in April 1923 as a laborer shoveling dirt. He considered the $4.40 wage he earned for a twelve-hour day "a lot of money."[20] After only a week, Castillo moved to a contract position, paid by volume of production. Content working 8 a.m. to 8 p.m. during the week and 6 a.m. to 6 p.m. on Saturdays, Castillo stayed in this position until he retired.[21] García, de Avila, and Castillo are just a few examples of Mexican workers who were mobile—albeit with very limited mobility—within the mills. Some moved to better positions, but managers rarely promoted Mexicans to foremen.[22]

Working in the steel mills during the 1920s provided more economic opportunities than did other jobs available to Mexican men, but these jobs came with the same workplace discrimination and mistreatment common in other industries. Mexicans regularly complained about the discrimination in the mill's employment office, the difficulties in advancing up the job ladder, and the lousy pay. Laborers of other ethnic groups—such as the Polish, Irish, Croatian, and Hungarian—were slow to accept Mexican immigrants for reasons that included the inability of many Mexican immigrants to speak English, the growing level of ethnic prejudice, and the reputation of Mexican workers as strikebreakers. These attitudes were not limited to fellow laborers. The vast majority of foremen and managers, who were primarily Polish and Irish, refused to hire Mexicans to work in skilled or higher-paying positions for many of the same objections voiced by laborers.[23]

Mexican residents of Chicago sought to maintain what they considered the most important facets of their Mexican culture and tradition. They formed South

Chicago's "third space," the space that allowed for a Mexican South Chicago culture where they selectively blended what they saw as the best Mexican customs with the best Chicago influences.[24] They tailored their public and private physical environments to conform to these beliefs. From the purchase of Mexican religious and cultural trinkets at a neighborhood store to the gendered cultural expectations shaping the behavior and role of women, men, girls, and boys, the community-imposed pressure to maintain a Mexican culture fashioned a distinct but uniquely South Chicago Mexican environment.

Since many Mexican immigrants to South Chicago planned to return to Mexico, they did not actively pursue naturalization. Those Mexicans who took advantage of English classes in order to improve employment prospects nonetheless understood Spanish was a critical component of their identity. They believed themselves to be sojourners who were escaping political turmoil and would eventually return to Mexico in a better economic position. Moving into an existing, ethnic working-class neighborhood in a crowded industrial environment had drawbacks when compared to rural life or life in the urban U.S. Southwest, yet the opportunities provided by living in a densely populated neighborhood with a large Mexican population allowed for community-building opportunities. These opportunities, however, were gendered. Cultural limitations put on women and girls made it difficult for them to take advantage of many of the opportunities available in a large urban area.

It was common for Mexican men in Chicago to object to their wives' entrance into the workplace outside of traditional, home-based, "women's work." The most frequently mentioned reason was the bad influence the workplace would have on Mexican women. They feared women's "liberation," or an Americanization that provided more autonomy for women, giving men less control over the daily lives of their wives.[25] Some women also disapproved of such autonomy for their daughters. Many more traditional Mexican men did not approve of their wives or daughters working outside of the home, or outside of jobs such as doing laundry, preparing food, or working in retail stores. Local Spanish-language newspaper publisher Francisco Huerta used the distinctions in what was acceptable to define ethnic differences: "The Polish people put their women to work. The Mexicans don't want their women to work even if they are poor." Huerta contrasted immigrant women with women born in the United States: "The Mexican immigrants don't like freedom of women, but it is all right for those Mexicans born here. The women find out that freedom of the U.S. is pretty good for them." His wife disagreed: "I want to go to work, but my husband doesn't want me to." In Francisco Huerta's rebuttal to his wife's complaint, he spelled out the perceived fear of many Mexican immigrant men. It is okay, according to Huerta, to let American women, and Mexican women raised in the United States, to enter the wage-earning workplace, because they were "used to American customs." Contending that his demand that his wife stay home did not stem from the jealousy she accused him of, he argued that "if our wives went to work, they would meet some other men and would go away with them; I would not blame my wife, I would blame only myself, because I have control of her. She would meet a man and go with him. Others are used to it, but not the Latin girls."[26]

As is the case today, many Mexican immigrants to early twentieth-century Chicago did not plan to stay long. This popular concept of Mexicans as sojourners, of eventually returning to Mexico in a better economic condition and as an asset to Mexico, operated on two levels. First was the effect on Mexicans themselves, the choices they made, and the rhetoric they used to describe their experiences. Second was how the sojourner attitude affected the way non-Mexicans—city officials, social workers and reformers, European immigrants, and the federal government—perceived and treated Mexicans. A shared expectation of returning to Mexico created a common bond that helped solidify a sense of community despite the fact that most did not plan to be in Chicago for long. They changed their environment to improve their living conditions and sense of belonging. However, Mexicans' expectation of eventual mobility did intensify anti-Mexican sentiment, as outside groups equated low levels of naturalization resulting, in part, from the sojourner attitude with hostility toward the United States.

Historian Gabriela Arredondo points out that "Mexicans in Chicago were not simply another ethnic group working to be assimilated into a city with a long history of incorporating newcomers." Because of the discrimination surrounding them, "Mexicans fought the current of pejorative qualities ascribed to 'being Mexican' by constructing their own Mexicanness to battle anti-Mexican prejudices."[27] Although this identity created resistance to full assimilation, Mexicans still wanted to be racialized as white, not the predominate other-than-white status occupied by most working-class Mexicanos.

As with other immigrant groups, Mexican-owned businesses could become a locus of community for South Chicago Mexicans and a site of resistance to less direct cultural pressures. José Galindo opened a drugstore at 8901 Buffalo Avenue in 1923, at the same address as his residence.[28] By 1926, "everyone from the neighborhood came to buy." Customers came more often to buy the herbs for familiar healing practices, rather than the medicines regulated by the U.S. establishment. One customer who wished to purchase a medicine described the appearance of the container—"the medicine that is sold [in] a little somewhat greenish bottle this size"—rather than asking for it by name, an indication that even when people did use "American" medicines, they were still using them in their own cultural context. The store also drew Mexicans from as far away as Joliet, suggesting that there were not many options elsewhere that carried familiar products, were welcoming, and operated more like Mexican drugstores. One of the reasons people went to Galindo's drugstore, rather than the unfamiliar spaces that catered to the dominant culture, was that it was comfortable and "did not seem very elegant."[29] In addition to providing the ingredients for remedies learned in Mexico or from relatives, the drugstore was a place where Chicago Mexicans could gather and converse with others, sharing news about friends, family, and work possibilities. The drugstore was a business, but it was also a shared community space within the neighborhood that offered Mexicans the means to resist adopting a particular aspect of the dominant culture. By stocking different kinds of remedies, the store enabled community members to avoid absorption into dominant ways of understanding health and illness.

As was the case for other urban, ethnic immigrant communities, Chicago Mexicans formed clubs, cultural societies, mutual-aid societies, and other worker-based organizations for many reasons. They formed organizations to seek a better life, for economic or social security in case of illness, and for death benefits. For a minimal monthly fee, members were, in theory, assured of aid if unable to work or in case of death for any reason. From the early years of the Mexican community, mutual-aid societies emerged as organizations that attempted to improve Mexican lives through protection of workers. The first *mutualista* in Chicago, the Sociedad Mutualista Benito Juárez, was established in 1917 by a group of Mexican "workers, lawyers, doctors, engineers, businessmen, writers, and newspapermen."[30] It served as a longstanding mutual-aid society in addition to a social organization that provided members a forum for discussion and sponsorship of community activities.

Community organizations served as moral and cultural "flag bearers" for the community, keeping watch over cultural expectations and activities. As Chicago's Mexican community grew, and its members became more entrenched into Mexican South Chicago, the number of support organizations increased. Despite the fact that many Mexicans in South Chicago saw themselves as sojourners who would return to Mexico sooner rather than later, they established organizations to improve their quality of life while in Chicago and to maintain Mexican customs and a support base.

Catholics created two parish-based organizations soon after the founding of Our Lady of Guadalupe in South Chicago, Los Caballeros de Guadalupe and Las Hijas de María. Like the organizations mentioned above, Los Caballeros sponsored dances and celebrations. Members also established a church-sponsored mutual-aid society, but it split from the church when the parish priest, Father James Tort, insisted on control of the organization.[31] Another early Catholic South Chicago organization was La Unión Nacionalista Mexicana. Although it is not clear when the organization was started, it was in existence in 1920. Its mission was "to help bring about the downfall of the present liberal government in Mexico." This organization serves as an example of the close political and social ties between Mexican Chicagoans and Mexico and their continued desire to keep a hand in Mexican domestic affairs.

Mexican steelworkers turned to *mutualistas* for some of the same reasons other workers joined labor unions. Widespread labor union discrimination and harassment against Mexican workers was one reason Mexicano steelworkers turned to the Mexican-only societies for support and to organize against workplace grievances. Although the vast majority of Mexican steelworkers would eventually become members of the Steel Workers Organizing Committee (SWOC), recruitment of and participation by Mexicans was limited before 1936.[32] Discrimination experienced by rank-and-file Mexican workers—as well as Mexican workers who helped in the organizing drives—made organized labor a limited, albeit necessary, form of resistance.

In 1928 there were few Chicago Mexicanos involved in trade unions since many worked in the poorly organized steel and meatpacking industries. Even when unions did exist in a particular industry, they were often weak in the low and unskilled grades that most Mexicans occupied. Thus, very few track laborers were part of the Brotherhood of Maintenance of Way Employees. Other unions, such as those for the building trades, required U.S. citizenship for membership, preventing most Mexicans from joining.[33]

In some cases, Mexican workers sought to remedy difficulties left unaddressed—or even caused by—union organizers and members. Although the majority of Mexican steelworkers in South Chicago joined the SWOC, many were frustrated by the widespread prejudice and unfairness. As a result, some who had started off as active organizers chose to limit their time spent doing union work. In the fall of 1935, Alfredo de Avila, one of the early Mexican organizers for the SWOC, started as one of about thirty Mexicans who volunteered to organize during the early stages of the SWOC campaign.[34] Soon, de Avila accepted a position as a full-time, paid organizer with the union. After organizing seven days a week for six or seven months, de Avila asked to be a part-time organizer and return to the plant because of discrimination in the union hall.[35] Although de Avila was a successful organizer and believed in the union and its principles, he decided to return to work at the steel mill and lessen his time commitment to the union because of constant harassment by some non-Mexican labor organizers. Despite problems, Mexicans continued to organize and resist through organizations led and run by Mexicans before, during, and after the SWOC campaigns.[36]

Mexicans created these organizations, social clubs, mutual-aid societies, pro patria associations, and community service groups, not only because of their large numbers, but to combat the environmental, social, and economic isolation caused by white and ethnic European racism and discrimination. Mexicanos also felt a need to promote Mexican culture while serving those in the community.

Mexicans equated discrimination and most assimilation efforts as not only an attack on them and their skin color but on their culture. In response they created organizations that celebrated Mexican culture and Mexican national holidays, a goal that the Mexican consul in Chicago actively encouraged through his vocal presence at events and his encouragement of the formation of organizations.

Community members used the discrimination against them, a sojourner attitude, organized sports, mutual-aid organizations, and other groups to bring together a diverse community of Mexicans and Mexican Americans—some educated, most not—to find ways to change their physical and cultural environment in order to survive. The fortunes of the community were linked to the built environment, their access to green space, and to their ability to change their physical and cultural surroundings. Mexicans acted on the industrial landscape by creating physical and cultural communities.

Why should we care about the creation and development of distinct Mexican physical and cultural communities in South Chicago? In going beyond the question of whether organizations such as labor unions, community-based groups, and mutual-aid societies spoke for the majority of Mexicans in South Chicago, it is important to look at these organizations as pieces of a puzzle where the most dynamic struggles took place outside of, or in spite of, the established traditional organizations. Analysis of labor unions and other formal organizations are important to understanding part of Mexicano life in South Chicago, but focusing alone on organized resistance limits our ability to see the full story. By recognizing and not underestimating the significance of everyday forms of resistance and the politics of culture, as well as institutions and organizations not normally seen as vehicles for everyday and working-class change, we can delve into the strategies that helped Mexicans in South Chicago cope with the oppressive environment that surrounded them. Labor union hostility toward Mexican workers further reinforced the importance of alternative sites of resistance. These sites included *mutualistas*, pro patria organizations, and local Spanish-language newspapers. These individual and community histories—the stories of people, organizations, and their physical surroundings—shed light on Mexicano life in a place far from the border and at the industrial heart of the United States. Ninety-five years after the first wave of Mexican immigrants came to Chicago to work the railroads, Mexican Chicagoans have developed into a major political, economic, cultural, and social force.

Notes

1. Sophenisba P. Breckinridge and Edith Abbott, "Chicago Housing Conditions, V: South Chicago at the Gates of the Steel Mills," *American Journal of Sociology* 17, no. 2 (1911): 174.
2. Ibid.

3. Zaragosa Vargas, *Proletarians of the North: A History of Mexican Industrial Workers in Detroit and the Midwest, 1917–1933* (Berkeley: University of California Press, 1993); Dionicio Nodín Valdés, *Barrios Norteños: St. Paul and Midwestern Mexican Communities in the Twentieth Century* (Austin: University of Texas Press, 2000). For more on Mexicans in Chicago, see Gabriela F. Arredondo, *Mexican Chicago: Race, Identity, and Nation, 1916–39*, Statue of Liberty–Ellis Island Centennial Series (Urbana: University of Illinois Press, 2008); Lilia Fernández, *Brown in the Windy City: Mexicans and Puerto Ricans in Postwar Chicago* (Chicago: University of Chicago Press, 2012); and Michael D. Innis-Jiménez, *Steel Barrio: The Great Mexican Migration to South Chicago, 1915–1940* (New York: New York University Press, 2013).

4. D. P. Thompson and Clyde M. Brading, interviews by Paul S. Taylor, 1928, box 11, file 32, Paul Schuster Taylor Papers, BANC MSS 84/38 c, the Bancroft Library, University of California, Berkeley.

5. Mark Reisler, *By the Sweat of Their Brow: Mexican Immigrant Labor in the United States, 1900–1940* (Westport, Conn.: Greenwood, Press, 1976), 5. As early as the 1880s, U.S. farmers hired labor agents to cross into Mexico and contract Mexicans to perform agricultural work.

6. José Hernández Alvarez, "A Demographic Profile of the Mexican Immigration to the United States," *Journal of Inter-American Studies* 8, no. 3 (July 1966): 473–74; Jeffrey Marcos Garcilazo, *Traqueros: Mexican Railroad Workers in the United States, 1870–1930* (Denton: University of North Texas Press, 2012), 49–53; Vargas, *Proletarians of the North*, 13–14, 19–22, 36.

7. For more on the United States as a safety valve and source of inspiration, especially in the Southwest, see Vicki L. Ruíz, *From Out of the Shadows: Mexican Women in Twentieth-Century America* (New York City: Oxford University Press, 2008), 8–9.

8. Sylvia Hood Washington, *Packing Them In: An Archaeology of Environmental Racism in Chicago, 1865–1954* (Lanham, Md.: Lexington Books, 2005), 78.

9. Elizabeth A. Hughes, *Living Conditions for Small-Wage Earners in Chicago*, (Chicago: City of Chicago Department of Public Welfare, 1925), 8–9.

10. For more on environmental racism against Mexicans and African Americans in the urban United States, see Laura Pulido, "Rethinking Environmental Racism: White Privilege and Urban Development in Southern California," *Annals of the Association of American Geographers* 90, no. 1 (2000): 12–40; as well as Washington, *Packing Them In.* For more on environmental racism specifically against Mexican and Mexican American communities, see Char Miller, "Streetscape Environmentalism: Floods, Social Justice, and Political Power in San Antonio, 1921–1974," *Southwestern Historical Quarterly* 118, no. 2 (2014): 158–77. To better understand urban environmental racism today, see J. Tom Boer et al., "Is There Environmental Racism? The Demographics of Hazardous Waste in Los Angeles County," *Social Science Quarterly* 78, no. 4 (1997): 793–810.

11. Robert Redfield, "Robert Redfield Journal," box 59, folder 2, Robert Redfield Papers, Special Collections Research Center, University of Chicago Library; Dorothea Kahn, "Mexicans Bring Romance to Drab Part of Chicago in Their Box-Car Villages: 30,000 Now Make City," *Christian Science Monitor*, May 23, 1931.

12. Kahn, "Mexicans Bring Romance."

13. Chapter 5 of Garcilazo, *Traqueros*, provides a thorough description of various Mexican boxcar camps throughout the country. Garcilazo argues that generalizations about boxcar colonies are almost impossible to make given "diversity of experiences around the country" (111). Using interviews and descriptions from the Paul Schuster Taylor Papers, Garcilazo gives examples of Chicago area boxcar camps on pages 125–28.

14. Paul Frederick Cressey, "The Succession of Cultural Groups in the City of Chicago" (Ph.D. diss., University of Chicago, 1930), 152.

15. South Chicago resident, interview by Paul S. Taylor, box 11, file 32, Paul Schuster Taylor Papers.

16. Ibid.

17. Justino Cordero, "Interview by Jesse J. Escalante," in Jesse Escalante Oral Histories, Global Communities Collection, Chicago History Museum.

18. Serafín García, "Interview by Jesse J. Escalante," in Jesse Escalante Oral Histories.

19. Alfredo de Avila, "Interview by Jesse J. Escalante," in Jesse Escalante Oral Histories.

20. Benigno Castillo, "Interview by Jesse J. Escalante," in Jesse Escalante Oral Histories. This interview is in Spanish; translation by the author.

21. Castillo, "Interview by Jesse J. Escalante." For a discussion of discrimination in the workplace and the establishment of occupational patterns for Mexicans in the South Chicago and Northwest Indiana steel mills, see Jorge Hernandez-Fujigaki, "Mexican Steelworkers and the United Steelworkers of America in the Midwest: The Inland Steel Experience (1936–1976)" (PhD diss., University of Chicago, 1991), 53–87. Hernandez-Fujigaki argues that the "incorporation of Mexicans in the labor markets of the Southwest, primarily as menial laborers, strongly influenced the range of occupations available to them in the steel mills of the Great Lakes" (54). He also argues that "the initial occupations that Mexicans occupied in the Midwest were shaped both by their late arrival and by the perceptions of the representatives of growers, mine owners and, particularly, the railroads in the Southwest. Historically it was in the Southwest where the association between Mexicans and their lowly occupational status had been initially made" (57–58).

22. Only one Mexican was listed as a steel mill foreman in the 1920 census enumeration districts within the South Chicago neighborhood. Gerardo Ríos, boarding on the 9200 block of Burley Avenue, was listed as a foreman at an unnamed steel mill. He immigrated in 1914, knew English, was twenty-nine years old, and was listed as single. 1920 U.S. Census, Chicago, Il., ED 504, p. 11a.

23. Castillo, "Interview by Jesse J. Escalante." Castillo remembered that, when starting at Illinois steel as a laborer working with a shovel "cleaning and gathering dirt," they made less money the first day because the other ethnic groups, primarily Polish, Irish, Croatian, and Hungarian, "didn't tell us how to start."

24. For more on the third space in Mexicano communities, see David G. Gutiérrez, "Migration, Emergent Ethnicity, and the 'Third Space': The Shifting Politics of Nationalism in Greater Mexico," *Journal of American History* 86, no. 2 (1999): 481–517.

25. Carlos Perez Lopez, "Interview by Manuel Gamio," transcript, box 2, Manuel Gamio Papers, the Bancroft Library, University of California, Berkeley; Francisco Huerta,

"Interview by Paul S. Taylor," Paul Schuster Taylor Papers. Perez Lopez believed that women in Chicago were more aware of their rights and were more assertive toward their husbands. He also added "the women of better social standing are more aware of their social responsibilities and do more social work than in Mexico."

26. Huerta, "Interview by Paul S. Taylor."

27. Arredondo, *Mexican Chicago*, 7.

28. 1930 U.S. Census, Chicago, Il., ED 2458, p. 5A.

29. Manuel Gamio, "South Chicago: Sr. Galindo," 1926, Manuel Gamio Papers, 1930 U.S. Census, Chicago, Il., ED 2458, p. 5A.

30. Francisco Huerta, "Las Organizaciones Méxicanas," *Correo Méxicano*, Chicago, Sept. 6, 1926.

31. Malachy Richard McCarthy, "Which Christ Came to Chicago: Catholic and Protestant Programs to Evangelize, Socialize, and Americanize the Mexican Immigrant, 1900–1940" (Ph.D. diss., Loyola University, 2002), 221.

32. Between 1933 and 1934, steelworkers in South Chicago and throughout the country turned to the American Federation of Labor (AFL) craft union, the Amalgamated Association of Iron, Steel and Tin Workers (AAISTW), that had represented the steelworkers during the unsuccessful organizing campaign that culminated in the 1919 Great Steel Strike. There is little evidence of Mexican involvement or recruitment of Mexicans by union organizers during this drive. Associated Employees of South Works held its first public meeting in 1935 and affiliated with the newly formed SWOC in 1936. It was not until the affiliation with SWOC, and the targeted recruitment of Mexican workers, that Mexican rank-and-file workers joined the union. For more on the organizing drive of 1933–34, the creation of Associated Employees and SWOC, see Lizabeth Cohen, *Making a New Deal: Industrial Workers in Chicago, 1919–1939* (New York: Cambridge University Press, 1990), 293–95.

33. Paul Schuster Taylor, *Mexican Labor in the United States: Chicago and the Calumet Region*, University of California Publications in Economics, vol. 7, no. 2 (Berkeley: University of California Press, 1932), 118–19, 123.

34. de Avila, "Interview by Jesse J. Escalante"; John V. Riffe, "Interview by Nicolas M. Hernandez," Dec. 14, 1936, transcript, *Foreign Language Press Survey*.

35. de Avila, "Interview by Jesse J. Escalante."

36. For more on the Mexican involvement in the Steel Workers Organizing Committee (SWOC) and later the United Steel Workers of America (USWA), see Hernandez-Fujigaki, "Mexican Steelworkers." See esp. 88–109 for involvement before World War II.

Latina/o Immigration before 1965

Mexicans and Puerto Ricans in Postwar Chicago

LILIA FERNÁNDEZ

In the twenty-first century, the Midwest is often hailed as a "new destination" for Latina/o immigrants, a place that heretofore had not received people of Latin American descent in significant numbers. Yet, as Latina/o historians of the region know, it is actually a "reemerging destination": Mexicans, Mexican Americans, and other Latinas/os have lived in midwestern towns and cities for generations.[1] Some migrants formed rural settlements as early as the late 1800s. Though the Latina/o population in the region remained small for decades, in the years after World War II, their numbers increased dramatically. Chicago became a primary destination, attracting thousands of women and men recruited to work in nearby agricultural fields, railroads, industrial workplaces, and other employment. Significantly, these communities began forming before the oft-cited 1965 immigration reform that precipitated a new wave of Latin American migration. As is outlined below, thousands of Mexicans, Mexican Americans, and Puerto Ricans made their way to the nation's third largest city and called it home in the years during and after World War II, thus creating a base for the communities that would continue to form in the late twentieth century.

The migrant flow of these three distinct groups converged in the urban Midwest and initiated an unparalleled process of social and physical integration. Nowhere else in the country did similar numbers of Mexicans, Mexican Americans, *and* Puerto Ricans come to settle in a major urban area, drawn both by direct, state-sponsored labor recruitment and the promise of industrial wages. Moreover, they came to places that had an earlier wave of immigrants. Chicago first recruited Mexican workers in significant numbers during World War I. Though this population declined during the Great Depression and the city experienced an immigration hiatus, Mexicans, Mexican Americans, and Puerto Ricans began migrating as part of the Bracero Program, Operation Bootstrap, or simply through personal and familial networks in the 1940s and 1950s.[2] By this time, European immigration dropped off sharply, and European immigrants were assimilating and consolidating their identity as "Americans" and, by extension, as "white." This racial identity became particularly salient when contrasted with the hundreds of thousands of southern African Americans migrating north also in search of industrial jobs. Ethnic Mexicans and Puerto Ricans, not surprisingly, experienced processes of integration and assimilation that differed from both earlier European immigrants and African Americans. Although Mexicans and Puerto Ricans came from distinct origins, had cultural idiosyncrasies and linguistic differences, both ethnic groups found themselves repeatedly racialized as "nonwhite" in the postwar era. This essay focuses on three areas they encountered this process of racial ascription—employment, housing, and the local and federal interpretation of migration policies.[3]

*   *   *

The migrations precipitated by the Bracero Program and Operation Bootstrap have become well-known in recent years, thanks to the work of historians and other scholars. Several have written extensively on the U.S.-Mexican binational labor agreements, known popularly as the Bracero Program, which placed hundreds of thousands of Mexican men as guest workers in the country's agricultural fields, particularly in the Southwest.[4] Others have written about the great Puerto Rican migration during the island's Operation Bootstrap campaign.[5] Mexican American migrant farm laborers, including many who had worked the seasonal circuit from Texas to the Midwest (Michigan, Ohio, Wisconsin, Indiana, and Illinois), also began to settle in the north as a result of the competition from the very *braceros* that farmers began favoring for lower wages. The Bracero Program thus drove increasing numbers of Mexican Americans out of the migrant labor circuit in search of more lucrative and stable work in urban areas.[6] The economic boom also inspired Mexican immigrants without *bracero* contracts—both men and women, authorized and unauthorized—to migrate, especially by the late 1940s and 1950s, in search of reportedly plentiful work opportunities. In an era of European immigration restriction and in the midst of the second Great Migration of southern African Americans, Puerto Ricans, Mexican nationals, and Mexican Americans came with the hope of gaining economic security just as employers hoped to hire them at the lowest wages possible.[7] Considered together along with domestic migrations, these labor flows offer a more comprehensive understanding of the wartime United States, its population movements, and economic shifts.

These simultaneous Latino migrations and their significant encounter in the Midwest have often been overlooked by the traditional bicoastal attention to Mexicans in the Southwest and Puerto Ricans on the East Coast. By the mid-1950s, however, Puerto Ricans and Mexicans had settled in the Midwest—specifically the industrial and population magnet of Chicago—in large numbers, and their migration would keep going strong for many years. By 1957 the Puerto Rico Migration Division estimated that 25,000 Puerto Ricans lived in Chicago.[8] Ethnic Mexicans were projected to be at least double, if not triple, this number. By 1970 the census reported nearly a quarter of a million "Spanish-speaking" or "Spanish-surnamed" people. Community leaders suspected this was a serious undercount, particularly of the Mexican population and of the undocumented. Nonetheless, according to official numbers, Mexican-origin people and Puerto Ricans constituted the overwhelming majority of the Spanish-speaking—nearly 75 percent—numbering 106,000 and 78,000 people, respectively.[9] Other Latin Americans, including Cubans and Central and South Americans, began arriving in growing numbers after 1965.

Racialized Labor in the Urban North

The Bracero Program and Puerto Rico's Operation Bootstrap economic development program proved to be guiding forces in directing Mexican and Puerto Rican migration to the United States. The Midwest, however, appealed to these migrants for the unique opportunities it offered. Industrial cities like Chicago, Milwaukee, Cleveland, Lorraine, Illinois, and Youngstown, Ohio, promised potentially higher wages than the low-wage agricultural work of Southwestern or Northeastern farms. Steel mills, meatpacking plants, factories, and railroads seemed much more attractive than toiling in the fields from sunup to sundown. Service jobs also abounded in downtown Chicago's hotels and restaurants, for example. Even those migrants who found themselves in agricultural communities in the Midwest, however, found labor markets that had a high need for farm and food processing workers and that actively recruited laborers through personal and family networks. For Mexican Americans who had migrated from Texas to the Midwest doing seasonal farm labor for years, "settling out" or leaving the migrant labor stream became increasingly appealing as employment opened up or as wages on local farms declined due to competition from recent immigrants.

Yet industrial work and life in the urban North was not as ideal as some may have expected. Mexican immigrants, Mexican Americans, and Puerto Ricans who came to Chicago in search of work experienced conditions similar to those of any recent immigrant group—they often had access only to the lowest-paid, most difficult, and unskilled positions. European immigrants initially encountered the same but usually experienced upward occupational mobility after a period of time. African Americans, in contrast, remained in the lowest-paid entry-level jobs—if they were hired at all. More often, employers systematically excluded them from job opportunities based on personal racial prejudices or discriminatory company policies. Employers often favored Mexicans and Puerto Ricans in comparison to black workers but often restricted them to the least desirable positions. Ironically, the labor migration of both had been facilitated by the Mexican and Puerto Rican governments, often at the behest of mainland employers. The contracts, however, were often temporary arrangements, thus marking them as a short-term, expendable workforce. They were often the last hired and first fired during economic downturns. Mexicans and Puerto Ricans thus had access to employment opportunities that were denied African Americans, yet in an era of automation, declining industrial employment, union-busting, and deskilling of labor, Mexicans and Puerto Ricans collectively represented an unskilled, low-wage labor force.[10]

State-sponsored employment arrangements did not always deliver the big earnings or favorable conditions promised. In October 1946, shortly after arriving at a foundry in North Chicago, Illinois, Enrique Baiz Miró and forty-six of his fellow workers sent a letter of complaint to the Puerto Rico Department of Labor about intolerable living conditions and excessive pay deductions. The Puerto Rico Department of Labor commissioner, Manuel Pérez, replied that he had recently received a similar letter from another foundry worker and had explained the following: First, workers were free to provide their own meals if those provided by the company were unsatisfactory. The deductions about which workers complained had been set forth in their contracts; such deductions would pay for round-trip transportation from San Juan to Chicago and remittances to Puerto Rico, among other expenses that the workers might incur. Pérez explained that "the [Puerto Rico] Department of Labor . . . is happy to receive and handle all questions and complaints that our compatriots there may have at any moment, but workers are asked to read their contracts carefully once and again, before filing complaints or protestations regarding the conditions outlined therein." He further explained that, prior to their departure, workers should have read the information provided regarding the vicissitudes of traveling to a foreign environment with new food, language, customs, and climate. "Acclimating to work such as that in a foundry, takes time even for those who are used to certain types of manual labor," he lectured. Pérez summarily dismissed the workers' complaints.[11]

Mexican and Mexican American migrants encountered similar and sometimes worse conditions and sought various means of resolving their issues as well. The few who had access to union representation turned to their locals for labor disputes. Others sought help with the Mexican consulate, local churches or local Mexican American organizations such as the Mexican Civic Committee

(MCC) or the Mexican American Council (MAC), which had formed the guidance of longstanding residents. Mexican American leaders, however, were not well positioned to help recent (im)migrants. As the MCC noted, "The Mexican population of Chicago has long occupied the status of a labor reserve . . . utilized in times of need and displaced in times of low production."[12] Viewed as temporary workers, not full-fledged citizens, despite being in the city for over two decades, Mexican Americans' status mirrored that of the thousands of *braceros* in the region. Thousands of Mexican immigrants and their U.S.-citizen children had been deported or repatriated during the Great Depression. Those who remained had not fared well in the local labor market. In 1935, one survey found that 66 percent of Mexicans occupied unskilled jobs compared to 31 percent of native-born whites, 35 percent of foreign-born whites, and 58 percent of African Americans. Only 5 percent of Mexicans held skilled positions compared to 35 percent of foreign-born whites. This was not due to differences in education or language skills, for European immigrants arrived in the United States with just as little education and limited English-language skills as Mexicans did. Nonetheless, longstanding Mexican residents of Chicago had much higher unemployment rates: 30 percent.[13] This racially based differential in employment seemingly affected Mexicans as severely as African Americans, if not more, at least during the Depression. Moreover, these figures reflected a Mexican labor force that already had been reduced artificially by repatriation and deportation.

Nearly fifteen years later, the employment status of Mexican Americans had changed little. In 1949, Mexican American community leader Frank Paz described the position of ethnic Mexicans in the local labor market and the racial discrimination that kept them in the lowest positions. Why, he asked, were there no Mexican brakemen, conductors, firemen, or switchmen on the railroads? "There is nothing wrong with working as a railroad section hand," he asserted, "but when a group of people are branded for employment only in one particular task there is something radically wrong." He cited similar patterns in the steel mills and packinghouses: Mexicans worked only in the dirtiest, most dangerous, lowest-paid, and unskilled jobs. Why did they hold no positions within the Steel Workers Union? Citing a 1927 report, which stated that Mexicans occupied only unskilled jobs in these industries, he asked why they had not been able to move up the occupational ladder despite more than three decades in Chicago.[14] Paz magnified the subtle and often invisible systemic exclusions that Mexicans experienced as a population. While this discrimination was not as severe as that practiced against African Americans, who were sometimes denied employment altogether, it contrasted dramatically with the mobility of many European immigrants who also started in the lowest entry-level employment but gradually ascended into skilled work.

Looking for Housing in a Racially Polarized City

Beyond the workplace, everyday life among other Chicagoans presented other challenges. As newcomers in a city that had not witnessed large-scale European immigration in several decades, Puerto Ricans and Mexicans stood out for their cultural, linguistic, and phenotypic differences. Although some Chicagoans welcomed them, many were hostile to the migrants, who were arriving on the heels of massive African American migration from the South. White Chicagoans violently repelled and rebuffed African Americans seeking housing in white neighborhoods.[15] When they encountered Mexicans and Puerto Ricans, however, they struggled to make sense of who they were racially and whether or not they were acceptable neighbors. Most determined that they were not. Thus, although relations with neighbors could be complex and varied depending on the context, most ethnic Mexicans and Puerto Ricans experienced racism and discrimination in housing and social relations. Chicagoans developed their opinions about them based on perceived characteristics, popular stereotypes, and personal encounters. Spanish speakers had varying experiences with Italians, for example. Some Mexicans remember positive relations with Italian landlords and neighbors who readily accepted them as just the latest immigrant group. Longtime Mexican American residents who had been in the neighborhood for years tended to be more socially integrated with Italian Americans.[16] In fact, the two groups seemed to get along well in the early 1920s. Over time, however, friction between them increased.[17] Italians who saw Mexicans as racially distant and unfamiliar adamantly strove to keep them out of their neighborhoods. Frank Paz's 1948 study notes, for example, that "Mexicans live within this larger community in small islands. . . . Although they have been living there for the last twenty-five or thirty years, they are still looked upon by the Italian-Americans as outsiders and intruders. . . . There are sections in this large area where Mexicans are restricted. 'They have been kept out,' as someone from the Italian group has boasted."[18]

Many Mexicans did indeed encounter discrimination in trying to find housing, being turned away sometimes based upon their appearance or demeanor. Some discovered that "passing" for Italian or Greek, whenever possible, could help them in their search for an apartment. Puerto Ricans similarly believed that "real estate agencies and private owners of buildings refuse to rent houses or apartments to Spanish speaking families."[19] Landlords often discriminated based on skin color, something which Latina/o families of varying skin tones quickly discovered. Monse Lucas-Figueroa recalled a time when her mother found an apartment for the family but then lost it once her husband arrived at the building.

Lucas . . . sounds more Italian than Puerto Rican. So my mom went to look for an apartment and they thought that her accent was due to an Italian accent. My mom was very white because her family was from Spain . . . the guy was willing to give my mom the apartment, so my mom gave him the rent and the deposit . . . when my mom took my dad—my dad is Puerto Rican, but *él es trigueño* [he is brown-skinned—lit. "wheat-colored"]—the guy said "no." He gave my mother back her deposit and we were without an apartment . . . When he saw my father, [he must have thought] "Ahh! He's black!"[20]

Another dark-skinned Puerto Rican man recounted a similar story of having trouble securing an apartment for his family. As soon as he appeared to answer an ad, the landlord would reject him. Finally a friend recommended he send his wife instead of going himself since "'she looks more white than you.'" The man explained, "do you know that the first time she went out to look for an apartment, she found one?"[21] For many Puerto Ricans, the search for housing became an exercise in evading negative racial judgments and masking one's origins.

2.2.1 Puerto Rican women on the steps of a building in the near north side of Chicago in the 1950s. University of Chicago Library, Special Collections Research Center, Mildred Mead Photographs, Apf2-09033.

As more and more Spanish-speaking people moved into the city and the white population increasingly headed to new suburban developments, however, landlords had to decide if the difference between themselves and these recent migrants was more important than the rents they could collect. Absentee landlords, for example, were much less discriminating in selecting tenants and renting out run-down apartments at inflated prices to desperate new arrivals. Especially during the dramatic housing shortages of the 1940s and early '50s, landlords could command premium prices for even the most dilapidated shelter.[22] When they rented to Puerto Ricans or Mexicans, however, neighboring white residents often resented and intimidated the new arrivals. One community worker pointedly described dynamics on the Near North and Northwest Sides: "As soon they [Puerto Ricans] move to this particular neighborhoods [sic] they feel the old residents do not like and want them as neighbors."[23]

Mexicans and Puerto Ricans negotiated complicated racial hierarchies as they sought to find a place within the local social order. In working-class, white ethnic neighborhoods where a community's integrity was often the only social capital that residents possessed, and where access to housing and employment depended on perceived ethnic and racial identity, ethno-racial difference took on paramount importance. New arrivals assimilated this lesson quickly.

Despite the sometimes hostile climate, however, some residents did form close personal relationships across ethno-racial lines. Frank Paz notes that "in spite of this feeling [of animosity,] there have been a number of inter-marriages between Italians and Mexicans." Indeed, some Mexicans and Puerto Ricans intermarried with Italians, as they also did with African Americans.[24] They also married one another. In an environment where people encountered "difference," negotiating space, resources, and social well-being could be complicated. Ultimately, each group had to look after its own, and interracial and interethnic alliances and cooperation more often represented the exception rather than the rule.[25]

Targets of Repatriation

The end of the Korean War brought economic recession in 1953–54. While it was mild in comparison to other periods of decline, it hit the manufacturing sector especially hard, resulting in high unemployment rates. Puerto Ricans and Mexican migrants were coming to the city just as industrial jobs were declining. Since many of them found work in manufacturing, they suffered significantly during the downturn.[26] Both groups became targets of suspicion and scorn, though for very different reasons.

The county welfare commissioner decried the influx of Puerto Ricans, who, he claimed, strained local relief rolls. Similarly, local newspapers regularly reported on the "wetback" invasion of Mexican "illegal aliens," who purportedly took U.S. jobs and depressed wages. The simultaneity of these phenomena could be gleaned on February 2, 1954, on the pages of the conservative *Chicago Tribune*, which carried stories on that day about both the Puerto Rican welfare "menace" and the Mexican "hordes" invading the border.[27] As in other periods of distress, native-born Americans looked on the most recent newcomers and foreigners as the cause of economic decline.[28]

Alvin E. Rose, commissioner of public welfare for Cook County, stood out among those who expressed concern over the new migrants. His agency had started taking notice of the growing numbers of Puerto Ricans seeking public assistance and the "problems they were creating."[29] Rose observed that many agricultural workers who went to neighboring states eventually arrived in Chicago at the end of the harvest season and struggled to find work. While the department had a one-year residency requirement in Illinois (six months in Chicago) in order to qualify for public assistance, Rose stated that he would make exceptions to the policy only to help needy families return to the island, and ostensibly relieve pressures on his agency. He would not help single men, however, nor families who wanted to stay in the city. Following this strategy would seemingly prevent what had happened in New York, "which now must deal with a Puerto Rican population of 450,000 which strains their public welfare system." Rose traveled to the island to discuss plans to "repatriate" migrants with local authorities. He also wanted to publicly discourage any other unskilled workers from coming to Chicago. He flew to Puerto Rico that February to meet with island officials and coordinate a publicity campaign to warn islanders not to come to Chicago.[30]

In a speech he made on the island, Rose apparently reassured listeners that neither he nor his agency were expressing racial prejudice: "Please believe me above all else that Puerto Ricans in Chicago are not now and never have been treated differently by the Chicago Department of Welfare than anyone else of any other race, creed, color or national origin." He explained further that his office was merely helping those who wanted to return to the island. "We are not sending anybody back," he said in defense of the "repatriations." In private, however, Rose expressed a very different policy. He reportedly told a staff member at the Welfare Council of Metropolitan Chicago his policy to "ship them back in plane lots" and allegedly urged the agency to "not make it too easy for them to stay and bring others in."[31]

Rose's concerns about Puerto Rican welfare dependency were exaggerated, as Puerto Ricans made up less than 1 percent of the relief rolls in Chicago, a fact that Rose himself revealed. Out of over 18,000 cases of public assistance, Puerto Ricans accounted for only 148 cases. The island Department of Labor cited this in a January 1954 press release, headlined "Puerto Ricans Go in Search of Work, Not Aid." Island officials adamantly defended them as labor migrants, not drifters in search of handouts. Former governor of Puerto Rico and member of President Roosevelt's liberal New Deal "brain trust" Rexford Guy Tugwell, who had since become a lecturer of political science at the University of Chicago, publicly criticized Rose's efforts to discourage Puerto Rican migration, stating that Puerto Ricans had as much right to migrate as "Texans, New Yorkers, and the mountain people of Mississippi."[32] Anthony Vega, of the Puerto Rico Migration Division office in Chicago, emphatically noted that the main issue in the city was one of economics, not Puerto Rican dependency. "This is a problem of unemployment, not a Puerto Rican problem," he explained. Indeed, economic recession and high unemployment rates strained the most vulnerable families and workers during this period. But Chicago officials singled out this population as a burden. In reality, very few Puerto Ricans received public assistance, although many more may have been eligible.[33]

At the same time that Puerto Ricans were receiving negative attention for their unemployment rates and being encouraged to "repatriate," unauthorized Mexican immigrants were increasingly becoming the targets of public hysteria and facing official deportations. The 1924 immigration law, which had established quotas for European immigration and created the Border Patrol, had also created an "illegal" status for Mexicans who entered the United States without authorization.[34] The Immigration and Naturalization Service (INS, now three entities) had been deporting unauthorized immigrants from Chicago, including those who overstayed *bracero* contracts, for several years. While Americans did not seem to mind the *braceros* during World War II, many increasingly insisted on removing suspected "illegal" immigrants, especially in the midst of economic decline. In 1954, the federal government unveiled an aggressive nationwide roundup campaign it callously called Operation Wetback. The sweeps started on the West Coast in January and reached Chicago by that September. Community agencies like the MAC tried to educate immigrants on their legal rights and their options should they be arrested. Still, the INS deported as many as a hundred people a day.[35]

The deportation campaign targeting undocumented Mexican immigrants and the attempts to "repatriate" Puerto Ricans reveal the ways in which white Americans, especially as represented by local and federal government officials, identified Mexicans and Puerto Ricans as foreigners, noncitizens, and interlopers. Although these populations generally were welcomed by employers when their labor was needed, as European immigrants were in the early twentieth century, Mexicans and Puerto Ricans could ostensibly be removed, expelled, and denied the right to employment when their labor was no longer desired, unlike their European predecessors. This was the result of a convergence of factors—the timing of their migration, the geographical proximity of Mexico and Puerto Rico, which made

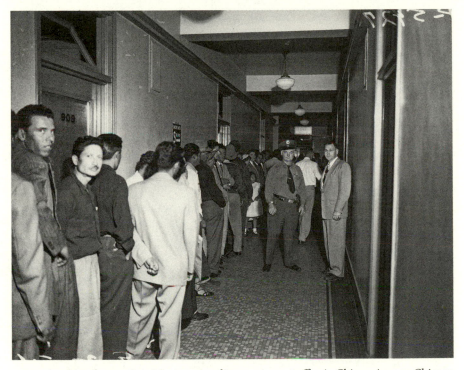

2.2.2 Awaiting deportation, Mexican men line up at a post office in Chicago in 1954. Chicago History Museum, ICHi-59815; Chicago Daily News.

it relatively easy to deport or repatriate migrants, and the ways in which Americans were understanding these populations as racially different from white or European Americans in the mid-twentieth century. Mexicans and Puerto Ricans were clearly not "white," but neither were they "black" in the same way African Americans were. Instead, they were conceived of collectively as nonwhite "foreigners" who could be removed from the nation at will. This characterization was a *collective* phenomenon: Latinas/os' *individual* experiences with regards to racial ascription may vary widely, particularly based on skin color, phenotype, class status, and English-language proficiency. Overall, however, Latinas/os who fit the stereotype of darker-skinned, foreign-looking or foreign-sounding, and working class, tend to be racialized in this way.[36]

Throughout the 1950s, 1960s, and 1970s, Mexican immigrants—both men and women—continued to enter unskilled and semiskilled manufacturing work in Chicago, where many employers welcomed them regardless of legal status. The availability of workers became such common knowledge that local factories such as Zenith Corporation, Western Electric, Motorola, National Video Corporation, National Radio, Florsheim Shoe, and food processors such as Nabisco, Jays Potato

Chips, Wilson, and Swift regularly inquired with pastors at Spanish-speaking parishes when they were hiring. They also employed U.S.-born Mexican Americans and Puerto Ricans.[37] With notable exceptions in steel and meatpacking, Mexican Americans and Puerto Ricans were often excluded from unions and, in general, increasingly became part of a nonunionized industrial labor force. Ironically, however, industrial employment opportunities began waning. From 1955 to 1965, the Mid-Chicago Industrial Development Area lost four hundred companies (more than 70,000 jobs).[38] Industrial flight to regions with even cheaper labor (both in the United States and abroad) meant fewer jobs in the urban north, a growing surplus of workers, and precipitously declining wages.[39] This would make it more difficult for (im)migrants to achieve economic mobility and more likely that they would retain their racial and class location as low-wage laborers.

Conclusion

Mexican, Mexican American, and Puerto Rican migrants who came to the Midwest in the years between World War II and the watershed 1965 Immigration Act represent a bedrock of the growing post-'65 Latina/o population in the region. Though their presence has been little noted by immigration scholars and overlooked by some Latina/o historians, their migration signals the beginning of a postwar surge of Latinas/os in the middle of the country. In the 1960s, '70s, and '80s, Latina/o immigration continued in great numbers. The diversity of sending countries in Latin America expanded too as a result of civil wars, political instability, and austere economic restructuring. Political and economic refugees were now coming not only from Mexico but from Central and South America, Cuba, and the Dominican Republic.

These earlier migrants who came to the Midwest paved the way for later generations. Indeed, many of the dynamics they experienced in employment and housing, and the public debates over the costs and benefits of new immigrants, have been replayed in different iterations in the "new" destinations where these migrants are arriving—in small towns and cities throughout the Midwest, South, and East Coast. The earlier settlement of ethnic Mexicans and Puerto Ricans provides some important lessons to help us understand these dynamics in the twenty-first century.

Notes

1. Lourdes Gouveia, Miguel A. Carranza, and Jasney Cogua, "The Great Plains Migration: Mexicans and Latinos in Nebraska," in *New Destinations: Mexican Immigration in the United States*, ed. Victor Zuñiga and Rubén Hernández-León (New York: Russell Sage Foundation, 2005), 23–49.

2. On Mexicans in Chicago in the early twentieth century, see Louise Año Nuevo Kerr, "The Chicano Experience in Chicago, 1920–1970" (PhD diss., University of Illinois, 1976); Gabriela F. Arredondo, *Mexican Chicago: Race, Ethnicity and Nation: 1916–1939*, Statue of Liberty–Ellis Island Centennial Series (Urbana: University of Illinois Press, 2008); and Michael Innis-Jiménez, *Steel Barrio: The Great Mexican Migration to South Chicago, 1915–1940* (New York: NYU Press, 2013).

3. I define "racial ascription" as the process by which people are assigned a racial identity or location on the local racial hierarchy. While racial identity can be both internally produced and externally assigned, here I focus on the external labeling of Mexicans and Puerto Ricans—how outsiders perceived and classified them racially.

4. Richard B. Craig, *The Bracero Program: Interest Groups and Foreign Policy* (Austin: University of Texas Press, 1971). Erasmo Gamboa, *Mexican Labor and World War II: Braceros in the Pacific Northwest, 1941–1947* (Austin: University of Texas Press, 1990). Juan R. García, *Operation Wetback: The Mass Deportation of Mexican Undocumented Workers in 1954* (Westport, Conn.: Greenwood Press, 1980). Barbara A. Driscoll, *The Tracks North: The Railroad Bracero Program of World War II* (Austin, Tex.: Center for Mexican American Studies, 1999). Peter N. Kirstein, *Anglo over Bracero: A History of the Mexican Worker in the United States from Roosevelt to Nixon* (San Francisco: R and E Research Associates, 1977), 15. Manuel García y Griego, "The Importation of Mexican Contract Laborers to the United States, 1942–1964," in *Between Two Worlds: Mexican Immigrants in the United States, ed. David G. Gutiérrez* (Wilmington, Del.: Scholarly Resources, 1996): 45–85.

5. Carmen Teresa Whalen, *From Puerto Rico to Philadelphia: Puerto Rican Workers and Postwar Economies* (Philadelphia: Temple University Press, 2001). Gina M. Pérez, *The Near Northwest Side Story: Migration, Displacement, and Puerto Rican Families* (Berkeley: University of California Press, 2004). J. Hernández-Alvarez, "The Movement and Settlement of Puerto Rican Migrants within the United States, 1950–1960," in *Latinos in the United States: Historical Themes and Identity*, ed. Antoinette Sedillo-López (New York: Garland Publishing, 1995). Edwin Maldonado, "Contract Labor and the Origins of Puerto Rican Communities in the United States," *International Migration Review* 13, no. 1 (1979): 103–21. History Task Force Centro de Estudios Puertorriqueños, *Labor Migration under Capitalism: The Puerto Rican Experience* (New York: Research Foundation of the City University of New York, 1979). Lorrin Thomas, *Puerto Rican Citizen: History and Political Identity in Twentieth-Century New York* (Chicago: University of Chicago Press, 2010).

6. See Angelica Rivera, "Re-inserting Mexican-American Women's Voices into 1950s Chicago Educational History" (PhD diss., University of Illinois at Urbana-Champaign, 2008), 40, 112, 122. *Braceros* themselves have testified to the hostility and animosity they felt from Tejano migrant farmworkers, for example, who resented *braceros* for being cheaper labor and driving down wages. See, for example, Pedro Pineda interview with the author, Sept. 1, 2005, Bracero Oral History Archive, http://braceroarchive.org/.

7. These population movements disprove the idea that the period between 1924 and 1965 witnessed no significant migration, an argument that is based on the absence of

widespread European immigration but completely overlooks the influx of "nonwhite," non-European migrants. See Whalen, *From Puerto Rico to Philadelphia*, 5.

8. "A Summary of Facts and Figures," January 1959 edition, produced by the Migration Division, Department of Labor, Commonwealth of Puerto Rico, folder 5, box 148, Welfare Council of Metropolitan Chicago Records, Chicago History Museum (hereafter WC-CHM).

9. Miriam Cruz, Carmen Rivera, Pastora Cafferty, and Arthur Velasques, "Chicago's Spanish Speaking Population: Selected Statistics" (Chicago: City of Chicago, Department of Development and Planning, 1973).

10. For more on the similarities and distinctions between Mexican and Puerto Rican migrants as racialized labor, see Lilia Fernández, "Of Migrants and Immigrants: Mexican and Puerto Rican Labor Migration in Comparative Perspective, 1942–1964," *Journal of American Ethnic History* 29, no. 3 (spring 2010): 6–39.

11. Manuel Pérez to Mr. Enrique Baiz Miró, Oct. 29, 1946, folder 277, box 15, series 2, section 4, Archivo Histórico, Fundación Luis Muñoz Marín, San Juan, Puerto Rico. See also Mérida Rúa, *A Grounded Identidad: Making New Lives in Chicago's Puerto Rican Neighborhoods* (New York: Oxford University Press, 2012). On the relationship between Puerto Rican migrants and the Puerto Rico Migration Division agency, see Thomas, *Puerto Rican Citizen*, esp. chaps. 4 and 5.

12. Progress Report of Mexican Civic Committee, 4, MCC flyer, box 108, Fair Employment Practices Commission, National Archives and Records Administration, Great Lakes Region. For more on the MCC and MAC, see Lilia Fernández, *Brown in the Windy City: Mexicans and Puerto Ricans in Postwar Chicago* (Chicago: University of Chicago Press, 2012), chap. 2.

13. Año Nuevo Kerr, "Chicano Experience in Chicago," 70, 78–79.

14. "Report on the Conference on the Mexican Americans in Chicago"; and Frank Paz, "Status of the Mexican American in Chicago," speech, 7, folder 4, box 147, WC-CHM. Jeffrey Garcilazo makes this same observation about Mexican railroad workers throughout the United States. Employers and bosses often hired only in the most menial, itinerant, purportedly "unskilled" jobs despite the fact that some track work actually required significant skill. Jeffrey Marcos Garcilazo, *Traqueros: Mexican Railroad Workers in the United States, 1870–1930* (Denton: University of North Texas Press, 2012).

15. See, for example, Arnold Hirsch, *Making the Second Ghetto: Race and Housing in Chicago, 1940–1960* (Cambridge: Cambridge University Press, 1983).

16. Phil Ayala, interview with the author, March 25, 2004; Gerald Suttles, *Social Order of the Slum: Ethnicity and Territory in the Inner City* (Chicago: University of Chicago Press, 1968), 49; and Thomas Guglielmo, *White on Arrival: Italians, Race, Color and Power in Chicago, 1890–1945* (New York: Oxford University Press, 2003), 47–48. Mexicans experienced a sort of "in-betweenness," much as Charlotte Brooks describes about Japanese Americans resettled after internment. Because of their much larger numbers and other factors, however, anti-Mexican prejudice seemed much more prevalent than that against Japanese Americans. Charlotte Brooks, "In the Twilight Zone between Black and White: Japanese American Resettlement and Community in Chicago, 1942–1945," *Journal of American History* 86, no. 4 (March 2000): 1657, 1669.

17. Thomas Philpott, *The Slum and the Ghetto: Neighborhood Deterioration and Middle-Class Reform, Chicago, 1880–1930* (New York: Oxford, 1978)), 285; Guglielmo, *White on Arrival*, 47–48; and Año Nuevo Kerr, "Chicano Experience in Chicago," 29.

18. Frank X. Paz, "Mexican-Americans in Chicago: A General Survey," Committee on Mexican Interests, Council of Social Agencies, Chicago, January 1948, 6, folder 4, box 147, WC-CHM.

19. José Muñiz, Community Project Report, January 1960, folder 12, box 93, Chicago Area Project, Chicago History Museum. Also, Migration Division, Annual Report, 1959–60, 160, box 1, folder 7, Offices of the Government of Puerto Rico in the U.S., Centro de Estudios Puertorriqueños, Hunter College. For a study of how a white working-class neighborhood in Brooklyn excluded Hispanics and maintained its racial composition, see Judith DeSena, *Protecting One's Turf: Social Strategies for Maintaining Urban Neighborhoods* (Lanham, Md.: University Press of America, 1990).

20. Monse Lucas-Figueroa interview with the author, June 21, 2004. She also noted landlords discriminated against large families, in some cases refusing to accept families with many children.

21. Cited in Felix Padilla, *Puerto Rican Chicago* (Notre Dame, Ind.: University of Notre Dame Press, 1987), 60. This was a common experience for Puerto Rican migrants in their search for housing. On this dynamic in Philadelphia, see Whalen, *From Puerto Rico to Philadelphia*, 191.

22. On Chicago's housing shortages in the 1940s, see Guglielmo, *White on Arrival*, 146–71; Hirsch, *Making the Second Ghetto*, 17–28; and Laura McEnaney, "Nightmares on Elm Street: Demobilizing in Chicago, 1945–1953," *Journal of American History* 92, no. 4 (2006): 1265–91. On the housing shortage and Japanese Americans, see Brooks, "In the Twilight Zone," 1674.

23. Muñiz, Community Project Report. Also, Chicago Commission on Human Relations, "Puerto Rican Americans in Chicago," Chicago: Mayor's Committee on New Residents, 1960, Municipal Reference Collection, Harold Washington Branch, Chicago Public Library. See also Whalen, *From Puerto Rico to Philadelphia*, 188.

24. Paz, "Mexican Americans in Chicago"; Ayala, interview with the author; Suttles, *Social Order of the Slum*, 61; and Joe Escamilla, interview with the author, Aug. 31, 2004. See also Guglielmo, *White on Arrival*, 54.

25. Suttles, *Social Order of the Slum*, 144; Hirsch, *Making the Second Ghetto*; and Guglielmo, *White on Arrival*. For more on how Italian Americans in Chicago consolidated their white identity, especially vis-à-vis African Americans by the 1940s, see Guglielmo, *White on Arrival*, 47–48, 57n54.

26. On the recession, see Harold G. Vatter, *The U.S. Economy in the 1950s: An Economic History* (New York: Norton, 1963), 63–97. National unemployment had actually reached a dramatic low of 1.8 percent in October 1953 but then climbed precipitously to over 6 percent by mid-1954.

27. See "News Summary," *Chicago Tribune*, Feb. 2, 1954, including "Puerto Ricans Pour into City and Ask Dole" and "Mexican Horde Repulsed by Border Patrol."

28. Puerto Ricans were clearly not "foreigners," as they held U.S. citizenship and were residents of a U.S. colonial possession. Still, the status of Puerto Ricans and their claims

to U.S. citizenship have been highly contested and fraught with racial politics ever since the matter was initially debated during the insular cases. See for example, Sam Erman, "Meanings of Citizenship in the U.S. Empire: Puerto Rico, Isabel Gonzalez, and the Supreme Court, 1898 to 1905," *Journal of American Ethnic History* 27, no. 4 (summer 2008): 5–33; Thomas, *Puerto Rican Citizen*; Christina Duffy Burnett and Burke Marshall, eds., *Foreign in a Domestic Sense: Puerto Rico, American Expansion, and the Constitution* (Durham, N.C.: Duke University Press, 2001).

29. "Puerto Ricans Pour into City." Other scholars have documented this episode as well. See Gina M. Pérez, "An Upbeat West Side Story: Puerto Ricans and Postwar Racial Politics in Chicago," *Centro Journal* 13, no. 2 (2001): 50; Rúa, *Grounded Identidad*. This characterization of Puerto Ricans as welfare dependent predates the academic discourse that emerged with the publication of Oscar Lewis's *La Vida: A Puerto Rican Family in the Culture of Poverty—San Juan and New York* (New York: Random House, 1966); and Nathan Glazer and Daniel Patrick Moynihan, *Beyond the Melting Pot: The Negroes, Puerto Ricans, Jews, Italians, and Irish of New York City* (Cambridge, Mass.: MIT Press, 1963).

30. "Puerto Ricans Pour into City"; "Puerto Rican Influx Brings New Inquiry," *Chicago Tribune*, Feb. 3, 1954; "Agree to Stem Puerto Rican Immigration," *Chicago Tribune*, Feb. 8, 1954; and "Boricuas piden ayuda en Chicago," *El Mundo* (San Juan, P.R.), Feb. 3, 1954, 1. See also Luis Sanchez Cappa, "Funcionario Chicago llega hoy a discutir situación de boricuas," *El Mundo*, Feb. 4, 1954, 5. Luis Sanchez Cappa, "Vino a discutir su plan de repatriar obreros," *El Mundo*, Feb. 5, 1954, 1. An editorial in the same paper opined that Puerto Rican migrants in Chicago should not be treated with prejudice and discrimination in their search for public aid, as they are citizens and are free to move about the country as they wish. "Puertorriqueños en Chicago," *El Mundo*, Feb. 4, 1954, 6. On the "Puerto Rican problem" in New York City, see, for example, Thomas, *Puerto Rican Citizen*, esp. chaps. 4 and 5.

31. Alvin Rose, speech, Jan. 9, 1954, and Mary A. Young to Mr. MacRae, Jan. 29, 1954, both in folder 3, box 148, WC-CHM.

32. "Rexford Tugwell señala boricuas tienen derecho a ir a Chicago," *El Mundo*, Feb. 6, 1954, 1.

33. "Boletin de información: Puertorriqueños van a trabajar no en busca de ayuda," Departamento del Trabajo, Estado Libre Asociado de Puerto Rico, March 26, 1954, Fondo Departamento del Trabajo, tarea 61-55, box 25, Archivo General de Puerto Rico, San Juan.

34. Año Nuevo Kerr, "Chicano Experience in Chicago," 144, 146. See also Mae Ngai, *Impossible Subjects: Illegal Aliens and the Making of Modern America* (Princeton, N.J.: Princeton University Press, 2004), chap. 2.

35. "Set Up Patrol to Seize Mexican Aliens Here," *Chicago Tribune*, Feb. 1, 1952; "135 Mexicans Begin Trip Home," *Chicago Tribune*, Feb. 7, 1952; "Move to Speed Deporting of Aliens in Jail," *Chicago Tribune*, March 5, 1952, B9; "100 'Wetbacks' Sent South on Way to Mexico," *Chicago Tribune*, Sept. 3, 1953, A4; "Midwest Drive on Wetbacks to Open Friday," *Chicago Tribune*, Sept. 15, 1952, A2; "Drive on Aliens by U.S. Brings 320 Detentions," *Chicago Tribune*, Sept. 28, 1954, 23; and "¿Está usted viviendo ilegalmente en este país?," *Vida Latina*, October 1954, 18, 20.

36. For a more extended discussion of this racialization, particularly in relation to the colonization of Mexicans and Puerto Ricans, see Fernández, *Brown in the Windy City*, chap. 1. On contemporary racialization and identification of Latinas/os in the United States, see Tanya Golash-Boza, "Dropping the Hyphen: Becoming Latino(a)-American through Racialized Assimilation" *Social Forces* 85, no. 1 (2006): 27–55.

37. See, for example, Marta Isabel Kollmann de Curutchet, "Localization of the Mexican and Cuban Population" (master's thesis, University of Chicago, 1967), 72; and A. Rivera, "Re-inserting Mexican-American Women's Voices," 57, 126.

38. See Adam Cohen and Elizabeth Taylor, *American Pharaoh: Mayor Richard J. Daley: His Battle for Chicago and the Nation* (Boston: Little, Brown, 2000).

39. The Border Industrialization Program, for example, which began immediately after the Bracero Program ended, signaled one form of "offshore" flight of U.S. industry to lower-wage foreign labor markets. On the Border Industrialization Program, see Jefferson Cowie, *Capital Moves: RCA's Seventy-Year Quest for Cheap Labor* (Ithaca, N.Y.: Cornell University Press, 1999), chaps. 4 and 6.

Not Just Laborers

Latina/o Claims of Belonging in the U.S. Heartland

MARTA MARÍA MALDONADO

Since the 1990s, Latina/o populations have increasingly settled into a range of "new gateways." In the rural Midwest, recruitment by employers in meatpacking and other food processing industries has been a key factor leading to a growing Latina/o presence.[1] Other contributing factors include the militarization of the United States–Mexico border, the passage of restrictive policies (such as Proposition 187 in California) along with growing anti-immigrant sentiment in "old" gateways, social networks, lower cost of living and availability of affordable housing in new gateway communities, the desire to move away from areas of high crime and gang activity, the desire to live and raise kids in areas with better schools, and generally the desire for greater tranquility.[2]

In this chapter, I draw from ethnographic and interview data to examine how Latinas/os articulate the meanings of nationhood and of their own presence in a new gateway in the rural Midwest. My focus is on the discourses of Latinas/os who live and work in Perry, Iowa, a small town that had few Latinas/os prior to 1990, in a region that can be characterized as emblematic of white America. I ask, how are stories of the U.S. nation reproduced or interrupted by diverse Latina/o populations who have settled in Perry? How do Latinas/os in this small town make claims to community and nation? To what extent are they able to develop a sense of belonging? I argue that Perry, and new gateways in general, constitute a sort of last socio-spatial frontier of immigrant incorporation in the United States; they are the spaces in which the new border politics are embodied and enacted, where the sociopolitical boundaries of culture and nation are played out in and through everyday interactions.

Latinas/os in Dominant Representations of the United States

While Latinas/os arrive in the United States from many different countries in the vast regions of Mexico, Central and South America, and the Caribbean, and while they have varied cultures and diverse languages, U.S. institutions and mainstream cultural outlets often racialize and represent them as one monolithic group, with a single "Hispanic" culture. Furthermore, while Latinas/os have been part of U.S. history and integral to the nation's development since the mid-1800s, and while most Latinas/os—63 percent, according to the 2010 U.S. Census—are, in fact, Americans by birth, dominant representations and discourses frequently portray them as foreigners and recent arrivals.[3] As Suzanne Oboler notes, "the ongoing exclusion of . . . historical minorities from the historical memory of the American imagined community means that Puerto Ricans and many second and later generations of Mexican Americans/Chicanos continue to be treated as second-class citizens when they are not perceived as newly arrived immigrants."[4]

This routine construction of Latinas/os as foreigners within U.S. public discourse is anchored on multiple elements, which include, notably, language, specifically the assumption that Latinas/os do not speak English, and also the belief that Latinas/os are unassimilable and forever foreign.[5] These elements permeate the discourses through which, on a quotidian basis, individuals, the media, conservative politicians, a growing number of anti-immigrant groups, and even some scholars, place Latinas/os irremediably outside the boundaries of the United States. In so doing, the imagined unity of the United States is reaffirmed, and U.S. history and national space are mythologized as white-Anglo America. As Paul Allatson argues, "the U.S.A.'s imaginability is unique because of the particular ways by which hegemonic rhetoric disclaims certain sectors as non-, un-, or even anti-American. Such sectors provide the internal loci of disavowal required for the U.S.A. to be mythologized as a community. . . . Pivotal in this regard are the ways in which Latino populations have been selectively included in or excluded from, or imaginatively fixed as peripheral in or even disruptive to, an array of U.S. national myths and an associated conglomerate of longstanding official or governing cultural logics."[6]

Racialized and outright racist constructions of Latinas/os as not just different from "Americans" (i.e., White Americans) but alas, also inferior, have even cropped up packaged as research findings, as in the case of Jason Richwine's 2009 dissertation for Harvard University. In a column published by the Huffington Post, Jason Ward notes that Richwine's dissertation claimed to demonstrate that "Hispanic immigrants have substantially lower IQs than do Whites." Ward quotes

Richwine's dissertation: "No one knows whether Hispanics will ever reach IQ parity with whites, but the prediction that new Hispanic immigrants will have low-IQ children and grandchildren is difficult to argue against. From the perspective of Americans alive today, the low average IQ of Hispanics is effectively permanent."[7] Richwine's arguments were anchored partly in old-fashioned biological racism: lower IQs among Hispanics in the United States are caused partly, he claimed, by genetics, though "the extent of [genetic] impact is hard to determine." There was also an element of "culture of poverty"[8] in Richwine's arguments. He characterized "the growing Hispanic underclass" as "a socially isolated group of people for whom crime, welfare, labor force dropout, and illegitimacy are normal aspects of life." Assimilation into U.S. culture and values is, according to Richwine, the only thing that will save some Hispanics in later generations—specifically those who will go to U.S. schools, learn English, and in sum, abandon all things non-U.S.

Sloppy as Richwine's arguments are, even when they clearly reflect the same faulty and discredited thinking that characterized scientific racism in the seventeenth and eighteenth centuries— Richwine's dissertation was still supervised *and approved* by a scholarly committee at Harvard University, earning him a doctorate in public policy. Furthermore, Richwine's arguments were spread and ventilated as valid "research findings" in national media outlets. For example, on September 11, 2009, the *New York Times* cited Richwine's work in an "Idea of the Day" column focusing on Robert Putnam's controversial finding that "ethnic diversity isn't an unqualified good." As the credibility of Richwine's work, and other "reports" and proposals for immigration restriction informed by it, came under growing scrutiny, some, including ultraconservative pundit Rush Limbaugh, defended Richwine and his research. Limbaugh declared on his radio program: "So, now it's trash the messenger time. . . . You're not supposed to bring that kind of stuff up. You're not supposed to talk about it. It's not politically correct, even if it's true. You're not supposed to bring it up."[9]

Others have similarly fanned the flames of anti-Latina/o sentiment using overtly racist claims.[10] As a result, a climate of "Hispanophobia" has become entrenched throughout the nation.[11] This entrenchment is especially visible in the context of the Department of Homeland Security state, which has not only militarized the United States–Mexico border but has extended border politics to the heartland and beyond, through heightened immigration controls and practices such as massive raids in worksites and communities, and the deputizing of local law enforcement to enforce immigration laws.[12] As the Latina/o presence reaches new gateways throughout the nation and continues to grow, and as more Latinas/os face such dominant discourses and their consequences in community contexts, their responses will help alter the national character of the United States through the renegotiation of the material and symbolic boundaries of culture and nation. How Latinas/os respond, how they speak back, has the potential to not only challenge "Hispanophobia" but also to interrogate and transform the social and political content of U.S. categories of race or ethnicity, class, nation, and citizenship.

The Study Site

Perry is a small meatpacking town of 7,702 residents located along the North Raccoon River, northwest of the city of Des Moines, in Central Iowa.[13] There were few, if any, Latinas/os living in Perry prior to 1990. Census data show that the town had forty-seven Latina/o residents in 1990. After just two decades, Latinas/os have come to constitute 35 percent of the town's total population. The "Latinization" of Perry is even more drastic and apparent if one looks at the younger segments of the town's population. As of 2016, 50.1 percent of Perry's elementary school students were Latino (National Center for Education Statistics).[14]

The demographic shift experienced in Perry has been driven to a great extent by restructuring of meatpacking and, more specifically, by the changes that such restructuring set forth in the local meatpacking plant. The plant first opened in

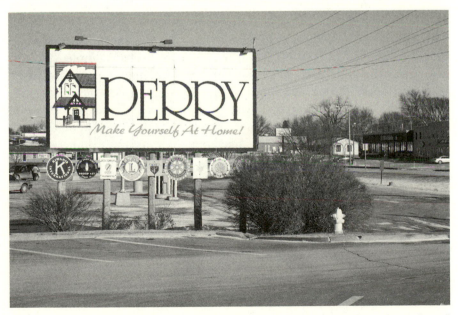

2.3.1   A welcome sign at the entrance of town invites visitors to "make themselves at home" in Perry, Iowa. Photo by Marta María Maldonado.

Perry in the 1920s, becoming a lead employer in subsequent decades.[15] In the early decades of the plant's operations, its workforce consisted predominantly of local residents, the vast majority of whom were whites of European ancestry. In the 1980s, industry restructuring resulted in a change in the conditions associated with meatpacking jobs, as well as changes in who constituted the labor force. As a strategy to reduce labor costs, employers moved away from unionized labor and began aggressively recruiting Latina/o (and also some Asian) workers. Employers recruited Latinas/os from established gateways such as California and Texas. As the first Latinas/os began to take jobs in the plant, informal recruitment practices and social networks continued to replenish the workforce and enabled recruitment of other Latinas/os, including some who came to Perry directly from their countries of origin. Latinas/os have since become the primary low-wage labor force in this meatpacking town.[16]

Perry is an ideal site for exploring how ethnicity, nation, and identity are discursively articulated and experienced, and how narratives of community and nation are reproduced and/or interrupted by Latinas/os. For one, new gateways such as Perry constitute a sort of last geographical and sociocultural frontier of immigrant (and more broadly, of Latina/o) incorporation. Given the newness of the Latina/o presence in these spaces, long-term residents often experience demographic change as a "shock" and as a threat to community identity and quality of life.[17] Additionally, in recent years, the rural Midwest and Iowa in particular have received much national media attention as the site of the most massive and visible anti-immigrant raid in U.S. history. As Étienne Balibar has noted, the border is everywhere. The geographic, sociopolitical, and cultural boundaries of the United States are enacted and contested in communities across the nation, with new gateways such as the rural Midwest being among the newest sites of heated border politics. Borders are not simply geopolitical—they are also embodied.[18] In Perry, Latina/o bodies and accents stand out by virtue of being different from what is assumed to be the ethno-racial norm in "the heart of America." As more and more Latinas/os circulate in community spaces, the community landscape has been and continues to be reconfigured. Local supermarkets have incorporated products aimed at Latina/o consumers. Latina/o business establishments have opened up. Some non-Latina/o-owned businesses have begun incorporating Latina/o (or at least Spanish-speaking) personnel. The presence of Latina/o iconographies (use of Spanish in signs, newspapers, and in materials produced by schools and other local institutions), and of generally recognizable sights of Latina/o cultures also attest to the Latinization of the town. In this chapter I explore how Latinas/os who live and/or work in Perry make sense of this unfolding transformation, whether and how they make connections to place, and develop a sense of belonging.

Space and Senses of (Un)Belonging

Latina/o sense(s) of place, their sense of belonging in the U.S. communities where they live and labor, offer a useful vantage point from which to explore Latina/o articulations of the United States, and the meanings they afford to their own presence on U.S. soil. Most Latinas/os I interviewed characterized Perry as "a tranquil place" and highlighted similar factors when describing what attracted them there. The most recurrent attractive dimensions of Perry reported by Latinas/os include jobs, the availability of affordable housing, and the importance of being able to raise children away from the crime, violence, and gang activity that tends to characterize urban areas of established Latina/o settlement. However, the stories told by Latinas/os reveal differences among segments of the Latina/o population in their ability to make connections to place, and to develop a sense of belonging. Some who had lived in Perry for a relatively long time (since the early 1990s), and some who were second generation (who grew up in Perry), described their relationship with neighbors as cordial, spoke about Perry as their home, and reported feeling free to circulate through community spaces and to interact with community institutions. These participants were typically bilingual or had at least some English fluency. They were either U.S. citizens by birth or had legal resident status.

The majority of Latinas/os interviewed, however, spoke of Perry as a place where quality of life and the ability to live peacefully and "without trouble," require a kind of tiptoeing around community space, so as not to bother or cause discomfort to "Americanos," their White American neighbors. Indeed, one recurrent theme throughout the interviews entailed a range of day-to-day practices Latinas/os undertake to remain mostly invisible and unheard, in order to avoid trouble with neighbors and local authorities, and to defy discourses of immigrants as problems.[19] Some rationalized this need to stay "below the radar" by noting that they are not in *their* country, but "in Americans' country." When one is in someone else's home, they explained, one should behave well. Benito's comments illustrate this position: "Sometimes we (Latinas/os) bring [to the United States], we could say, misbehaving, lack of respect for others, and this implies annoying the neighbor, the American community. . . . We are in their house and we don't know how to behave. [Interviewer: Do you feel that it is your house too?] . . . . It's more theirs . . . I feel like I'm a visitor, and as such, I should behave well. This is their country and you're not going to come here to cause them discomfort."[20]

Not all those interviewed, however, shared this sense of "estando en casa ajena," or living "in someone else's home." Some expressed resentment of the discourses, practices, and contexts that make them feel that they do not belong in Perry or in the United States. Interviewees expressed such resentment in response to the ways immigrants are often criminalized or represented as problems, and they contextualized this in relation to Latinas/os' role in the economic vitality of Perry and the larger U.S. economy. Recalling an anti-immigrant radio talk show discussion in which the caller argued that immigrants only come to take away jobs, Maria said, "they give us the jobs they don't want to do because they don't like to work as much as we do. They need our labor, and that is something good that one brings. If no Latinos were here in Perry, I don't believe IBP [Iowa Beef Processors] or what is now Tyson would be here. The same is true for construction work. . . . Hispanics are always the ones who do the hardest labor and I believe that in one way or another, we always contribute more to this community." Likewise, Jorge noted, "the Latino has helped the economy of this town. For example, the store Hy-Vee was small and they made it big. There's another one too called Fareway."[21]

Latina/o stories display an awareness of the ways in which dominant discourses as well as *the American gaze* render them not just raced, but also classed (a marginalized class), with consequences for everyday life in the community. Many expressed resistance to a range of practices and discourses that produce Latinas/os as always only laborers. This was evident in their discussions about being "more than just laborers," about a desire to be accepted and engaged by the community beyond their capacity as workers. Berta stated Latinas/os need Americans "to see us . . . not like we're invading this country, not like strangers, but like neighbors, like people who have just arrived but are not foreign to this country or to the community . . . and maybe for both cultures [Americans and Latinas/os] to get more involved with each other. . . . I would like to see more minorities working in different types of businesses—not just low-end businesses—I would like to see, more [Latina/o] teachers and administrators."[22]

The narratives of Latinas/os in Perry display an awareness of what Alexandra Dobrowolsky has referred to as "instrumentalization." Instrumentalization can be defined as the social processes by which we come to think of and treat certain populations as instruments or tools. Dobrowolsky notes that instrumentalization entails a parallel process of "invisibilization." States, localities, and businesses call on certain labor practices, such as the massive recruitment of immigrant populations—especially those who are most vulnerable economically and politically by virtue of being undocumented—while simultaneously producing and maintaining conditions for the continued "invisibilization" of the laboring immigrant population.[23] The threat of deportability forces the undocumented, and those to whom they are connected by kin, to remain in the shadows, unable to denounce abuses or mistreatment, and without legal recourse or protection by the state.[24] Put differently, immigrants are at once wanted in particular contexts (as laborers), and unwanted and even rejected in other contexts, lacking realistic opportunities to live and work in the United States legally, being shrouded with a stigma of illegality and criminality by the media, and facing hostility in everyday encounters.

Across the United States, Latinas/os are incorporated into rural communities such as Perry as laborers first and foremost, always in a position of economic marginality, and mostly as an underclass.[25] The narratives of many Latinas/os in Perry suggest a keen awareness that they are recruited into tough, low-wage jobs and are accepted in Perry strictly as laborers, but that they are otherwise not accepted as full members of the community. Many Latinas/os expressed resentment because they saw themselves and other Latinas/os as contributors to the economic well-being of Perry and of the United States, but felt they were not regarded as neighbors and equals in community contexts. Several young men specifically related their sense of unbelonging in Perry to an awareness of instrumentalization. They felt pressured to conform to expectations of Latinas/os as always only laborers. Manny, who was nearing high school graduation, mentioned that he wanted to leave Perry because there are no attractive jobs, or at least no work he wanted to pursue. "There are just, like, two main jobs here in Perry, which is picking corn and Tyson." Similarly, Luisa, a mother, explained that her eldest son refused to get a job through the subcontracting job agency that many Latinas/os use when they first arrive in Perry. "He doesn't want to work there or at Tyson— he says that only when he has his papers [he will work]." Luisa noted that "he wants to go to college. . . . He says 'I'm not going to work at Tyson . . . I'm going to be able to look for work elsewhere.' He has his ideas, his dream is to become a police officer, but he doesn't have papers. He graduated [high school], and he can't continue his studies because we don't have the means to pay, so he can go on to college."[26] These young Latinos actively resist and reject instrumentalization and the pigeonholing of Latino males as manual laborers. They demand a different type of belonging, one in which Latina/o youths do not simply fill an underclass, but where they have full access to resources and opportunity.

Ethnographic observation also reveals the existence of "parallel worlds" in Perry.[27] Latinas/os and non-Latinas/os in Perry live, for the most part, segregated lives, with little opportunity for sustained interaction across ethno-racial lines. There are few everyday contexts where there is considerable interaction between Latina/o and those who Latinas/os refer to as "Americanos." Church communities are separated by language, and Latinas/os and "Americanos" work at different jobs and tend to practice civic engagement in different ways. In these ways, different ethno-racial segments of community, with their unique concerns, needs, and experiences as well as their ways of contributing to the community, remain invisible to each other. In fact, when I asked Latinas/os in Perry about their connections to community, they often appeared to interpret this to mean their connections to other Latinas/os in Perry, as if Latinas/os and non-Latinas/os belonged to separate and different communities.[28]

One specific instance of parallel worlds takes the form of segregated labor practices that are spatialized and configured around ethnicity and immigrant status.

These segregated labor practices were consistently described by interviewees who worked at the local meat processing plant. Latina/o descriptions of that workplace reveal that whites occupy most, if not all, management positions. Several Latinas/os suggested that a given job's level of risk and strenuousness correlates with who performs that job. The most dangerous jobs, for instance, are undertaken during the night shift and are often performed by those without papers (unauthorized immigrants).[29] Segregated labor practices are one example of how the day-to-day production of parallel Latina/o and non-Latina/o worlds hinges, in part, on different timing for daily activities and circulation through community spaces. Further evidence of the existence of parallel worlds in Perry is apparent in Latinas/os' descriptions of their leisure activities. Latinas/os (especially immigrants, but also those who have family members who are undocumented) spoke of going fishing or picnicking in isolated places, where they were not likely to encounter other people, and where they were not likely to call attention to themselves and get in trouble.[30]

Altogether, Latina/o descriptions of their lives in Perry show how they see themselves as contributors to the material well-being of the United States, and how, on that basis, they make claims to community space. They allude to work as a key nation-building process in which they are full and vital participants, as they not only work hard, but often tackle the toughest jobs that are unwanted by most Americans. However, Latinas/os in Perry reject characterizations and sociocultural scripts that confine them to low-wage work and include them in the United States solely as a marginalized class of manual laborers. They call for full inclusion in all spheres and ranks of economic, social, and political life ("I would like to see more [Latinas/os and minorities] working in different types of businesses—not just low-end businesses—I would like to see, more teachers and administrators"). In the following section, I examine how Latinas/os also interrogate and reject dominant visions of the United States as a monocultural, monolingual nation.

Talking Back, *en español*

Nativist politics in the post-1970s era of U.S. immigration have accorded a great deal of attention to the issue of language. An insistence on monolingualism and the privileging of the English language have been key concerns within the nativist agenda of recent decades in the United States. At the broader systemic level, language itself has been racialized, much in the same way as have been those who speak it. Dominant cultural politics have entailed the devaluing—sometimes even the demonizing—of the Spanish language. The use of Spanish, the mixing of Spanish and English into the hybrid Spanglish, and Latina/o accents have all been racialized as inferior within the U.S. sonic and linguistic landscapes. U.S.

institutions, including schools, the media, and scholars in a variety of disciplines have often assigned negative characteristics to Spanish usage, and frequently invoke perceptions of Spanish language dominance among Latinos as explanation for their marginalized position in U.S. society.[31] As Ofelia García argues, "the Spanish language and bilingualism have become markers of being non-white, of being 'out of place,' thus minoritizing the position of U.S. Latinos and excluding them. . . . No longer viewed as the language of original settlers, or even of the conquered and colonized who might be entitled to language and civil rights, but characterized as the language of foreign immigrants, often undocumented, and blamed for the poverty and the low level of education of U.S. Latinos, Spanish is held in contempt in political and educational circles."[32]

At the micro level of day-to-day interactions between individuals, and at the level of institutional practices, the regulating and policing of linguistic landscapes and boundaries is a central aspect of community and nation building. The state of Iowa has formalized English-only as a purportedly unifying force. In 2002, the Iowa General Assembly passed the Iowa English Language Reaffirmation Act (IELRA), mandating English as the state's "official" language. Representative Dwayne Alons, of Hull, who led the language initiative in the Iowa House, compared the state to a salad: "When you put together your salad, the one item that really brings it together is a dressing. For Iowa, I believe English is that one ingredient for us."[33] The law mandates English-only in the printing of all government documents and forms, except for driver's education materials, trade and tourism documents, and documents discussing the rights of victims of crimes, criminal defendants, and constitutional issues. In Perry, demographic change has entailed the remapping of the linguistic, and more broadly, sonic landscape.[34] The sights and sounds of Spanish are often coded negatively and managed through practices of linguistic surveillance in the dominant cultural context. There is a spatialized everyday policing of language boundaries. Latinas/os who speak Spanish in some community spaces, specifically in those spaces in which conversations in Spanish enter the radar of "Americans," such as schools and hospitals, report being reproached for speaking Spanish and instructed to speak English. For example, Doris noted that speaking Spanish made her feel vulnerable to the constant gaze of her "American" neighbors. "Wherever we went," Doris noted, "I was a bit scared of not knowing English because the Americans would laugh at us, and when you'd go someplace to eat they'd keep staring at you, and that would make me mad. . . . They'd be staring at me while I ate, and if I went to the store they'd keep staring."[35]

In effect, Latinas/os who were primary speakers of Spanish articulated being scolded by "Americans" for speaking Spanish across community and employment contexts in Perry, and they explained experiencing Perry as an English-only context. The practices they described constitute not only a kind of linguistic boundary surveillance, but also a type of everyday violence that seeks to render immigrants silent and invisible. Interestingly, discussions about such policing of language practices were frequently contextualized by Latinas/os in relation to the sense of instrumentalization described earlier. Several Latinas who worked at a health clinic reported being yelled at and admonished for speaking Spanish. These women specifically expressed resentment about how Americans silence Latinas/os and deny them a right to speak Spanish, while also actively seeking out and recruiting Latinas/os for the most labor-intensive and lowest-skilled jobs. Latina/o interviewees consistently expressed an understanding that their labor was valued while their presence was devalued, an experience that had implications for their sense of belonging. For example, Jacinta explained that "in both of the places where I've worked here there was a lot of racism. . . . In the free classes [training] that were offered most of us were Hispanic, and [the personnel] didn't want us there, they forbade us from speaking Spanish [when we were] working, and also in class we were not allowed to speak Spanish. . . . One person was scolded for speaking Spanish." Jacinta experienced linguistic discrimination, even in a context where Latinas/os constituted the majority.[36] Similarly, Doris, pointed to the speaking of Spanish as something that resulted in a kind of hypervisibility for her and other Spanish-speaking Latinas/os.

2.3.2   A Salvadoran restaurant on Second Street, next to a Spanish Learning Center. Photo by Marta María Maldonado.

She emphasized how the comfort with which she circulated as a "Spanish-speaking immigrant" in California, where she had lived before, has turned into discomfort and even fear in Perry. She noted a great deal of fear associated with being the object of unwanted attention due to her lack of English skills. Notably, she connected the unwanted attention for speaking Spanish that is directed at her in Perry to a continual surveillance of her presence at restaurants and stores.[37]

The interviews with Latinas/os show that linguistic practices are enacted within a broader sonic or auditory community landscape. In their daily lives in Perry, Latinas/os routinely pay attention to Americans' perceptions of music and "noise." Some spoke of practicing a kind of noise regulation, or even muteness, at home, in their cars, and in public spaces, as a way to live peacefully and not get into trouble with "Americanos." For example, Josefina noted, "I've lived next door to Americans, and I've never had problems with them because . . . everyone lives their life. . . . This is their country and you're not gonna come here to make them uncomfortable with all that music, and all of that stuff that makes them uncomfortable." Similarly, Maria spoke about how she tries to be a good neighbor, "you just have to not mess with them, simply don't be playing music. . . . It's true, each one is in their property, but you're not going to make other people who don't like your music uncomfortable. And more as a Hispanic, where we play music so loud that . . . it's deafening. (*Laughs.*)"[38]

Other interviews were less concerned with disrupting their white American neighbors. For example, Hector noted that "if we're neighbors and you don't like loud music, sorry, this is who we are, if you don't like it, move elsewhere—And they are moving elsewhere!" Likewise, Luisa commented, "40 percent of Anglos don't know us very well and they prefer to keep their distance. . . . Many don't like noise, but for us it's not noise: it's happiness." Benjamin also pointed to the contest over sonic landscapes as an area of tension between Latinos and non-Latinas/os in Perry. "The American is jealous in the sense that they say we take away from them," Benjamin explained. "For example, they're mad because we took away their radio [station]. What's now the Spanish radio [station] used to be an Anglo radio station, and it got bought [by Latinas/os] and taken to Des Moines, and they're mad about that."[39]

Benjamin's remarks are a reminder that the contest over soundscape also has institutional and political dimensions. The emergence of Latina/o media in Perry, in particular, a radio station, has relevance beyond the strictly cultural. Latinos alluded to "the Spanish station" as a source of information that allows them to ascertain and navigate locally the threat of deportability, and through which they learn about community resources relevant to their needs. Petra shared the following.

The majority [of Latinos] live with fear and without information. But we have the radio, which is an excellent means of communication. . . . We have it playing all day long, it keeps us informed about raids, and above all else, about everything that is happening with immigration. There was an attorney that came to Des Moines every Monday for an hour and a half, taking calls, answering any question one had.[40]

Pedro told a similar story.

On the radio we heard that there was a sheriff that used to stop Latinos [who were driving] between Perry and Des Moines, and he was found out—and we learned about it on the radio, that there were going to be some meetings that people who ever encountered problems with this guy should attend.[41]

These examples regarding Latinas/os' need to remain invisible in a context of negatively coded hypervisibility, and their concomitant reliance on radio broadcasts as an informational, culturally relevant, and culturally and legally transgressive tool, suggest that Dolores Inés Casillas is right when she argues that

it is the need to seek legal advice and documentation without being visually recognized that privileges (for Latinos) the medium of sound. . . .

U.S.-Spanish language radio is an acoustic tool for listeners, specifically its most legally vulnerable immigrant listeners, to navigate the U.S. immigration system during moments of political discrimination and heightened security. . . .

In the face of visual-based surveillance and legislative tactics, Spanish-language broadcasting offers a transgressive possibility to patrol la migra in both its physical and its bureaucratic manifestations.[42]

The stories shared by Latinas/os challenge the imposition of English-only through various practices including linguistic and sonic surveillance. These discriminatory and silencing procedures are incongruent with the demographic reality of Perry and the United States, and further, are practices that deny Latinas/os the space to be themselves fully, in their cultural complexity and specificity within U.S. communities. While some Latinas/os monitor their use of Spanish and the emission, so to speak, of Latina/o sounds, as a strategy to survive and coexist in community, others make overt claims to space through what may be characterized as a sonic takeover of community.

Conclusions and Implications

The Perry example shows that, while there are differences among Latinas/os in the extent to which they see themselves as belonging in the rural Midwest and in the United States, many challenge dominant discourses and practices that welcome them as laborers and yet deny them full belonging as members and contributors to community and nation. Overwhelmingly, Latinas/os in Perry described their lives as lives of work. In their accounts of daily activities, they recognize themselves as vital contributors to the material, economic foundation of Perry and indeed of the nation. There is a discernible sense of pride in Latina/o descriptions of their commitment to work in the United States. Significantly, several Latinas/os punctuated that the fact that Latinas/os are willing to tackle hard jobs (jobs that Americans often do not want) does not mean they are disinterested in or incapable of tackling better jobs, or that they are content simply being constricted to manual labor. As Berta, quoted above, noted, "I would like to see more (Latinas/os and) minorities working in different types of businesses—not just low-end businesses—I would like to see, more (Latina/o) teachers and administrators."[43] Young Latinas/os, including several who are Americans by birth, expressed their rejection of what they saw as a pervasive expectation in the community and in the overall society that they become workers in the local meatpacking plant, or low-wage laborers elsewhere. Young males especially relayed a keen awareness of such expectation, and their desire and intention to not fulfill it.

Further, Latinas/os in Perry, independently of age or length of residence in Perry or in the United States, often interrogated the incorporation of Latinas/os into the country strictly as a marginalized class of workers, while otherwise being denied their full humanity, with its particular cultural manifestations. From Latinas/os own accounts, this denial of full humanity takes multiple forms, ranging from a context of reception that makes them uncomfortable when they circulate throughout the community as Latina/o-looking, Latina/o-sounding bodies, to downright hostility, surveillance, and persecution associated with the extension of border politics to the heartland, and the racialization of Latinas/os as criminals and "illegals." To this point, Latinas/os spoke about wanting "Americans" to see them and engage them, not as strangers, but as neighbors.

I interpret these recurrent themes as a critique of the racialized class relations implicit within dominant visions of the nation as a whole, and as the starting point for an alternative vision of the United States and of rural America from a Latina/o perspective. Across industries, regions, and communities, the United States relies heavily on Latina/o labor for its everyday functioning and prosperity. Latinas/os take those jobs others do not want, jobs that would remain vacant, productivity that would be lost, were it not for Latina/o workers.[44] The discourses articulated and embodied by growing numbers of Latinas/os in Perry (and arguably, in other similar communities across the country) bring to the fore the question of how dynamic and contested relations of race, ethnicity, and class affect the structure and cultural content of the United States. They specifically point to the contradiction inherent in inviting and recruiting Latinas/os to perform jobs in the United States, while simultaneously and systematically precluding them from living and participating fully in community. As discussed, most Latinas/os interviewed in Perry articulated a vision of the nation in which they are included as integral, not just to the economic vitality, but also to the sociocultural and political fabric of communities and the nation. The case of Perry also suggests that a community's sonic landscape is a key arena in which the cultural and linguistic boundaries of the nation are contested on a quotidian basis. Latinas/os spoke about choosing to regulate (or not) the volume and type of music and noise emerging from their homes and cars, and the sound of their interactions with others (volume of conversations, the language in which they speak), as a way to make claims to place and belonging in Perry. Several Latinas/os who were recently arrived described Perry as a site in which English is dominant and there is little room for linguistic diversity. In fact, they described an everyday policing of language boundaries in which they were reprimanded through hostile words or stares for speaking Spanish. They rejected the monoculturalist vision of the United States in which such policing practices are anchored. Further, they criticized these silencing practices as symptomatic of instrumentalization and of the dehumanizing of Latinas/os in the United States.

The lived experiences of Latinas/os in Perry illustrate that the content and meaning of the heartland and of the nation itself are neither fixed nor stable, but rather contested and always in flux. Community spaces across the United States are always contingent and becoming—a reflection of historically specific social relations and "stories so far." As the "Latinization of America" continues to unfold, the stories embodied and told by Latinas/os bespeak a larger story about social relations of power and about sociocultural change as necessarily formative of community and nation. In the course of ongoing and rapid demographic change, dominant notions of community and national identity are likely to be challenged, complicated, resisted, and reshaped from the margins, in part through the everyday practices and from the perspectives of transcultural subjects.

Notes

1. Lourdes Gouveia and Donald Stull, "Dances with Cows: Beefpacking's Impact on Garden City, Kansas, and Lexington, Nebraska," in *Any Way You Cut It: Meat Processing and Small-Town America*, ed. Donald D. Stull, Michael J. Broadway, and David Griffith (Lawrence: Kansas University Press, 1995), 85–107; Nancy Naples, *Economic Restructuring and Racialization: Incorporation of Mexicans and Mexican-Americans in the Rural Midwest*, Working Paper 7, Center for Comparative Immigration Studies at UC San Diego, 2000; Mark Grey and Anne Woodrick, "'Latinos Have Revitalized Our Community': Mexican Migration and Anglo Responses in Marshalltown, Iowa," in *New Destinations: Mexican Immigration in the United States*, ed. Víctor Zúñiga and Rubén Hernández-León (New York: Russell Sage, 2005), 133–54; and William Kandel and Emilio Parrado, "Restructuring of the US Meat Processing Industry and New Hispanic Migrant Destinations," *Population and Development Review* 31, no. 3 (2005): 447–71.

2. See, for example, Jorge Durand, Douglas S. Massey, and Chiara Capoferro, "The New Geography of Mexican Immigration," in Zúñiga and Hernández-León, *New Destinations*, 1–20; Rubén Hernández-León and Víctor Zúñiga, "Making Carpet by the Mile: The Emergence of a Mexican Immigrant Community in an Industrial Region of the U.S. Historic South," *Social Science Quarterly* 81, no. 1 (2000): 49–66; Douglas S. Massey, ed., *New Faces in New Places: The Changing Geography of American Immigration* (New York: Russell Sage Foundation, 2008); and Katherine Fennelly and Helga Leitner, *How the Food Processing Industry Is Diversifying Rural Minnesota*, Working Paper 59, Julian Samora Research Institute, Michigan State University, East Lansing, 2002.

3. Rogelio Sáenz, "Latinos in America 2010," *Population Bulletin Update* (December 2010). An example of Latinas/os being characterized as "foreign" is that neither Mexican Americans nor Puerto Ricans have been fully accepted as U.S. citizens despite their history as laborers and property holders on land now under U.S. control. Mexicans have been on U.S. soil since 1848, when a large portion of Mexican land was made U.S. territory, and have been massively recruited as laborers since the beginning of the twentieth century. Similarly, large shares of the Puerto Rican population were incorporated as laborers for various industries across the United States immediately following U.S. intervention on the island in 1898.

4. Suzanne Oboler, *Ethnic Labels, Latino Lives: Identity and the Politics of (Re)Presentation in the United States* (Minneapolis: University of Minnesota Press, 1995), 171.

5. Linda Martín Alcoff, "Latinos beyond the Binary," *Southern Journal of Philosophy* 47, no. 2 (2009): 112–28; Otto Santa Ana, *Brown Tide Rising: Metaphors of Latinos in Contemporary American Public Discourse* (Austin: University of Texas Press, 2002), 289.

6. Paul Allatson, *Latino Dreams: Transcultural Traffic and the U.S. National Imaginary* (New York: Rodopi, 2002), 24.

7. Jon Ward, "Jason Richwine Dissertation on Low Hispanic IQ Puts Heritage on Defensive," *Huffington Post*, May 8, 2013.

8. The "culture of poverty" idea was first advanced by anthropologist Oscar Lewis based on his studies of poor Mexican and Puerto Rican communities. In a nutshell, the culture of poverty "theory" presumes that the attitudes, values, and behaviors of the poor are what leads them to and keeps them in poverty. Lewis argued the burdens of poverty lead to the formation of an autonomous subculture, as children are socialized into behaviors and attitudes that perpetuate their inability to escape the underclass. Lewis's ideas have long been widely critiqued and discredited by scholars from a variety of disciplines—see, for example, Jack Roach and Orville Gursslin, "An Evaluation of the Concept 'Culture of Poverty,'" *Social Forces* 45, no. 3 (1965): 383–92; Eleanor Burke Leacock, ed., *The Culture of Poverty: A Critique* (New York: Simon and Shuster, 1971); Paul Gorski, "The Myth of the Culture of Poverty," *Poverty and Learning* 65, no. 7 (2008): 32–36.

9. *The Rush Limbaugh Show*, Premiere Radio Networks, broadcast May 9, 2013.

10. See, for example, Peter Brimelow, *Alien Nation: Common Sense about America's Immigration Disaster* (New York: Harper Perennial 1996); Patrick Buchanan, *The Death of the West: How Dying Populations and Immigrant Invasions Imperil Our Country and Civilization* (New York: St. Martin's Press, 2002).

11. Heidi Beirich, "The Anti-Immigrant Movement," Southern Poverty Law Center, Intelligence Files, 2011, http://dialogic.blogspot.com/2011/03/heidi-beirich-anti-immigrant-movement.html, accessed Dec. 19, 2016.

12. Matthew Coleman, "Immigration Geopolitics Beyond the Mexico–US Border," *Antipode: A Radical Journal of Geography* 39, no. 1 (2007): 54–76.

13. U.S. Census Bureau, 2010.

14. Perry Elementary School statistics, school ID 192253000051, Institute of Education Sciences and National Center for Education Statistics, Common Core of Data, http://nces.ed.gov/ccd/schoolsearch, accessed Dec. 19, 2016.

15. The plant changed owners at various points and has been operated by Oscar Meyer, Iowa Beef Processors, and Tyson Foods.

16. Ferro Trabalzi and Gerardo Sandoval, "The Exotic Other: Latinos and the Remaking of Community Identity in Perry, Iowa," *Community Development* 41, no. 1 (2010): 76–91.

17. Lionel Cantú, "The Peripheralization of Rural America: A Case Study of Latino Migrants in America's Heartland," *Sociological Perspectives* 38, no. 3 (1995): 399–414.

18. Étienne Balibar, *We, the People of Europe? Reflections on Transnational Citizenship* (Princeton, N.J.: Princeton University Press, 2004).

19. The experiences of Latinas/os in Perry suggest that many pursue invisibility routinely as a tactical response to imposed, structural hypervisibilities, which are coded with a range of negative connotations. For a detailed discussion of "the social production of Latino hypervisibilities and invisibilities," see Adela C. Licona and Marta María Maldonado, "The Social Production of Latino/a Visibilities and Invisibilities: Geographies of Power in Small Town America," *Antipode* 46: 517–36 doi:10.1111/anti.12049.

20. Benito, interview with author, Perry, Iowa, March 25, 2007. To protect the confidentiality of the interviewees, all names of those interviewed are pseudonyms.

21. Maria, interview with author, Perry, Iowa, March 27, 2007. Jorge, interview with author, Perry, Iowa, March 28, 2007.

22. Berta, interview with author, Perry, Iowa, March 28, 2007.

23. Alexandra Dobrowolsky, "Interrogating 'Invisibilization' and 'Instrumentalization': Women and Current Citizenship Trends in Canada," *Citizenship Studies* 12, no. 5 (2008): 465–79.

24. Nicholas De Genova, "Migrant 'Illegality' and Deportability in Everyday Life," *Annual Review of Anthropology* 31 (2002): 419–47.

25. Leif Jensen, *New Immigrant Settlements in Rural America: Problems, Prospects, and Policies*, Reports on Rural America, vol. 1, no. 3 (Durham: University of New Hampshire / Carsey Institute, 2006).

26. Manny, interview with author, Perry, Iowa, March 28, 2007. Luisa, interview with author, Perry, Iowa, July 14, 2007.

27. Lise Nelson and Nancy Hiemstra, "Latino Immigrants and the Renegotiation of Place and Belonging in Small Town America," *Social and Cultural Geography* 9 (2008): 319–42.

28. When they described their life trajectories, experiences, and interactions in Perry, Latinas/os spoke of and acknowledged differences in national origin among Latinas/os, but they also acknowledged common ground along ethno-racial lines, identifying simultaneously in terms of their particular national origin, and also as "Latinos" or "hispanos."

Several spoke of other Latinas/os as "their people" or "their brothers and sisters." However, Puerto Ricans, who occupy a different structural location in Perry, holding the better-paid jobs (supervisory positions in meatpacking, and jobs in real estate and a range of local institutions), discursively distanced themselves from other Latinas/os, with several identifying, not as Latinas/os, but as Americans. Central Americans and Mexicans also often described their experiences and interests as different from those of Puerto Ricans.

29. Lupe, interview with author, Perry, Iowa, March 29, 2007.

30. Rosa, interview with author, Perry, Iowa, March 28, 2007.

31. Elizabeth Aranda and Guillermo Rebollo-Gil, "Ethnoracism and the Sandwiched Minorities," *American Behavioral Scientist* 47, no. 7 (March 2004): 910–27. See also Ofelia García, "Racializing the Language Practices of U.S. Latinos: Impact on Their Education," 101–15, and Jane H. Hill, "English-Language Spanish in the United States as a Site of Symbolic Violence," 116–33, both in *How the United States Racializes Latinos: White Hegemony and Its Consequences*, ed. Jose A. Cobas, Jorge Duany, and Joe R. Feagin (Boulder, Colo.: Paradigm Publishers, 2009).

32. García, "Racializing the Language Practices," 101, 109.

33. United Press International, "Iowa Passes English-Only Measure," Feb. 26, 2002, www.upi.com.

34. Philip Boland, "Sonic Geography, Place and Race in the Formation of Local Identity: Liverpool and Scousers," *Geografiska Annaler*, series B, *Human Geography* 92, no. 1 (2010): 1–22. David Matless, "Sonic Geography in a Nature Region," *Social and Cultural Geography* 6, no. 5 (2005): 745–66.

35. Doris, interview with author, Perry, Iowa, April 17, 2007.

36. Jacinta, interview with author, Perry, Iowa, May 9, 2007. Jacinta's discussion of linguistic discrimination relates directly to the notion of linguistic terrorism described by Anzaldúa as intentional silencing and intimidation. See Gloria Anzaldúa, *Borderlands/La Frontera: The New Mestiza,* 3rd ed. (San Francisco: Aunt Lute Books, 2007), 80.

37. Doris interview.

38. Josefina, interview with author, Perry, Iowa, March 21, 2007. Maria interview.

39. Hector, interview with author, Perry, Iowa, April 17, 2007. Luisa interview. Benjamin, interview with author, Perry, Iowa, Nov. 14, 2007.

40. Petra, interview with author, Perry, Iowa, March 27, 2007.

41. Pedro, interview with author, Perry, Iowa, March 27, 2007.

42. Dolores Ines Casillas, "Sounds of Surveillance: U.S. Spanish-Language Radio Patrols La Migra," *American Quarterly* 63, no. 3 (2011): 808–29, 809, 810, 826.

43. Berta interview.

44. The recent farmworker shortages experienced in states such as Alabama and Georgia after the passage of legislation restricting opportunities for undocumented immigrants, and the subsequent exodus of Latina/o populations there, lends support to this argument articulated by Latinas/os in Perry. See for example, "How Alabama's Immigration Law Is Crippling Its Farms," *Washington Post*, editorial, Nov. 3, 2011, www.washingtonpost.com, accessed March 27, 2012.

PART 3

La educación adelanta

Spanish Language and Education in the Midwest

KIM POTOWSKI

It is widespread knowledge that the U.S. Latina/o population is large, consisting of approximately 56.6 million as of 2015.[1] What tends to surprise some people is that the United States is the third-largest Spanish-speaking country in the world. According to the 2010 U.S. Census, approximately 37 million people reported speaking Spanish in the home. To this, we can add approximately 9 million undocumented Latin American immigrants (the vast majority of whom are Spanish-speaking) for a total of 46 million Spanish speakers in the United States. Only Mexico and Spain have more Spanish speakers—and the U.S. Latina/o population is predicted to increase to 30 percent of the national population by 2050.

Yet Spanish in the United States exists under very different circumstances compared with countries where it is the dominant, prestigious language. This chapter explores connections between minority languages, education, and identity through a focus on Spanish in the Midwest. It seeks to answer questions: Why do some Midwest Latinas/os speak Spanish while others do not, and how does their Spanish use compare to that of Latinas/os in other parts of the nation? What factors, including educational programs, promote or hinder the development of Spanish proficiency? What is the role of the Spanish language in the construction of a Latina/o identity in the Midwest, and is this connection different compared to other regions of the United States? The chapter is divided into three main sections: Spanish use, Spanish language educational opportunities, and the role of Spanish in Latina/o identity.

First, we must lay out some basic facts about language shift. Around the world, when people immigrate across linguistic boundaries, it is common to learn the language of the new country.[2] This can happen slowly or quickly, and it can happen with or without losing the family language. One study compared how quickly the family language was lost among immigrants in thirty-five different nations around the world, and found that immigrants to the United States experienced the fastest rate of loss of the family language.[3] Adoption of English is well underway even among very recently arrived groups to the United States. C. Veltman, for example, found that after zero to five years, 20 percent of immigrants aged from infancy to the age of fourteen at the time of arrival had already adopted English as their usual language. After five additional years, the number rose to 40 percent.[4]

Over the past several decades, linguists and sociologists of language have focused on Spanish use in the United States. A majority of U.S. Latinas/os (75%) report speaking Spanish to some degree, while the other 25 percent say they are monolingual in English. However, the number of Spanish-proficient Latinas/os is projected to decline as a result of *intergenerational language shift*. This process has been amply attested among U.S. Latinas/os (as well as the majority of non-English languages spoken in the United States—see Kim Potowski, *Language Diversity in the USA*) and is summarized in table 3.1.1.[5]

What we notice in the table is a low percentage of passing down Spanish from the second to the third generation. Many Latina/o adults in the second and third generations, even those who speak Spanish quite well, have family members (cousins, nieces, nephews, younger siblings, or children) who do not know Spanish. There are

Table 3.1.1. Intergenerational language shift

Sociolinguistic Generation*	Definition	Self-Reported Language Dominance†		
		Spanish	Bilingual	English
1st generation	Immigrants who arrive over the age of 12 monolingual in Spanish. May or may not learn English.	61%	33%	6%
2nd generation	Children of the 1st generation, born in the U.S. or brought before the age of 6. May arrive to school monolingual in Spanish, or bilingual. Usually English becomes stronger than Spanish, and they speak to their own children in English.	8%	53%	40%
3rd generation	Children of the 2nd generation; grandchildren of the 1st generation. Very common to only understand but not speak Spanish; some do not understand Spanish.	2%	29%	69%
	All U.S. Latinas/os	38%	38%	24%

† Source: Paul Taylor, Mark Hugo Lopez, Jessica Martínez, and Gabriel Velasco, *When Labels Don't Fit: Hispanics and Their Views of Identity* (Washington, DC: Pew Hispanic Center Report, April 4, 2012).
* Youths who immigrate between the ages of 7 and 11 are often called the "1.5 generation." The older they are when they arrive, the stronger their Spanish tends to be.

many reasons why this happens. People who grow up in the United States usually attend English-language schools and are surrounded by English-language speakers, movies, television, popular culture, and music. It is quite natural for English to become their stronger and preferred language. There is also tremendous pressure from hegemonic U.S. forces against languages that are not English. This pressure ranges from nationally publicized cases of employees being fired for using a non-English language, to individuals being challenged in public places (elevators, shopping centers, parks, etc.) for doing so. Some family practices can contribute to stronger proficiency in Spanish, including parents who insist on Spanish use; monolingual grandparents living in the home; and visits to Spanish-speaking countries. Birth order is also shown to correlate with Spanish proficiency: older siblings tend to have stronger levels of Spanish than younger siblings, primarily because younger siblings are spoken to in English very frequently by older siblings, and because some parents speak increasingly more English each year.

Overall, though, studies in all parts of the United States show that Spanish is eventually abandoned in favor of English, including in the Southwest, New York, and Miami.[6] As we see in the next section, the Midwest is no exception to this pattern of intergenerational language loss.

Two factors have been suggested as potential decelerators of this shift to English. The first is the local concentration of Spanish-speakers. For example, Richard Alba and colleagues found that a third-generation Cuban child living in Miami—which is in a county that is 60 percent Spanish speaking—is twenty times more likely to be bilingual than a child living in another town where just 5 percent of the population speaks Spanish.[7] The second factor is the proportion of recently arrived Latin American immigrants. That is, the generational loss of Spanish shown in table 3.1.1 has been offset by a steady flow of new immigrants from Latin America. However, with U.S. Latina/o birthrates rapidly outpacing immigration rates, the proportion of U.S. Latinas/os who speak Spanish speakers will likely decline over the course of the twenty-first century. And although one might think that the strong levels of immigration of monolingual Spanish speakers might slightly "revitalize" the Spanish of second- and third-generation Latinas/os, this effect does not appear to be large. Several researchers have shown that second- and third-generation Latinas/os in the United States, instead of speaking frequently in Spanish with newly arrived immigrants, in fact reject them as neighbors, friends, and schoolmates for a variety of social reasons.[8]

Spanish Language in the Midwest

Scholarship on Latinas/os in the Midwest is abundant and cannot be summarized here; these communities are found not just in cities but also in rural locations, as exemplified by the title of Ann Millard and Jorge Chapa's edited volume, *Apple Pie and Enchiladas: Latino Newcomers in the Rural Midwest*.[9] But compared to the rest of the country, relatively few studies have been done on Spanish language use in the Midwest, perhaps because the region is home to only 7.6 percent of all U.S. Latinas/os, as per the 2010 U.S. Census. But two demographic facts indicate that the Midwest is an important area for Latina/o-oriented sociolinguistic research: this region experienced almost a doubling of its Latina/o population between the 2000 and 2010 censuses; and in eight of the twelve states that make up the Midwest, the Latina/o population grew more than 73 percent over the same period.

One of the first studies about Spanish use in the Midwest, conducted in Minneapolis–St. Paul, showed that the second generation used much less Spanish than the first generation. A similar study in a small Iowa town showed the same pattern: 90 percent Spanish use with parents, under 80 percent with siblings, and 60 percent with children. In Northwest Indiana immediately outside of the metropolitan Chicago area, John Attinasi examined self-reports of language use and attitudes and compared them with those of Latinas/os in New York City. He found evidence of bilingualism that included stronger fluency in English but very positive attitudes toward bilingual education and cultural allegiance to the Spanish language. Shift to English was further along in Northwest Indiana than in New York City, and the low Spanish use and proficiency in Indiana led the author to conclude that it was unlikely that Spanish would be transmitted to future generations.[10] This more rapid shift in Indiana may be due to the overall lower concentrations of Latinas/os there in the 1980s compared to New York City.

In Chicago—home to the largest concentration of Midwest Latinas/os at 856,000—Potowski (2004) conducted a survey with 815 Latina/o high school and college students, asking them how often they spoke Spanish with different people. She found the same thing that has been found everywhere else in the country: a clear and steady decline in Spanish use from first- to second- to third-generation speakers. The average amount of Spanish the third generation reported speaking each day was 33 percent with parents and 24 percent with peers. Although the overwhelming majority of respondents emphatically stated that it was important for their future children to know Spanish, people typically find their future mates from within peer groups—and when peers speak mostly English together, it seems less likely that Spanish will be transmitted to future children. The factors in that study that appeared to hold back a complete shift to English included positive attitudes toward Spanish as well as strong preferences for musical artists who sing in Spanish.

Shifting focus away from *how much* Spanish is used to *how well* people speak it, Kim Potowski and Lourdes Torres in Chicago interviewed thirty-nine Mexicans and forty Puerto Ricans in Spanish and found a clear pattern of declining proficiency across generations. Thus, midwestern patterns of Spanish language loss and shift to English across the generations appear to be similar to those in the rest of the country. They also found that, among the second and third generation, Mexicans were slightly more proficient in Spanish than Puerto Ricans.[11] Other work that has examined issues related to the Spanish language in the Midwest include the chapters in Marcia Farr's edited volume and the studies of "transnational" families who live between Chicago and Michoacán, Mexico carried out by Juan Guerra, Marcia Farr, and Elias Dominguez Barajas.[12]

As we saw in the previous section, a primary characteristic that makes Spanish in the United States different from other Spanish-speaking countries is that, in the United States, Spanish is a minority language that is pushed out by English rather quickly. Another important difference is that the United States is home to a wide variety of different national varieties of Spanish. This means that varieties of Spanish spoken by Mexicans, Puerto Ricans, Dominicans, and many other groups are in contact with each other. Table 3.1.2 lists the top ten countries of origin of U.S. Spanish speakers.

The Spanish dialect of each of these groups has important differences in pronunciation, vocabulary, and pragmatics. All Spanish speakers, for example, can quickly distinguish spoken Puerto Rican Spanish from Mexican Spanish. But what happens when members of different dialect groups live in close proximity? Do their ways of speaking Spanish begin to influence each other? In the Midwest, contact between Mexicans and Puerto Ricans has existed in Chicago since the mid-twentieth century, and the current population of the city is 69 percent Mexican and 9 percent Puerto Rican, making it an excellent location for research on Spanish dialect contact.[13] Kim Potowski and Lourdes Torres sought to discover whether the Spanish dialects of these two groups were affecting each other in vocabulary and in accent. For vocabulary, they created a list of ten common items that are referred to differently by Mexicans versus Puerto Ricans.[14] Some examples are listed in table 3.1.3.

Table 3.1.2. Origins of U.S. Latina/o population

Rank	Country of Origin	Number	Percent
1	Mexico	31,797,000	63.0
2	Puerto Rico	4,634,000	9.2
3	Cuba	1,786,000	3.5
4	El Salvador	1,649,000	3.3
5	Dominican Republic	1,415,000	2.8
6	Guatemala	1,044,000	2.1
7	Colombia	909,000	1.8
8	Spain	635,000	1.3
9	Honduras	633,000	1.3
10	Ecuador	565,000	1.1

Source: U.S. Census 2010. Only the top ten countries of origin are listed here; the remaining 10.6 percent are dispersed among other Spanish-speaking countries.

Table 3.1.3. Examples of cross-dialectal vocabulary differences

English	Mexican Spanish	Puerto Rican Spanish
pacifier	chupete/chupetón	bobo
red beans	frijoles	habichuelas
drinking straw	popote	sorbeto
earrings	aretes	pantallas

Source: Kim Potowski and Lourdes Torres, *Spanish in Chicago* (New York: Oxford University Press, forthcoming).

Showing pictures of these items to thirty-seven Mexicans and thirty-nine Puerto Ricans, they found that Puerto Ricans are more familiar with Mexican words than Mexicans are with Puerto Rican words. This expected result is probably related to at least three factors: the numerical dominance of Mexicans in Chicago, the higher international status of Mexican Spanish compared to Puerto Rican Spanish, and the fact that a large proportion of internationally broadcast Spanish-language television is from Mexico.[15] Researchers have found that Puerto Rican Spanish is often stigmatized around the Spanish-speaking world, but this is not due to any inferiority of Puerto Rican Spanish, but rather to a series of complicated factors including media exposure and racial prejudice.[16]

In addition to examining vocabulary words, a handful of studies have started looking at whether different U.S. Spanish accents are influencing each other. Three of these have taken place in the Midwest, again with Mexicans and Puerto Ricans. There are two sounds that are noticeably different between Mexican and Puerto Rican Spanish. The first is the *s* at the end of a syllable, which Mexicans pronounce as *es* but that Puerto Ricans often weaken or eliminate, such that "los mismos" sounds like "lo mimo."[17] The second is the double *rr*, which Mexicans trill, but which some Puerto Ricans velarize (pronounce in the back of the throat), as in the pronunciation of the name of the German musician "Bach," such that "Ramón" sounds like "jamón" and "carro" sounds like "cajo." Michelle Ramos-Pellicia found that, even though Puerto Ricans in rural Lorain, Ohio, had higher status than the recently arrived Mexican immigrants, Mexicans were not adopting Puerto Rican *s* or *rr* pronunciations. In Chicago, E. Ghosh Johnson wondered whether Mexican-origin high school students in a predominately Puerto Rican high school would adopt Puerto Rican phonology. However, she found that these students not only avoided each other, but they also spoke English whenever they had to interact—so there would be no reason for either group to change their Spanish features. Finally, E. O'Rourke and Kim Potowski examined whether eighteen Mexican and twenty-four Puerto Rican adults in Chicago would change their accent based on whether they were being interviewed by a Mexican or a Puerto Rican. They found that Mexicans do not change their features at all. Puerto Ricans, however, more frequently used velarized *r* when speaking with other Puerto Ricans than when speaking with Mexicans (their use of *s* did not vary when speaking with either group).[18]

The previous section describes several linguistic results of the contact between these two groups. But what happens when the dialect contact occurs right in the home—for example, when one parent is Mexican and the other is Puerto Rican? The "mixed Latina/o" individual, such as "MexiRicans," are another product of inter-Latina/o connections. This is becoming increasingly more common around the United States, as evidenced by New York City marriage records, but the only linguistic studies to date about the Spanish of mixed Latinas/os have been conducted in Chicago.[19] In *Intra-latino Language and Identity*, Potowski has shown that the dialect of the mother has a considerable effect: a MexiRican will more often show stronger Puerto Rican vocabulary and phonological features like *s* and *rr* when the mother is Puerto Rican. In addition, alongside ardent claims to being "equally Mexican and Puerto Rican," the majority of the seventy MexiRican individuals interviewed in Spanish exhibited more features from one dialect over the other. This has interesting implications for identity claims, because family and friends will often "other" MexiRicans for using language traits from the other dialect—that is, their Mexican family will tell them that they are "not really Mexican" when they use a Puerto Rican feature, and vice versa with their Puerto Rican family.[20]

This section on Spanish use and dialect contact concludes with a discussion of Spanish print media. When a family's language is different from the language of wider society, it is very common for children not to develop literacy in the family language. For example, many members of the second and third generations can speak Spanish to varying degrees but do not feel comfortable reading or writing it. Scholars in heritage language maintenance have pointed out that reading to children in the heritage language can go a long way in bolstering their proficiency in that language. Easily accessible reading material is also an important component of literacy maintenance and educational development among Spanish-speaking adults. Thus, we need much more research on the availability of Spanish print materials in the United States. The sole survey to date is by Sandra Pucci, who compared newsstands, supermarkets, libraries, and bookstores in Los Angeles with those in the general Milwaukee metropolitan area. Although she found no Spanish-language newsstands in Milwaukee, the three large Mexican-owned supermarkets carried a wider range of popular reading materials in Spanish than did supermarkets in L.A. However, the public library in the heart of the Milwaukee Mexican community, despite its primarily Spanish-speaking clientele, had a relatively limited collection of books. Yet there were several racks of *bolsilibros*—a small, softcover pocketbook in a wide range of genres, some in comic book style, others as short novellas—which were well-worn and very popular. These were not available in L.A. libraries. Finally, L.A. had a large bookstore with exclusively Spanish materials, although orders for some political and literary titles took months to fill. Milwaukee only had one Spanish-language bookstore in a community center.[21]

Literacy is one of the main goals of formal education. The next section addresses the question: What opportunities are available for Midwest Latinas/os to engage in the formal study of Spanish?

Spanish Educational Opportunities

Young people spend about half of their waking hours in school. While Latina/o children comprise fully one-quarter of all school-age children in the United States, they attend school in even higher concentrations in cities like Chicago, where Latinas/os make up almost half (44%) of the public district's enrollment. Commenting on the numerous difficulties that the Chicago public schools faced during 2013—including school closures, massive budget reductions, neighborhood violence, and high dropout rates—Latino Policy Forum executive director Sylvia Puente stated that Chicago is a litmus test of educational realities across the country and specified three factors that can contribute to three improved outcomes for Latina/o children: increased access to quality preschool programs; training for teachers, as Illinois phases in required bilingual education for English language learners in preschool; and quality teachers, more of whom are themselves Latina/o.[22] This section addresses two questions: To what extent do schools play a role in Spanish language development and maintenance among Midwest Latinas/os? And, more importantly, to what extent can Spanish play a role in improving Latina/o children's' academic success?

Guadalupe Valdés argues that because third-generation immigrants have relatively little exposure to the minority language both at home and within the community, the direct involvement of educational institutions is essential if youths are to have the opportunity to develop their competence in the minority language. The field known as *bilingual education* studies the efficacy of different school models that are available for children who are considered not sufficiently proficient in English when they enter the U.S. school.[23] The vast majority of these programs are called *transitional* bilingual education because they have as their goal a rapid transition of English language learners (ELLs) to all-English classrooms. They do not seek to maintain or develop the heritage language. In our case, transitional bilingual education programs use Spanish typically a few hours a day for one to three years, which is seen as a "crutch" until the children are considered able to function in all-English classrooms. The city of Chicago, for example, serves most of its 70,000 English-learning students (84% of whom are Spanish speaking) with a preK/K through fourth-grade transitional bilingual education program. The vast majority of Latinas/os in the Midwest and across the United States participate in transitional bilingual education with the exception of Arizona, California, and

Massachusetts, where they were outlawed and replaced with English immersion programs (in November 2016, California voters passed Proposition 58, repealing the eighteen-year-old bilingual education ban in the state).

It may seem logical to assume that instruction delivered 100 percent in English would be the best way to help ELLs. After all, most things a person seeks to improve are accomplished through time on task. For example, if I want to improve my tennis, I should play tennis more frequently. If I want to become a better car mechanic, I should spend a lot of time working on cars. But for ELLs to learn English more quickly, surprisingly, the best route is giving them quality instruction in their home language. Several nationwide studies have demonstrated this by comparing student outcomes in three different elementary school programs for Spanish-speaking ELLs: 100 percent English instruction; transitional bilingual education, just discussed above; and *dual-language immersion*. In dual-language immersion, students receive between 50 to 90 percent of their instruction in the heritage language from kindergarten through eighth grade. Dual language is also designed to rebalance power imbalances, because it integrates into the same classrooms native-speaking-language minority children along with English-speaking children whose parents want them to learn the minority language. In other words, instead of the ELL children being the only language learners in the school, approximately half of the students speak English at home but are expected to learn the minority language taught in the school. In this way, the Spanish-speaking children are positioned as knowledgeable linguistic and cultural models.

So, is it true that 100 percent English instruction leads to better English learning? Figure 3.1.1 compares the English reading scores of graduates of these three program types once students had advanced to eleventh grade.

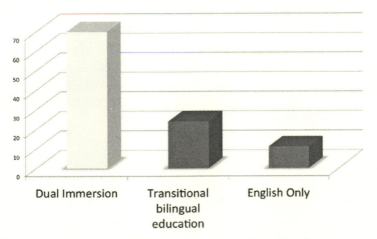

3.1.1   Eleventh grade English readin scores of Spanish-speaking ELLs (from Thomas & Collier 2009)

Although it may seem counterintuitive, these findings clearly show that the more time spent learning in Spanish, the greater the *English*-language achievement of Spanish-speaking ELL students. This is due in part to the fact that, in the earliest years of school, ELLs are taught in a language they understand, so there is less chance they will fall behind on academic subject matter. As they gradually develop English proficiency, their subject matter knowledge transfers across languages. Not only does their English benefit, their overall academic achievement is higher and their Spanish is likely to develop more strongly than in other program types.[24]

How common are dual immersion programs in the United States? According to a 2007 Center for Applied Linguistics report, there are 421 programs in eight different languages, with 93 percent of them operating in Spanish. In the twelve states that form the U.S. Census–designated Midwest region, there are a total of sixty-one Spanish dual-immersion programs listed in this report.[25] Table 3.1.4 demonstrates that, despite being only the fifth most populous state, Illinois has the third largest number of reported Spanish dual-language programs in the nation.

Interestingly, only ten of the Illinois programs are in Chicago (all of which are in free public schools), meaning that many smaller communities in the state and across the Midwest offer this innovative model of dual language education. For example, Carla Paciotto and Gloria Delany-Barmann document how a group of teachers in a rural Illinois town (with 6,000 residents and a Latina/o population of 18%) founded a successful dual-immersion school in response to the influx of ELL students. Another dual-immersion program worth mention is located in West Liberty, Iowa (documented by Elaine Shenk), a town that is 41 percent Latina/o in a state that is only 2.8 percent Latina/o.[26]

Once in high school or college, most students have the option of studying a foreign language, and Spanish is the most commonly chosen language across the country (69% of high school language enrollments, and 52% in colleges). In the late twentieth century, educators began realizing that their Latina/o stu-

Table 3.1.4. Dual-language Spanish schools in the seven most populous states

State	Population, in millions	Number of Spanish Dual-Language Schools
California	38.0	116
Texas	26.0	61
New York	19.5	28
Florida	19.3	9
Illinois	12.8	32
Pennsylvania	12.7	1
Ohio	11.5	1

Source: Center for Applied Linguistics, Directory of Two-Way Bilingual Immersion Programs

dents who had learned some Spanish in the home were not well served by traditional foreign-language programs. The first publications about teaching Spanish
to "heritage speakers" came out of the Southwest in the 1980s, and high schools
and universities in both Miami and the New York metropolitan area also showed
early development of this kind of instruction. Other areas of the country used
to be able to ignore this issue, because their Spanish classes only had "foreign"-
language students. However, the growth of the Latina/o population means that
Spanish teachers everywhere in the country need some kind of preparation to
work with heritage speakers and schools everywhere need to offer specialized
Spanish courses for heritage speakers.[27]

The Midwest has responded well to these demographic changes. For example,
the American Colleges of the Midwest held a session on heritage speakers at their
2012 annual meeting, and many other Midwest campuses have begun investi-
gating ways to develop heritage speaker programs.[28] The University of Illinois at
Chicago's heritage speaker program has been in place since the mid-1980s, serves
approximately 150 students per semester, and has pioneered empirical research
on effective placement exams for heritage speakers, in addition to launching a
heritage speaker study abroad program in Oaxaca, Mexico.[29] At the high school
level, the Chicago Public School district regularly offers professional development for instructors of heritage speakers, and the Network of Illinois Educators
of Spanish for Heritage Learners has held annual pedagogical workshops since
2005. Two of the twenty organizations belonging to the National Association of
Latino Fraternal Organizations were founded in the Midwest: Alpha Psi Lambda
and Gamma Phi Omega.[30] Although as yet no published research exists on this
topic, I hypothesize that membership in these organizations leads to higher rates
of graduation among Latina/o college students.

However, despite the fact that many high schools and universities across the
nation now offer courses for heritage speakers of the language, the majority of
Spanish heritage speakers in the United States does not have access to them. At
the secondary school level, just 9 percent of schools surveyed in 2008 offered
heritage Spanish speaker instruction. At the postsecondary level, Sara Beaudrie
found that 40 percent of universities nationwide are now offering heritage Spanish speaker courses—which means that 60 percent of them do not.[31] Offerings
in the Midwest likely look very similar to those in the nation at large. A positive
pedagogical footnote for the Midwest comes in the form of Foreign Languages
in the Elementary Schools (FLES) programs. These teach languages other than
English for thirty to fifty minutes each day, three to four times a week, in grades
K–6. Currently, only 25 percent of U.S. elementary schools offer FLES programs,
and in districts with large Latina/o populations, the FLES classes often include
heritage Spanish-speaking children.[32] Chicago offers FLES at about thirty schools

and, given that 44 percent of the district's students are Latina/o, a federally funded grant project was undertaken by a group of local educators to develop a K–8 heritage Spanish curriculum.[33]

Many U.S. language minority groups have organized local Saturday schools that offer language and culture classes in Chinese, Japanese, Polish, and other languages. Such programs in Spanish appear to be largely missing from the U.S. landscape. This may be due to family beliefs that children will acquire sufficient Spanish, constraints on family time and budget, and perhaps concern about children's English development. There are a few community-based programs in the Midwest, including the En Nuestra Lengua program in Ann Arbor, Michigan; the Latino Cultural Academy and Son Chiquitos in Chicago; and two programs in Minneapolis–St. Paul. Finally, at least one organization supported by another Spanish-speaking nation invests in Spanish heritage language education in the United States: Spain's Cervantes Institute in Chicago offers a heritage speaker course for children.

The Role of Spanish in Latina/o Identity

The preceding discussion about Spanish language education opportunities leads to a question that guides this section of this chapter: For what purposes might Latinas/os seek to develop proficiency in Spanish among themselves and their children? Sociolinguistic studies around the world have shown that language is a key component of how ethnicity is experienced and expressed.[34] To what extent does one "need" Spanish to be Latina/o?

In California, Susana Rivera-Mills asked fifty U.S. Latinas/os of various nationalities and across three generations of immigration whether Spanish is necessary to be Latina/o. She found that only 30 percent strongly agreed, while another 30 percent moderately disagreed. Also in California, one hundred Latinas/os interviewed by García Bedolla responded differently according to their generation: the first generation said that being Latina/o meant speaking Spanish; the second generation said it meant speaking both Spanish and English; and the third generation defined "Latina/o" as "of Latin American descent," with rare mention of language ability. All of the third-generation participants had a strong ethnic identity, even though they did not consider themselves fluent in Spanish. Thus, as Spanish proficiency decreases across generations, individuals seem to drop the requirement of knowing Spanish to be Latina/o.[35] Aside from generation, ethnic background might also play a role in the connection between Spanish and Latinidad. De Genova and Ramos-Zayas present evidence that U.S.-raised Mexicans in Chicago experience greater pressure to speak Spanish than do their Puerto Rican peers. Zentella, too, found that Puerto Ricans raised on the mainland lay absolute claim to being Puerto Rican even if they are 100 percent monolingual in English.[36]

Also in Chicago, a small study found that twenty-one of twenty-four Latinas/os claimed that Spanish was *not* necessary to be Latina/o, and Potowski and Torres found similar trends with a larger group of individuals there. Also recall the study cited earlier in which Latinas/os in northwest Indiana insisted less on the need for Spanish than did their counterparts in New York City.[37] These findings illustrate that, as in other parts of the United States, Spanish-language proficiency does not play a deal-breaking role in the construction of Midwest Latina/o ethnic identity, although it may be more important for Mexicans than for Puerto Ricans.

Finally, in a study combining language and ethno-cultural studies, Potowski and Gorman examined the extent to which the Spanish language plays a role in Chicago *quinceañera* celebrations. Sixty percent of the surveyed girls who had *quinceañeras* replied that Spanish was useful in their celebrations in order to communicate with family members, understand the Mass and offer a short reading from the Bible, and send out invitations. However, they stated that an English-language Mass was "acceptable," which acknowledges the possibility of being Latina and not knowing Spanish. Although Spanish was not seen as required, the majority of respondents indicated that knowledge of Spanish was important because "the tradition of a *quinceañera* is from a Hispanic background."[38]

Conclusions

The continued growth of the Latina/o population, the mix of urban and rural locations, and a fair amount of diversity of ethnolinguistic groups make the Midwest a critical site for studying issues of language and identity among Latinas/os. In particular, this region of the nation stands out for at least three factors. The first is its fairly large number of Spanish-English dual-language schools and other types of heritage language education, which contribute to innovative models of Spanish language maintenance education. The second is the significant contact between dialect groups for more than half a century and the existence of "MexiRican" individuals, both of which lead to innovative uses of the Spanish language and Latina/o identity constructions. The third is that the Midwest is home to the nation's third largest public school district (Chicago), which as noted by Puente and McElmurry is a "litmus test" for the educational experiences of Latinas/os across the nation.[39] As educators in other parts of the country seek to understand best practices in teaching Latina/o youths, including heritage language maintenance, and as linguists seek to explore the results of dialect contact, both intergroup and intra-familial, the Midwest can provide significant insight.

Notes

1. U.S. Census Bureau, "FFF: Hispanic Heritage Month 2016," Newsroom, Facts for Features, release CB16-FF.16, Oct. 12, 2016, www.census.gov/newsroom/facts-for-features/2016/cb16-ff16.html, accessed Dec. 24, 2016.

2. Some U.S. Spanish-speaking communities, particularly in New Mexico, are not immigrant groups but rather original settlements of Spanish speakers before the United States became an independent nation.

3. Stanley Lieberson, Guy Dalto, and Mary Ellen Johnston, "The Course of Mother-Tongue Diversity in Nations," *American Journal of Sociology* 81 (1975): 34–61.

4. C. Veltman, "The American Linguistic Mosaic: Understanding Language Shift in the United States," in *New Immigrants in the United States: Readings for Second Language Educators*, ed. Sandra Lee McKay and Sau-ling Cynthia Wong (New York: Cambridge University Press, 2000), 58–93, 75.

5. Kim Potowski, *Language Diversity in the USA* (New York: Cambridge University Press, 2010).

6. Southwest: MaryBeth Floyd, "Spanish in the Southwest: Language Maintenance or Shift?," in *Spanish Language Use and Public Life in the United States*, ed. Lucía Elías-Olivares, René Cisneros, and John Gutiérrez (New York: Mouton, 1985), 13–25; Susana Rivera-Mills, "Acculturation and Communicative Need: Language Shift in an Ethnically Diverse Hispanic Community," *Southwest Journal of Linguistics* 20 (2001): 211–23; and Carmen Silva-Corvalán, *Language Contact and Change: Spanish in Los Angeles* (New York: Oxford University Press, 1994). New York: Ana Celia Zentella, *Growing Up Bilingual* (Oxford, U.K.: Blackwell, 1997); and Pedro Pedraza, "Language Maintenance among New York Puerto Ricans," in Elías-Olivares et al., *Spanish Language and Public Life*, 59–71. Miami: Ricardo L. Garcia and Carlos F. Diaz, "The Status and Use of Spanish and English among Hispanic Youth in Dade County (Miami) Florida: A Sociolinguistic Study," *Language and Education* 6 (1992): 13–32; Alejandro Portes and Richard Schauffler, "Language and the Second Generation: Bilingualism Yesterday and Today," in *The New Second Generation*, ed. Alejandro Portes (New York: Russell Sage, 1996), 8–29; Barbara Zurer Pearson and Arlene McGee, "Language Choice in Hispanic-Background Junior High School Students in Miami: A 1988 Update," in *Spanish in the United States: Linguistic Contact and Diversity*, ed. Ana Roca and John Lipski (New York: Mouton de Gruyter, 2000), 91–102; and Ofelia García and Ricardo Otheguy, "The Language Situation of Cuban Americans," in *Language Diversity: Problem or Resource?*, ed. Sandra Lee McKay and Sau-Ling Cynthia Wong (New York: Newbury House, 1988), 166–92.

7. Richard Alba, John Logan, Amy Lutz, and Brian Stults, "Only English by the Third Generation? Loss and Preservation of the Mother Tongue among the Grandchildren of Contemporary Immigrants," *Demography* 39, no. 3 (2002): 467–84.

8. In California: Norma Mendoza-Denton, "Sociolinguistics and Linguistic Anthropology of U.S. Latinos," *Annual Review of Anthropology* 28 (1999): 375–95; and Lisa García Bedolla, "The Identity Paradox: Latino Language, Politics, and Selective Dissociation," *Latino Studies* 1, no. 2 (2003): 264–83. In Chicago: Lillian Gorman and Kim Potowski, "Spanish 'Recontact'

between U.S. Born and Recent Arrival Latinos in Chicago," paper presented at the 22nd Conference on Spanish in the United States, Coral Gables, Fla., 2009.

9. Ann V. Millard and Jorge Chapa, eds., *Apple Pie and Enchiladas: Latino Newcomers in the Rural Midwest* (Austin: University of Texas Press, 2004).

10. Rene Leone and Elizabeth Cisneros, "Mexican-American Language Communities in the Twin Cities: An Example of Contact and Recontact," in *Spanish in the U.S. Setting: Beyond the Southwest*, ed. Lucía Elías-Olivares (Rosslyn, Va.: National Clearinghouse for Bilingual Education, 1983), 181–209. Nora González and Irene Wheritt, "Spanish Language Use in West Liberty, Iowa," in *Spanish in the United States: Sociolinguistic Issues*, ed. John J. Bergen (Washington, D.C.: Georgetown University Press, 1990), 67–78. John Attinasi, "Hispanic Attitudes in Northwestern Indiana and New York," in Elías-Olivares et al., *Spanish Language Use and Public Life*, 27–58.

11. Kim Potowski and Lourdes Torres, *Spanish in Chicago* (New York: Oxford University Press, forthcoming).

12. Marcia Farr, ed., *Latino Language and Literacy in Ethnolinguistic Chicago* (Mahwah, N.J.: Lawrence Erlbaum, 2005); Juan Guerra, *Close to Home: Oral and Literate Practices in a Transnational Mexicano Community* (New York: Teachers College, 1998); Marcia Farr, *Rancheros in Chicagoacán: Language and Identity in a Transnational Community* (Austin: University of Texas Press, 2006); and Elias Dominguez Barajas, *The Function of Proverbs in Discourse: The Case of a Mexican Transnational Social Network* (New York: De Gruyter Mouton, 2010).

13. There has been excellent scholarship on relationships between Mexicans and Puerto Ricans in Chicago, including Feliz M. Padilla, *Latino Ethnic Consciousness: The Case of Mexican Americans and Puerto Ricans in Chicago* (Notre Dame, Ind.: University of Notre Dame Press, 1985); Gina M. Pérez, "Puertorriqueñas rencorosas y mejicanas sufridas: Gendered Ethnic Identity Formation in Chicago's Latino Communities," *Journal of Latin American Anthropology* 8, no. 2 (2003): 96–125, Nicholas De Genova and Ana Yolanda Ramos-Zayas, *Latino Crossings: Mexicans, Puerto Ricans and the Politics of Race and Citizenship* (New York: Routledge, 2003); and Lorena García and Mérida Rúa, "Processing Latinidad: Mapping Latino Urban Landscapes through Chicago Ethnic Festivals," *Latino Studies* 5, no. 3 (2007): 317–39. The present chapter focuses on the Spanish language.

14. Potowski and Torres, *Spanish in Chicago*.

15. Arlene Dávila, "Talking Back: Hispanic Media and U.S. Latinidad," *CENTRO Journal* 12, no. 1 (2000): 37–47.

16. See Zentella, *Growing Up Bilingual*.

17. Jesse Aaron and José Esteban Hernández found that Salvadorans in contact with Mexicans in Houston more likely pronounce the *s* at the end of syllables the way Mexicans do—in order to avoid teasing and to possibly "pass" for Chicanos and avoid harassment by immigration authorities. Jesse Aaron and José Esteban Hernández, "Quantitative Evidence for Contact-Induced Accommodation: Shifts in /s/ Reduction Patterns in Salvadoran Spanish in Houston," in *Spanish in Contact: Policy, Social, and Linguistic Inquiries*, ed. K. Potowski & R. Cameron (Eds.), (pp.). (Amsterdam: John Benjamins, 2007), 329–44.

18. Michelle Ramos-Pellicia, "Language Contact and Dialect Contact: Cross-Generational Phonological Variation in a Puerto Rican Community in the Midwest of the United States" (PhD diss., Ohio State University, 2004); E. Ghosh Johnson, "Mexiqueño? A Case Study of Dialect Contact," Penn Working Papers in Linguistics, vol. 11, no. 2, *Selected Papers from NWAV 33* (2005), 91–104; E. O'Rourke and K. Potowski, "Phonetic Accommodation in a Situation of Spanish Dialect Contact: /s/ and /r/ in Chicago," *Journal of Hispanic and Lusopone Linguistics* 2, no. 9 (2016): 1–44.

19. Greta Gilbertson, Joseph P. Fitzpatrick, and Lijun Yang, "Hispanic Intermarriage in New York City: New Evidence from 1991," *International Migration Review* 30, no. 2 (1996): 445–59; S. Lee, "Love Sees No Color or Boundaries? Interethnic Dating and Marriage Patterns of Dominican and CEP (Colombian, Ecuadorian, Peruvian) Americans," *Journal of Latino/Latin American Studies* 2 (2006): 84–102.

20. Kim Potowski, *Intra-latino Language and Identity: MexiRicans* (Amsterdam: John Benjamins, 2014).

21. Sandra Pucci, "Spanish Print Environments Implications for Heritage Language Development," In *Mi Lengua: Spanish as a Heritage Language in the United States, Research and Practice*, ed. Ana Roca and M. Cecilia Colombi (Washington, D.C.: Georgetown University Press), 269–90.

22. Silvia Puente and Sara McElmurry, "Chicago's Next Education Crisis Isn't Limited to Chicago—Here's Why," *Huffington Post*, Sept. 4, 2013, www.huffingtonpost.com, accessed Dec. 6, 2016.

23. Guadalupe Valdés, "Ethnolinguistic Identity: The Challenge of Maintaining Spanish-English Bilingualism in American Schools," in *Bilingual Youth: Spanish in English-Speaking Societies*, ed. Kim Potowski and Jason Rothman, 113–48 (Amsterdam: Benjamins, 2011). One of the best overviews of bilingual education in the United States is Colin Baker, *Foundations of Bilingual Education and Bilingualism* (Clevedon, U.K.: Multilingual Matters, 2011).

24. Kathryn Lindholm, *Dual Language Education* (Clevedon, U.K.: Multilingual Matters, 2001); S. Montrul and K. Potowski, "Command of Gender Agreement in School-Age Spanish-English Bilingual Children," *International Journal of Bilingualism* 11, no. 3 (2007): 301–28.

25. Center for Applied Linguistics, *Directory of Two-Way Bilingual Immersion Programs in the U.S.*, 2007, http://webapp.cal.org/duallanguage/. The number of dual-language programs listed in midwestern states are as follows: Illinois has 32; Nebraska has 8; Wisconsin has 7; Iowa, Michigan, and Minnesota each have 4; Indiana and Ohio each have 1; Kansas, Missouri, North Dakota, and South Dakota have none. This list is based on schools' self-reports, so there are likely additional schools in existence that are not included in this database.

26. Carla Paciotto and Gloria Delany-Barmann, "Planning Micro-Level Language Education Reform in New Diaspora Sites: Two-Way Immersion Education in the Rural Midwest," *Language Policy* 10, no. 3 (2011): 221–43. Elaine Shenk, "Choosing Spanish: Dual Language Immersion and Familial Ideologies," in *Bilingualism and Identity: Spanish at the Crossroads with Other Languages*, ed. Jason Rothman and Mercedes Niño-Murcia (Amsterdam: John Benjamins, 2008), 221–56.

27. Kim Potowski and María Carreira, "Towards Teacher Development and National Standards for Spanish as a Heritage Language," *Foreign Language Annals* 37, no. 3 (2004): 421–31.

28. These include DePaul University, Indiana University, Monmouth College, Northwestern University, Ohio University, St. Olaf College, University of Nebraska–Omaha, University of Wisconsin (Eau Claire and Madison), Western Illinois University, and Western Michigan University.

29. Kim Potowski, MaryAnn Parada, and Kara Morgan-Short, "Developing an Online Placement Exam for Spanish Heritage Speakers and L2 Students," *Heritage Language Journal* 9, no. 1 (2012): 51–76.

30. I am grateful to several members of Gamma Phi Omega at the University of Illinois at Chicago for bringing NALFO to my attention.

31. Nancy C. Rhodes and Ingrid Pufahl, *Foreign Language Teaching in U.S. Schools: Results of a National Survey* (Washington, D.C.: Center for Applied Linguistics, 2010). Sara Beaudrie, "Research on University-Based Spanish Heritage Language Programs in the United States," in *Spanish as a Heritage Language in the United States: The State of the Field*, ed. Sara Beaudrie and Marta Fairclough (Washington, D.C.: Georgetown University Press, 2011), 203–21.

32. Rhodes and Pufahl, *Foreign Language Teaching*.

33. Jorge Berne, Amy Clark, Amy Hammerand, and Kim Potowski, "Spanish for K–8 Heritage Speakers: A Standards-Based Curriculum Project," *Hispania* 91, no. 1 (2008): 25–41.

34. Joshua Fishman, *Language and Ethnicity in Minority Sociolinguistic Perspective* (Clevedon, U.K.: Multilingual Matters, 1989).

35. Susana Rivera-Mills, "Intraethnic Attitudes among Hispanics in a Northern California Community," *Research on Spanish in the United States: Linguistic Issues and Challenges*, ed. Ana Roca (Somerville, Mass.: Cascadilla Press, 2000), 377–89. García Bedolla, "Identity Paradox." Although it seems that Spanish is not *necessary* to be considered Latina/o around the United States, Guadalupe Valdés shows that Spanish is not *sufficient* for Latina/o identity, either. G. Valdés, "Ethnolinguistic Identity."

36. De Genova and Ramos-Zayas, *Latino Crossings*. Zentella, *Growing Up Bilingual*.

37. Kim Potowski and Janine Matts, "Interethnic Language and Identity: MexiRicans in Chicago," *Journal of Language, Identity and Education* 6, no. 3 (2008): 137–60; Potowski and Torres, *Spanish in Chicago*. Attinasi, "Hispanic Attitudes."

38. Kim Potowski and Lillian Gorman, "Quinceañeras: Hybridized Tradition, Language Use, and Identity in the U.S.," in Potowski and Rothman, *Bilingual Youth*, 57–87, 81.

39. Puente and McElmurry, "Chicago's Next Education Crisis."

Contesting the Myth
of Uncaring
Latina/o Parents Advocating
for Their Children

CAROLYN COLVIN, JAY ARDUSER,
AND ELIZABETH WILLMORE

Our work with immigrant adults residing in a rural midwestern community began twenty years ago and was prompted by comments from local school administrators who wondered why immigrant parents were not active participants in the school.[1] When pressed, administrators and teachers expressed concern that because of immigrant parents' perceived lack of school participation, they had come to believe these parents cared less about their children's academic success. It seems clear that faculty and administrators in this rural site have internalized unofficial and yet commonly held standards for what constitute "good" parents regarding school involvement and participation. Local school officials had often referred to patterns of parent participation for immigrant families to explain why some students and not others experienced academic success. In research examining the lives of Mexican-origin families in border communities, Guadalupe Valdés discusses the relationship between immigrant parent involvement and their children's academic success as framed by theories of cultural difference or deficit.[2] While researchers have pursued a coherent theory that would take into account multiple factors to explain the lack of academic success for Mexican-origin students, Valdés notes that these researchers continued to return to language differences and family characteristics to explain school failure, thus reinforcing the difference-as-deficit notion.

We describe conversations with Latina/o parents as they "talk back" to the myth of uncaring and describe how they construct their roles as advocates for their children.[3] Our goal is to place at the center of parent-teacher communication, the voices of Latina/o parents to challenge this myth of uncaring that regularly frames discussions of immigrant parent participation. These parents reveal where U.S. educational practices are confusing and culturally at odds with their own educational experiences and describe their strategic acculturation to local school expectations of parent participation.

Parent participation in schools is a culturally constructed practice and is emblematic of unwritten educational expectations held by teachers that dictate the ways in which good parents participate and communicate with faculty and administrators.[4] As Carola Suárez-Orozco, Marcelo Suárez-Orozco, and Irina Todorova report, "parents who came to school and helped with homework were viewed as concerned parents, whereas parents who did neither were thought to be disinterested and parents of poor students."[5] Some researchers advocate for the positive effects of parent involvement by suggesting that parent participation is an important factor in raising student achievement among low-income and minority youth, developing parent abilities to raise children, establishing positive parental attitudes toward working with teachers, reducing drop-out rates, and increasing home-school communication.[6] Few scholars would disagree that parents have a consistent, positive, and convincing influence on their children's academic achievement in school and throughout life.[7] Recent scholarship documents criticism of educators and legislators' ready endorsements of strong home-school connections and urges caution when there are gaps in understanding what involvement means for *all* parents.[8] On the surface, it makes sense that teachers and schools would create partnerships with parents to ensure student success. The relationship between parents and schools has been the subject of extensive study; however, these relationships are deeply complex and seldom understood.[9]

It is against this research backdrop that we spoke with immigrant parents who participate in our literacy program regarding their school involvement. The literacy program is a part of a university-community partnership to provide quality literacy instruction to immigrant adults who seek greater literacy. Preservice teachers participate in training to serve as literacy tutors for adult students who attend the weekly literacy program housed in a local school. The adult students receive individual or small-group instruction working with tutors; in turn, the tutors create literacy activities specifically designed for the adults for whom they work. School faculty and administrators, also project partners, make school facilities and materials, including computers and books (in English and Spanish), available to tutors and adult students.

Extensive research on commonsense notions urging parent participation to enhance their children's success has shown how children, and ultimately the school, will benefit when parents are involved.[10] While we endorse parent-teacher collaborations so that children experience success, we call for a more nuanced understanding of the complexities of parent involvement when institutional hi-erarchies continue to frame parent participation in terms of power. The rituals and traditions framing many K–12 educational experiences are unfamiliar and culturally distant from what immigrant parents know, so they may experience heightened confusion and tension because often they have not attended U.S. schools and lack familiarity with these practices.

Reviewing the parent involvement research, we noted that voices of parents were often missing. Further, much of the literature focuses on models for middle-class parents, most of whom are Anglo and themselves successful in school. Increasingly, researchers are examining parent involvement from the perspective of nonmainstream parents.[11] While parent voices are more evident, immigrant parents' perspectives deserve greater attention than they have received, so that their negotiations of this complex terrain become visible. Failing to include par-ent voices may doom educators to continue to marginalize the very individuals whose experiences we seek to understand.

The Southeastern Iowa Context

Rural midwestern school districts have been transformed by the arrival of Latina/o and other immigrant families.[12] Teachers, administrators, and immigrant parents face cultural and linguistic challenges as they learn to communicate effectively. The context for communications most often takes place around the unique prac-tice of parent-teacher conferences, the primary venue for sharing *and* discussing information concerning academic progress for children.[13] The experiences and rituals that occur around parent-teacher conferences occupies a special, almost sacred, place in East Town—the community where we work.[14]

East Town is not unlike other midwestern rural sites where small-town demo-graphics reflect dramatic transitions: from the largely European American families who have resided in the community for two-plus generations to the "new" trans-national communities where the majority of students speak a first language other than English. In East Town, 58 percent of the students are Latina/o and 3 percent are Asian (Lao and Vietnamese) students. Since the early 1900s, Mexican-origin residents have lived in the community following the recruitment of Mexican work-ers to assist in building the railroad. Two workers remained in the town after the railroad's completion and were eventually joined by extended family members. Subsequently, the town's Latina/o population grew by chain migration. Anecdotal reports from East Town residents reveal that the first Salvadoran immigrants ar-rived in the mid-1980s. Families from Laos and Thailand began arriving in Iowa in 1975 at the invitation of former governor Robert Ray, who endorsed Laotian and Vietnamese resettlement in Iowa. The Lao and Vietnamese families who eventu-ally settled in East Town arrived first in Des Moines and then moved east to sites in southeastern Iowa where employment opportunities were available. Leadership opportunities in East Town for Latinas/os have been few despite the numbers of Latina/o residents in the community. At the turn of the twenty-first century, after Latinas/os had been residents in East Town for almost a hundred years, a longtime Latino resident and local businessman was elected to serve on the city council. More recently, there are elected Latina/o representatives on both the local city council and school board. A walk down East Town's Main Street reveals a thriving business district with approximately one-third of the storefronts housing local businesses owned and run by Latinas/os and Asian families. A burgeoning arts community is in evidence supported by the local arts council, with regional music from Mexico and Central America in the local town square on Friday evenings throughout the summer. Like its rural counterparts, East Town is largely a working-class community that depends on a local meatpacking plant for employment.

3.2.1 Romana D. Moralez in front of Santa Fe Railroad boxcar, ca. 1923, Fort Madison, Iowa. Courtesy of State Historical Society of Iowa.

Even with East Town's history with Latina/o residents, the challenges to this rural school district have increased as more immigrant families moved to the community. These challenges include hiring teachers who speak Spanish, funding issues that face many rural schools, providing culturally competent instruction, and on occasion, outward Anglo student enrollment to other districts (resulting in lost state funding dollars).[15] Many local teachers come from and were educated in predominantly Anglo rural schools themselves and were unprepared for the rich diversity in language and culture. Thus, pedagogy and practices have tended to reflect educational perspectives appropriate for the mostly middle-class English-speaking schools these teachers attended.

In our roles as tutors in an adult literacy program, we interact with immigrant parents from Mexico, Guatemala, El Salvador, Laos, Vietnam, and Cambodia whose children attend the local schools. Because of the program's longevity, we have established relationships with program participants and they may share concerns and seek our assistance. Some adult students who are also parents raised questions related to expectations around parent-teacher conferences. Their questions were generated by teachers who questioned how parents understood their roles as parents. In conferences, teachers asked whether parents monitored and explained homework to their children, and asked what they, as parents, hoped for regarding their students' academic success. Scholars report that while teachers

3.2.2   In 1962, Mexican American children play at the Muscatine Child Care Center and School in Muscatine, Iowa. Courtesy of Joan Liffring Zug-Bourret, State Historical Society of Iowa.

may be quite positive in their assessments of immigrant youth, they tend to think less highly of immigrant parents. Again, Suárez-Orozco and her colleagues report that "they tended to see them as uninterested in their children's academic welfare and reported that immigrant parents were often absent and uninvolved."[16] Sadly, we find that some East Town teachers held similar views of immigrant parents, which profoundly shaped parent-teacher relationships. While teachers wanted *all* parents to attend conferences, they specifically noted the importance of immigrant parent attendance to discuss their concerns of academic achievement. More often, teachers spoke in deficit terms, echoing Valdés's notion of "difference as deficit" that opens this chapter. Teachers seemed unaware of the positive effects that come with immigrant parents and transnational communities to reshape and transform East Town.[17]

Teachers and Scholars Invested in East Town

We come to the East Town adult tutoring program as teachers and researchers who have special interests in literacy and learning for immigrant families, particularly adults who are recent arrivals and who maintain identities with their home countries. As tutors, we can find ourselves at odds with schools-as-institutions whose larger purposes are to socialize parents and students into particular ways of believing and performing. We remain strong advocates for opportunities made available through learning literacy and have been involved in providing literacy instruction for adult students in various contexts over time. As researchers, we work against the invisibility of immigrant parents when well-funded research agendas focus exclusively on studying K–12 ELL students. To overlook adult immigrant parents is to misunderstand the ways in which their own educational needs are critical and complex, mostly invisible, and largely unfunded.

Conversations with Parents from El Salvador

Because we already have ongoing informal conversations with parents, we invited immigrant parents to talk about parent-teacher conferences and their perceptions of communicating with teachers in general. Both Lao and Latina/o parents responded, so we arranged individual appointments and had a translator present so parents had the option of talking in their first language. The parent conversations occurred at the school site where the tutoring program meets. We conducted conversations with elementary teachers to discuss similar topics; these conversations serve as a backdrop for this chapter.

There is no singular Latina/o parent experience, and we do not intend to represent the perceptions and beliefs of all parents from El Salvador or, indeed, of all immigrant parents who reside in East Town. Our conversations were typical in tone and content to all immigrant parent conversations. Our goal is to address research gaps by bringing Latina/o parent voices regarding immigrant parent involvement to the center. We use a case study approach to create a richly complex narrative of one parent describing how she serves as an advocate for her children. Case portraits lend themselves to an examination of processes and to tell a story that is particularistic and descriptive. We generated questions around key topics such as teacher communication to frame conversations with parents with a particular focus on how parents understood their roles as advocates for their children. For Latina/o parents, an experienced Spanish translator who is not a member of the local community assisted with translation. She provided translation during the interviews so that we could pose follow-up questions for clarification.

Before addressing our themes, we share four key observations common across all Latina/o parent conversations. First, none of the parents could recall or describe any similar experiences in their home country that involved talking with teachers in the context of promoting academic success. Second, all participating parents described language as a complicating factor for effective parent-teacher communication. School administrators have dedicated their efforts to assist Spanish-speaking parents and English-speaking teachers communicate; however, the translators are often local residents—a neighbor, a friend of the parent, or even a relative and thus privy to private information about families. Finally, when East Town teachers and parents navigate language differences (e.g., Spanish, Lao, and Vietnamese), they must also deal with the preponderance of educational jargon that has come to define teaching and learning in rather unfortunate ways. As examples, we share acronyms often used in discussing student academic status: ITBS, IEP, NCLB, SAT, NGE, ACT, AYP, GPA, FAFSA.[18] While these terms are common to teachers, they are rarely understood by parents and certainly not self-evident. Given language and cultural differences that frame communication as mediated through translation or interpretation and informed by the expectations that each party brings to this educational "third space," we found the critical moments Latina/o parents described worth deeper investigation.[19]

Case Portrait of a Salvadoran Parent

We draw a portrait of one mother from El Salvador in order to share relevant stories and details that emerged in our conversations. We place Margarita's case at the center of our discussion and use as a backdrop comments from two other mothers from El Salvador. The women chose to speak Spanish and use the translator so they could understand questions and respond in Spanish. These women are approximately the same age (late thirties to early forties) and members of extended family/friend networks—not surprising given that immigration patterns often bring families and extended families to the same location by virtue of "labor mobility sustained by interpersonal networks bridging points of origin and points of destination."[20] Extended family networks offer invaluable support to newly arrived parents. Within a two-year time period, the three women became naturalized U.S. citizens and made use of the tutoring program to prepare for and pass the U.S. Naturalization Test.[21] The women reported that they attended public schools in rural El Salvador until the sixth grade, when they stopped attending for reasons that included helping out with younger siblings, assisting their families with farm work, or traveling with family to the United States. They reported that discontinuing school attendance after the sixth grade was common practice in rural sections of their country.

MARGARITA'S BACKGROUND

Margarita has been a dedicated student attending the tutoring program for almost seven years. She regularly brings her children to participate in the children's program. Each year, Margarita describes her literacy goals; at the top of the list are her desires to improve as an English speaker and to enhance her skills as a reader and writer. Though she did not mention it as a goal, Margarita wants to serve as a model for her children so they can see her improve as a reader, writer, and speaker. Margarita often brings friends to the program and serves as our unofficial program recruiter. She and her husband have resided in East Town for almost twenty years and are employed at a nearby meatpacking plant. They are parents to two sons and a daughter. Like many adults in our program, they chose a work schedule that allows one of them to be at home with their children before and after school. However, this work schedule also means that only one parent (Margarita) is available to attend parent conferences.

Margarita and her husband left El Salvador to travel to Los Angeles, tracing the journey of family members who lived in California. Once there, they struggled with living costs and finding stable employment, so they relocated to Iowa for work, more affordable housing, and safety—all improvements over the quality of life they had in California. When they left El Salvador, Margarita and her husband also left their five-year-old son in the care of relatives. Their plan was for him to join them once their living situation was stable. However, because of unanticipated difficulties and immigration restrictions, months turned into years, and their son eventually joined them when he was twenty-two. The family separation exacted a painful toll evident in quiet moments when Margarita spoke of her need to become a naturalized citizen so that she could bring her son to the United States, her rationale for spending many long hours preparing for the U.S. citizenship test. She attended the tutoring program to get assistance preparing for the test; at home, she taught her husband so that he could also pass the test.

We know Margarita for her ever-present smile and the constant cheer she brings, even after a long workday at the plant. We have observed her recall childhood memories in El Salvador as a frame for understanding and making sense of rural Iowa. She delights in sharing stories of cooking treasured family recipes, memories of holiday celebrations, and her extended family members. As you will see, she has found ways to negotiate a bicultural stance that bridges her native country and the United States, where she is a new citizen.

MARGARITA'S ROLE AS ADVOCATE FOR HER CHILDREN

Our goal in engaging Latina/o parents in conversation was to better understand how they make sense of school practices where they are expected to communicate with teachers as though they are equals who speak the same language and live by the same social and cultural frameworks. We selected Margarita because of her ability to reflect on the complexities of talking with teachers. Conducting the interview in Spanish, we noted how she spoke with confidence and assurance. Margarita's English skills, her histories of communicating with teachers, and her regular attendance at conferences also position her as a valuable resource for other Latina/o parents who do not bring the same participation history. She reports that her conferences have gone well but she is aware that other parents have not had similar experiences so they seek her advice: "So, for me personally they've [conferences] been good. . . . A lot of other parents who don't go will ask me, 'So, what did they tell you?' They're wondering probably, like how does your child like this teacher, because my, my child does not like this teacher—things like that."

A major theme evident in conversations with Margarita and echoed by other Salvadoran parents is fear or embarrassment because they believe their English to be limited. In parent-teacher conferences, Latina/o parents may comprehend some of what teachers say but find they are unable to generate appropriate responses to teachers' questions. A choice for parents who anticipate such conferences is to attend the conference but remain silent. Some parents may attend and attempt to ask questions and risk feeling stupid when they can't convey what they mean. (All three mothers described that, as parents of young children, they were fearful, uncertain, and found the conferences with teachers to be "difficult" so they rarely attended.) When they did attend, their choices would be to use the school translators or to ask their children to translate for them. Neither option is good. A translator hears personal family information, and in small towns, the translator may be someone the parents know. Margarita was motivated to learn English so that she could negotiate the teacher conferences without assistance of school translators or without asking her children for assistance. When asked about translators, she replied, "yeah, there are a few times when I've used them [a translator]. It hasn't been that they'll call someone specifically [for me], but it's more like if another parent had just left the room and the interpreter is there, then I will use them as well. The translators haven't ever been my neighbor, but they have been friends, and . . . my, my son's pretty well-known around town from his soccer team so . . ." For translation to be effective for parent-teacher communication, far more is involved than knowing two languages. There is great variability in the skill of translators and in the nuance of the various world languages spoken by Latina/o parents.[22]

A more complex choice is to allow one's child to translate for parents and teachers during a conference. The three mothers from El Salvador admitted with regret that at one time or another they have relied on their children to assist with translation during parent conferences. Margarita explained her misgivings when asking her children to translate. "I . . . I think sometimes the child might feel bad, but I think it's more that I feel bad having to use my child as an interpreter, and I don't like to use my child as an interpreter, but I . . . I feel bad. I think my children also wind up feeling embarrassed, um . . . because if . . . the teachers speak in English and they [the children] have to translate . . . for their parent, they're embarrassed that they might have a dumb parent."

We asked if the practice of translating for children at the bank or the post office was qualitatively different than translating for parents during conferences. Margarita said it was, noting that stakes are different for parents and children. She described children as really intelligent so, in contexts where their futures hang in the balance, children may learn that they have leverage and can wield power over both teacher and parent. Margarita and other parents worry that children might not be translating everything the teacher said and question what is omitted. Margarita's anecdotes address the potential disruption of hierarchy within the family, allowing for an unsettling of respect for elders critical in Latina/o families, and dispersing of power that belongs with parents. And on this point, all three Latina mothers agree: allowing children to serve as translators for parents can, over time, upend the family balance that Latina/o parents strive to maintain while they are learning in cultural, economic, and political contexts that are largely English speaking, and White. Margarita describes what happens when a child sees a parent in a diminished role because he or she cannot speak the language of the teacher and may not understand the social context or implications of the language in use.

> I think it can wind up being really bad because a child can turn rebellious and . . . and spoiled because they'll use that role that they have and . . . the parent wants them to be, um, to be their interpreter all the time, and, the child can turn back and say, "Well, I'm not gonna interpret for you unless you get me this," and they wind up kind of abusing the situation. So you'll ask them, what, what did they [teacher] say? And the child will be like, no, nothing, and, but no one knows.

When we asked Margarita what she understood as the purposes of conferences between parents and teachers, she described opportunities for teachers to provide updates to parents on the child's academic progress.

> They tell you a bit about everything, they'll tell you how their reading is progressing, what their writing is like in English and in Spanish . . . they'll talk about their behavior, if they raise their hand when they want to speak, . . . they'll tell you if they're asking for permission if they need to use the bathroom, if they're making lots of noise, how their behavior is controlled, if they have to move them from one seat to another because they're talking too much—all little things like that.

Margarita's son is a student in a highly regarded dual-language program with instruction in both English and Spanish. She is attentive to his behavior because he is a lively, engaging, and active student and three of his cousins are in the same class. Not only does Margarita carefully monitor his academic progress, but she oversees whether he completes his homework each night. "So, I also ask about homework, because there's a lot of times where my son will say, 'Oh, no, I finished my homework—I did it at school,' and I'll be like, 'Hmm, I'm gonna ask the teacher about that.'"

We have come to believe, and research supports our claim, that for Latina/o parents to garner the respect they deserve in the conference setting, they are expected to ask questions of the teacher (another unwritten but firmly held standard that constitutes a good parent in a teacher's eyes). Suárez-Orozco and coauthors report that "in American schools parents are expected to come to the school and question the school. They are expected to be more active in the educational process."[23] We wondered whether Margarita questioned the teacher about her son's academic performance. "Yeah, I have definitely taken the chance to speak with teachers about that. For instance, my son does not like reading in Spanish—it's really difficult for him to read in Spanish, and there's a lot of parents who think that the language of our children is gonna be English, so they should just be practicing English, but . . . the teachers are saying that's exactly the problem: they need to be practicing Spanish and they need to be reading Spanish, so I've talked with the teacher about how my son has difficulties reading in Spanish."

We have known Margarita for years and understand that posing questions to the teacher is a learned behavior. As she has increased her ability to converse with English-speaking teachers, she has become more assertive in questioning the teacher while sharing her perspectives and concerns. In short, she has learned how to advocate for her children in U.S. schools by adopting strategies that teachers would categorize as those of good and concerned parents.

Margarita continues. "And, the teachers respond well in explaining, like, the need for both languages and explaining how, uh, when you grow up, you will need to have both languages and you'll be able to do really well having both languages. So, the teachers recommended that your child reads at home the books that interest them. Like, my son likes soccer, and so he should be reading a book about soccer because he's gonna be interested in the book and he'll read it faster, and that's all good."

At this juncture, readers might praise this teacher who provides valuable advice to support Margarita's son while also addressing her concerns. Clearly, this teacher understands how success in both English and Spanish portends overall academic success. However, not to be missed is the fact that this communication comes as a negotiation and collaboration between both teacher *and* parent. This interaction is positive because Margarita actively participates in advocating for her son, yet Margarita needed time and experience to assume an agentic identity as a parent advocate. Similarly, for other Latina/o parents to acquire identities as parent advocates, they need experience and time to learn to speak with teachers in direct fashion, all while acknowledging that these communicative acts may be at odds with their cultural frameworks.

In conversations with both Lao and Latina/o parents, we were struck by how often the term *expectation* was used. In this regard, we are not unlike teachers who fail to examine and question the encompassing pervasive discourse of school. The notion of expectations and, importantly, teacher expectations is at the core of how student success is understood and the manner in which teachers assess student progress. We entered these parent conversations *assuming* that we were all guided by common definitions of this word, failing to question whether our meanings for the word *expectation* were the same. However, each parent was confused by this term. In follow-up conversations, we discovered that for Latina/o parents, the word expectation (*esperar* from the same root as *expectativas*) has multiple meanings: to expect (anticipate, hypothesize about possible outcomes) and to hope (for something, or that something will happen).[24] While subtle, the distinctions in the context of communication between teachers and parents are profound and critically shape one's interpretation. More important are the culturally different meanings that Latina/o parents may apply to understand the word *expectations*. Latina/o parents' expectations may be so embedded in their understanding of schooling—teachers teach, students learn, students do what they are told, parents do not have expectations of the school or the teachers other than that they should do their jobs, which goes without saying—that they cannot be articulated and understood outside the cultural frames parents bring to these experiences. And the same may be said of teachers and their uses of and conceptual understandings for expectations. The discourse of school catches all of us! Our point is that East Town teachers are likely unaware of Latina/o parents' cultural understandings of the word and other words equally critical to understanding local educational practices.

Seeking Hope in Transnational Communities

Our goal has been to place at the center of parent-teacher communication the voices of Latina/o parents to challenge the myth of uncaring that continues to frame discussions of immigrant parent participation in East Town. During our conversations with parents, we wondered why this myth of uncaring is perpetuated. For those who work with immigrant families and the challenges they face, the research continues to endorse what Margarita's case represents—caring, supportive, and concerned immigrant parents involved in learning new languages while coming to understand how to work effectively with schools and teachers.[25] Latina/o parents seek to advocate for their children and to develop personal identities, all while respectfully acknowledging the historical, cultural, and linguistic traditions that continue to shape the people they are in the process of becoming. We call on researchers and practitioners to develop relationships with parents as one step in dismantling the myth of uncaring.

We see three implications from our work. First, educators must seek new visions for the many forms and practices inherently part of parent participation and communication. Communication can no longer exist in narrow linear pathways that intend to exclude rather than include. Models of parent involvement that have served as *the* standard must be reconsidered; those dated models were constructed for mostly White, middle-class parents and are no longer relevant to transnational communities like East Town. We see promise in models where parents and teachers work in educational third spaces as conceptualized by Gutiérrez and colleagues who describe how in jointly constructed activities, parents and teachers will work to assume shared roles of learning, to collaborate in solving problems, and to learn across diverse experiences. Educational third spaces draw on linguistic and cultural hybridity and allow participants to discuss misconceptions and misunderstandings that exist when crossing language and cultural borders.[26] Misconceptions and misunderstandings occur when there is a lack of meaningful contact between parents and teachers.

Some East Town teachers expressed hope for a return to a romanticized and prosperous past that existed for some but not all residents. These romantic notions of earlier rural communities framed life and living as homogeneous, safe, comfortable, and familiar.[27] Unfortunately, such visions do not permit Anglo residents to see beyond what was and discover what is possible in reenvisioning rural spaces as exciting sites where cultural and linguistic boundaries do not define learning and opportunity.

If schools and teachers seek to partner with Latina/o parents, they must work from a desire to build relationships to collaborate and listen, and to learn from their stories and journeys. Immigrant parent voices deserve a central place in educational research so that practitioners understand the complex navigation required of parents who advocate for children. The optimism and drive that teachers admire in immigrant students is often the result of enormous parental sacrifices and aspirations they hold for their children. We believe that the limited research on adult immigrants' educational perspectives, particularly Latina/o immigrants, has allowed misunderstandings to exist and myths to be perpetuated. And, it has delayed our taking up new visions for what transnational communities offer for the longtime rural residents of East Town and newly arrived families. There is power and vision to be found in transnational communities, so working to understand residents in these communities is a goal we should embrace. Great potential and substantial challenges await rural residents, Latina/o and Anglo, as they engage with local educational institutions and local economies in productive and critical fashion.

Notes

1. We use the term *immigrant* to describe participants who attend the adult tutoring program. Immigrants, as we use the term, may have arrived in the United States in the last five years or more than twenty years ago, but as a group they tend to view themselves differently from white Americans and live lives based on standards from their home country. Guadalupe Valdés and Marjorie Faulstich Orellana explain their use of the term. Valdés describes immigrants as those individuals who are born both in and outside the United States but maintain an "immigrant mentality" (6)—and remain oriented toward their home country. Orellana uses the term to refer to actions of children and families in a country to which they have moved; her use of the term *immigrant* "presumes the vantage point of the receiving context" (147). Guadalupe Valdés, *Con Respeto: Bridging the Distances between Culturally Diverse Families and Schools: An Ethnographic Portrait* (New York: Teachers College Press, 1996). Marjorie Faulstich Orellana, *Translating Childhoods: Immigrant Youth, Language, and Culture* (New Brunswick, N.J.: Rutgers University Press, 2009).

2. Valdés, *Con Respeto*.

3. We reference bell hooks's use of the term "talking back" in her *Teaching to Transgress: Education as the Practice of Freedom* (New York: Routledge, 1994).

4. Jeanne R. Paratore, Alisa Hindin, Barbara Krol-Sinclair, and Pilar Durán, "Discourse between Teachers and Latino Parents during Conferences Based on Home Literacy Portfolios," *Education and Urban Society* 32, no. 1 (1999): 58–82.

5. Carola Suárez-Orozco, Marcelo M. Suárez-Orozco, and Irina Todorova, *Learning a New Land: Immigrant Students in American Society* (Cambridge, Mass: Belknap Press of Harvard University Press, 2008), 76.

6. See for example, Joyce L. Epstein, "School/Family/Community Partnerships: Caring for the Children We Share," *Phi Delta Kappan* 76, no. 9 (1995): 701–12, and Joyce L. Epstein, *School, Family, and Community Partnerships: Preparing Educators and Improving Schools* (Boulder, Colo.: Westview Press, 2011).

7. Anne T. Henderson and Karen L. Mapp, *A New Wave of Evidence: The Impact of School, Family, and Community Connections on Student Achievement*, Annual Synthesis 2002 (Austin, Tex.: National Center for Family and Community Connections with Schools, and Southwest Educational Development Laboratory [SEDL], 2002).

8. Edward M. Olivos, Oscar Jiménez-Castellanos, and Alberto M. Ochoa, *Bicultural Parent Engagement: Advocacy and Empowerment* (New York: Teachers College Press, 2011).

9. Ibid., 11.

10. Susan Auerbach, "From Moral Supporters to Struggling Advocates: Reconceptualizing Parent Roles in Education through the Experience of Working-Class Families of Color," *Urban Education* 42, no. 3 (2007): 251.

11. Ibid.

12. Osha Gray Davidson, *Broken Heartland: The Rise of America's Rural Ghetto* (New York: Free Press, 1996), 125.

13. Paratore et al., "Discourse between Teachers and Latino Parents."

14. The names of all people and locations are pseudonyms.

15. Michelle Young and Carolyn Colvin, "Diversity and Open Enrollment in a Rural Midwestern School Community," paper presented at the annual meeting of the American Educational Research Association, Seattle, Wash., April 2002.

16. Suárez-Orozco et al., *Learning a New Land*, 76.

17. Carola Suárez-Orozco and Marcelo M. Suárez-Orozco, *Children of Immigration*, the Developing Child series (Cambridge, Mass.: Harvard University Press, 2001), 30–31. We recognize the many meanings applied to the term transcultural. For our purposes, we borrow from the Suárez-Orozcos to suggest that "immigrants are players—economically, politically, and culturally in their newly adopted lands and in their communities of origin." Similarly, we believe communities like East Town may embody transcultural characteristics.

18. ITBS (Iowa Tests of Basic Skills), IEP (Individual Educational Plan), NCLB (No Child Left Behind), SAT (Scholastic Aptitude Test), NGE (National Grade Equivalent), ACT (American College Testing), AYP (Annual Yearly Progress), GPA (Grade Point Average), FAFSA (Free Application for Federal Student Aid).

19. Kris D. Gutiérrez, Patricia Baquedano-López, and Héctor H. Alvarez, "Literacy as Hybridity: Moving beyond Bilingualism in Urban Classrooms," in *The Best for Our Children: Critical Perspectives on Literacy for Latino Students*, ed. María de la Luz Reyes et al., Language and Literacy Series (New York: Teachers College Press, 2001), 126–27.

20. M. Patricia Fernández-Kelly and Richard Schauffler, "Divided Fates: Immigrant Children and the New Assimilation," in *The New Second Generation*, ed. Alejandro Portes (New York: Russell Sage Foundation, 1996), 32.

21. The Naturalization Test is found at https://www.uscis.gov/us-citizenship. This series of tests includes the civics test (100 questions about U.S. government, history, etc.). On a given day, ten questions are randomly selected. Applicants must be able to successfully answer six of the ten questions. Applicants must also now demonstrate their ability to write and read in English. Applicants are expected to know, understand, and perhaps use specific vocabulary in written form. The English portion may include dictated sentences

that applicants must write and read in English. See https://www.uscis.gov/citizenship/learners/study-test/study-materials-english-test.

22. Soria Elizabeth Colomer and Linda Harklau, "Spanish Teachers as Impromptu Translators and Liaisons in New Latino Communities," *Foreign Language Annals* 42, no. 4 (2009).

23. Suárez-Orozco et al., *Learning a New Land*, 76.

24. Judith Liskin Gasparro, email to authors, May 25, 2013.

25. Olivos et al., *Bicultural Parent Engagement*.

26. Gutiérrez et al., "Literacy as Hybridity," 128–31.

27. Patrick J. Carr and Maria J. Kefalas, *Hollowing out the Middle: The Rural Brain Drain and What It Means for America* (Boston: Beacon Press), 17.

Latina/o Studies and Ethnic Studies in the Midwest

AMELIA MARÍA DE LA LUZ MONTES

"Se me enchina el cuerpo al oír tu cuento . . ." (I get goosebumps hearing your story . . .). This is the title of a short story written by author and professor Norma Cantú.[1] "How the day after graduating as valedictorian from the high school in the Rio Grande Valley you helped your family board up the door and windows of the frame house and pack the old pick-up truck to make your annual trek north" (125). The valedictorian, the character in the story, takes his family to the Midwest for agricultural work. Because he is the educated one, he speaks for the family and stands up to the bosses who disrespect and cheat the family of decent wages. It is when he sees his father drowning in chicken feathers that he says "enough!" Not only does he take his family away from the oppressive labor practices the bosses have created, he drives "the Midwest farm road" to complain to the labor relations board. "No one had ever done that before. But you read the language of the bosses. You move on with your family, and your father is pleased; your mother beams but is afraid in her heart for her son who speaks the language of the bosses" (125). Cantú's story is only a page long and yet it "speaks volumes" about class and the dynamics that occur when one acquires the language and behaviors of the privileged and uses that privilege to assist others. In the story, the father is pleased, as is the mother. However, the mother fears for her son, too, because she knows there are also consequences.

Two years ago, with only two weeks left in the spring semester, I was summoned to the Dean of Arts and Sciences Office. The email indicated only that the meeting had to do with the Institute for Ethnic Studies, and no other information was revealed. Three years before that, I had led the reorganization of our institute and program, fending off a top-down restructuring from the administration. The university had been experiencing diminution in economic support from the state and in student enrollment, specifically in the humanities. As director of the University of Nebraska–Lincoln's (UNL) Institute for Ethnic Studies, I was the one negotiating with the dean on behalf of the institute. At that time, we understood that cuts were imminent, but we requested autonomy in the process. "Let us [Ethnic Studies] decide how to streamline our program," we asked. The dean acquiesced. With the help of neighboring interdisciplinary program and department directors and chairs, such as Dr. Phil Deloria from the University of Michigan (Program in American Culture) and Dr. Arlene Torres from the University of Illinois at Urbana-Champaign (Latino Studies Department), our faculty retained agency in the process, made the necessary cuts, and streamlined our program into a much more efficient administrative structure. Our cuts made sense to us because I made sure the faculty were included. And that is what I learned as director of a program: transparency and inclusion are key in maintaining a functional community of scholars who are researching, publishing, teaching, and serving the community. Serving, making direct connections to community is key. In our Ethnic Studies program, I have twenty-one joint appointed faculty from seven other departments: anthropology, English, history, modern languages, political science, psychology, and sociology. We also have over thirty affiliated faculty.

Although no program or department is perfect, the commitment to including faculty in decisions, giving them the necessary information, and listening to their ideas is essential. Three years later, as stated, I was summoned to the dean's office, but not to see the dean. I was to meet with the associate dean of research, who was given the job to tell me that before the end of the semester (which was in two weeks), the entire Institute of Ethnic Studies was to pack its bags and move to a building that, as I soon discovered, was already a condemned building. The directive, this time, was coming from the senior vice chancellor's office.

Since its inception in the 1970s, Ethnic Studies at UNL had been housed in a small office on the margins of campus. Its last home was not centralized and quite invisible. It was difficult, even with a campus map, to find the tiny office. Then, in 2007, we finally moved into a beautiful space large enough to share with other interdisciplinary programs: Women's and Gender Studies, Judaic Studies, and Global Studies. These other programs, like Ethnic Studies, had been in tiny spaces far from each other. The move in 2007 gave us airy offices and a large conference room to share for meetings and receptions. Ethnic Studies was also given its own book and video library, and administrative offices. There are many advantages to having interdisciplinary programs together on one floor or building. Students can visit all the faculty at once, and often when we have had student events, we have had higher attendance because the advertising comes from all the programs, so the students see them as integrated. The close office proximity allows informal interdisciplinary discussions and collaborations. As well, some of our newer faculty had noted that seeing our well-appointed offices during their interviews here encouraged them to feel that our programs were respected, that the administration was committed to interdisciplinary work. The kind of space we had been given, and where the space was, in relation to campus life, contributed greatly to the recruitment and hiring of faculty. Now I was in a meeting with the associate dean informing me that all the programs were being dispersed again to various areas of the campus and that all this had to happen very soon.

A note about the way the interdisciplinary programs were informed: the associate dean did not meet with all the program directors at once. Each director was called in separately and without much explanation as to why this was occurring. The directive: we had two weeks (without taking into consideration our end-of-semester teaching and finals schedules) to get out of the building. I immediately called all the program directors to discuss this abrupt decision. Later, we learned that the senior vice chancellor's office had been searching for building spaces and, without consulting any of the interdisciplinary programs, had decided to requisition our space to house International Affairs while their building was undergoing renovation. The University of Nebraska–Lincoln Physical Master Plan 2006–15, in the "Building Efficiency Goals" section, states: "make space more flexible or adaptable and promote shared core facilities that serve the needs of multi-disciplinary activities." Our third-floor space created optimal multidisciplinary activities. Now we were to be, once again, separated and placed in a condemned building, and the time frame was next to impossible.

Our efforts immediately went into organizing against this decision instead of packing up our offices. After calling the senior vice chancellor's office and not receiving any response, we called the school newspaper, informed all of our students, and planned a protest. Ethnic Studies printed poster-size maps of our existing space and how we were using it to fulfill the university's mission for diversity and interdisciplinary research and teaching. I located the floor plan of the condemned space and had it blown up into a poster to hang on the wall next to our existing floor plan in order to reveal the stark difference in working spaces. I then went into the condemned building and took photographs of rotting wood, broken windows, numerous broken desks and chairs, windowless offices without air-conditioning or ventilation, and cracks in the walls and ceiling. Those photographs were posted alongside the floor plans. The students from Ethnic Studies, Women's and Gender Studies, Judaic Studies, Global Studies, and from other interdisciplinary fields also mobilized. They informed the Associated Student Body (ASU)—UNL's aggregate student government. Word spread and the students were ready for a day of protest.

The evening before the day of protest, I received a phone call from the senior vice chancellor. To her credit, she admitted that she had made a mistake. She told me the directive would be canceled if I stopped the protest. She hadn't realized what it meant for these programs to be moved. I negotiated with her by requesting that she come to our third-floor space the next day. We would not protest. Instead, all the program directors would inform her about what we do and why the space these programs inhabit is vital to the university's core mission. The next day, she and other administrators sat down with us in our building and learned about what we do. They had never been there before. What was made clear that morning was the disconnect that happens between upper administration and nontraditional programs or departments. Three years before, the dean of Arts and Sciences had informed us of a budget crisis, had listened to our request, and agreed to include our faculty in the decision-making process to streamline our program. In contrast, the senior vice chancellor's office simply sent out what they called a building czar to look for possible space. No one asked us anything. Instead, they informed us that we had to leave without any explanation. Luckily, the risk we took to mobilize, to threaten to protest, brought about a positive outcome because we wound up not having to leave our building. It is now 2017, and we are still there. However, we were also reminded that we do not have ownership of any space on campus, a reminder that has a double meaning. It puts us in our place and reinscribes a culture of distrust and insecurity. Had the senior vice chancellor's office approached us to say, "Next time, we will approach you and explain the situation to get your input, so we can work together to solve the problem," the issue would have ended on a more secure note. Unfortunately, it is rare for this to happen in academia.

The lack of transparency in the workplace is not endemic to the Midwest or to academia. It happens everywhere and in every kind of employment setting—and it's never a positive work practice. A lack of transparency sets up a hierarchy that mirrors a rigid class structure. And when it involves academic programs and departments whose research focus and whose faculty by and large reflect working-class backgrounds, diverse races, ethnicities, cultures, there exists, as Cantú's story describes, "a scar . . . it hurts when the weather changes or the memory intersects with this time and place" (125). Swift action and mobilization helps to strengthen community ties. But it won't happen without first creating communities of understanding and making connections with differences among each other within the programs and departments. If a lack of transparency exists there, then the possibility of a strong Ethnic Studies or Latina/o Studies, or any other program, may take longer to achieve.

Midwest Personality

Regarding the Midwest, there is a generalization about the Midwest personality as being one that shies away from confrontation. I'm thinking of the cover of cultural critic Edén Torres's book, *Chicana without Apology*. The photograph on the cover reveals a protest underway and two Chicanas at the forefront marching with many others. One is yelling, the other (in front) also has her mouth open, as if in a chant, her arm lifted defiantly, hand in a fist. The photograph is dramatic and fierce. Now that I've lived in the Midwest (specifically Nebraska) for a number of years, I can say that I have not often seen such a depiction of fervent emotion here. Interestingly, the cover photo of *Chicana without Apology* is a photo originally published in the *Los Angeles Times*. However, I don't want to perpetuate stereotypes. While I was a postdoctoral fellow at the University of Illinois in Urbana-Champaign during the 2004 academic year, students there were fervently protesting the Chief Illiniwek mascot, and in 2007, they were successful, and the university retired the mascot name. At the University of Michigan, students in Latino Studies have mobilized to protest the affirmative action ban. All of these examples contradict the Midwest idea of complacency. And yet, complacency and a reserved environment is present in my classroom when I begin the semester. I have had to create strategies to engender a classroom space where student discussion can happen organically. In *Creating Minnesota: A History from the Inside Out*, Annette Atkins writes about the term "Minnesota nice." This refers to the stereotypical behavior of people born and raised in Minnesota as courteous, reserved, and mild-mannered (Nebraska has the equivalent term: "Nebraska nice"). "The cultural characteristics of Minnesota nice includes a polite friendliness, an aversion to confrontation, a tendency toward understatement, a disinclination to make a fuss or stand out, emotional restraint, and self-deprecation.... Critics have pointed out negative qualities, such as passive aggressiveness and resistance to change" (242). When I first arrived to Nebraska from Los Angeles, I asked students (in my matter-of-fact way) why they were so hesitant to speak in class.

One student answered, "Well I've always been told not to stand out. It's embarrassing."

Another said, "It's egotistical—like you know more than anybody else."

I thought about this and asked the students to think instead about being genuinely curious about other students' ideas. I said, "If you stop thinking about yourself and whether or not you're going to stand out, then you will be able to shift away from silence. You'll be able to think instead about (1) making a contribution to the community of people in the room, and (2) making a commitment to genuinely hear and understand your colleague's contribution. In this way, we become a community of speakers, of individuals witnessing and considering each other instead of making assumptions and living in fear of speaking due to another person's judgment." This reasoning has helped, along with acclimating the students by putting them in pairs at the beginning of the semester, moving to larger groups of three and four, and finally working toward a robust full-class discussion format.

Along with student reticence to speak inside the classroom, during my years at UNL, I have never seen students organize a major protest en masse or go on a hunger strike, as students did from April 27 to May 5, 1994, at the University of California Santa Barbara, when students demanded more faculty lines and a doctoral degree program in the Chicana/o Studies Department. In 2010, students at the University of Texas, San Antonio, chanted for hours and were arrested at a sit-in, demanding the DREAM Act be passed for undocumented students. Not here. Change can happen at a slower pace among midwesterners for whom politeness remains front and center, and this also impacts transparency. The commitment to politeness and protocol inhibits transparency because transparency necessitates debate, faculty thoughts, and opinions, which may lead to uncomfortable conversations. In Atkins's book, she points out that instead of direct discussions and/or (peaceful!) confrontations, passive aggressive behavior will occur as a reaction to the cultural climate of silence.

Edén Torres, who teaches at the University of Minnesota, seeks to encourage the Chicana voice and Chicana agency rather than allow silence, which can lead to passive aggressive behavior. In the Midwest, I have found direct and honest disclosure somewhat more difficult than in Los Angeles, where I was born and raised. Yet, I also see the merits in striking a balance between harsh confrontation and politeness. *Politeness*, however, is not a word I favor. I would choose the word *respect*, instead: to respect another individual while also speaking frankly and with confidence (not cockiness) is a rhetorical art to continually practice. My years in administration have led me to this conclusion. Merging *respect* with "voice and agency" creates the ability to be receptive and understanding while also being fearless and strong.

In what other ways might this work in the classroom and with faculty? I will always remember when a student spoke to me about "Nebraska nice." He was an African American student from a working-class area of Washington, D.C., and had been in the Midwest for two years.

"You know what 'Nebraska nice' feels like sometimes, Dr. Montes?"
"What?" I asked.
He looked at me with a wry smile, "Nebraska shady." He laughed.
"Say more," I said.
"Well, you know, they're thinking something else while they are smiling and being polite. They don't say the truth. They stand behind their lie with a smile. It's lying by omission. But then, it forces me to just smile too. It doesn't feel good."
"Why doesn't it feel good?"
"Because I'm not being heard and understood, and then I'm doing what they're doing."

To students and faculty of various backgrounds, "Nebraska nice," "Minnesota nice," "Fill-in-the-blank nice" can feel like a huge wound—a divide between the privileged and the working class. The privileged remain silent, and they go about their business. Anything challenging the norm is a threat. Therefore, the Chicana/Chicano (working-class minority) student or faculty member, the Other, is left to "conform," to "assimilate" in order to survive in the academic culture, or not. The atmosphere either becomes one of complacency or one where students are given the opportunity to learn skills to engender a vibrant and meaningful way to engage with their fellow students. Among the professoriate, faculty members fear retribution during tenure, promotion, or merit considerations. Faculty may worry that their interdisciplinary programs and departments will not receive the support they need to flourish. To remain silent, as Edén Torres points out, only creates an erasure that serves no one.

In my example, Ethnic Studies and the other programs at UNL refused to remain silent. We did not dutifully pack up our offices. Instead, we carefully mapped out a number of steps in our refusal to set ourselves up in the shabby rooms of the condemned building. (1) We wrote the vice chancellor requesting the decision to be revoked. When that did not work, (2) we investigated the condemned building. (3) We had a meeting to discuss the severe problems of the building and next steps. (4) We took the photographs and hung the floor plans of our building and the condemned building side by side to demonstrate the differences. Along with the floor plans, we posted pictures of the broken windows, chairs, and discolored and moldy walls of the building. (5) We called the newspapers and informed our students, who then began to mobilize. (6) Writing this article creates an archival document. We can take from these examples to determine future steps for much more subtle challenges to come.

The phenomenon of "Nebraska nice" is not a culture or a personality. I see it as "fear" enacted to fend off difference. When placed in an academic setting, it contradicts the core mission to engender cultural expression at the very intersections of race, class, gender, and sexuality. "Nebraska nice" or any other "nice" negates the presence of difference and instead establishes only one story, one way to behave, which then leads to stereotypes, because if one does not behave in the "Fill-in-the-blank nice" way, the individual is described as having a lack of "emotional restraint" or humility. Here are some examples: The person-of-color chair, or faculty member, who talks with her hands, who is loud, who makes her point with a lengthy narrative, is shunned because she refuses to (1) remain quiet or (2) negotiate in an understated, restrained way. The term "presenting your point elegantly" is sometimes code for speaking in a linear and minimalist narrative. Do not reveal your emotions. Keep your hands by your sides or in your lap. A person of color will be speaking and after she (it's more often a woman) makes her case, a person of privilege will then say to the group, "So let me explain to everyone what you were trying to say here . . ." Agency is taken away over and over again.

I think of fiction writer Chimamanda Ngozi Adichie's TED talk, "The Danger of a Single Story." Adichie explains how ashamed she was to realize when she went to Mexico that she had fallen into believing the "single story" about Mexicans as " abject immigrants . . . fleecing the [U.S.] health care system." Only by going to Mexico did she actually see the highly diverse aspects of the Mexican people and their cultures. The single story, she reminds her audience, is about power.[2] To perpetuate just one story works to control a people and establish a normative culture. Even though the Midwest personality seems to be one of reticence, I do see a very different story when I witness the many midwestern farm owners uniting with the Lakota Sioux Tribe to stop the Keystone XL Pipeline. The danger here is when people are not acknowledged for standing up, for not speaking when academic freedom is in peril, when programs, departments, and faculty that are vital to an understanding of our racial and cultural diversity are disregarded, and disrespectfully, silently transferred to a condemned building or worse.

Shrinking Curriculum and Interdisciplinary Programs

Consolidating interdisciplinary programs and/or departments by combining them or, as previously discussed, shunting them into smaller or menial spaces is one way to diminish these units. Another way is to cut course requirements. When I began teaching at UNL, students were required to take six humanities general education courses. My classes were full. Not only were classes full, but I felt very supported in my commitment to optimal teaching and learning. Every semester I would also receive a list of possible visiting artists. I would choose the artist who would complement what I was teaching, and the university would commit to bringing two artists a semester. Chicana/Chicano and Latina/Latino artists came to speak to my classes, to give a reading, a performance, to even take over the class to teach the students to create a performance or write a poem, flash fiction piece, or journal entry. The students were enthralled. Many of the visiting artists remain my friends today. The students (who were mainly born and raised in Nebraska) were meeting artists from Texas, New York, California, and Florida, and the artists were also asking the students many questions about the Midwest. They were discovering each other. It was an interactive cultural experience.

I remember a fiction writer from Los Angeles who excitedly asked the students what it was like living on a farm. No one answered. Finally, one student said, "I've never lived on a farm." Another student answered, "I grew up here in Lincoln." The fiction writer then asked, "Okay—has anyone here lived on a farm?" One student raised his hand but said he was very young when his family's farm was sold to a corporation after being in the family for generations. During this exchange, I learned from some of the students that when they've traveled outside of Nebraska, they've been asked if they have chickens and if they use outhouses instead of bathrooms. (By the way, in all my years teaching at UNL, I know of no student born and raised in Nebraska who had an outhouse on the family property.) Further, the students asked questions of the fiction writer that revealed their own stereotypes about California and Los Angeles. They assumed that she had been mugged because she lives in Los Angeles. They also assumed she lived near a movie star. Instead, she talked about her working-class upbringing in East L.A.

This program inspired so many of my students. After four years, though, funding for this program ended, and the college did not want to renew it. A number of us wrote letters, even asked the students to write letters. The program never returned. One by one, such programs have ended with today's challenge of a shrinking curriculum.

In 2013 at the college faculty meeting, the science professors proposed cutting the already severely shaved number (since the year I began) of required humanities courses to two. By a large margin, they won the vote. I was there at the meeting, in total disbelief as to what was happening. Where were the rest of my humanities colleagues? I had been to many Arts and Science College faculty meetings—hardly anyone present, and that day felt like a party. All these (primarily) male professors walked in together, took seats in the front row. They raised their hands in unison. The few humanities professors sprinkled about the room voted against, but without a chance of prevailing. And now the absentee humanities professors are complaining. Last year, I had to cancel two of our ethnic studies courses because fewer than five students had registered for each.

I think about our building protest and our success at keeping the space. Then I think about the shrinking curriculum, and the loss of students. You may be in the building space you want, but you won't have a program if you don't have the students, and each year I have seen diminishing numbers in various humanities departments. This is a much larger issue and an ongoing challenge. And in today's world, these classes are vital for all students. Ethnic studies and other interdisciplinary courses are braided tightly within the mission of educating students to navigate a very diverse, global world.

In her contribution to a book about Latino and women of color in higher education, Latina/o studies professor Carmen R. Lugo-Lugo writes that

> Ethnic Studies is different from disciplines like sociology, political science, and anthropology, which tend to hide behind the curtain of scientific objectivity and present issues by discussing numbers and an array of calculated theories designed

to provide some explanation for the numbers. In fact, listening to my colleagues and friends in those disciplines discuss their student evaluations, it appears that if professors in any of these (and related) disciplines try to move beyond mere presentation of facts, they are told to "shut up and teach." Because of its transdisciplinary methodology, ethnic studies is not a shut-up-and-teach kind of discipline. Ethnic Studies does not hide behind the veil of objectivity, and in fact, to be effective, it has to advocate and strive for a fundamental transformation of race relations. Stating that there is inequality is not enough. And here is where I come in: I am a Latina telling my mostly white students that racism, discrimination, and inequality still exist and affect all our lives (theirs included), both in ways that can be measured and ones that cannot. I also tell them that they are implicated in those things, that they must do something about them, and that their comforts come at the expense of others. And, of course, they do not want to hear that. Especially not from me.[3]

I can relate to what Lugo-Lugo describes in her classroom. However, imagine trying to explain these concepts to other administrators and faculty—to ask them to consider their own implications and, further, to request that they do something about this so that they will consider "color insight" best practices at the level of faculty reappointments and tenure reviews. Like Lugo-Lugo's students, many do not want to hear it. They want to hold fast to a numerical metric system of evaluation, to online courses that create a virtual space that leaves out human interaction and confrontation. No explanations are needed, no room for discussion, it is easy—just fill out the multiple choice tests or complete the Blackboard assignment.

Lugo-Lugo's words remind me of an independent study student I taught last year who is a Chicano major. She wanted to do a comparative unit (reading Chicana/Chicano literature with what is considered traditional Anglo-American literature). I chose stories from authors who seek to problematize our class structure. I had her read the very powerful short piece by Norma Cantú that begins this chapter, "Se me enchina el cuerpo al oír tu cuento." The reader is able to experience the disrespect and just anger the son feels when the farm owner directs his farmworker family to sleep in the chicken coop. The son is straddling two worlds. He is educated, but he also belongs to this family of exploited workers. In his story "The Paradise of Bachelors and the Tartarus of Maids," Herman Melville describes two strikingly different worlds: the highly privileged world of a fraternal club of lawyers, while across the way is the paper mill, a kind of Juárez *maquiladora* filled with women who will lose their job if they marry or become pregnant (therefore staying "maids" the rest of their lives), women whose faces look pale and empty, whose limbs repeat the same monotonous movements in order to provide the fancy paper on which the jaunty young male lawyers write.

Cantú's story is contemporary, illustrating a North American social condition of exploitation. Melville's world is a nineteenth-century preindustrial revolutionary one. He wrote this story so that such a social condition would not exist in the United States, a cautionary tale that did not at all prevent what we have now, which is what Cantú describes. Placing these two stories together broadens student discussions toward historical, global, and gendered considerations.

Ethnic studies, Latina/o studies, and other interdisciplinary programs in the Midwest reflect multifarious and labyrinthine challenges. What Cantú's story has, which Melville's lacks, is that Cantú's main character has connections in both worlds (the privileged world and his poor, working-class family), which allows him to protect and nurture his family. Cantú creates a character whose educational background does not prevent him from continuing to be a member of that family. Instead, he takes what he has learned (understanding the language of the bosses) to become the activist and secure the money owed the family by locating and speaking to the labor relations office. In Melville's story, there is no one in the paper mill to assist the maids. The two worlds are stoically segregated. Those of us who come from poor and working-class families, those of us who are first-generation graduates, we have all jumped the fence to the other side. It is what we do "on the other side," what we do with this privilege that makes Latina/o studies and ethnic studies in the Midwest especially prescient. We are in the flyover, disregarded, checkered lands of the United States that Thomas Jefferson imagined ("each man in his own square"). It is within this space that the existence of ethnic studies, Latina/o studies, and other interdisciplinary programs allow for further problematizing of the academic arena.

Notes

1. Norma Cantú, "Se me enchina el cuerpo al oír tu cuento . . . ," in *Latino Boom: An Anthology of U.S. Latino Literature*, ed. John S. Christie and José B. Gonzalez (New York: Longman, 2006). Citations to this work appear in text.

2. Chimamanda Ngozi Adichie, "The Danger of a Single Story," filmed July 2009, TED Global video, 18:49, www.TED.com.

3. Carmen R. Lugo-Lugo, "A Prostitute, a Servant, and a Customer-Service Representative," in *Presumed Incompetent: The Intersections of Race and Class for Women in Academia*, ed. Gabriella Gutiérrez y Muhs, Yolanda Flores Niemann, Carmen G. González, and Angela P. Harris (Boulder: University Press of Colorado, 2012), 40–49.

PART 4

Performeando the Midwest

The Black Angel

Ana Mendieta in Iowa City

JANE BLOCKER

I work with the earth, with nature, and I make sculptures out of
landscapes and the environment. I think this has much to do with
Cuba, in the sense that I was attracted to nature because I didn't
have a land, a Motherland.

—Ana Mendieta

A patriot bids farewell, she bids farewell, at the midnight hour. She
leaves her birthplace, she clutches her child to her breast, in order to
find bread for him in faraway places.

—Terezie Doležal Feldewert

It is a clear, sunny autumn day. The deep blue sky, across which the branches of
bare trees draw a veil of black lace, turns a pale aqua green as it imprints itself on
the Super 8 film stock. The camera, mounted on a tripod, beautifully frames a dark
winged statue, which sits atop a granite monument. The waning afternoon light
creates long shadows as the sun drops toward the southwest. As the film stutters
through the projector, we see a young woman of about twenty-seven years of
age, dressed in black, lying face down on the flat tombstone that stretches from
the sculpture's base. The woman, Cuban-born artist Ana Mendieta (1948–1985),
rises to her feet, her back to the camera, dwarfed beneath the bronze angel rising
over twelve feet into the air. A dark outline of Mendieta's body—arms upraised,
feet together—remains on the stone. She walks backward toward the camera to
retrieve a cardboard box, which lies on the grass in front of the tripod, just beneath the film frame. She carries it to the foot of the grave, where she sets it on
the grass, its top flaps open. We have not yet seen her face. She bends at the waist,
scoops handfuls of black dirt or powdered pigment (it's hard to tell which) from

the box, and sprinkles it gradually to fill in the dark outline, creating a black silhouette. As she turns toward the camera to walk out of the frame to the right, the cool wind blows her long, straight, dark hair across her face like a shadowy veil.

The film cuts.

She emerges again from the right with a second box, lays it on the grass next to the first. This time she scoops handfuls of a red powdery substance, possibly dry tempera, and uses it to outline the black figure, first along the right side from foot to head, then along the left side.[1]

The film cuts abruptly, making her seem to disappear with a snap from beneath the dark sculpture like a magic trick. It has been three minutes, the end of the first roll of film.

Having loaded a new roll of film, she now enters the frame once again from the right, this time using the red powder to fill in a section of the dark figure's upper torso as though to indicate a human heart. Again she exits the shot to the right, and again she returns, this time taking more dark powder from the box on the left and using it to inscribe a large black X across the figure. She exits to the right for the third and last time. Returning, she stands for a brief moment at the foot of the

4.1.1   Ana Mendieta, *Black Angel*, ca. 1975. Still from super-8mm film transferred to high-definition digital media, color, silent. Running time 6:37 min. © The Estate of Ana Mendieta Collection, LLC. Courtesy of Galerie Lelong, New York.

grave looking up at the dark bronze angel perched above her. She steps onto the stone crypt and, in a broad gesture of erasure, swings her right leg in a wide arc and sweeps the dirt and pigment away with her foot (fig. 4.1.2). She exits the shot on the left this time, and the camera catches a glimpse of her expressionless face as her eyes move upward to meet the distant horizon, and she disappears.

This film, which is today simply known as *Black Angel*, is thought to have been made in 1975 at Oakland Cemetery in Iowa City, Iowa. Mendieta, as is well-known, was born in Havana in 1948 but was sent with her sister Raquelín to the United States on September 11, 1961, shortly after the Cuban Revolution. A reluctant beneficiary of Operación Pedro Pan, she was just twelve years old.[2] With no relatives in the United States to claim them, the girls spent nearly a month in Camp Kendall in Miami and then were sent to St. Mary's, a Catholic group home for "juvenile delinquents" in Dubuque, Iowa. Alienated and homesick, like many of the Pedro Pan children, for the next four years Ana and her sister were shuttled among foster homes in Cedar Rapids (about 25 miles north of Iowa City). She graduated from Regis High School in 1965. The following year, her mother and younger brother Ignacio joined Ana and her sister in Cedar Rapids, while her

4.1.2   Ana Mendieta, *Black Angel*, ca. 1975. Still from super-8mm film transferred to high-definition digital media, color, silent. Running time: 6:37 min. © The Estate of Ana Mendieta Collection, LLC. Courtesy of Galerie Lelong, New York.

father remained in prison under the Castro regime. In 1967, Ana transferred from Briar Cliff College in Sioux City, on the western border of the state, to the University of Iowa (the state's original capitol building is on that campus), where, over the course of the subsequent ten years, she completed her undergraduate and two graduate degrees in fine art.

It is common in the literature on Mendieta to see references to and explanations of her Cuban heritage, her study of pre-Columbian cultures in Mexico, her fascination with Afro-Cuban religious practices such as Santería, her research into the Taíno and other native Cuban peoples, as well as her interest in African religious and artistic customs. Although she spent nearly half of her short life in the Midwest (she died at the age of thirty-six), critics and scholars rarely discuss Iowa—its people, landscapes, history, or culture—as a significant influence on her art.[3] In part this has to do with Mendieta's own repeated characterization of her work as a direct response to her traumatic experience of exile and feelings of displacement and alienation in Iowa, and it is surely a reflection of scholars' desires, since her tragic death in 1985, to establish her reputation as an important late-twentieth-century artist, a task that requires locating her in relation to urban centers (New York and, to a lesser degree, Los Angeles) as the locus of significant artistic innovation in the United States.

The one notable exception to this tendency is Julia Herzberg's 1998 dissertation, "Ana Mendieta, the Iowa Years," and her subsequent essay for the major retrospective exhibition catalog, *Ana Mendieta, Earth Body: Sculpture and Performance, 1972–1985*.[4] Despite the crucial importance of Herzberg's work, and despite that it provides a detailed history of Mendieta's life in Iowa, including descriptions of some of the sites where she created her work, it too may be read in such a way as to distance the artist from the cultural and historical specificity of the Midwest. For example, Herzberg repeatedly emphasizes Mendieta's exposure to a long list of New York artists and critics through the University of Iowa's Intermedia Program (Vito Acconci, Willhoughby Sharp, Lucy Lippard, Robert Wilson, and others), and documents her study of ancient Mesoamerican cultures and of anthropology in the courses she took but has little to say about her interests in and relation to Iowa itself. Nor does Herzberg discuss *Black Angel*, which, because of its incorporation of a famous local landmark, reads perhaps more than any other work that she executed in the state as distinctly in conversation with Iowa.[5]

Thus it is on this film, and on this site, that I intend to map (with a broad X like the one Mendieta makes at the base of the statue) the artist's engagement with the Midwest, her intervention in the history and culture of eastern Iowa. I argue that *Black Angel* makes direct reference to Iowa as a site of immigration and cultural crossings, not only for immigrant Latinos and exiles like Mendieta, but also for displaced Europeans, especially Czechs, a significant though often maligned ethnic group in the region.[6] Moreover, I read the film as an engagement with immigrant trauma—the trauma of displacement, alienation, acculturation, and loss—which is always negotiated and expressed through an amalgam of alien languages, customs, and symbols. As Michel de Certeau writes, "There is no place that is not haunted by many different spirits hidden there in silence, spirits one can 'invoke' or not. Haunted places are the only ones people can live in."[7] In this case, the hidden spirits manifest themselves in Czech and English inscriptions, a broken tree and an angel, ghosts and shadows, and the voice of a grieving mother. This is significant not only because it draws attention to Iowa as an important influence on and subject matter in Mendieta's art, but also because it offers further evidence for the assertion I have made elsewhere that the scholarship on the artist has been (and in some cases continues to be) focused detrimentally on her work as solely a direct outgrowth of her own personal experiences of displacement (a form of self-therapy) rather than as engaging with and offered to her audiences and their larger cultural concerns.[8] But I am getting ahead of myself and want to cut back to the film, to enter the shot from off camera and begin again.

On this autumn day, Mendieta took her Super 8 camera, at least two rolls of film, two boxes of pigments, and probably a plywood or cardboard template of her own body, which she would have used to trace her outline on the stone, and went to Oakland Cemetery on the north side of Iowa City to create this work of art.[9] In several ways *Black Angel* is typical of Mendieta's larger oeuvre. It deploys her well-known iconography, materials, and methods. By the time she created this work, for example, she had already made several important pieces in outdoor locations, had used her body in a wide range of performances, had incorporated references to Christ's bleeding heart, and had, since the previous year, been integrating her immediately recognizable *silueta* iconography (lit. silhouette; the female figure in outline or shadow, its arms upraised) with which her work has since become synonymous. The piece also utilizes materials that were common in her practice, dirt and/or powdered pigments as well as Super 8, of which she created around a hundred films in her short career.[10]

In addition to its materials, methods, and iconography, the work's location is also typical for the artist. She was no stranger to cemeteries and burial grounds, having created works in Zapotec tombs in the Yagul archaeological site in Oaxaca and in the Xochimilco borough of Mexico City in 1973. In 1977, two years after producing *Black Angel*, she created a series of mud tombs on the banks of Old Man's Creek in Sharon Center, Iowa, inspired by ones she had seen in Mexico, and in 1981 created an untitled grass-covered *silueta* in Holy Rood Cemetery in Georgetown. But this film is unique in her oeuvre for its incorporation of someone else's work of art, a bronze statue of an angel by Czech-born sculptor Josef Mario Korbel (fig. 4.1.3). The imposing angel, rendered in a late nineteenth-century

4.1.3   Josef Mario Korbel, Doležal Feldewert Monument ("the Black Angel"), 1913, Oakland Cemetery, Iowa City. Photo by Joseph Mischka.

modernist style, introduces a realist mode of depiction into Mendieta's film that is unprecedented even by those of the artist's earlier works in Mexico, which were sited in the large sculptural niches of the Cuilapan Church in Oaxaca.

About Mendieta's interest in death and burial, art historians frequently comment. Historian and curator Olga Viso writes that "traditions of ritual sacrifice in some Mesoamerican cultures, Day of the Dead celebrations across the country, and the distinctive culture surrounding death in the Valley of Oaxaca served as rich subject matter throughout the 1970s."[11] What if, in addition to Mendieta's interests in pre-Columbian cultures of Mexico, she had also been aware of the Native American peoples of eastern Iowa, the Sauk and Meskwaki, or if she had been aware of pre-historic earthworks such as the Effigy Mounds in the northeast part of the state?[12] Further, what would it mean if, just as she studied the cultures of Mexico and Cuba, integrated herself in specific landscapes and historical sites there, and therefore inserted her work into complexly layered histories, geographies, cultures, and politics, so too she marked and was marked by, crossed and was crossed with, the landscape, history, geography, culture, and politics of Iowa? Reading most of the literature on this artist, one is hard-pressed to find a framework for interpreting her work through a midwestern lens; indeed in Viso's book, while there are maps of important sites in Mexico and Cuba, there is no map of Iowa, no indication of the spatial relationships between Dubuque, the Mississippi and the Iowa Rivers, the Coralville Dam and Reservoir, the university campus, Old Man's Creek, Sharon Center, Amana, or even of Cedar Memorial Cemetery in Cedar Rapids, where Mendieta and her parents are buried. That absence may be symptomatic of our inability as historians to reconcile the artist's complex performances, films, and earthworks with Iowa's other, more famous contribution to art—American regionalism—and the state's most famous artist—Grant Wood. But it also implies that Iowa is unimportant, or that it is already familiar, or that it is somehow unrepresentable.

The Black Angel monument has been something of a famous landmark in Iowa City since it was erected in 1913. As early as the 1920s, a relative of the woman who commissioned the monument was already trying to dispel rumors about it. More recently, local historian Timothy Parrott published an entire book on the sculpture, the purpose of which was to demystify it and debunk the supernatural aura that is said to surround it:

> Most local Iowa City residents will have heard that the statue was created of white marble in Italy and the ocean air turned it black on its voyage to America, or that it fell into the sea! Others allege that the statue turned black when it was struck by lightning, or as a sign "of the sins of one of the errant daughters in the family." It has even been claimed that a repentant preacher erected the sculpture over the grave of the son he had murdered, and it turned from white to black due to the "foulness of the misdeed."[13]

In addition to speculation about the figure's black appearance, many superstitions have developed suggesting that the sculpture is haunted by dark forces. Any virginal girl who is kissed at the angel's feet in the moonlight, it is said, will die within six months. A pregnant woman who passes by the sculpture will miscarry. And anyone who touches the figure's feet on Halloween night or dares to kiss the angel will be instantly struck dead. The cemetery thereby becomes a theater of superstition, audacity, and in some instances vandalism on moonlit nights and on All Hallows' Eve, when local residents, tourists, and university students test their bravery in its obscure shadow. And indeed it may have been the statue's macabre reputation that drew Mendieta to it, for she displayed an ongoing interest in ghosts and specters, natural and supernatural forces, and an array of what were referred to in the 1970s, when she was a student at Iowa, as "primitive" beliefs.

But I wonder too if, on this bright autumn day she wasn't also drawn more directly to the small monument that stands just to the left of the bronze angel: a six-foot-tall stone sculpture depicting a tree stump with a ragged top, as though the tree had been blown down and cracked in two by a strong wind, or struck by lightning (fig. 4.1.4). Mendieta created numerous sculptures out of tree trunks during her career, such as the *Untitled (Totem Grove)* series from 1985, and staged a variety of pieces in and around trees, including *Árbol de la vida/Tree of Life* from 1976 (fig. 4.1.5). This suggests to me that at the very least she would have taken a

4.1.4 Unknown sculptor, monument to Eddie Doležal, 1891, Oakland Cemetery, Iowa City. Photo by Josef Mischka.

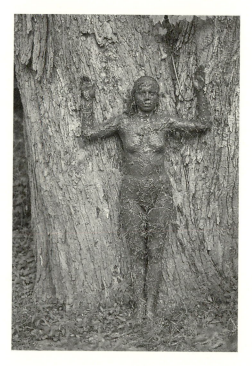

4.1.5 Ana Mendieta, *Tree of Life*, 1976. Lifetime color photograph, 20 x 13¼ inches (50.8 x 33.7 cm). Collection of Ignacio Mendieta. © The Estate of Ana Mendieta Collection, LLC. Courtesy of Galerie Lelong, New York.

second glance at this unusual grave marker, and perhaps she might have read its inscription, which, unlike the Czechoslovakian epitaph etched in the base of the Black Angel (sometimes described as a "strange language" and seen as evidence of the figure's mysterious power), is written in English.

The two grave markers are in fact related. The stricken tree was erected by Terezie Doležal Feldewert (1836–1924) for her son Eduard, or Eddie, who died suddenly in 1891 at the age of eighteen. She had already lost her two-week-old son, Otto, in 1868, when she still lived in Strmilov (now part of the Czech Republic).[14] Feldewert, a Czech immigrant who came to eastern Iowa in March 1878 (just as thousands of Czechs, drawn to the available farmland and to the meatpacking industry, had done before her), also commissioned the Black Angel in 1911 for the grave of her third husband, Nikolaus Feldewert. Eddie's body and Terezie's and Nikolaus's ashes are all buried there. The front of the sculpted tree bears a trompe l'oeil parchment inscribed with a text in English, which Parrott speculates is likely a translation of a poem written in Czech by Feldewert:

Like a bud just opening
Commenced my life to be
But death came without mercy, without pity
The Lord had sent for me
I was not granted time to bid adieu
Do not weep for me dear mother
I am at peace in my cool grave.[15]

This mournful poem, written from the point of view of the dying child who bravely consoles his grieving mother, would certainly have struck a chord with a young artist who had herself been separated from her mother at a young age. "Having been torn from my homeland (Cuba), during my adolescence," Mendieta writes, "I am overwhelmed by the feeling of having been cast out from the womb (Nature). My art is the way I reestablish the bonds that unite me to the Universe. It is a return to the maternal source."[16]

To the degree that trees were important figures with which Mendieta was in dialogue, living beings through which she could "return to the maternal source," I suspect that she would have recognized in this severed tree (with its ragged top symbolically representing a young life cut short) a familiar sort of trauma. I suggest that the film she produced on this site (about which virtually nothing has been written in the scholarship on Mendieta) is an effort to bear witness to the trauma of immigrant exile, of familial loss and separation, of having one's deepest sorrow spoken in a foreign language, and of the suddenness of death, traumas which she shared with other Iowans such as Feldewert.[17] Iowa is, after all, a state populated by immigrants, refugees, and exiles who began to settle across its plains in the mid-nineteenth century when the U.S. government forced the native peoples who lived there farther and farther west and offered the rich farmland with its black soil to Norwegians, Swedes, Dutchmen, Germans, Irish, Englishmen, and Czechs. In the twentieth and twenty-first centuries, with increasing globalization, farm and factory workers from central and South America, India, and Southeast Asia have replaced those earlier waves of immigrants. By making this claim, I do not wish to psychoanalyze Mendieta for the purpose of exposing her own mental scars, as Donald Kuspit does in an essay about which I have already expressed my reservations.[18] Rather I wish to understand *Black Angel* as a work that speaks in conversation with the immigrant or exile experience more broadly. Having spent her adolescence and young adulthood in Cedar Rapids, with its large Czech population, its Czech Village neighborhood (once colloquially known as Boheemie Town), and its grade school curriculum emphasizing the history of Czech immigration, Mendieta would certainly have been aware of that experience. Therefore, I suggest, *Black Angel* exists in conversation with those who, like Mendieta and her sister, ended up living—buffeted by strangers' cold repudiation and warm kindness; by isolation and familiarity; by exile and belonging—in the rolling green hills, prairie grasses, and fecund farmland of eastern Iowa.

One example of how her own experience might have made her more sensitive to Feldewert's wrenching grief over the death of her son, may be found in a distant memory of her childhood in Cuba. We can get another glimpse at how Mendieta might have approached these monuments, how she might have thought about this sad tree through her sister Raquelín's recollection of the Cuban folksong "Y tú qué has hecho," which they sang and performed as children in Havana:

> In the trunk of a tree a girl
> engraved her name filled with pleasure
> and the tree, touched in its bosom
> let a flower drop to the girl . . .
> I am the tree, moved and saddened
> you are the girl that wounded my trunk
> I always save your beloved name
> and you . . . what have you done with my poor flower?[19]

The romantic song gives voice to the silent tree, which yields its bark to the girl's knife, endures the wound she inflicts, retains her memory, but is itself forgotten by her. In these performances, Raquelín remembers that Ana always played the girl dramatically carving her name in the tree, sculpting it, wounding it again and again. Like the *árbol triste* in the song, the stone tree in Oakland Cemetery saves the name of its beloved, Eddie Doležal.

Raquelín's memory of this old song, with its theme of inscription and remembrance, combined with the setting for Mendieta's film, with its lapidary monuments periodically decorated in flowers, suggest the work's engagement with the problem of death and memory, grief and the monument, trauma and history. In this context, it is difficult not to think of Cathy Caruth's beautiful and provocative reading of Freudian trauma theory. Freud uses Tasso's epic story of Tancred, the medieval knight who accidentally kills his beloved Clorinda, because she is disguised in the armor of his enemy. Grief stricken, Tancred enters an enchanted forest and madly strikes his sword against the bark of a tall tree. Clorinda, whose soul is magically imprisoned in the tree, cries out again in anguish. Freud uses this story to illustrate the ways in which psychic trauma is always a wound that is repeated neurotically in the mind, just as Clorinda's slaying recurs in the cutting of the tree, because by its very desubjectifying nature, trauma is beyond comprehension. It is experienced, Caruth writes, "too soon, too unexpectedly, to be fully known and is therefore not available to consciousness until it imposes itself again, repeatedly, in the nightmares and repetitive actions of the survivor." She concludes from this that trauma is "always the story of a wound that cries out, that addresses us in the attempt to tell us of a reality or truth that is not otherwise available."[20] She argues that acts of witness or of history are therefore a matter of listening to such wounds, responding to such cries.

Like the story of Clorinda, *Black Angel* bears witness to the wound that cries out from the stone tree, violently cut down and permanently stunted; it records the inscription and then erasure of the artist's own image at the base of the monument, an image that, like the fragile flower, is lost. Thus we might read the work as a performative act of memorialization, of bringing Feldewert's pain into the present, skirting past the sensational stories that have betrayed and obscured it. Five or six years after Mendieta performed and filmed *Black Angel*, she created a sculpture by carving and then burning a figural shape into a seven-foot section of tree trunk (fig. 4.1.6). That she titled this piece *Árbitra* (Witness) (1982) suggests that, like Caruth, Mendieta recognized in the cutting of the tree a re-wounding, a symbolic return to the scene of trauma. I want to think about her cutting of this later tree as a reenactment of the Czech mother's loss, the felling of one tree repeating the felling of another in a cycle of traumatic return.

A similar doubling and return takes place in Mendieta's filmed performance at the base of Josef Korbel's strange sculpture. According to Parrott, a friend of Feldewert recommended Korbel, a young Czech immigrant (forty-six years her junior) to create her late husband's monument.[21] Though representational, the figure is somewhat roughly modeled, the hair rather lumpy and lacking in detail, the folds in the drapery stylized in a nascent modernist fashion. Critic Arnold Genthe, reviewing Korbel's first major exhibition in New York in a 1916 issue of

4.1.6   Ana Mendieta, *Árbitra*, 1982. Lifetime color photograph, 10 x 8 inches (25.4 x 20.3 cm). Collection Raquelín Mendieta Family Trust. © The Estate of Ana Mendieta Collection, LLC. Courtesy of Galerie Lelong, New York.

International Studio, explains of Korbel that "instead of being satisfied with a faithful presentation of the characteristic features he goes considerably beyond giving a mere likeness."[22] With its head cast down and its right arm and pointed wing sweeping across horizontally rather than raised upward in an ascending motion, it seems to be an angel of death rather than an angel of protection, mercy, or resurrection. This composition, which appears from the side like an enormous blade, or scythe, surely contributes to the macabre lore that surrounds the sculpture to this day (fig. 4.1.7).

At the feet of this dark specter, Mendieta traced an outline of her own body. The film begins with her slowly getting up from the stone as though she were emerging, like a ghost (the echo or repetition of a now dead body), rising from a crypt. By filling in the outline of her own inert figure, she makes of it a dark shadow so that we are not sure whether it is she or the silhouette that is the trace or ghost of the other. By outlining the *silueta* in red, the artist mobilizes the visual trope of blood, which pervades her work either in the actual use of or illusionistic references to it. Here the blood-red pigment piles up around the figure's heart, thus seemingly reanimating it, bringing it to life. Though shocking and grotesque in some of her works, blood is for Mendieta a potent life force, one of the media (along with sap rising in plants, breath escaping the body, and water flowing in

4.1.7 Josef Mario Korbel, Doležal Feldewert monument ("the Black Angel"), 1913, Oakland Cemetery, Iowa City. Photo by Joseph Mischka.

rivers) through which *àshe*, or life force, moves. "My art is grounded in the belief of one universal energy," she writes, "which runs through everything: from insect to man, from man to spectre, from spectre to plant from plant to galaxy. My works are the irrigation veins of this universal fluid. Through them ascend the ancestral sap, the original beliefs, the primordial accumulations, the unconscious thoughts that animate the world."[23]

In light of her mythic characterization of her own work as part of a universal fluid, a primordial and galactic energy, Mendieta's childlike gesture of erasure—the giant X, the kicking up of the pigment—seems at first disillusioning. The act of destroying her drawing is like a giggle in the midst of a ghost story or an impolite sound in church; it punctures the inflated drama of ghosts and gods and turns them into so much dust. Because this film was not exhibited extensively during her lifetime, and because, unlike many of her other films, she made it without an audience or any assistance from friends or teachers, it is difficult to know what she meant by this act; whether she would have thought of the film itself as a sketch, an experiment with which she was dissatisfied and that would be realized in more definitive form later, or if indeed she saw it as a completed work, for which her act of cancellation constituted a fitting end. But I am struck by the way she pauses at the foot of the grave just before wiping away her drawing.

It seems to be a respectful gesture of recognition in which she looks, for the first time in the film, directly at the angel under whose wings she has been working. To the degree that we can view her actions over the course of the short film as a reenactment of the Feldewerts' living and dying, and their ultimate reunion with the universal energy, we might read the gesture of erasure as a merciful act of forgetting, of consigning an immigrant mother's pain and sorrow to oblivion.

Ana Mendieta could not have known this when she made *Black Angel*, but there is another way in which it stages a symbolic return from exile, a reunion with the mother. Josef Mario Korbel spent some time in Havana, Cuba, during and after his honeymoon in 1917. His son Ivan was born there in 1918, and the following year Korbel completed two commissions, one a portrait of the country's president, Mario Menocal, and the other the monumental figure *Alma Mater*, installed at the University of Havana.[24] This famous sculpture, which Mendieta would likely have seen during her childhood and from which her exile separated her, is seated at the top of a massive staircase leading to the university entrance. The figure represents a mother goddess in classic robes, her arms outstretched in a sign of affection welcoming her lost children home.

Thus it was that to this spot marked with an X, in this cemetery, in the midst of rolling hills, along the Iowa River valley, in a prairie land patched with farms, that a Cuban exile, a family of Czech immigrants, and a Czech sculptor all came together. Mendieta's film serves as silent witness to their respective sorrows, and to the place where their lives crossed.

Notes

The first epigraph is Ana Mendieta, interviewed by Tony Martinez in Cuba, 1980, film clip included in Nereida García-Ferraz, Kate Horsfield, and Branda Miller, *Ana Mendieta: Fuego de Tierra*, videocassette (VHS) (New York: Women Make Movies, 1987). "Yo trabajo con la tierra, con la naturaleza, y hago esculturas en el paisaje, en el ambiente fuera, ¿no? Y yo creo que tiene mucho que ver con Cuba en el sentido que, a mí me sentí a traído por la naturaleza, por que yo no tenía la tierra, que yo no tenía patria" (translation by Alejandro Velasco). The second epigraph is Timothy C. Parrott, *The Enigma of Theresa Dolezal Feldwert and the "Black Angel"* (Iowa City, Iowa: self published, 2007), 10.

1. Julia Herzberg mentions red tempera as among the media that Mendieta employed in this period. Julia A. Herzberg, "Ana Mendieta, the Iowa Years: A Critical Study, 1969 through 1977" (PhD diss., City University of New York, 1998), 289.

2. Operation Peter Pan, or Operacíon Pedro Pan, was initiated by the CIA and carried out with the help of the Roman Catholic Archdiocese of Miami and Monsignor Bryan O. Walsh, which brought fourteen thousand Cuban children to the United States between 1960 and 1962. Their travel was made possible by an extension of the rules on "student" visas, which allowed them to be issued to unaccompanied minors as young as five years

old. The program was a response to rumors, fed by CIA propaganda, that Fidel Castro would take children away from their families to work on communal farms, to go to military schools, or go to Soviet labor camps. Some of the children who participated were able to live with relatives in the United States, but others, like the Mendieta girls, were not. Forced into exile and seemingly abandoned by their parents, many of the children were emotionally wounded and alienated. See Yvonne M. Conde, *Operation Pedro Pan: The Untold Exodus of 14,048 Cuban Children* (New York: Routledge, 1999) and Bryan O. Walsh, "Cuban Refugee Children," *Journal of Inter-American Studies and World Affairs* 13, nos. 3–4 (July–October 1971): 378–415.

3. My own writing on the artist is only a slight exception in that I discuss the importance of Mendieta's work in performatively producing the experience of exile in spectators who would otherwise unproblematically assume an identificatory relationship with Iowa or the United States more broadly. Jane Blocker, *Where Is Ana Mendieta? Identity, Performativity, and Exile* (Durham, N.C.: Duke University Press, 1999); see esp. chap. 3, "Exile."

4. Herzberg, "Ana Mendieta, the Iowa Years"; see also Julia A. Herzberg, "Ana Mendieta's Iowa Years, 1970–1980," in *Ana Mendieta: Earth Body; Sculpture and Performance, 1972–1985*, ed. Olga Viso (Washington, D.C.: Hirshhorn Museum and Sculpture Garden, Smithsonian Institution; Ostfildern-Ruit, Germany: Hatje Cantz Verlag, 2004).

5. The first mention of *Black Angel* in the scholarship on Mendieta appears in Olga M. Viso, *Unseen Mendieta: The Unpublished Works of Ana Mendieta* (Munich: Prestel, 2008). Of the work she writes, "*Black Angel* (c. 1975) was executed in a well-known Iowa City cemetery distinguished by the bronze sculpture of a winged angel. In the Super 8 film that documents the action, the artist is seen fully clothed lying on the concrete slab at the base of the sculpture. There she renders in powdered pigments the dark silhouette of her form with her arms extended" (110–11).

6. For more on the relation between Latino and other immigrants in the Midwest, see José Límon's chapter in this book.

7. Michel de Certeau, *The Practice of Everyday Life*, trans. Steven F. Rendall (Berkeley: University of California Press, 1984), 108. I warmly thank Santiago Vaquera-Vásquez for bringing my attention to this passage and to the metaphor of crossings at work in Mendieta's film.

8. Blocker, *Where Is Ana Mendieta?*, 11–16.

9. Although she does not mention this particular work, Herzberg explains that in early 1975 Mendieta had begun using a template as "a model for her body" in works that have come to be known as the Silueta Series. Herzberg, *Ana Mendieta*, 291.

10. The actual number of films is somewhat unclear since at the time of her death they were not cataloged or titled by the artist. The catalog of a 2015 exhibition organized by the Katherine E. Nash Gallery at the University of Minnesota claims there were 104. See Lynn Lukkas and Howard Oransky, curators, *Covered in Time and History: The Films of Ana Mendieta* (Minneapolis: Katherine E. Nash Gallery at the University of Minnesota, in association with University of California Press, 2015). Since she was working primarily in Super 8, which was sold in three-minute reels, in some instances her works have been

counted by reel. In some cases, however, such as *Black Angel*, the artist likely intended the reels to be spliced together into a single six-minute film, and in others, it is obvious that there are several versions of a single film, complicating the question of whether the artist would have considered them separate works.

11. Viso, *Unseen Mendieta*, 110.

12. Herzberg notes in passing that "at the end of the Iowa years, Mendieta did a series of sand figures with markings, pieces, I suggest, referring to Native Americans who formerly inhabited the area along Old Man's Creek where she worked in private for many years." Herzberg, *Ana Mendieta*, 345.

13. Parrott, *Enigma of Theresa Doležal Feldewert*, 6.

14. Ibid., 8.

15. Terezie Doležal Feldewert, quoted in ibid., 17.

16. Ana Mendieta, quoted in Viso, *Unseen Mendieta*, 297.

17. While Mendieta commented on her status as an exile, someone who was ripped from the Motherland, she did not discuss the question of immigration and exile more broadly. My book on the artist postulates that she embraced her status as exile, however, in terms of her art making, because it allowed her strategically to occupy an un-locatable position relative to questions such as race, nationality, and identity. See *Where Is Ana Mendieta?*

18. Blocker, *Where Is Ana Mendieta?*, 14. Here I discuss Donald Kuspit, "Ana Mendieta, Autonomous Body," in *Ana Mendieta*, ed. Gloria Moure (Barcelona: Fundación Antoni Tàpies; Santiago de Compostela: Centro Galego de Arte Contemporánea, 1997), 35–63.

19. Raquel Mendieta, "Childhood Memories: Religion, Politics, Art," in Moure, *Ana Mendieta*, 225. "En el tronco de un árbol una niña / Grabó su nombre henchida de placer / Y el árbol conmovido allá en su seno / A la niña una flor dejó caer . . . / Yo soy el árbol conmovido y triste / Tú eres la niña que mi tronco hirió / Yo guardo siempre tu querido nombre / Y tú . . ¿qué has hecho de mi pobre flor?"

20. Cathy Caruth, *Unclaimed Experience: Trauma, Narrative, and History* (Baltimore, Md.: Johns Hopkins University Press, 1996), 4.

21. Parrott, *Enigma of Theresa Doležal Feldewert*, 20–21.

22. Arnold Genthe, "The Work of Mario Korbel and Walter D. Goldbeck," *The Studio International* 57, nos. 225–28 (November/December 1915 and January/February 1916), xix.

23. Ana Mendieta, "Personal Writings," in Moure, *Ana Mendieta*, 216.

24. Janis Conner and Joel Rosenkranz, "Josef Mario Korbel," in *Rediscoveries in American Sculpture, Studio Works, 1893–1939* (Austin: University of Texas Press, 1989), 95–103.

History in Drag

Latina/o Queer Affective Circuits in Chicago

RAMÓN H. RIVERA-SERVERA

This chapter began as an obituary for Ketty Teanga, a Chicago-based trans-Latina drag queen whose performances I had been following since my arrival in Chicago in 2007 and who died in 2011.[1] In what follows, I propose Miss Ketty, her practice as theory, as an important example of Latina/o queer gesture as a world-making procedure. These world-making practices (theoretical and performative) are hopeful, but never naive, realms of imaginative survival amid a political economy that renders queer of color nightlife and life, vulnerable. I am especially invested in how gesture tells the story and history of Latina/o queer life in the midwestern city of Chicago.

My account of Miss Ketty's significance to Latina/o queer history was motivated by Jill Austin and Jennifer Brier's groundbreaking exhibition at the Chicago History Museum, *Out in Chicago: LGBT History at the Crossroads*, and their invitation to contribute an essay to the edited volume that accompanied the exhibition.[2] The exhibition, concerned as it was with documenting queer history in Chicago, found limited archival holdings documenting Latina/o experience. In my essay on Latina/o queer history in Chicago, coauthored with Lawrence La Fountain-Stokes and Lourdes Torres, I recurred to Teanga's performances of queer Latinidad and their limited circulation through non-Latina/o Chicago LGBT circles as an example of Latina/o history's general marginalization within larger mainstream projects that memorialize and remember queer, mostly white, lives in Chicago, the Midwest, and beyond.

Teanga was born in Ecuador and since age eleven lived with her mother and Puerto Rican stepfather in New York City and then Puerto Rico. She began performing in the drag scene in Puerto Rico and briefly moved back to New York City, where she performed at Latina/o queer nightlife venues. Eventually, Teanga made her home in Chicago, where she was critical in the founding of

4.2.1   Promotional flyer for Circuit Night Club (el Circuito), featuring Miss Ketty Teanga, Chicago. Photo courtesy of Ramón H. Rivera-Servera.

the well-known Latina/o drag bar La Cueva in the Southwest Chicago Mexican enclave of La Villita. She also went on to anchor the Latina/o queer nightlife of Chicago's North Side queer district in the Lakeview neighborhood, popularly known as Boystown. There, she hosted multiple nights a week at Club Circuit, which alternated its programming between mainstream contemporary dance club fare and Latina/o nights (from vaquero to urban hip-hop) under a variety of banners, including the Spanish translation to Circuito during Ketty's reign of the club and themed parties such as La Noche Loca and Noche Latina.

At the time I coauthored that essay, I was interested in Miss Ketty's work at La Cueva as an example of the often tacit presence of Latina/o queer life in the city of Chicago.[3] I was interested in ameliorating what I saw as the lack of mainstream recognition by queer historians, including those working on the museum exhibition for which the essay was commissioned, of La Cueva's and Miss Ketty's pioneering roles in the development of a Latina/o queer public in the city. I focused on the history and location of La Cueva as indicative of that marginal position.

Located in the southwest corridor of the city, a combination of nineteenth-century industrial and residential development initially occupied by Bohemian and Irish immigrants and now constituting the largest Mexican neighborhood in Chicago, La Cueva began as a single-night event hosted by Ketty Teanga at another historic gay La Villita watering hole, El Infierno. Because of the event's popularity, it became a regular feature at the owner's larger establishment, La Cueva.[4] Credited as being one of the oldest Latina/o drag clubs in the country still in operation, La Cueva was, until a remodeling in 2014, not identified by a flashy street sign, nor did it feature roped-off entrances commonly found in Chicago's Boystown establishments. Instead, the plain white wood-paneled facade of the single-story building insinuated itself subtly within the Mexican commercial neighborhood that surrounds it. Here, the second-largest business district in the city, working-class gay Latinos and trans-Latinas, and increasingly cis-gendered Latinas and trans-Latinos, have drunk, danced together, and witnessed, for over three decades, the spectacular performances of Latina drag queens impersonating the vast repertoires of Latin American and U.S. Latina/o popular musicians, from bolero and ranchera divas to salsa queens and the more recent bubble-gum Mexican pop stars.[5]

Despite the long history of the queer Latina/o presence in the city and the existence of pioneer spaces and performers such as those found in La Cueva, I argued in the museum exhibition catalog that our Latina/o queer history remains for the most part unknown. Hidden behind the unassuming facades of marginal geographies often rendered mute by the LGBT mainstream, the history of Latina/o queer Chicago often recedes into the realm of invisibility. La Cueva is but one such site, historical event, and community in need of recognition, documentation, and celebration as part of queer, Latina/o, and Chicago history.

On first impulse, my analysis relied on an economy of visibility and its potential achievement in the development of the archive. With such an argument I sought to frame contributions by my two coauthors, Lawrence La Fountain-Stokes, who in that essay addressed Latina/o queer literary and visual art works, and Lourdes Torres, who related the history of Latina lesbian activism in Chicago assembled from interviews, ephemera, and personal experience. Collectively we argue that "the archives, written histories, and media representations of gay and lesbian activism and culture in the United States, and in Chicago especially, have not generally acknowledged a Latina/o presence. When accounts have focused specifically on queer Latinas/os, they have rarely landed in Chicago, offering us instead a bi-coastal map that almost exclusively focuses on that well-rehearsed triumvirate of Latina/o queer mythology: New York, Los Angeles, and San Francisco."[6] In turn, it proposes our archival labor into Chicago Latina/o queer history as supplement to the histories of queer and Latina/o queer lives generally circulated in the mainstream.

I revisit the critical strategy I just outlined in order to question the premise under which my and my coauthors' contributions were framed. I want to return to the figure of Miss Ketty, this time less as the sad figure of the neglected queen to be rescued by us historians, and more as an agentive force, a critical irritant in the homonormative progression of queer history. That is, I am interested in pursuing a slightly different relationship to the work of the archive. In doing so, I am perhaps less invested in bringing La Cueva out of the cave and into the visibility of the history museum than in dwelling within its walls, attending to its own logics of the historical. I argue that Miss Ketty's performance labor, the gestural and oratorical repertoires of Latina drag queens, function as practices of "queer homemaking" that rely on the affective weight of Latina/o popular culture to instantiate publics not just "in the know" of Latina/o queer history but in the practice of historical memory.[7] Advancing an understanding of history that invests as much on conscious awareness of past events as in the often less conscious reenactments of embodied knowledge, I want to position the labor of the drag performer as that of the history lesson.[8]

Let me remind you that the history I am interested in addressing here is not a history of ascendancy into the mainstreamed status of the history museum. In fact, I argue that Miss Ketty sought to slow down, at times even stop, that particular mode of "past looking" to animate deliciously anachronistic modes of historical becomings that touch the past. I see this as a similar strategy to what scholars such as Carolyn Dinshaw and Elizabeth Freeman have understood as queer modes of history whereby connections are established across time without requiring absolute fidelity to fact nor yielding to notions of historical progression.[9] But I am also invested in offering a specifically Latina/o queer take on what J. Jack Halberstam has described as queer time and space, or the ways in which queer lives unravel through different life schedules and spaces not always congruent with mainstream notions of forward motion into heteropatriarchal reproductive adulthood.[10] I am particularly interested in how performing through and in relation to historical memory instantiates Latina/o queer social intimacies, a question that in part frames the analysis in my *Performing Queer Latinidad: Dance, Sexuality, Politics*.[11] I see performance as an intimate realm of public assembly where the archives of Latina/o queer history are continuously activated in the present through embodied communicative action. I borrow here from Diana Taylor's influential distinction between the archive as those historically sanctioned and privileged practices that record the past, even if partially, in the certainty of the object (writing, recording), and the repertoire that "enacts embodied memory: performances, gestures, orality, movement, dance, singing—in short, all those acts usually thought of as ephemeral, nonreproducible knowledge."[12] My focus has generally been movement: gesture, choreography, and dance.

When performing at the mainstream center of queer life in Chicago, Miss Ketty functioned as critical irritant to the homonormative progression of queer economics and history. Her performance aesthetic was anachronistic: bolero songs from the 1960s, '70s, and '80s; big hair and makeup from yesteryear; grand and slow upper-body gestures. Miss Ketty's performance labor functioned as practices of "queer worldmaking," a term coined by José Esteban Muñoz, that relied on the affective weight of Latina/o popular culture to instantiate publics not just "in the know" of "old-school" Latina/o queer repertoires but in the practice of re-enacting them across generational divides. This labor of the drag performer as pedagogue offers an alternative account for Miss Ketty as an agent of history.

José Muñoz's theorization of queer gesture is key here. I first encountered this investment in how gesture facilitates queer of color minoritarian engagements with the historical in his 1995 essay on Richard Fung, published in the journal *Screen*, later revised and published in his landmark first book, *Disidentifications: Queer of Color and the Performance of Politics*. Muñoz opens the essay with that marvelous and poignant sequence in Fung's 1990 film, *My Mother's Place*, where "the pasty specter of the monarch born to the throne helps to formulate an entirely different type of queen."[13] In this sequence, the visual aesthetics of old technologies (8mm film) image schoolchildren in Trinidad waiting along a procession route where the British queen is to and eventually does pass by. A voiceover narration, at once apprehending the event as in the moment of performance and in the pastness of childhood experience, fixates on the greeting gesture of the queen and its appropriation by the young Filipino queer and his sister, who, as the narrator explains, playfully rehearse the royal wave, white socks standing in as white gloves, in the intimacy of their home. Muñoz reads the "double articulation" of gesture here, vis-à-vis Homi Bhabha, as "colonial mimicry."[14] Understanding the queer child's performance as one shaped not only by colonized/colonizer but gay/straight divides, he explains, "this moment of protodrag 'flaunting' not only displays an ambivalence to empire and the protocols of colonial pedagogy, but also reacts against forced gender prescriptions that such systems reproduce."[15] Muñoz then pursues the queer hyperbole of this gesture in other disidentificatory visual narrative techniques that allow Fung to work between ethnographic and pornographic filmic economies, grounded in the history of colonialism and its aftermath, for queer of color ends.

These gestural interventions into the historical past and their enduring consequences in politico-economic arrangements that disadvantage queer of color lives, are beautifully staged in the nightlife geographies of Latina/o queer club cultures, especially in Miss Ketty's own interventions. Let me offer a brief example from 2010.

On a typical Thursday night in Chicago, a crowd of young queer Latina/o men, women, and other-gendered folk enter La Noche Loca, a weekly party advertised as "Chicago's longest-running Latin night" and hosted by none other than La Cueva's grand dame, Miss Ketty Teanga.[16] The evening features a diverse musical program as the DJ spins *cumbia*, hip-hop, salsa, merengue, and pop sets frequently enhanced by an add-on techno beat or Latin house arrangement. It also showcases lip-synching performances by a rotating roster of Latina drag queens anchored by Miss Ketty's sharp wit and typically flirtatious rapport.

Miss Ketty's girls, as she calls them, rely on a repertoire of contemporary pop music in both English and Spanish. But every so often an old bolero or pop song will sneak in, and Miss Ketty will inquire from her audience whether they recognize or remember the song. She will often remark teasingly on her audience's youth and school them on the appreciation of Latina/o queer anthems of yesteryear. This then sixty-three-year-old pioneer of Chicago's Latina/o queer public culture and her fellow divas perform these songs to new generations of young audiences with incredible gusto and passionate commitment. Their performances not only honor the shared experiences of Latina/o queer community in music and dance but stage for a new generation the labor of the drag queen as an important convener of this social scene.[17] Miss Ketty and her fellow queens participate in what performance scholar David Román has termed "archival drag," or performances that "set out to reembody and revive a performance from the past."[18] Miss Ketty's performances of history, invested as they are in accessing the archives of Latina/o memory queerly, transfer among the gathered youths knowledge about the ways we live, love, and struggle as queers and Latinas/os.

Miss Ketty's evocation of history, her embodiment of anachronistic aesthetics in fashion, hair, makeup, and musical taste, are also a slap in the face to a disturbingly disciplinary logic of progress that governs drag performance in popular media, and many homonormative LGBT establishments, in the present. I see this temporal logic inextricably tied up to a spatial one. Think here of *RuPaul's Drag Race*, perhaps today's best-known platform for drag performance. The very premise of searching for "America's next drag super model" over and over again instills a fast-paced formula of surrogacy anchored on narratives of the "new" and highly dependent on evaluations that rely on geographically specific trends as universal ones. That is, generally, with some exceptions, Los Angeles and New York drag stand as drag now and moving forward, and drag from other regions of the country get narrated as past or passé styles, especially midwestern or southern drag.

The *RuPaul's Drag Race* phenomenon is a good example in which the politics of visibility, that is the presentation of the archive of drag performance under an aspirational politics of circulation, is attached to a political economy of mainstreaming. Granted, this mainstreaming is only partial relative to a majoritarian public sphere. As Jenna Wortham commented in the *New York Times*, *RuPaul's Drag Race* is "as mainstream as a show about drag can get" but still "flourishes in cultlike purgatory."[19] Nonetheless, the *Drag Race* franchise has infiltrated a large number of LGBTQ establishments nationwide with an army of rent-a-drag performers sponsored by marquee vodka producers and the performance aesthetics they in turn import into these spaces. That is, the more diverse history and ecology of drag performance is rendered more and more as a cookie-cutter industry in its centralized and prepackaged, speeded-up-to-the-race quality.

Miss Ketty slows down this progression. She does this by making the past, even the recent past, available for contemplation in a performatively intensified deceleration, and thus, extended present. Miss Ketty always moved slowly. Not just in her later years when the frailty of her health limited her choreography, but always. The grand gestural embellishments of bolero that were her specialty demanded this. Unlike much of the pop-oriented, fast-paced choreography we are most accustomed to spectating in contemporary Latina/o queer dance clubs, Miss Ketty focused on numbers by Rocío Durcal and other divas who dominated the bolero airwaves of the Spanish-language musical scene from the mid-1960s to the early 1980s. Their music, and boleros more generally, continue to circulate and have received special attention from Latino queer artists.

The choreographic aesthetics of the bolero singer's number rarely focus on footwork. Instead the diva traverses slowly across the stage, often pausing to accentuate a particularly emotional turn in the song with an abdominal contraction, a dramatically poignant facial expression, or the space-occupying and ornate articulation of her upper extremities. That is, bolero choreography moves a lot but barely emphasizes travel or speed. This focus on slowly and gently executed upper-body choreography contrasts significantly with the high-energy virtuosic hip-hop or techno soundscapes and movementscapes that dominate the club.

Instead of the quick steps, splits, and drops of vogue-influenced drag perform-ers, Miss Ketty offered the upright melodramatic posing of the bolero diva. Both traditions strike a pose, but they do so at significantly different paces. Miss Ketty slows us down. And this slowdown is a serious one.

In his 2006 book on contemporary dance in the United States and Europe, An-dré Lepecki describes mainstream dance critics who, reading dance experiments of the 1990s and early 2000s that slowed down choreography to focus gestural effort or even stillness, dismissed the work as not dance. Because these works did not properly offer skillful movement arrangements for spectatorial pleasure, critics complained of the frequency with which dance simply stopped. Lepecki makes the case for how these anxieties over the slowing down or stopping of dance as continuous movement were founded on an anxiety over the dismantling of an established relationship, since the 1930s, between dance and modernity. This relationship is instituted on their shared investments on a state of constant agita-tion, motion. For North American and European concert dance traditions, this meant a shift from choreography as the scripting of sequential posing into the seamless articulation of movement.[20] The connection to modernity, and the way in which the transition in dance becomes emblematic of it, has all to do with the increasing speed of the world economy and its movement of goods, people, and ideas across an increasingly expanded geography. Lepecki goes on to champion the work of dance artists who "exhaust dance" as a form of philosophical and practical interruption of the relationship between dance and modernity; a chal-lenge to the unquestioned focus on forward progression in historical conceptu-alizations of the world economic and political realms.[21] To slow down, or to be still, is to momentarily offer a challenge to the seemingly unstoppable progress of neoliberal logics and their attendant aesthetic partners.

The slowdown of bolero is purposely intended to enhance the affective impact of the singer's performance. It is a lingering in the service of emotional depth. Elegantly and softly moving her arm from a forward extension toward her chest, fingers fluttering (ever so slowly that they exhaust the very capacity of the verb to describe the movement), hand rotating gently at the wrist, before a dramatic clenching of the fist and a punch against the chest, Miss Ketty captivates the au-dience with an emotional performance that echoes the excesses of the recorded track. But this gestural display also grounds the recorded track on the liveness of performance as shared time and space. Throughout the early 2000s, when I started to frequent her performances at La Cueva and then at Circuit, her perfor-mances offered dramatic pauses, even interruptions, to the otherwise hyperactive and hypersensorial orientation of the club, and the violences that characterized living queer and Latina/o in Chicago at a time where black and brown presence was and continues to be actively evicted from Boystown by an alliance of wealthy homonormative and hetero whites and their trending focus on family start-ups, neighborhood watch, and urban "revitalization." These performances always occurred late in the night and served as moments of rest for dancers already exhausted from hours of dancing, as transition between the flirtatious together-ness of the dance floor and the sweaty follow-ups in the bedrooms or other more public intimate contexts of sex, and as a critical moment's reflection, where we could, if for an instant, feel each other, Latinos and queer. We became a collective through the emotional labor of our queen, Miss Ketty, who demanded that we just pay attention, that we simply stop time to spend time with one another. Her retro knowledge was life sustaining. In the midst of all the fast-paced RuPaul Queer mainstreaming, Boystown gentrifying dreams that sought to push queer youths of color out of the white queer boy oasis, she was there to slow us down.

I see Miss Ketty's performances, and those of other queens who have followed in her path, as much-needed interventions into these dynamics. I propose that her self-presentation as dragging the forward march of history into a Latina/o speed or at least slowing down its progress to allow us to insert ourselves in, perhaps on our own terms. In his theorization of archival drag, Román teases out the term *drag* as a draw on the past (as in dragging material forward into the present) and as an acknowledgment of the bad affect toward the scholarly return to discussions of performance and the archive or drag queens altogether (as in "what a drag that we have to talk about this yet again").[22] I want to add to this understanding of *drag* and its relationship to the archive by mobilizing both *drag* as an action and as a sentiment backward. As I mentioned above, I want to suggest that Miss Ketty strategically slows down historical progression. This deceleration as extension and intensification of shared time positions the work of history into a social scene of collective, pleasurable, action. These are the moments of performance queer theorist Jill Dolan has termed utopian performatives. A category of intersubjective, affectively charged moments in performance when we are slightly elevated from the present in richly embodied experiences of what the world could feel like if every moment of our lives was offered to us as fully affective in the everyday.[23]

In closing, I turn to José Muñoz's other beautiful and critically influential engagement with queer gesture. In "Gesture, Ephemera, and Queer Feeling," which first appeared as a response essay to some of the contributors of *Dancing Desires*, the foundational queer dance studies anthology edited by Jane Desmond and published in 2001 (and revised and published as a chapter in his tour de force *Cruising Utopia*, 2009), Muñoz gifts us with one of his most powerful autobiographical accounts, about the casual ridiculing of femme walking in an intimate family scene to make a case for the vulnerable state and punishing environments under which queer corporality moves.[24] He also finds, in queerly cultivated gesturality, especially as exemplified in the extraordinary performance work of nightlife diva Kevin Aviance, strategies to move otherwise, in indulgently queer manner. As Muñoz explains, Aviance "uses gestures that permit them," the white gym-bodied Chelsea boys that dance about and spectate her, "to see and experience the feelings they do not permit themselves to let in."[25] In taking on the labor of queer gesture, Miss Ketty also allows Latina/o dancers at Circuito to pause and admire the trans-Latina diva move and move them, us, into utopian possibilities for being and being together that invest in working-class queer and Latina/o experience and aesthetics, even within the hostile environs of gentrifying Boystown.

Notes

Earlier versions of sections of this essay have appeared in my "José E. Muñoz's Queer Gestures," *QED: A Journal of GLBTQ Worldmaking* 1, no. 3 (2014): 146–49, and in Lawrence La Fountain-Stokes, Lourdes Torres, and Ramón H. Rivera-Servera, "Toward an Archive of Latina/o Queer Chicago: Art, Politics, and Social Performance," in *Out in Chicago: LGBT History at the Crossroads*, ed. Jill Austin and Jennifer Brier (Chicago: Chicago History Museum, 2011), 127–53.

1. I use the phrase "trans-Latina drag queen" to describe Teanga's identity as a transgender Latina as well as her performance labor within the Chicago drag scene.

2. *Out in Chicago* was on display in the Bessie Green-Field Warshawsky Gallery, the Mazza Foundation Gallery, and the Benjamin Benedict Green-Field Gallery of the Pritzker Foundation Special Exhibition Wing at the Chicago History Museum from May 21, 2011, through March 26, 2012.

3. La Villita (also known as the Little Village or South Lawndale) is also the setting of Tadeo García's film *On the Downlow* (2004), which is about "the relationship between Isaac and Angel, two young Latinos involved in a Southside Chicago gang" (Gilberto Magaña, "On the Downlow" plot summary, imdb.com).

4. Kay Lyndersen, "La Cueva: The Oldest Latino Drag Club in the Country Has Done Much to Change Attitudes in Chicago's Mexican Community," *Colorlines Magazine*, July 1, 2006.

5. For an excellent discussion of La Cueva, especially the performances that take place there, see Achy Obejas, "Juanga Forever," *TriQuarterly Online*, July 5, 2010, http://triquarterly .org, accessed July 26, 2010.

6. Lawrence La Fountain-Stokes, Lourdes Torres, and Ramón H. Rivera-Servera, "Toward an Archive of Latina/o Queer Chicago: Art, Politics, and Social Performance," in *Out in Chicago: LGBT History at the Crossroads*, ed. Jill Austin and Jennifer Brier (Chicago: Chicago History Museum, 2011), 127.

7. On queer homemaking, see Marivel T. Danielson, *Homecoming Queers: Desire and Difference in Chicana Latina Cultural Production* (New Brunswick, N.J.: Rutgers University Press, 2009).

8. My interest in the work of gesture raises the question as to the conscious nature of the strategy at hand or the success with which the knowledge imparted in gesture lands on its intended audience. The concept of a semipublic transcript, as developed by urban historian Earl Lewis, is helpful in identifying forms of knowledge and resistance imparted through creative means that are neither the official public realm nor the hidden off-stage strategies outlined by James Scott. Miss Ketty's work can be seen to reside precisely between the mainstream platform of the LGBTQ club stage and the quotidian strategies of survival required to maintain Latina/o queer lived in inhospitable contexts. See Earl Lewis, "Connecting Memory, Self, and the Power of Place in African American Urban History," *Journal of Urban History* 21, no. 3 (1995): 347–71.

9. See Carolyn Dinshaw, *How Soon Is Now? Medieval Texts, Amateur Readers, and the Queerness of Time* (Durham, N.C.: Duke University Press, 2012), and Elizabeth Freeman, *Time Binds: Queer Temporalities, Queer Histories* (Durham, N.C.: Duke University Press, 2010).

10. See Judith Halberstam [J. Jack Halberstam], *In a Queer Time and Place: Transgender Bodies, Subcultural Lives* (New York: New York University Press, 2005).

11. Ramón H. Rivera-Servera, *Performing Queer Latinidad: Dance, Sexuality, Politics* (Ann Arbor: University of Michigan Press, 2012).

12. Diana Taylor, *The Archive and the Repertoire: Performing Cultural Memory in the Americas* (Durham, N.C.: Duke University Press, 2003): 20.

13. José Esteban Muñoz, *Disidentifications: Queers of Color and the Performance of Politics* (Minneapolis: University of Minnesota Press, 1999), 77. Richard Fung, *My Mother's Place*, documentary film (Chicago: Video Data Bank, 1990), videocassette (VHS), 49 min.

14. Homi Bhabha, *The Location of Culture* (London: Routledge, 1994).

15. Muñoz, *Disidentifications*, 78.

16. See the Circuit's weekly events calendar, www.circuitclub.com, accessed Aug. 17, 2010.

17. For a discussion of performance resource sharing in Latina/o queer clubs, see Ramón H. Rivera-Servera, "Choreographies of Resistance: Latina/o Queer Dance and the Utopian Performative," *Modern Drama* 47, no. 2 (2004): 269–89.

18. David Román, *Performance in America: Contemporary U.S. Culture and the Performing Arts* (Durham, N.C.: Duke University Press, 2005), 140.

19. Jenna Wortham, "A Bold Struggle for Acceptance," *New York Times* (New York edition), May 6, 2016, C1.

20. Literally, the writing of choreographic script had been historically the focus of dance until the advent of modern ballet in the Western tradition.

21. André Lepecki, *Exhausting Dance: Performance and the Politics of Movement* (New York: Routledge, 2006).

22. Román, *Performance in America*, 140.

23. Jill Dolan, *Utopia in Performance: Finding Hope at the Theater* (Ann Arbor: University of Michigan Press, 2005).

24. José E. Muñoz, "Gesture, Ephemera, and Queer Feeling: Approaching Kevin Aviance," in *Cruising Utopia: The Then and There of Queer Futurity* (New York: New York University Press, 2009), 65–82. Originally published in Jane C. Desmond, ed., *Dancing Desires: Choreographing Sexualities on and off the Stage* (Madison: University of Wisconsin Press, 2001).

25. Muñoz, "Gesture, Ephemera, and Queer Feeling," 78.

El Museo del Norte

Passionate Praxis on the Streets of Detroit

MARÍA EUGENIA COTERA

We want to document a history of Latina/os by Latina/os for Latina/os in a space where the stories of our grandparents are honored and new stories are generated from the old. We want a site for the production of art, music, literature, and performance that gives voice to our experience and leads to new ways of imagining our world. We want, most of all, a place of community, where the various paths of our lives can come together in mutual support and respect.

—Mission statement, El Museo del Norte, Detroit

This is a story about Latina/o placemaking in the Midwest, and about the particular "midwestern conditions" that complicate and enrich that process. It is a story that centers on the struggle to create a community space in the heart of Detroit—El Museo del Norte, a museum envisioned as a place where the community can come together to document the particular experiences of Latinas/os in the Midwest. As El Museo's mission statement suggests, this story is less about building a brick-and-mortar structure than it is about responding to *a structure of feeling* that invites us to reimagine the museum from the bottom up as "a place for our stories" and to engage history as a community-building project. As I hope to show in this overview of the ongoing process behind its formation, El Museo del Norte is something more than a museum (if we imagine the museum as simply a building that houses artifacts or documents histories); it is a space of dialogue where new collectivities are being nurtured, and with them new ways of imagining the place of Latinas/os in the Midwest. In this chapter I weave together the various strands of this process—ranging from the events, actors, and contexts that were central to it, to my personal experiences as a scholar negotiating the boundaries of my outsider-insider status—in an effort to convey something about the project and the complexities of community-engaged scholarship in the Midwest.

El Museo del Norte began in 2009, as a community-university collaboration between me and Elena Herrada, a Detroit community organizer and scholar. It was during a period of heightened scrutiny of Latina/o immigrants in Michigan and throughout the country; a moment marked by the proposal and sometimes passage of numerous anti-immigrant laws at both the national and local levels as well as efforts on behalf of Immigration and Customs Enforcement (ICE) agents to increase surveillance and detention of undocumented immigrants.[1] As an historically Latina/o neighborhood that is also home to the busiest international border crossing between the United States and Canada (the Ambassador Bridge), the community of Southwest Detroit, where this project originated, was uniquely impacted by this heightened climate of scrutiny. Elena Herrada, who at the time was director of the Centro Obrero / Workers' Center in Detroit, was concerned about this situation and about how it might affect the relationship between long-standing Latina/o communities of Detroit and newer arrivals. Because she had spent over a decade documenting the impact of state-sponsored repatriation campaigns on the Mexican community of Detroit, Elena understood that there were important and unexplored historical affinities between the experiences of older Latina/o Detroiters and newer Latina/o immigrants, who were experiencing their own "crackdown" is the form of punitive legislation, law enforcement harassment, and policies to encourage "self-deportation."[2] So when Elena and I came together in 2009, our initial objective was fairly simple: to reveal these historical interconnections and thereby create new avenues for solidarity and understanding among Latina/o communities in the Detroit area. Elena initially proposed that we cosponsor a tour of "Latino Detroit" to acquaint recent residents

4.3.1 Flor B. Walker (left) and Elena Herrada (right), *We Are Not Undocumented* exhibit, 2012. Photo by Jennifer García Peacock.

with the history of Latinas/os in the region and thereby foster ties between old Detroit and new Detroit, but our conversation quickly lead to a key question: is there a place for our history in the Midwest? Should there be, in other words, a permanent site, or project, that recorded that history and made it available not just to new arrivals, but also to a new generation of locals who might have forgotten it?

This sense—that there had to be a central site, or a series of connected sites, that recorded the long history of Latinas/os in the state (and the region)—was the nucleus for the El Museo del Norte project. In 2009, the project applied for and received funding from the University of Michigan Arts of Citizenship Program to explore the possibility of creating a museum and cultural center that could document the historical presence of Latinas/os in Michigan and establish their key role in the life of the state. Realizing that finding a name for the museum that would satisfy multiple Latina/o constituencies would be a drawn-out, perhaps even conflictual process (more on this later), we initiated the project with a descriptive, albeit bland, placeholder name—the Latino Museum and Cultural Center Project—and invited community stakeholders to the table for a yearlong exploration of the "museum idea" that involved visits to regional cultural institutions (Charles H. Wright Museum of African American History, Ziibiwing Center of Anishinabe Culture and Lifeways, Arab American National Museum) and a series of community conversations about the role of museums in public life and the centrality of both history and storytelling to cultural citizenship and belonging. Our university-community dialogue generated a great deal of excitement about the role that a "Latina/o museum" could play in enriching and sustaining Latina/o communities in Detroit and throughout Michigan, but it also revealed the multiple challenges that we face in bringing such an institution to life. Primary among these was the economic crisis inflicted on Detroit in the wake of the collapse of the auto industry, and made worse by diminishing state and federal support for basic infrastructure (especially public humanities initiatives).

But there were also less obvious pressures, both external and internal, that made the process of developing a brick-and-mortar institution extraordinarily challenging. External pressures around the complicated (and not always beneficial) role of the nonprofit industrial complex in the "rebuilding" of Detroit made finding safe institutional partners for cost-sharing extremely difficult.[3] There were also internal differences around language, culture, and the very meanings of "Latinidad" that complicated the process of coming to agreement on the museum's mission and goals. Who would decide the story that our museum would tell about the Latina/o community in Michigan? What *is* our history, and how far back does it go? Should we conduct meetings in Spanish or in English? However, outweighing these potential sources of disagreement were several important points of agreement: that the museum project should respect the autonomy of the Latina/o community in Michigan; that it should represent their history from their point of view, not an academic vantage point; and that what the museum should preserve for Latinas/os was a sense of belonging to this place—a right to be here.

These points of contention—and agreement—index the unique historical realities that shape Latina/o culture and community in the Great Lakes region of the Midwest, realities that seemed entirely new to me when I first toured the streets of Detroit with Elena Herrada. I came to Michigan from Texas by way of California, places in the Southwest where, at least since the emergence of the Chicana/o Movement of the 1960s, a relatively stable narrative of origins had shaped our collective historical imaginary and our sense of belonging. And so I faced a steep learning curve when it came to sorting through the ways in which this midwestern community of Latinas/os imagined these things. As a child of 1960s radicals, I grew up with a steady stream of images, texts, and cultural events that asserted my right to belong in the Southwest. Indeed, the now common refrain "I didn't cross the border, the border crossed me" encapsulates the discursive reversal enacted by powerful movement ideologies that allowed for the consolidation of disparate communities across the region. Almost overnight, Mexicans throughout the Southwest were transformed from outsiders, "aliens," and permanent "foreigners" to a people who had been wrongly stripped of their prior claim through the machinations of imperial swindlers and the demagoguery of Manifest Destiny. Never mind that this narrative bracketed out complicating factors (such as the conquest of Indigenous people by Spanish and later Mexican settlers), its usefulness as a unifying tool was manifest. New Mexicans, Californians, Coloradoans, Arizonians, Texans, and other Mexicans living in the geographic region that has come to be known as Aztlán felt a renewed sense of belonging and even ownership of space, which lead, inevitably, to the reclamation of public space in murals, Chicano Parks, and cultural centers throughout the Southwest.

Midwestern Chicanas/os and Latinas/os experienced the social, political, and cultural upheavals of the 1960s and 1970s as viscerally as did those living in the Southwest. In the case of Puerto Ricans, they even initiated some of their own upheavals (the Young Lords Party originated in Chicago). However, their historical experience of racialized oppression differed in key ways from that of Mexicans in the Southwest—which has inevitably complicated their claims to space. Though there were deep historical connections between Texas and Michigan, forged through long-standing networks of migratory labor, Mexicans in Michigan could not as easily make historical claims about prior belonging in the Midwest. Their history carried its *own* of pain of unbelonging, shaped through decades of economic and political policies that brought Latinas/os into the demographic fold of the Midwest while nevertheless scripting them as permanent outsiders to the cultural and economic life of the region. This history of unbelonging, or perhaps more accurately, *temporary* belonging, has been documented by scholars of the Latina/o experience, but its primary features, especially in the context of Latina/o settlement in Michigan, are worth briefly rehearsing here because they inevitably shaped the ways in which the community responded to our call to think about what a museum would look like, and more importantly what it would *do*, in the context of Latina/o Detroit.[4]

Latinas/os have been in Michigan since at least the beginning of the twentieth century, and from the start their laboring lives have been marked by cycles of departure and return and shaped by the ebbs and flows of the state's two primary industries: agriculture and auto manufacturing. In his book on Latinas/os in Michigan, David A. Badillo notes that the first Latinas/os to arrive in the early twentieth century were largely U.S.-born Mexicans from the Lower Rio Grande and Winter Garden agricultural areas of Texas.[5] These Tejanos (as they self-identified) were drawn to the region by the promise of seasonal agricultural jobs, primarily in the sugar beet industry. They replaced an earlier workforce comprised primarily of Eastern European immigrants, who had abandoned field work for higher-paying jobs in the emerging auto industry. Many of the early Latina/o immigrants came with their families, establishing small but thriving communities in agricultural areas throughout Michigan. Some members of these early settlements followed their earlier immigrant counterparts into industrial work, which brought them to Saginaw, Detroit, Pontiac, Flint, Lansing, and other cities in Southeastern Michigan. As in the region more generally and the United States as a whole, the upheavals of the Mexican Revolution (1910–20) brought a new influx of Mexican laborers to Michigan, drawn by the promise of peace and stability. By the end of World War I, Latina/o immigration into Michigan had swelled considerably, largely due to the increased need for labor in both agriculture and industry as a result of the wartime industrial boom and the lack of traditional immigrant labor sources.[6]

The flow of immigrants into the state was halted, and even reversed, during the Great Depression, when concerns over the cost of maintaining an underemployed labor pool led to punitive "repatriation" campaigns in which Mexicans (many of them U.S. citizens) were forced return to Mexico. But as the auto industry and agribusiness began to rebuild after the ravages of the Great Depression, Mexican immigrants were inevitably called into the fields and the factories once more, and by the 1940s, when wartime labor shortages stepped up demand for both agricultural and industrial workers, Mexicans (and increasingly Puerto Ricans) once again saw Michigan as a place of opportunity. Many new and returning

immigrants came to Michigan in the 1940s through the Bracero Program, a bi-
lateral agreement between Mexico and the United States that allowed for the
temporary employment of Mexican workers in industries experiencing labor
shortages (primarily agriculture). While the Bracero Program offered opportunities to economic migrants coming from Mexico, it did not offer them a path to
citizenship, a situation that contributed to the general impression of Mexicans as
permanent outsiders or at best as "temporary" residents. As Badillo observes, by
the 1960s, "prevailing prejudices since the 1920s portrayed Mexicans and Mexican
Americans in Michigan, particularly those in agriculture, as cheap, docile, and
temporary laborers to be forgotten when no longer needed."[7] These ideas also
shaped the experience of Latina/o immigrants who were not Mexican, particularly Puerto Ricans, who like many Mexican and Mexican American economic
migrants had come to the state through governmental programs designed to create a cheap and flexible labor pool at the service of industry, and who also saw
their employment opportunities (and their sense of belonging) wax and wane
along with the labor needs and economic fortunes of agribusiness and the auto
industry.

This brief sketch of the history of the Latina/o presence in Michigan provides
a bit of context for the challenges and contradictions that our community advisory board faced as we tried to collectively imagine "a place for our stories,"
especially given the urgency that such a project took on as efforts reignited to
script working-class immigrants as an inherent threat to the economic and social
stability of the nation. It also explains the particular investments that community members had in the proposed museum and its meanings. Indeed, questions
around content emerged very early on in the process. How would we narrate
our history? Where do we begin? What communities will be represented in this
narrative? At one level, these questions were holdovers from earlier community
efforts to establish a museum in Detroit—efforts that proposed a very particular
historical vision—but at another level they pointed to what can only be termed
an existential dilemma for Latina/o cultural citizenship in the Midwest. I turn
first to these earlier efforts, as they help to illuminate the larger existential question of belonging.

The first of these earlier efforts to establish a Latina/o museum was initiated in
the 1980s, when Dr. Lucille Cruz Gajec (known as Dr. Luci), a community expert
on Mexican history and culture and one of the first PhDs to graduate from Wayne
State University's Chicano Boricua Studies Program, opened her own museum, El
Museo Indigenista (figs. 4.3.2–4). According to Elena Herrada, Cruz Gajec's museum housed a massive personal collection of artifacts that included homemade
models of the Aztec Empire, mannequins wearing Mexican regional costumes,
handcrafts of ceramic, artwork from places she had traveled in Mexico, and "all

4.3.2 Interior, El Museo Indigenista, Luci Gajec (left), standing behind her Styrofoam scale model of Tenochtitlán. Courtesy of Harness family collection.

4.3.3 El Museo Indigenista, display case with Meso-American artifacts. Courtesy of Harness family collection.

4.3.4   El Museo Indigenista, religious artifacts display. Courtesy of Harness family collection.

manner of collected material which she herself archived and displayed." As noted in her obituary, "hundreds of school children and community members in Detroit passed through this humble setting, by appointment only. Dr. Luci ran the whole operation herself, without government funds or much outside assistance so that she could maintain autonomy over the project."[8]

In 2005 an "exploratory committee" that included Cruz Gajec was organized to investigate the feasibility of establishing a more permanent and sustainable institution, tentatively called the Michigan Museum of Native Latin American Cultures in the heart of Southwest Detroit. The white paper they collectively drafted, which clearly found its initial inspiration in Cruz Gajec's storefront museum, proposed a museum that would offer a "historically accurate" depiction of "Latin American Culture from both a pre-Columbian and present day indigenous folk culture." The exploratory committee's interest in historical "accuracy" was not just a nod to conventional museological norms. The committee clearly felt that the deep traditions of Latin American culture and history had been ignored or misrepresented in existing museums, and that the general public's engagement with these traditions had been unduly shaped by popular expressive culture:

So often, the general population views Latin American Culture through a lens that is limited to experiences of restaurants, festivals, and modern music. In addition, it is often not widely understood that Latin American culture is as old as most of the great civilizations of the Eastern hemisphere such as Egypt, India, China and Mesopotamia. At the time of the Spanish conquest, some Mesoamerican cities were as large as the cities of Europe with populations of several hundred thousand and large satellite regions under their control. In the first millennium AD, the Mayan empire was the most densely populated area of the earth.[9]

The exploratory committee hoped to counteract the public's one-dimensional view of Latina/o culture by proposing a museum that would inspire and educate while bringing tourism and much-needed revenue to southwest Detroit. They made a case for rehabilitating the headquarters for the third police precinct, a vacant building in close proximity to both the international crossing and a planned welcome center (which was finished in 2008). The structure was not only ideally situated to attract tourism to the area, but it had the added benefit of a facade that would lend itself to a renovation that was "evocative of a pre-Columbian pyramid." The building itself would house a permanent exhibit in a main gallery, which would be arranged in a "time line manner to expose patrons about the development of pre-Columbian culture." It would also include a large exhibit hall detailing "present day folk cultures" that focused on the "regions and peoples" of Latin America. Smaller rooms would host rotating exhibits, a theater, a place for instruction, a research center, and a gift shop. A reproduction of a Mayan ball court was proposed for the exterior, as a way to attract neighborhood children to the museum.[10]

In the detailed and (in retrospect) achingly hopeful descriptions of the white paper we can see Cruz Gajec's homemade museum transformed into a "real" museum: a monumentalist building that evoked the community's ancient roots in the Americas through its architecture, exhibit halls, collections of valuable artifacts, and robust educational programs, all authorized by institutionally recognized "experts" (the exploratory committee consulted with Dr. Joyce Marcus, a cocurator of the Pre-Columbian Latin American Collection at the University of Michigan). The proposed Michigan Museum of Latin American Cultures was of course far more costly in terms of financing and human effort than Cruz Gajec's rather more homespun vision, and not surprisingly given the long-standing economic hardships of Detroit, the project did not come to fruition. Nevertheless, the community effort to give form to such a place was a vital and important step in the process of imagining the role that an institution like El Museo del Norte might play in the cultural life of Michigan. Indeed, the white paper for the Michigan Museum of Latin American Cultures is much more than a dead letter for a project that never came to be. In its efforts to connect the "pre-Columbian" past to "present day folk cultures" and its insistence on creating a place where that could happen (in an former police building no less), the white paper revealed the community's desire to grant Latinas/os an historical presence. It also revealed the ways in which that desire had been shaped by their economic, political, and cultural marginalities in the life of the state.

The white paper provided invaluable insights to me—as an outsider, a scholar, and a Tejana with my own ideas about history, space, and belonging—about the ways in which my understanding of these things had to be recalibrated in the context of the Midwest. For example, it might be easy for a scholar of the Chicana/o experience to read the exploratory committee's focus on pre-Columbian history and "traditional" folk culture as a throwback to the neo-indigenism of the 1960s and 1970s; an impulse to re-create Aztlán in the Midwest. In a less charitable analytic, one could read the effort to create a museum of Latin American cultures that reached deep into the past for a vision of "culture" that could rival those of "Egypt, India, China and Mesopotamia" as a discourse of "racial uplift" in which the standard to aspire to was one set by dominant valuations of "civilization." But these readings do not capture the complexities of the placemaking practice at the heart of both Cruz Gajec's vision for the Museo Indigenista or the white paper it inspired in 2005. Because these two visions for a museum shared something more than just an interest in pre-Columbian culture and a commitment to educate the public. As placemaking gestures that should be understood as narratives of belonging, they not only insisted on the centrality of Latinas/os to the cultural imaginary of Detroit's borderlands, they also gestured toward much deeper historical roots on the continent.

These earlier iterations of the museum idea also revealed the representational dilemmas that museums present to diasporic communities whose relationship to the "traditional" culture of their countries of origin is necessarily attenuated, and whose presence in the U.S. cultural imaginary is marginal at best. Can a traditional museum tell a story it seems designed to ignore—a story of movement and transit, of displacement and settlement, of the intangible meanings of "place" to a people who have been scripted as having no place in the cultural imaginaries of both "sending" and "receiving" nation states? How can we reimagine the museum so that it can tell this story and make a place for us somewhere in-between? These existential questions guided us as we delved deeper into the process, and they led, inevitably, to one conclusion: that form mattered, and that instead of trying to find stories that made sense in a traditional museum, we needed to imagine a place that made sense for our stories. In other words, if museums, as we have come to know them, are repositories of culture, places where artifacts and historical "truths" are shaped into coherent narratives that tame the messiness of history, and if what we are after is the *unleashing* of this messiness for the truths it can tell, then we need to "rethink" the museum.

Toward the end of our yearlong conversation, stakeholders came together for a final retreat to discuss possible future steps for the project. Despite the real barriers to building an actual museum, participants at the retreat felt strongly that models did exist for a long-term strategy that could build community interest across the state and thereby lay the groundwork for a sustainable future for the project. The project would move into a new phase as a "museum without walls" that would essentially perform the functions of a brick-and-mortar museum without the benefits (and liabilities) of owning and maintaining a building. In the "museum-without-walls" model, the community develops and curates exhibits, and teaches and shares with its members their history, art and culture. Our museum without walls would sponsor oral history projects, speaker series, art walks, movie nights, musical performances, and "pop-up museums" throughout the city (and even the state). We would also cocurate exhibits with established institutions eager to diversify their content and audiences.

Stakeholders at the final retreat also proposed a new name for the project, El Museo del Norte. This renaming was vitally important to reimagining the project more generally, as it touched on some of the key principals of the points of agreement I noted earlier. First, the new name reflected an experience of migration that linked various Latina/o communities to a place—El Norte—through a geospatial metaphor (i.e., we may come from different places, and at different times, but we have all come to "El Norte," and that is an experience we share). Drawing on the oral history of El Norte, the name also importantly connects the project to community-based knowledge systems and thus signals (both linguistically and historically) that El Museo del Norte represents the history of Latinas/os not from an institutional vantage point (hailed by the term "Latina/o") but from the community's point of view. The multi-referentiality of the name for the project, as well as its intentional lack of geographical specificity (El Norte as opposed to Michigan) reflects another important dimension of the community thought process that lead to the final decisions of the retreat. Throughout the yearlong process, the project hosted meetings, lectures, and community forums. At these gatherings, community members shared their suggestions for the kinds of collections, programming, and educational content they wanted to see in the museum. Some community participants wanted a place that could reverse negative stereotypes of the Latina/o community as perpetual laboring outsiders to the state ("cherry-pickers," migrant farmworkers, immigrants). Others, particularly those with historical connections to the Chicana/o movement in Michigan, wanted a deeper exploration of the Chicana/o community's indigenous roots. Given the diversity of the Latina/o community in Michigan, this could have become a major rift in terms of moving the concept forward, but we were able to come to a vision that brought the strands of these two stories together.

In both these desires—the desire to not be perpetually scripted through our migratory labor and the desire to mark our connections to indigeneity—one can see a common thread: the desire to belong. And not coincidentally, this common thread links these expressions of museological desire to Cruz Gajec's museum and the white paper, both of which sought to mark Latina/o's long-standing presence in North America through the recuperation of indigenous histories and folkloric traditions. Our name for the museum taps into this desire, paradoxically by pointing to a process not usually associated with belonging—migration. "El Norte" could reference Michigan, the Great Lakes, the Midwest, but what it *meant* was less a place than an experience that has been a fact of life in the Americas for millennia. Working through these tensions, which arose around something as seemingly trivial as the "naming" of our museum, I realized that regardless of the real gains we have made since the 1960s, Latinas/os as a whole and especially Mexican Americans continue to be figured as permanent "aliens" as a result of our histories of migration. But it is precisely those histories of migration that connect us to this continent, that ground us in this place, and that ultimately respond to the xenophobic discourse that would figure us as perpetual outsiders. In short, I came to realize that migration is as "indigenous" as a Mayan ball court.

The community dialogue process that gave birth to El Museo del Norte upended fixed notions of space (as perpetually bounded by the nation-state) and proposed a new politics of belonging (in which migration indexes belonging, not its opposite), but it also forced many of us to reconsider what a museum could be. For some involved in the project, letting go of the idea of a "brick-and-mortar" museum was freeing in that it allowed us to shift our focus, as I put it at the start of this chapter, from a "structure" to a structure of feeling—a new way of imagining ourselves, in all of our multiplicity, as historical subjects in this place. Which is to say that we began to think of El Museo del Norte not as a building for housing new collections, but as a catalyst for building new collectivities. That said, many people (especially Detroiters) who have participated in this process continue to feel that acquiring a building is a vital necessity for a community that remains invisible in the state's cultural life. These two visions are not irreconcilable; a brick-and-mortar museum needs more than just capital investment to function properly, it needs human investment, and a sense of commitment to its mission. El Museo del Norte is slowly building that investment, through a variety of activities ranging from ongoing oral history projects, to archive collection and digitization, to our annual pop-up exhibits that feature materials that we have collected from the community. Through these initiatives we are building both our collection and our audience from the ground up. But

4.3.5 *A Place for Our Stories* exhibit, El Museo del Norte, Detroit, Michigan. Photo by Jennifer García Peacock.

we are also building investment in the process of community history, and in the idea that the Latina/o community has a history to tell. We are building—as our 2012 pop-up exhibit put it—"a place for our stories" (fig. 4.3.5). That place may be temporary (for now), but it is nevertheless a place built by us, shared by us, and meant for us. In the words of Elisa Gurulé, a member of our community task force and Elena's daughter: "If we don't tell our own stories, someone else will. And I'm certain that they will get them wrong. The first act of self-determination is to tell one's own story. Once we have possession of our history, the world is wide open. El Museo del Norte is one step on this journey."[11]

As an outsider to Latina/o Michigan but one who has experienced her own privileged form of labor migration, I came to the scene in Detroit and to the El Museo del Norte project with both a sense of connection and an awareness of the potential contradictions of my role as a scholar and a participant in a collective process of *concientización* already underway. As a young girl in Texas, I had learned, like Elisa Gurulé, that culture, history, and storytelling were central sites for transformational change in embattled communities. As a scholar working in Detroit I learned new lessons: about the delicate negotiations of space, power, and voice, about the differences that divide Latina/o communities, and about the real work necessary to reclaim our place in a history that offers us no quarter. I have written elsewhere about "passionate praxis"—the intimate, dangerous, and transformational work that so many scholars of color find themselves doing when they move from observation to encounter and enter into the borderlands between "insider" and "outsider."[12] Through my engagement with Elena and the others who have for so long pushed their dreams for a museum forward, I found myself entering into that world on the streets of Detroit, in a place far from home, but surprisingly close to my heart. Their efforts to imagine a museum are therefore inextricably woven into my own story of coming home to Detroit. It is a collective story—and like so many of the stories that El Museo del Norte seeks to document—it is marked by a cycle of departure and return.

Notes

1. For an example of federal anti-immigrant legislation, see Sensenbrenner Bill in the glossary.

2. See the glossary for an explanation of self-deportation.

3. The "nonprofit industrial complex" describes the late-twentieth-century corporatization of the nonprofit sector characterized by new institutional relationships between nonprofits, governmental agencies, educational institutions, and corporations. These relationships create systems of control that undermine grassroots initiatives and propose top-down solutions for struggling communities. Over the last several decades in Detroit, highly resourced and powerful nonprofits have emerged to address the city's ills, often with very little input from the communities that they serve.

4. Dennis Nodín Valdés, *Al Norte: Agricultural Workers in the Great Lakes Region, 1917–1970* (Austin: University of Texas Press, 1991); Zaragosa Vargas, *Proletarians of the North: A History of Mexican Industrial Workers in Detroit and the Midwest, 1917–1933* (Berkeley: University of California Press, 1993); David A. Badillo, *Latinos in Michigan* (East Lansing: Michigan State University Press, 2003).

5. The earliest Latina/o community in Detroit predated the arrival of former migrant workers. In 1917, Henry Ford began recruiting young men from Mexico and Latin America for training in the production systems at his Highland Park and Fordson plants. These young men were to return to their home countries to establish car dealerships and manage fledgling subsidiary plants. However, as Badillo notes in *Latinos in Michigan*, many of these young recruits stayed in Michigan, settling in Detroit and its surrounding suburbs (8).

6. Another "pull" factor was undoubtedly the shift in U.S. immigration policy that culminated in the passage of the 1924 Immigration Act, which restricted Eastern European and Asian immigration while leaving the door (relatively) open to immigration from Mexico and Latin America.

7. Badillo, *Latinos in Michigan*, 25.

8. Elena Herrada, "Obituary for Dr. Lucille Cruz Gajec," personal email communication to the author, October 2013.

9. Latin American Museum Exploratory Committee, "A Concept Paper on the Feasibility of a Michigan Museum of Native Latin American Cultures," 2, El Museo del Norte Archives, Detroit, Mich., 2005.

10. Ibid., 3–5.

11. Elisa Gurulé, "We Will Be Heard," wall text, El Museo del Norte, June 2013.

12. María Eugenia Cotera, "Epilogue: 'What's Love Got to Do with It?' Toward a Passionate Praxis," in *Native Speakers: Ella Cara Deloria, Zora Neale Hurston, Jovita González, and the Poetics of Culture* (Austin: University of Texas Press, 2008), 225–32.

PART 5

Movimientos

Religious Migrants

The Latina/o Mennonite Quest for Community and Civil Rights

FELIPE HINOJOSA

Daniel Tijerina was only five years old when he first remembers making the trip north with his family. "I didn't know where exactly we were going," remembered Daniel, "all I heard was '*ibamos pa'l norte*' [we were going north]. . . . The only other kid I remember that night was my cousin Ben, who we called Chamín." The annual trips usually began in May and took the family from their starting point in Brownsville, Texas, to multiple work sites across the Midwest. On their way north, the family passed through Houston, then Hope, Arkansas, where they stopped at a migrant camp for a shower and where Daniel's mother cooked a hot meal for the family. From there it was up through Little Rock to Indianapolis and then on to their first destination, Sebewaing, Michigan, where they hoed sugar beets. In mid-July they traveled to Traverse City, Michigan, where they picked cherries, and by mid-August they were on their way to Archbold, Ohio, to pick tomatoes until mid-October. After that it was back home to South Texas, although on occasion they made a quick stop in Missouri to pick cotton.[1]

Each stop brought hard labor, swimming trips to nearby lakes when possible, and of course, church services. In Sebewaing, the Tijerinas joined other migrant families at a nearby Pentecostal church for services in Spanish on Sunday afternoons. In the Traverse City area, migrants and their families met in a farmer's barn, which he had outfitted with benches and a small lectern for migrants to hold their own services. In Fulton County, Ohio, the Tijerinas gathered with the local missionary outreach that Mennonites had established for migrant farm workers. "We were Methodists in Texas," Daniel admitted, "but on our migrant travels, we worshipped with Pentecostals and Mennonites."[2]

Stories of faith on the migrant trail, like the one documented above, demonstrate the importance of religion in the everyday lives of Latina/o migrants. Here, in the heart of the U.S. Midwest, Latinas/os blended their religious faith traditions with those of other migrant laborers and in some cases with the white farmers whose barns and farm fields served as makeshift sanctuaries. In the unfamiliar surroundings of the Midwest, church services provided a much-needed sense of community and a place for Latinas/os to ask for God's continued protection.

This chapter follows the stories of Latinas/os who joined the Mennonite Church during the middle part of the twentieth century.[3] Some Latinas/os joined the church because of the positive experiences they had as migrant workers. Others joined the Mennonite Church as a result of the efforts of Mennonite missionaries who in the 1930s set out to evangelize Latina/o communities in Chicago, South Texas, and later Puerto Rico and New York City. But regardless of their origin stories, Latina/o Mennonites carried a shared history as migrants—religious migrants—when they joined the Mennonite Church. The Midwest, as the land of perpetual out- and in-migration, provided a particularly important backdrop for the development of new expressions of faith that in this case brought religious migrants to the Mennonite Church.

During the mid-twentieth century, the Midwest was a region characterized by missionary flows southward and labor flows northward. Places like the Moody Bible Institute in Chicago, for example, served as an important training ground for evangelical missionaries destined for urban centers in the United States or Latin America, Asia, and Africa.[4] For Mennonites, the central mission agency—Mennonite Board of Missions and Charities (MBMC)—was located in Elkhart, Indiana. In the 1950s the MBMC launched its greatest missionary efforts to Latina/o communities in places ranging from Chicago's Near West Side to the cotton fields of South Texas. But while religious historians have given plenty of attention to missionary flows south, few have studied the religious lives and experiences of Mexican American and other Latina/o migrants in the Midwest during much of the twentieth century.[5]

This chapter flips the script on historical studies whose focus on the postwar evangelical thrust has led to an oversight of Latina/o religious migrants headed north and the implications this history carries for religion in the U.S. Midwest. I argue that religion served as an important platform for Latina/o civil rights movements in the Midwest. With a focus on the Mennonite Church, this chapter shows how religious activism was part of the larger project of community formation for Latina/o migrants who were making the Midwest their new home. The quest for civil rights included building an interethnic alliance between Mexican Americans, Puerto Ricans, and African Americans, which organized in 1968 and called itself the Minority Ministries Council (MMC). This group helped organize a K–12 educational program that created a pathway for black and brown youths to attend Mennonite schools. They were also at the center of controversy when they exposed the poor treatment of migrant farmworkers by white Mennonite farmers in northern Indiana. While these movements were for the most part dominated by Latino men, Latinas created their own spaces by organizing conferences that brought together women from across the country. This flurry of activity led to an unprecedented rise of Latinas/os within the Mennonite Church. In a span of about ten years, Latinas/os went from zero representation on national Mennonite Church boards to having Latinos and Latinas on every major church board from the East Coast to the Midwest.[6]

As a region defined by migration, the Midwest served as the crossroads where religious and labor migrants met and interacted. These interactions, however, were fleeting and to a large degree tempered by the racialized geography of midwestern communities. In other words, even in religious contexts, white and Latina/o Mennonites lived very separate lives. Churches were segregated along lines of race and language, with Latina/o Mennonite churches emerging in Chicago in the 1930s and later in Davenport (Iowa), and Goshen (Indiana) in the late 1960s. The emergence of these churches reveals the intricate ways in which Latinas/os created a new "homeland" in what to many was an unfamiliar region far from their homes in Texas or Mexico. If "religions make sense of the nomadic as well as the sedentary in human life," as Thomas Tweed has suggested, then examining the churches and religious lives of Latinas/os can open new avenues for understanding community formation in the heart of the U.S. Midwest.[7]

The religious impulse to "preach the Gospel" emerged for white Mennonites right at the moment that they took note of the rising number of Latina/o immigrants coming to the United States in the years prior to and immediately after World War II. Nelson Kauffman, a leader of the MBMC, wrote that "tens of thousands of Puerto Ricans are coming to the states annually, and immigrants from other countries are coming in large numbers and are unevangelized."[8] Kauffman was referring not only to Puerto Ricans coming to Chicago and New York, but also to the growing number of Mexicans arriving in the Midwest. Much of this immigration was spurred by the rising demand for laborers in agriculture and manufacturing industries. In the years after World War II, labor shortages in the Midwest spurred on recruiting efforts for Mexican American workers, most of whom migrated from Texas.[9] As a result, thousands of Tejano migrants like the Tijerina family set off to states such as Wisconsin, Michigan, Indiana, and Ohio.[10]

As Mexican and Puerto Rican migrants traveled north, Protestant missionaries organized "trackside churches" along the Santa Fe and Union Pacific rail lines and reached out to agricultural laborers on their breaks, eager to offer them pamphlets with the Gospel message.[11] In the Mennonite Church, mission leaders like Kauffman feared that ignoring the migrant flow north carried grave consequences for the future of the church. What followed was the most direct and focused approach to church mission programs aimed at Latina/o communities in the history of the Mennonite Church: from Chicago to South Texas to New York.

In 1934 Mennonites established their first outreach to Mexicans in Chicago's Near West Side. Not long after the church had attracted a steady number of Mexican families, Mennonite missionaries tapped a young Pentecostal preacher named David Castillo to lead Bible studies. Mennonite leaders were so impressed with Castillo that they quickly arranged for him to begin taking Bible courses at the nearby Goshen Seminary (Goshen, Ind.) in 1934.[12] Two years later Castillo became the first Mexican American to be licensed for ministry in the Mennonite Church. The efforts of Mennonite missionaries in Chicago soon expanded to other regions of the country.

In the late 1930s, Mennonites organized churches in South Texas, and in the 1940s and 1950s missionary work extended into Puerto Rico and New York City. As Mennonite churches in these regions grew, Mexican American and Puerto Rican youths were offered scholarships to study at Mennonite colleges in the Midwest. The Puerto Rican students who started attending Goshen College (now Mennonite College in Goshen, Ind.) in the late 1940s and 1950s came via the connections they formed with Mennonite conscientious objectors working in Puerto Rico during World War II through the federal Civilian Public Service. Puerto Rican students arrived in northern Indiana from Bayamón, Río Pierdas, Barranquitas, and other places around the island.[13] In the late 1950s, Latina/o students from South Texas and Puerto Rico arrived at Hesston College (now Mennonite College in Hesston, Kans.) to take Bible classes to prime them for church leadership. The focus was on male Latino students who expressed an interest in ministry or showed leadership potential. The program worked. The students who attended Hesston College in the late 1950s and 1960s included José Ortiz (from Puerto Rico), Samuel Hernández (South Texas) and Lupe De León (South Texas), each of whom became important leaders for the church. For José Ortiz, who grew up in the small town of Coamo Arriba (Puerto Rico), the forays into the Midwest and Mennonite ethnic enclaves meant being both identified and misidentified. "On the island I was sure of myself, I was on my own turf, in the States, I was a guest . . . I moved to become the 'third man,' not necessarily Hispanic, not American, but perhaps both. . . . In Hesston college [Kansas] I was a foreign student, at Goshen College [Indiana] I was a Puerto Rican national, and later they called me a minority."[14]

This is why cultural identity became so important for Mexican Americans and Puerto Ricans who joined the Mennonite Church. For Latinas/os, ethnic nationalist movements that emerged in the late 1960s offered an opportunity for them to self-identify instead of perpetually being thought of as a "foreigner" in one context and a "minority" in another. As José Ortiz, Samuel Hernández, and

Lupe De León became Mennonite pastors, the emerging social unrest from the Vietnam War and the civil rights movement greatly affected their political and theological views. For Lupe De León, who remained suspicious of Mennonite pacifism, the casualties of Mexican American soldiers in Vietnam while young white Mennonites "hid behind the skirt of the church" raised his level of political commitment and made him somewhat of a rabble-rouser in the church.[15]

The fact that most Latina/o students arrived on Mennonite campuses just as the civil rights movements captured the attention of the nation had a great effect on how these students thought about faith, politics, and social engagement. The Latina/o migrants who made their way into the Mennonite Church in the 1960s and 1970s were no longer only coming from the migrant labor camps. During this time Latinas/os who moved to places such as Indiana and Kansas did so to pastor congregations and work in denominational offices. In most cases, these Latinas/os were the same kids who attended Mennonite vacation Bible schools in the 1950s in South Texas, Puerto Rico, and elsewhere. The religious migrants who entered the church during the mid-twentieth century became a permanent fixture in the church and blended their religious and cultural identities by calling themselves Meno-Latinos and Meno-Latinas.[16]

Not surprisingly, the center of this new religious identity was in Chicago, where the Mexican mission that started in the 1930s had grown to become the Lawndale Mennonite Church and, by the early 1970s, was attracting a large number of Mexican Americans every Sunday morning. The Lawndale church was the first self-sustaining and bilingual Latina/o Mennonite church in the States.[17] The church also developed somewhat of a folk following due to the famous Lawndale Choir. Led by two Latina religious migrants, Gracie Torres from New York City and Seferina De León from Mathis, Texas, in 1972 the choir produced an album titled *Everything Is Beautiful*. The music ranged from *música mexicana* to contemporary folk and traditional Mennonite hymns.

In April 1973, Latina/o Mennonites were featured in an article in the national Latina/o magazine, *La Luz*. "The Minority Ministries Council: Mexicanos, Puerto Ricans, Blacks, and American Indians Working Together" focused on the interethnic alliance built within the Mennonite Church.[18] The MMC was unique on two counts. First, it was one of the few interethnic movements found within a religious context. Most progressive religious movements were oriented around the cause of one particular ethnic group, whether African American or Latina/o.[19] Among secular movements, interethnic coalitions were often short-lived. The MMC had not only built an interethnic movement, but also sustained it and managed to avoid some of the pitfalls other interethnic alliances experienced, mainly competition over limited resources and an inability to think critically about intersecting oppressions.[20]

5.1.1 Lawndale Choir singing at St. Francis of Assisi Church, Chicago, Illinois, circa 1973. Courtesy of Mennonite Church USA Archives, Organizational Records, Mennonite Board of Missions Photographs, 1971–1995 (IV-10-7.3).

The MMC caught the attention of *La Luz* writers not only because it was an interethnic movement, but also because it worked within the religious structures of a small, ethno-religious community in the Midwest. MMC leaders hung "Chicano Power" posters on the walls of the organization's central office in Elkhart, Indiana. But more importantly, this was an overwhelmingly white denomination. In 1971, only 6 percent of people in the Mennonite Church were nonwhite. Of this 6 percent, 3 percent were African American, 2 percent Latina/o, and 1 percent Native American. This translated into a total of seventy-five churches of color across the United States, which represented approximately 3,100 members.[21]

Even with their small numbers, the religious movements of Latina/o Mennonites were more than historical quirks. Between 1968 and 1974, the MMC organized a Cross-Cultural Youth Convention in 1972 (fig. 5.1.2), helped to develop a K–12 educational program for Latina/o and African American children through a program called High-Aim, and challenged the mostly white Mennonite Church to be more responsive to the needs of black and brown communities. The programs established by the MMC helped usher in substantive change in the Mennonite Church. White pastors began leaving their leadership positions in Latina/o and African American congregations; white missionaries began to rethink their roles in minority communities; and the assumption that being Mennonite was tied

5.1.2   The Minority Ministries Council organized the Cross-Cultural Youth Convention, held in Epworth Forest, Indiana in 1972. Courtesy of Mennonite Church USA Archives, Organizational Records, Mennonite Board of Missions Photographs, 1971–1995 (IV-10-7.3).

solely to ethnicity became a point of contention. Mennonite identity in the 1970s was shifting away from its foundation in ethnic kinship to a belief system that appealed to a much broader audience—Latinas/os and African Americans were at the center of this shift.[22] But the road toward self-determination was bumpy. Nowhere was this clearer than in the battles that raged around the labor practices of Mennonite farm owners and the lack of racial diversity in K–12 Mennonite schools in the Midwest.

Apart from their evangelical concern for Latinas/os, white Mennonites knew little about the daily struggles of the Mexican migrant workers who arrived each summer and fall to work the harvest season. That all changed during the summer of 1969 in Goshen, Indiana, when Annas Miller, a Mennonite businessman, was accused of providing poor housing for large numbers of Mexican Americans who traveled from South Texas to work in his turkey processing plant. In an editorial that appeared in the Goshen newspaper, Don Klassen described the living conditions at Pine Manor as consisting of "a tar-paper shack hidden behind tall corn or over the hill . . . or a room 10 by 20 with two or three beds where three to five children sleep in the same bed."[23] But while no one agreed the living conditions of workers and their families were ideal, some disagreed with Klassen's descriptions. "It was crowded and it was a chicken house and it wasn't the nicest place to live," Mennonite pastor Moses Beachy remembered, "but it was temporary."[24] But the concerns raised by Klassan were legitimate. Reports noted that workers often felt that at Pine Manor they "lived like pigs," with no adequate trash disposal, no indoor plumbing, and increasing concern about the odor coming from a nearby pond where children often played.[25]

Two years after the scandal broke over migrant housing at Pine Manor, the MBMC agreed to help fund a fifteen-unit housing project for farmworkers that forced Pine Manor and its owner, Annas Miller, to close its inadequate living quarters.[26] Later that year, MMC leaders granted $10,000 to the Medical Aid to Migrant Employees project in the South Bend area. The funds were given to help provide medical care and prenatal care for migrant farm workers in six counties in northern Indiana.[27]

The Pine Manor incident captured the attention of white Mennonite church leaders and made the plight of Mexican migrant workers impossible to ignore. But the case also revealed just how disconnected white Mennonites were from Latina/o communities across the Midwest. Even as white Mennonite missionaries had lived among Mexican Americans in South Texas and Puerto Ricans on the island, building relationships on their home turf in the Midwest was another issue entirely. In 1968 an educational program initiated by African American Lee Roy Berry, and with the support of the MMC, set out to bridge these cultural divides. As a program focused on K–12 education, the High-Aim program opened avenues for Latina/o and African American youths to attend Mennonite schools across the Midwest and East Coast.

Lupe García, who directed the program during the mid-1970s and hailed from South Texas, noted that the program recruited black and brown students based on their "economic rather than racial status."[28] While the program had broad support, critics saw the program as only reproducing "white" education in a "white" context. Even though High-Aim numbers remained low, white Mennonites often complained about "their ability to adequately serve the minority church in view of their commitments to their own increasingly overcrowding, school constituency."[29] In other words, some white Mennonites worried that a focus on black and brown youths might affect the recruitment of white Mennonite students. For black and Latina/o students themselves, the experience in Mennonite schools was mixed.

Some students expressed their frustrations during an evaluation session where they made clear that "I want no part of Mennonites!" or "these white people haven't done a thing for me!" On the other side of the spectrum, some Latina/o and black students expressed positive emotions like "I don't know what I would've done without High-Aim." The program eventually floundered because it failed to garner sufficient support from Latina/o and African American Mennonite churches. Some Latina/o Mennonites argued that "the idea of Mennonite education brings the thought of white Swiss-German people who are imparting their beliefs and values on a culturally different people."[30] While the High-Aim program did have some success, the program failed to bridge cultural differences, as black and Latina/o students never quite fit in at the mostly white Mennonite schools. And yet even as the program remained mired in controversy throughout the 1970s, High-Aim did succeed in opening the doors of Mennonite education by creating possibilities for black, Latina/o, and other nonwhite youths to attend schools that had previously catered only to white Mennonite students.

The involvement of Latina/o Mennonites in educational and labor activism, however, was not unique. The civil rights movement in the United States coupled with the rise of liberation theology in Latin America inspired a wave of movements among U.S. Latina/o Christians. Groups like Católicos Por La Raza, PADRES (Chicano priest movement), Las Hermanas (women religious in the Catholic Church), La Raza Churchmen (Presbyterian) and Latin American Methodist Action Group, all clamored for institutional reform, more inclusion at denominational levels, and theological education that better represented the "Christ of the poor" across the Southwest.[31] What distinguished the movements of Latina/o Mennonites from these important groups, however, was the interethnic nature of its politics and the fact that it unfolded among white Mennonites in the rural Midwest.

Gender and the women's movement also became prominent during this era and touched the church as well. In 1973, Latina Mennonites carved their own space through a series of conferences they organized across the Midwest. Initially called Servicios de Inspiración (Services of Inspiration), the conferences were mainly about moving women, whose husbands often traveled or were involved in church work, out of the home and away from chores and child care into a space where they could share religious experiences with other women. "This was a time for women to come," remembered Seferina De León, "and where the husbands could stay with the children, so we can be refreshed . . . and we would sing, pray, and share."[32] The first conference took place on April 14, 1973, when close to sixty Latinas gathered at the Iglesia Evangélica Menonita (Evangelical Mennonite Church) in Moline, Illinois (fig. 5.1.3). Women came from as far away as Texas and New York and as close as Indiana, Chicago, and churches across the Quad Cities region (Moline and Rock Island in Illinois, and Bettendorf and Davenport in Iowa). According to María Bustos, one of the conference organizers, the women gathered "because there was a need to get to know each other and worship God together in Spanish."[33] María Bustos and her husband Mac were originally from Chicago,

5.1.3 Las Hermanas, with Seferina De León in the middle, at the first Servicios de Inspiración Conference in Moline, Illinois, 1973. Courtesy of Mennonite Church USA Archives, Organizational Records, Mennonite Board of Missions Photographs, 1971–1995 (IV-10-7.3).

but they moved to Davenport in 1963 to help start Segunda Iglesia Menonita (Second Mennonite Church) at the request of the Iowa-Nebraska Mennonite Conference. In Davenport, the Bustos became involved with the American GI Forum (a Mexican American civil rights organization) and the Minority Coalition, which advocated for the rights of Latinas/os and African Americans in the Quad Cities. After a few years in Davenport, the Bustos moved the church to nearby Moline, where they refurbished an old Catholic church to host their first services in 1970.[34]

Prior to meeting in Moline, Latinas had rarely held any positions of leadership within the church and for the most part remained behind the scenes. Although women attended MMC meetings, they mostly led worship sessions, cooked the meals, and prepared the coffee. In fact, the only woman to hold leadership on the MMC was Criselda Garza, a Mexican American woman from South Texas. In 1968, Garza was one of the few women to attend the MMC inaugural meeting in Chicago, where she was appointed to serve on the first executive committee.[35] After the first conference in 1973, the women organized biannual meetings and formalized their movement by changing the name of the conference from Servicios de Inspiración (Services of Inspiration) to Conferencia Femenil Hispana Menonita (Hispanic Mennonite women's conference).[36]

Each of the conferences had a special theme that appealed to Latinas who desired to play a larger role in church leadership: "la mujer decidida en un ambiente hostil" (the confident woman in a hostile environment), "embajadoras de Cristo" (ambassadors of Christ), and "libertad y responsibilidad en la familia cristiana" (liberty and responsibility in the Christian family).[37] Importantly, and impressively, these conferences were for the most part organized with funding raised by the women themselves, an accomplishment that the male leaders of the MMC never came close to matching.

The conferences that Las Hermanas organized, however, did more than prove that Latinas could be effective church leaders. This was already understood as Latinas were highly regarded as gifted preachers, Bible interpreters, singers, and musicians. These conferences helped shatter the universal grip of Latino and black male leadership and exposed the workings of sexism in the church, which often came through most clearly in the ways that Latinas and black women were laughed off or not taken seriously when they demanded stronger leadership roles in the church.

The work of Latinas/os in the Mennonite Church documents the ways in which religious migrants helped to transform a church steeped in Swiss-German culture and the simplicity of midwestern life. But these movements were more than just about making a predominately white church more inclusive. Programs established by the Minority Ministries Council and the Latina conferences were part of a larger project of community formation that also showcased the multiple formulations of ethnic nationalism. The religious movements of Latina/o Mennonites remind us that ethnic nationalist movements were rarely singular, rarely one-dimensional—rather, they expressed multiple ideologies that emerged in diverse sites, from the streets of urban America to Mennonite sanctuaries in the Midwest.[38]

Positioning the work of Latina/o Mennonites as one of the many cultural and political representations during the civil rights era helps magnify the multiple and sometimes hidden manifestations of ethnic nationalism. In this way we can begin to reimagine how politics, religion, and activism varied across time and space. The activism of religious migrants in the Mennonite Church also moves us to the Midwest; to the region where the struggles, hopes, and stories of community formation of Latinas/os remain, for the most part, overlooked.[39]

Scholars who write about the Midwest characterize it as a place that has defied definition, a "land of normalcy and niceness," and where generally "not much seems to happen."[40] And yet, the Midwest is a region of constant reinvention, on the down-and-out, postindustrial, yet carrying the burden of being the "real America." Well-manicured lawns, clean homes, and expansive farms are juxtaposed with the grinding poverty and postindustrial remains of old steel mills and automobile factories. In the winter the skies are cold and gray, and the summers bring unforgiving heat.

But more importantly, it is a region where Latinas/os have interacted daily with white ethno-religious communities—whether Mennonites in Indiana or the Dutch Reformed in Iowa—whose histories are engraved into the landscape via Amish buggy parking lots outside of local Walmart stores. And yet even as the Midwest is increasingly defined by cultural interaction, it remains clouded by the legacy of white supremacy that has its strongest support in states like Indiana, where Tejano migrant Lupe De León remembered seeing the KKK rally around the courthouse in downtown Goshen.[41] Even so, as has been evident in other regions, midwestern Latinas/os have carried with them that entrepreneurial spirit and hunger for social change that at the height of the civil rights movement propelled them to work to make the Mennonite Church a more inclusive place.

They did so by forming interethnic alliances with African American Mennonites, by organizing Cross-Cultural Youth Conventions and educational programs (fig. 5.1.4), working for better migrant and health services, and by moving the church to be more culturally relevant for Latinos and Latinas. Latina/o Mennonites spent the latter part of the 1970s staking out a political space in the church by drafting policy statements, planting more than fifty congregations, publishing Mennonite literature in Spanish, and organizing a Bible school with the specific aim of training Latinos and Latinas for church leadership. In 1975, Latina/o Mennonites organized their own group, the Concilio Nacional de Iglesias Menonitas (National Council of Spanish Mennonite Churches), and named José Ortiz, a Puerto Rican pastor, as its first leader.[42] They did all this against the backdrop of very "ordinary" places across the Midwest, where they merged the theological sensitivities of white Mennonites with their own expressions of Chicano and Puerto Rican activism. These religious stories, the process of community formation, are what make the cultures and politics of midwestern Latinas/os unique. The interactions, the alliances, and the identities that have emerged are a result of encountering a cultural milieu in the Midwest that is at once simple and dynamic. In other words, it is hard to imagine Latina/o Mennonites emerging in any other regional context.[43]

This chapter began with the story of the Tijerina family, who in the 1950s participated in the circular labor migration patterns along with thousands of other Mexican American families. And like many of those migrants, they practiced their faith on the road and in many cases blended their traditions with new and sometimes old ethno-religious traditions prevalent in the Midwest. In the mid-1960s, when parts of the Tijerina family decided to relocate to the small town of Archbold in northwest Ohio, they joined a church that grew out of the migrant

5.1.4   The Cross-Cultural Conventions brought young people of color together and helped develop interethnic alliances. Courtesy of Mennonite Church USA Archives, Organizational Records, Mennonite Board of Missions Photographs, 1971–1995 (IV-10-7.3).

mission, Iglesia Menonita Del Buen Pastor (Good shepherd Mennonite church).[44] Fifty-two years after that church was founded, it continues to be a space for Latinas/os who have lived in Ohio for decades and for Latina/o immigrants who today are making the Midwest their new home.

Notes

1. Daniel Tijerina, interview by author, Brownsville, Tex., 26 June 2010.

2. Ibid.

3. This chapter focuses on the (Old) Mennonite Church because this group had the largest missionary outreach to Latina/o communities. As an ethno-religious group with roots in the Radical Reformation of the sixteenth century, Mennonite theology is centered on peace and non-resistance, which has historically informed how white Mennonites have interacted with the state, modern life, and the question of war. See Harry Loewen and Steve M. Nolt, *Through Fire and Water: An Overview of Mennonite History*, 2nd ed. (Scottdale, Pa.: Herald Press, 2010).

4. George M. Marsden, *Fundamentalism and American Culture*, 2nd ed. (New York: Oxford University Press, 2006), 130–32. See also William Trollinger, *God's Empire: William Bell Riley and Midwestern Fundamentalism* (Madison: University of Wisconsin Press, 1991).

5. Works by sociologists and religious studies scholars that cover Latina/o religion in the Midwest include Jane Juffer, "Hybrid Faiths: Latino Protestants Find a Home among the Dutch Reformed in Iowa," *Latino Studies* 6, no. 3 (2008): 290–312; Luisa Feline Freier, "Religion, Ethnicity, and Immigrant Integration: Latino Lutherans versus Mexican Catholics in a Midwestern City," *Studies in Ethnicity and Nationalism* 8, no. 2 (2008); Manuel A. Vasquez, Chad E. Seales, and Marie Friedmann Marquardt, "New Latino Destinations," in *Latinas/os in the United States: Changing the Face of America*, ed. Havidán Rodríguez, Rogelio Sáenz, and Cecilia Menjívar (New York: Springer, 2008), 19–35; Karen I. Leonard, Alex Stepick, Manuel E. Vasquez, and Jennifer Holdaway, eds., *Immigrant Faiths: Transforming Religious Life in America* (Walnut Creek, Calif.: AltaMira Press, 2005).

6. Felipe Hinojosa, *Latino Mennonites: Civil Rights, Faith, and Evangelical Culture* (Baltimore, Md.: Johns Hopkins University Press, 2014), 174–76.

7. Thomas Tweed, *Crossing and Dwelling: A Theory of Religion* (Cambridge, Mass.: Harvard University Press, 2006), 75.

8. Nelson Kauffman, "Broadening Our Witness to Meet Expanding Needs at Home," Fifty-First Annual Meeting of MBMC, IV-6-3, box 4, file 18, Mennonite Board of Missions, 1906–2002, Mennonite Church USA Archives, Goshen, Ind. (hereafter MCA).

9. For more on Latina/o migration to the Midwest, see Dennis Nodín Valdés, *Al Norte: Agricultural Workers in the Great Lakes Region, 1917–1970* (Austin: University of Texas Press, 1991); Zaragosa Vargas, *Labor Rights Are Civil Rights: Mexican American Workers in Twentieth-Century America* (Princeton, N.J.: Princeton University Press, 2005); Lilia Fernández, *Brown in the Windy City: Mexicans and Puerto Ricans in Postwar Chicago* (Chicago: University of Chicago Press, 2012); Marc Simon Rodriguez, *Tejano Diaspora: Mexican Americanism and Ethnic Politics in Texas and Wisconsin* (Chapel Hill: University of North Carolina Press, 2011); Michael Innis-Jiménez, *Steel Barrio: The Great Mexican Migration to South Chicago, 1915–1940* (New York: New York University Press, 2013).

10. Rodriguez, *Tejano Diaspora*, 4–5.

11. Adam Morales, *American Baptists with a Spanish Accent* (Valley Forge, Pa.: Judson Press, 1964), 41.

12. David Castillo's name is in the student register for the Winter Bible School at Goshen College, Jan. 3 to Feb. 2, 1934, *Goshen College Bulletin*, May 1934, Mennonite Historical Library, Goshen College, Indiana (hereafter MHL).

13. Maple Leaf Year Book, Dec. 17–18, 1952, Mennonite Board of Education Minutes 1985–2001, V-1-8, box 2, MCA.

14. José Ortíz, interview by author, Goshen, Ind., April 17, 2007.

15. Lupe De León, interview by author, Mathis, Tex., June 2007.

16. Rafael Falcón, "La Iglesia Meno-Latina en Norte América: una interpretación," *Ecos Menonitas* 9, no. 3 (July 1983), MHL.

17. Nelson Kraybill, "The Birth of the Chicago Mexican Mission," unpublished paper, Goshen College, 1978, 33, MHL.

18. "The Minorities Ministries Council: Mexicanos, Puerto Ricans, Blacks, and American Indians Working Together," *La Luz* (Denver) 2, no. 1 (April 1973): 20–23.

19. There were some exceptions. Other interethnic religious movements during the middle part of the twentieth century included the Catholic Interracial Council that worked

in New York and places like Davenport, Iowa, and the Christian Friends for Racial Equality that worked in Seattle. Randi Jones Walker, *Religion and the Public Conscience: Ecumenical Civil Rights Work in Seattle 1940–1960* (Winchester, U.K.: Circle Books, 2012); Janet Weaver, "From Barrio to ¡Boicoteo! The Emergence of Mexican American Activism in Davenport, 1917–1970," *Annals of Iowa* 68, no. 3 (summer 2009): 215–54.

20. Dina G. Okamoto, "Toward a Theory of Panethnicity: Explaining Asian American Collective Action" *American Sociological Review* 68, no. 6 (December 2003): 813; Michael Banton, *Racial and Ethnic Competition* (New York: Cambridge University Press, 1983); Joane Nagel and Susanne Olzak, "Ethnic Mobilization in New and Old States: An Extension of the Competition Model," *Social Problems* 30, no. 2 (December 1982): 127–43; Karen M. Kaufmann, "Cracks in the Rainbow: Group Commonality as a Basis for Latino and African-American Political Coalitions," *Political Research Quarterly* 56, no. 2 (June 2003): 199–210.

21. Specific numbers are hard to get since the Mennonite church did not officially count churches as Latina/o or African American until their 1983 yearbook. José Ortíz did provide some leads when he stated that Latinas/os made up 184 members in 1955, 498 in 1970, and 1,583 in 1981. See José Ortíz, "The Spirit of Ebenezer" (Mennonite Yearbook, 1982), 10, MCA; John Powell, "Minority Ministries Council Program Projections, January 1974–1976," letter to Board of Directors of MBM, Jan. 9, 1973, IV-7-6, MMC folder, MCA; Dan Shenk, "Minorities Seek Closer Ties with Total Mennonite Church," *Happenings* 2, no. 2 (Dec. 5, 1972), MCA.

22. Mennonite historians are clear that questions of cultural assimilation, language, and culture take on increased salience during the 1930s. However, the civil rights movement introduced a new way to talk about Mennonite identity that included discussions on race and culture. See James C. Juhnke, *Vision, Doctrine, War: Mennonite Identity and Organization in America, 1890–1930* (Scottdale, Pa.: Herald Press, 1989).

23. Don Klassen, "Plea for Migrants," *Goshen (Ind.) News*, Nov. 14, 1969.

24. Moses Beachy quoted in Ben Noll, "A Community of Brotherhood," unpublished paper, Goshen College, 2009, 4–5, MHL.

25. Paul Hershberger, "Miller May Close Housing," *Goshen (Ind.) News*, December 1971; Kenn Washington, "Protesters to Boycott Pine Manor Products," *Goshen (Ind.) News*, Nov. 19, 1971.

26. Paul Hershberger, "Housing Project Proposed," *Goshen (Ind.) News*, Dec. 17, 1971.

27. John Powell, Compassion Fund Report, July 1969–July 1971, General Board Files 1, Minority Ministries Council, 1971–1973, box 3, file 38, I-6-5, MCA.

28. Lupe García, quoted in untitled article, *Gospel Herald*, Oct. 10, V-14, High-Aim file, MBE, Lupe García, MCA.

29. Arthur Griffin, "Proposal for Implementing High-Aim Redevelopment Program," Dec. 16, 1975, V-14, MBE box 2, High-Aim file, Arthur Griffin, MCA.

30. Ibid.

31. Works that cover these important movements include: Leo D. Nieto, "The Chicano Movement and the Gospel," in *Hidden Stories: Unveiling the History of the Latino Church*, ed. David Cortés-Fuentes and Daniel R. Rodríguez-Díaz (Decatur, Ga.: Asociación para la Educación Teológica, 1994), 146–50; Paul Barton, "*Ya Basta!*" in *Latino Religions and*

Civic Activism in the United States, ed. Gastón Espinosa, Virgilio Elizondo, and Jesse Miranda (New York: Oxford University Press, 2005), 127–44; Richard Martínez, *PADRES: The National Chicano Priest Movement* (Austin: University of Texas Press, 2005); Lara Medina, *Las Hermanas: Chicana/Latina Religious-Political Activism in the Catholic Church* (Philadelphia: Temple University Press, 2005).

32. Seferina De León, interview by author, tape recording, Goshen, Ind., April 17, 2007.

33. Lupe De León, "Entrevista con Mary Bustos," *Ecos Menonitas*, March 1974, MHL.

34. Letter from Ernest Rodriguez to Vicente Ximenes, American GI Forum, July 2, 1968, Ernest Rodriguez Collection, American GI Forum file, 1963–69, Iowa Women's Archives, University of Iowa Libraries; Rafael Falcón, *The Hispanic Mennonite Church in North America*, transl. Ronald Collins (Scottdale, Pa.: Herald Press, 1986), 111–22.

35. "Spanish-Speaking Churches Caucus," December 1969, Chicago, Mennonite Church Office of Latin Concerns, 1969–1972, I-6-6, MCA.

36. Mary Bustos, "Corta historia de la Conferencia hispana femenil," *Ecos Menonita*, April 1978, MHL.

37. Mary Bustos, "Asi fue el principio: Conferencia femenil hispana menonita, 1973–1982," Hispanic Mennonite Church, I-6-6.2, MCA; Lupe De León, "Letter to Beulah Kauffman," Jan. 22, 1974, Hispanic Mennonite Women's Conference, 1974–1980, MBM Home Missions, box 2, Lupe De León file, IV-16-21, MCA.

38. How historians define "ethnic nationalism" remains a heavy debate, but as historian Jeffrey Ogbar contends, there are fundamental qualities that center on "self-determination, unity . . . people must view themselves as an organic unit, bound together with common experiences, historical myths and culture." All of these characteristics fit how Latinas/os in the Mennonite Church saw themselves. See Jeffrey Ogbar, "Puerto Rico en Mi Corazón: The Young Lords, Black Power, and Puerto Rican Nationalism in the U.S., 1966–1972," *Centro Journal* (fall 2006): 150.

39. Historians such as Ernesto Chávez suggest that Mexican Americans practiced complex political forms that went beyond "narrow-nationalisms." Chávez's conceptualization of Chicano nationalism "as a truly American phenomenon that at times encompasses the tenets of American liberalism" is an important framework for understanding the religious activism of Latinas/os. Ernesto Chávez, *"¡Mi Raza Primero!": Nationalism, Identity, and Insurgency in the Chicano Movement in Los Angeles, 1966–1978* (Berkeley: University of California Press, 2002), 5.

40. Andrew R. L. Clayton, "The Anti-Region: Place and Identity in the History of the American Midwest," in *The American Midwest: Essays on Regional History*, ed. Andrew R. L. Clayton and Susan E. Gray (Bloomington: Indiana University Press, 2001), 141.

41. Lupe De León interview.

42. Falcón, *Hispanic Mennonite Church*.

43. In *Crossing and Dwelling*, Thomas Tweed argues that these processes suggest that "emplacement was as significant as displacement," 81.

44. Guillermo Tijerina, *Iglesia Menonita Del Buen Pastor*, May 25, 1986, booklet commemorating the church's 25th anniversary, author's personal archive.

The Young Lords Organization in Chicago

A Short History

DARREL WANZER-SERRANO

The Young Lords Organization was a street-gang-turned-political-entity that originated in the Lincoln Park neighborhood of Chicago. Emerging as a gang in 1959, the Young Lords organized in response to the verbal and physical abuse Puerto Ricans were enduring from white gangs in the neighborhood. The Young Lords shifted direction in 1968 after their leader, José "Cha Cha" Jiménez, experienced a political conversion during a sixty-day stint in Cook County Jail on drug charges. Befriended by a black Muslim librarian while in jail, Jiménez began reading widely, most importantly the works of Martin Luther King Jr. and Malcolm X. He also began learning more about the Black Panther Party and, according to a 2012 interview, thought he could do "something similar to what blacks were doing but within the Puerto Rican community."[1] By the fall of 1968, Jiménez had reorganized and renamed the group the Young Lords Organization (YLO), instigating a concomitant shift in focus away from gang dealings and socialization, and toward more revolutionary ideals and activism. The newly reformulated group began by focusing, largely, on issues of urban renewal, poverty, and police brutality. By 1969 they were operating in coalition with the Chicago chapter of the Black Panthers (under the leadership of Fred Hampton, who had a significant impact on Jiménez) and the Young Patriots (a group of white leftists), which constituted the original Rainbow Coalition (fig. 5.2.1). According to an editorial in the first issue of their *YLO* newspaper, dated 19 March 1969, the organization wanted "a new society in which all people are treated as equal; a society whose wealth is controlled and shared by all its members, and not by a few; a society in which men and women view other members as brothers and sisters and not as people to be exploited and hated." The editorial went on to denounce police

5.2.1 *YLO* newsletter, vol. 1, no. 2, Young Lords Organization, May 1969. Courtesy of Young Lords Newspaper Collections, DePaul University Library Digital Collections.

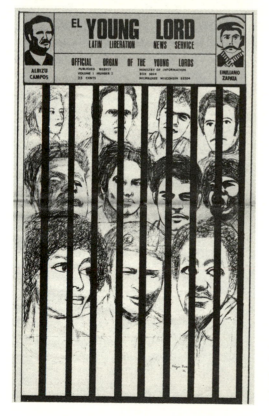

5.2.2 *El Young Lord Latin Liberation News Service*, vol. 1, no. 2, Young Lords, April 15, 1971. Courtesy of Young Lords Newspaper Collections, DePaul University Library Digital Collections.

brutality, advocate for a living wage, demand community control of institutions and land, and condemn all forms of colonialism. Featuring various programs organized around an insistence on self-determination, the YLO led numerous campaigns and takeovers, ran a breakfast program for children, addressed important health care needs, and fought gentrification. At one point or another, the YLO had branches in New York (where they published the *Palante* newspaper and split from Chicago to form the Young Lords Party), Milwaukee (where they published a newspaper called *El Young Lord*, beginning in April 1971), California, and throughout the Northeast (fig. 5.2.2). Faced with constant police repression, disorganization, and lack of resources, the Chicago YLO was defunct by 1972.

Note

1. José Jiménez and Ángel G. Flores-Rodríguez, "The Young Lords, Puerto Rican Liberation, and the Black Freedom Struggle: Interview with José 'Cha Cha' Jiménez," *OAH Magazine of History* 26, no. 1 (2012): 61–64. doi:10.1093/oahmag/oar058.

Additional Resources

DePaul University. "Young Lords Newspaper Collection." DePaul University Library, Digital Collections. http://digicol.lib.depaul.edu/cdm/landingpage/collection/younglords.

Fernández, Johanna. "The Young Lords and the Postwar City: Notes on the Geographical and Structural Reconfigurations of Contemporary Urban Life." In *African American Urban History since World War II*, ed. Kenneth L. Kusmer and Joe W. Trotter. Chicago: University of Chicago Press, 2009.

Jeffries, Judson. "From Gang-Bangers to Urban Revolutionaries: The Young Lords of Chicago." *Journal of the Illinois State Historical Society* 96, no. 3 (2003): 288–304.

Jiménez, José. *Tierra y Libertad: Two Interviews with Corky Gonzales and Cha Cha Jimenez*. Detroit: Radical Education Project, 1970. Accessed at http://alexanderstreet.com.

Vásquez Ignatin, Hilda. "Young Lords Serve and Protect." *Movement*, May 1969, 4–5.

¡*Viva La Causa!* in Iowa

JANET WEAVER

A pivotal period in Iowa Latina/o history occurred between 1967 and 1970, when a core group of Iowa Latinos and Latinas stood in solidarity with farmworkers employed in both California and in Iowa. These Iowa activists were the children of Mexican immigrants who had come to the Upper Midwest to work in the opening decades of the twentieth century. In the late 1960s, inspired by La Causa (The Cause), they led a coalition of activists to support the rights of California farmworkers to organize a union and bargain collectively (see fig. 5.3.1).

La Causa movement originated in the San Joaquin Valley in California after grape pickers went on strike in 1965 to protest an arbitrary reduction of their wages. When growers refused to negotiate with their union—the United Farm Workers Organizing Committee (UFWOC), AFL-CIO, led by Cesar Chavez—workers expanded their protest to encompass a consumer boycott of supermarkets across the country that continued to sell California table grapes. The grape boycott campaign was the brainchild of UFWOC cofounder Dolores Huerta. It heightened public visibility for La Causa and inspired Latinos throughout the United States not only to support the rights of California farmworkers but also to broaden that struggle into a movement for the rights of Latinas/os in other parts of the country across wide-ranging issues that included education, employment, and housing.

In Iowa, members of the Davenport council of the League of United Latin American Citizens (LULAC) Council 10 formed the Quad City Grape Boycott Committee. Together with representatives from unions, colleges, church groups, and civil rights organizations, they handed out leaflets, picketed supermarkets, organized rallies, and persuaded supermarkets, including A&P, to stop carrying California table grapes. Rita Vargas, the ten-year-old daughter of the head of the *huelga* (strike) committee, recalled that standing picket duty with her father in Davenport was controversial and sometimes frightening. People would yell,

5.3.1   Iowa governor Harold Hughes (center) with migrant worker activists José and Irene Guzman (right) after signing Iowa migrant child labor legislation into law in 1967. Courtesy of Irene and José Guzman papers, Iowa Women's Archives, University of Iowa Libraries, Iowa City.

swear, and even spit at them. Yet support for the grape boycott grew, and within a twelve-month period, UFWOC leaders Cesar Chavez, Dolores Huerta, Antonio Orendain, and Eliseo Medina had all visited Iowa.

The grape boycott campaign heightened public awareness of the plight of migrant laborers employed on Iowa farms. Each year over a thousand Mexican Americans traveled from Texas to work in the tomato fields around Muscatine, where H. J. Heinz Company operated a large cannery (fig. 5.3.2). Neither the collective bargaining provisions of the Wagner Act nor the overtime and child labor provisions of the Fair Labor Standards Act adequately covered agricultural laborers. LULAC members called for a tomato boycott to support a migrant child labor bill that would establish a minimum age for the employment of migrant children on Iowa farms. In a Republican-dominated legislature allied with corporate agriculture, the bill before the Iowa General Assembly in 1967 seemed likely to fail; it needed strong bipartisan support even to make it out of committee.

5.3.2   Muscatine Migrant Committee sign. Muscatine Migrant Committee records, Iowa Women's Archives, University of Iowa Libraries, Iowa City.

The bill faced opposition from H. J. Heinz Company and from tomato growers in eastern Iowa. Support for the bill came from church groups, unions, students, migrant agencies, and LULAC (figs. 5.3.3 and 5.3.4).

After months of heated debate, the bill not only made it out of committee but was passed and signed into law. This law had an important weakness, however, for it prohibited farmers from *knowingly* employing migrant children under ten and *knowingly* employing children under fourteen before and during school hours. The strategic word *knowingly* made the law unenforceable: farmers could always plead ignorance, placing the burden of responsibility with the parents.

IS THE PRICE
TOO HIGH?

The Earth buds forth its Savior.

SPRING! JOY!

The Earth is budding with life, and soon the migrant workers will be back in Iowa's rich fields to perform stoop labor — bending, hoeing, weeding, harvesting.

Their living conditions are generally deplorable. Let's act with Christian concern to change these conditions.

Bills to improve housing and sanitation in migrant camps and to regulate child labor are awaiting action in the Iowa Legislature.

Opponents of these bills include growers, legislators, and lobbyists from the Muscatine area, WHERE H. J. HEINZ CO. HAS A CANNING PLANT.

DON'T BUY HEINZ PRODUCTS
until the Legislature acts to correct deplorable conditions afflicting migrant workers in Iowa.

Contact the members of the Senate and House. Tell them you are a Christian who supports:

HF 146 – TO REGULATE MIGRANT CHILD LABOR.

HF 317 – TO IMPROVE HOUSING AND SANITARY CONDITIONS IN MIGRANT CAMPS.

"Whatsoever you do to
the least of My brothers . . . "

5.3.3   Flyer distributed at Iowa churches on Easter Sunday 1969. LULAC Council 10 records, Iowa Women's Archives, University of Iowa Libraries, Iowa City.

5.3.4   Iowa State LULAC director John Terronez (with sign), picketing National Food Stores in Davenport, Iowa. *El Malcriado: The Voice of the Farm Worker* (Delano, Calif.) 3, no. 12 (Sept. 15–Oct. 1, 1969): 13, retrieved from https://libraries.ucsd.edu/farmworkermovement/archives.

Iowa Mexican Americans stepped forward again in 1969 to support efforts to strengthen these provisions and regulate housing standards in migrant camps. Legislators heard testimonies of Latina/o activists describing deplorable conditions at migrant camps around Muscatine and Mason City. On March 19, 1969, fifteen hundred demonstrators gathered in Des Moines to show the strength of support for migrant worker legislation in Iowa. At the rally, the bill's sponsor, Representative John Tapscott from Des Moines, called for a boycott of Heinz Company products, while the director of UAW Region 4 called for a union organizing drive of migrant workers in Iowa.

Iowa legislators responded positively to these pressures. In May 1969, the Iowa legislature approved the migrant camp bill, effective immediately, and the next year Republican Governor Robert Ray signed a new Iowa child labor law that strengthened protections for migrant children on Iowa farms.[1]

Note

1. For a detailed account, see Janet Weaver, "From Barrio to '¡Boicoteo!': The Emergence of Mexican American Activism in Davenport, 1917–1970," *Annals of Iowa* 68, no. 3 (summer 2009): 215–54.

Work, Coalition, and Advocacy

Latinas Leading in the Midwest

THERESA DELGADILLO

JANET WEAVER

In this chapter we focus on the life and leadership experiences of Latinas in Wisconsin and Iowa.[1] Using oral histories and archival documents, we provide a view of how midwestern Latinas from a variety of occupations and ethnic backgrounds navigated barriers to opportunity throughout the twentieth century. Whether they worked at home, in factories or fields, or in white-collar and professional sectors, these Mexican, Mexican American, Puerto Rican, and Salvadoran women in the Midwest faced gender, ethnic, and racial discrimination in their efforts to build community, improve working conditions, and create new opportunities for themselves and their children. In responding to these challenges they often drew from the life lessons of their mothers and grandmothers, sometimes embraced feminist perspectives, and always cultivated solutions that took into account their gender, race, and ethnicity—known in feminist theory as an intersectional framework.[2] Because they engaged with Latinas/os as coworkers, small-business owners, professionals or managers, these differing economic positions influenced their activism and leadership. At times it focused on the interests of all Latinas/os as a racial or ethnic group and at other times it addressed the concerns of blue-collar workers, women, or businesses more broadly. We include Latina voices from varied ethnic and national backgrounds to consider how Latina experience shaped neighborhoods, workplaces, and organizations throughout the twentieth century.[3] We also recognize that the Latina/o experience may vary between an industrial city with a dense population like Milwaukee, Wisconsin, and that of smaller industrial hubs, like Davenport, Iowa. This research suggests that midwestern Latinas responded to and helped promote social and political movements and cultural changes leading to greater equity for Latinas/os in multiple spheres.

Our analysis of the significance of gender in Latina/o economic, social, political, and educational experiences contributes to a growing body of research on Latinas/os in the Midwest.[4] Creating an archive of Latina life in the Midwest that future researchers can draw from is a primary concern in our respective projects. In Iowa, little information existed about Latinas that had not been filtered through the eyes of outside observers. The records are *about* them, not *by* them. In both Iowa and Wisconsin there was little archival documentation of women's individual lives and experiences. As the women authors of *Telling to Live: Latina Feminist "Testimonios"* ask in their introduction, "after all this time, why are our stories still invisible in the academy?"[5] Oral history projects like ours have often gone hand in hand with efforts to gather written documentation on the lives of women. Such projects have been especially important for members of marginalized groups whose documents have not been valued by archivists, historians, or society at large.

The Iowa research discussed here comes from the collections of the Mujeres Latinas Project of the Iowa Women's Archives at the University of Iowa Libraries, launched in 2005.[6] The Wisconsin research discussed here is excerpted from oral history interviews conducted between 2008 and 2011. In our respective projects and in this chapter, we join historian Gabriela Arredondo in tracking the "whispers that remain of their migration processes, their settlement and adjustment experiences, and the decisions they made along the way."[7] Indeed, many of the women who participated in our research did so out of their own sense of having been left out of existing historical and scholarly accounts.

In these oral histories, Latinas discuss their reasons for leaving their homeland, the long and difficult journeys to far-off destinations, and the harsh living conditions they encountered as they constructed new lives in the Midwest. They describe themselves not simply as the partners of male migrants, along for the ride, but as agents of migration and immigration, workplace change and community building in their own right. Contrary to popular perception, Latina settlers in the Midwest often raised families while they worked outside the home in varied employment settings, including agricultural labor and factory work.

Most Latinas who came to the Midwest in the early twentieth century were either from Mexico or they were Mexican American migrants from the Southwest. Some who arrived in midwestern communities in the 1910s and 1920s journeyed *al norte* with families; others traveled alone with their children. In an example of step migration (from Mexico to Kansas and, later, Iowa), Martina Morado helps us understand her mother's decision to leave her home in the state of Guanajuato on the eve of the Mexican Revolution (fig. 5.4.1): "Soon after we left Mexico, the war of 1911 started. I don't know what would have happened to me if I had not come with mother when we did. We arrived in the United States on April 11, 1910. I was thirteen years and five months old. We settled in Kansas, a place mother didn't like much. We lived with mother's relatives and she worked to support me and my brother. We ran a rooming house and did laundry for people. As time passed, we got used to living in this place that we found so cold."[8] Mexicana migrants to the Midwest in this earlier time period managed boardinghouses, raised families, headed households and, in so doing, built a powerful sense of community in the face of discrimination and marginalization. They passed down their tenacity and resilience to daughters (and sons) who would continue to struggle for full economic and social inclusion and achieve legislative change in the 1960s and 1970s.

Mexican American Maria Monreal-Cameron attributes her family's migration from Texas to Milwaukee in the 1940s, after their migration from Mexico to Texas, to her mother's strong desire to improve the family's lot in life: "My older sister Juanita told me about these conversations between my parents, when they lived in Texas, about whether they would move to Wisconsin. . . . According to my sister . . . my mother would not give in. She insisted, 'No. I don't want to stay here. I want to go north, because I keep hearing that there's more opportunity

5.4.1   Martina Morado and her mother, Angela, Horton, Kansas, 1913. Courtesy of the Iowa Women's Archives, University of Iowa Libraries, Iowa City.

north.' That's what was important to her."[9] In recognizing their mothers as agents of change for their families, Morado's and Monreal-Cameron's narratives broaden prevailing conceptions of Latina/o migration to the region as largely driven by males in search of employment (fig. 5.4.2).

In the Iowa Mississippi River town of Davenport, Mexican women engaged in improving their community and employment situations in the tight-knit, interracial community of the Cook's Point barrio. A two-acre site with frame houses, boxcars, and boathouses, Cook's Point was home to roughly 270 residents, mostly Mexicans, but also African Americans and whites. Poverty was a defining feature of the barrio. Like many barrios scattered across the Midwest during this time, Cook's Point suffered regular flooding, its streets went unpaved, and its homes never had running water, electricity, or sanitary facilities. A city dump was nearby. Mexican nationals and their U.S.-born children inhabited this neighborhood in the 1920s and remained there until the early 1950s.

5.4.2   Julius and Martina Morado Vallejo with their children (left to right), James, Helen, Margaret, and Salvador, Horton, Kansas, 1921. Courtesy of the Iowa Women's Archives, University of Iowa Libraries, Iowa City.

Children raised in Cook's Point benefited from strong female role models like Mary Ramirez Terronez. Born in 1918 in the Mexican state of San Luis Potosí, Terronez had lived in Cook's Point since she was five years old. She married in 1936, raising five of her six children in the barrio. Like many women at "the Point," Mary supplemented the family income with seasonal work in the onion fields of nearby Pleasant Valley. She drove a truck, worked in a poultry-processing factory, and developed the practice of engaging onion growers in informal wage negotiations on behalf of barrio field workers. By the 1940s her fearless and outspoken nature had established the young, bilingual Terronez as a community leader and activist.

A Changing Demographic

By the mid-twentieth century, Latina/o life in the larger urban centers of the Midwest became increasingly inter-Latina/o as Puerto Rican and Cuban migrants made their way to the region. While Puerto Ricans were often recruited from the island for agricultural or industrial labor, Cubans arrived as refugees from the 1959 revolution that deposed dictator Fulgencio Batista. Latina/o neighborhoods, clubs, and organizations in Milwaukee, as in many other cities of the Midwest, took on an inter-Latina/o character. Specific ethnic or national groups established important cultural celebrations in their new midwestern homes, such as Puerto Rican Day parades or Mexican Independence Day festivities. Multiple Latinidades became a distinctive feature of Latina/o life in this region as Mexican, Tejana/o, Puerto Rican, Cuban, Central American, Dominican, and South American migrants encountered each other's cultural traditions and formed coalitions, but also experienced intra-Latina/o conflict.

Ramona Arsiniega, a working-class woman who moved to Milwaukee from her home country of Mexico in 1956, describes her involvement in Milwaukee's changing ethnic and cultural landscape through her involvement in the International Institute, an organization dedicated to the celebration and preservation of the world's ethnic life: "It was a big group. We met every month. We organized ethnic celebrations and parties—we'd take food and have a dance. We had one every month. It wasn't just Mexicans, either, there were Cubans and other Latina/o races involved. That's where I met many Cubans, who at that time were arriving in the U.S. There were also many other Latinos involved, Argentines and others—that's why it was called the International Institute!"[10] Arsiniega did not automatically relocate to Milwaukee to join her U.S.-citizen husband Jesus, but instead remained in Mexico for several years while her husband traveled back and forth for work. She chose to move only when she was sure of greater networks of support. In Milwaukee, Arsiniega kept a home for her husband and their six children. She contributed to the household income with work in leather and garment factories, a bakery, and finally as a drill press operator in a machine shop.

Elvira Sandoval Denk's father, Pedro Sandoval, settled in Milwaukee in 1924 with his brother Vidal, both of whom came directly from Mexico. Sandoval Denk, born in Milwaukee in 1942, was one of six children raised by Pedro and Margarita Sandoval. She and her sisters were strongly encouraged to pursue both education and music, and the sisters frequently performed as a singing quartet at family, cultural, and religious events in the Mexican community. Sandoval Denk was hired by the Milwaukee public schools in 1964 at the age of twenty-two, at a time when few if any Latinas/os were employed in K–12 education. She describes some of the intra-Latina/o tensions that she noticed among Latinas/os in the early 1980s when she worked as a bilingual guidance counselor. In this period, she worked at both Riverside High School on the northeast side of town, where the bilingual population was predominantly Puerto Rican, and at South Division High School on the near south side, where the bilingual populations was predominantly Mexican origin: "We were divided . . . I, myself, in order to be more 'authentic,' and even though my parents are both Mexican, I was Puerto Rican when I was on the North Side and Mexican when I was on the South Side. I could be 'one of us' in both places. . . . But it was planned and I knew about it . . . . and it opened doors."[11] In Denk's description, the deployment of "passing" among educators so that they might better serve students eventually led to greater acceptance among Puerto Ricans and Mexicans in the schools. Her story is one of several in the Milwaukee project that offer insight into how bilingual educators in the Milwaukee public schools bridged cultural and ethnic divisions to achieve a unified front between Puerto Rican and Mexican origin communities from which to work for change.

Daisy Cubias, who migrated from El Salvador to New York in 1965 then to Milwaukee in 1970, has a rich history in Milwaukee of involvement in feminist and Central American solidarity activism; Latina/o arts, education and labor advocacy; and creative writing (poetry). In one of several jobs she held in Wisconsin that involved working with multiple Latina/o groups, Cubias served the primarily Mexican immigrant laborers in rural areas of Wisconsin:

> The Latino migrant workers lived there in their own camps, provided by the employer. Most are from Mexico, and they work in Wisconsin every season. I talked to them. I did a very good survey of about seventeen pages long. I reported to the state. For every person that applied for residency, the state got money because it was a service for them. I found an old man, he was like seventy-something, and he came every year, crossing the border like he was undocumented when he was

a legal resident! I said to him, "*Señor*, you're a legal resident. Look at this paper; it says you're a legal resident." He was very surprised, and even more surprised when I told him that he could take a plane here, that he could travel here sitting down on a plane, and that the employer had to pay him minimum wage. . . . Yes, yes, I ran into those things. Oh, the employer never wants to tell them that because then they lose money. They were treating those workers like everybody's undocumented. Mmhmm, that's what big business is. . . . On that job, I went to all kinds of *fincas*, saw *vacas* and *lecherías* and pine gardens—everything. Those are areas where the work is all down by brown hands, brown sweat.[12]

The prominence of inter-Latina/o contact and collaboration in the life stories and leadership experiences of Latinas belies the assumption that Latinas/os engaged only with members of their own ethnic or national group, and it demonstrates how paths to leadership for Latinas often depended on their ability to work with other Latinas/os and forge inter-Latina/o collaborations.

Neighborhoods in Milwaukee and other large cities frequently housed multiple ethnic groups, while smaller industrial cities like Davenport, Iowa, and East Moline, Illinois, featured working-class enclaves that were both interracial and multi-ethnic. For example, Eva Savala grew up in the predominantly African American company town of Watertown in East Moline, just across the Mississippi River from Davenport. Originally from Mexico, Savala's parents had lived in the Midwest since the 1920s. She described the character of the neighborhood in the 1940s and 1950s: "It was really a wonderful neighborhood. Everyone took care of one another. We never locked our doors. When somebody needed help, it was there. It was like a big family. There were two more Hispanic families and three more white families, but the majority was a black neighborhood. It was more family than anything else."[13] In the 1950s and 1960s agricultural laborers from the Southwest, who had followed the migration stream through the Midwest for many years, began to "settle out" and live permanently in Iowa communities such as Muscatine and Mason City, where they found employment in local factories. Thus, in addition to seeing an interracial makeup of Latina/o neighborhoods in Iowa, we find an intergenerational mixing of old and new Mexican American residents in Iowa.

El Movimiento

Few women in our analysis pursued traditionally male-dominated routes to leadership. For Latino men in the region, leadership opportunities in the early to mid-twentieth century came in the form of traditional mutual aid societies organized along ethnic or national lines. From the mid- to late twentieth century, Latino men took on leadership in unions, social service agencies, and, in Milwaukee but not in Iowa, political office. However, for Latinas, the trajectory to leadership was more limited. In the early and mid-twentieth centuries, social networking and leadership options for many Latinas remained limited to their religious and parental roles. As Antonia Morales, who moved with her parents to Milwaukee from Mexico in 1926 at the age of two, observed, "After I married, I belonged to a group called the Society of Our Lady. . . . That was my only social life really, the church groups were the only social life then for me." Similarly, her involvement in a parent group was one a few avenues open to her to meet other women.[14]

In the 1950s and 1960s, however, Latinas in the Midwest joined and led civil rights organizations and movements throughout the region. In postwar Davenport, Mexican American women navigated traditionally patriarchal organizations such as the American GI Forum to achieve similar goals. Founded in Texas in 1948 to uphold the rights of Mexican American World War II veterans, the forum supported a wide range of civil rights issues. Mary Vasquez Olvera, a former Cook's Point resident whose two brothers were killed in the war, worked closely with her husband to form an Iowa chapter of the forum in 1958. She took a lead role in managing its affairs as well as its women's auxiliary, whose members were active in politics, education, and civil rights. By creating and demanding opportunities in leadership and political activism, forum women nurtured and passed on to their children an activist consciousness firmly rooted in their cultural heritage and identity. With the benefit of educational scholarships made possible by the fund-raising efforts of forum women, Olvera's children attended the University of Iowa.

When Council 10 of the League of United Latin American Citizens (LULAC) was founded in Davenport in 1959, its members included both women and men. While the council's predominantly male leadership served on the Davenport Human Relations Commission and local civil rights organizations, its women proved indispensable to the day-to-day running of the council, raising money for educational scholarships, supporting community projects, preserving cultural traditions, and fighting racial discrimination. Though they did not hold the top leadership posts in LULAC, these midwestern Mexican American women maneuvered deftly between family and community to uphold their rights in a largely patriarchal world. As a male leader of the council later recalled, "If the women didn't want to do it, it didn't get done."[15]

During the 1960s, Mexican American women in Iowa battled for the new opportunities embedded in the civil rights legislation of the day, moving outside Mexican American organizations to participate in community coalitions and fill leadership positions in local, state, and regional organizations. This activism follows the type of labor feminism described by labor historians.[16] In their efforts to achieve the privileges that define economic citizenship—such as access to better-paying jobs with decent working conditions, educational opportunity,

and adequate housing—Mexican Americans in Iowa challenged gender and racial inequity on multiple fronts.[17] In the eastern Iowa towns of Davenport and
Muscatine, their work encompassed a broad spectrum of progressive reform that
included picketing local factories and supermarkets. Collectively and individually,
these Mexican American mothers, daughters, breadwinners, and nuns worked
to end racial and gender discrimination.

The farmworker movement for justice led by Cesar Chavez and Dolores Huerta
had a profound impact in Iowa, where it found support from an interracial coalition of activists. This included members of LULAC, labor unions, the Davenport
Catholic Interracial Council (CIC), Congress of Racial Equity (CORE), the National Association for the Advancement of Colored People (NAACP), farmworkers, and women religious. Through this interethnic and interracial political work,
activists simultaneously supported the rights of grape pickers in California and of
migrant workers in Iowa's agricultural industry. Between 1967 and 1970, settled-
out migrant workers, Mexican American activist nuns, African Americans, and
Anglo allies fought high-profile battles in the Iowa legislature for the rights of
migrant workers, including the right to education for migrant children.[18]

In southeastern Iowa, Mexican American nuns Irene, Molly, and Lucinda Muñoz worked to improve health and safety standards for migrant workers on Iowa
farms. The children of first- and second-generation Mexican immigrants, they
grew up in a working-class neighborhood in West Des Moines. Irene Muñoz
trained as a public health nurse and joined the order of the Congregation of the
Humility of Mary (CHM) in Davenport. Responding to the ideals of liberation
theology and the principles set forth by the Second Vatican Council, Sister Irene
sought and received permission to live permanently in Muscatine where she participated in political and legislative battles in support of migrant worker rights.

In 1967, Sister Irene arrived in Muscatine, where for the next fifteen years she
provided health services to migrant workers. Working for the Muscatine Migrant
Committee in cooperation with doctors from the University of Iowa, she helped
organize the free medical clinic that served patients each Friday evening in the
basement of a local church. In 1973, with funding from the Department of Health,
Education, and Welfare, Sister Irene and her actual sister, Sister Molly, opened
the doors of the modest but welcoming Muscatine Migrant Clinic. Within four
years, the clinic was serving 2,500 migrant workers annually in thirty-two labor
camps in six counties along the Iowa–Illinois border. Growers did not always
welcome the sisters' regular visits to the homes of migrant workers living tem-
porarily on their property, as it afforded an opportunity for the nuns to inspect
the camps and report violations of Iowa's migrant housing law. Sister Irene had
"run-ins" with the farmers, and one farmer kept a shotgun to "throw her off [the
property]. . . Rabble rousers, they called us," she remembers.[19]

5.4.3 Margaret, Agnes, Florence, Benita, Dorothy, Linda, and Josephine Vallejo in front of their home in West Des Moines, Iowa, 1945, not far from the working-class neighborhood where nuns Irene, Molly, and Lucinda Muñoz grew up. Courtesy of the Iowa Women's Archives, University of Iowa Libraries, Iowa City.

Looking back on her years in Muscatine, Sister Irene Muñoz noted that "we really pushed for a lot of changes in the state of Iowa."[20] In 1969 she testified at a public meeting in Davenport called by the Iowa State Advisory Committee to the U.S. Commission on Civil Rights. Her testimony helped lay the groundwork for the creation of the Spanish Speaking Peoples Task Force, which led to the formation of the Iowa Spanish Speaking Peoples Commission in 1976, on which she served. She represented Iowa on a steering commission charged with the formation of a Midwest Council of La Raza in 1970. During this period, Sister Irene Muñoz identified with El Movimiento Chicano rather than the organizations of predominantly white, middle-class feminist movements. Yet by 1977, when the National Women's Conference convened in Houston, Sister Irene attended as the only Mexican American delegate from Iowa.[21]

The Late Twentieth Century

From the 1970s onward, Latinas in Iowa and Milwaukee forged new leadership experiences through involvement in the feminist movement and in professional employment opportunities made possible by the advent of affirmative action policies. Several Milwaukee Latinas cite their efforts to build bridges among groups and advocate for pan-ethnic Latina needs in the context of their new career paths. Yet even in these new venues women remained conscious of the need to continue to cultivate Latina and women's leadership and wrestled with ways to expand prospects for Latinas/os and women.

Olga Valcourt-Schwartz, voted Hispanic Woman of the Year by the United Migrant Opportunity Services and the Hispanic Chamber of Commerce in 1987, moved to Milwaukee from Puerto Rico to attend college in the early 1950s. She considered the coalitions she helped build among Latina/o groups as central to her sustained leadership role in the Milwaukee Public Schools Bilingual Education Program. She described her involvement in multiple Latina/o organizations, some of which are traditionally linked to particular ethnic or national groups:

> I have participated in the Puerto Rican parades, and was even the Marshall of the Parade one year. I was also active in Mexican Fiesta, taking part in committees to make sure that things ran smoothly. Among the many community organizations in Milwaukee where I have volunteered are the Spanish Center, the Great Milwaukee Chapter of the American Red Cross, and the Legal Aid Society of Milwaukee. Legal Aid helped lawyers to take cases for economically challenged people, especially in the Hispanic community. . . . I worked with several boards of Hispanic organizations, such as SER–Jobs for Progress [Service, Employment and Redevelopment], and the UCC [United Community Center]. I served different positions on the board of UCC for twenty-five years.[22]

For Valcourt-Schwartz, working full-time as an educator while also raising five children, coalition building among distinct Latina/o groups proved important to the ability of Latinas to make change. "When you put it all together," she recalled, "you're not just working for one faction but everybody has to come together for one vision. That's what happened."[23]

As the head of the Hispanic Chamber of Commerce of Wisconsin (HCCW), Maria Monreal-Cameron advanced three key initiatives to address women's needs: an Annual Salute to Hispanic Women Luncheon and Conference that recognizes women's leadership and promotes discussion of women's issues; proactive support for the formation of a new group, Hispanic Professionals of Greater Milwaukee, in which women figure more prominently than they do in the long-standing business organization she heads where members are predominantly male business owners; and a year-long and citywide effort to build resources to assist Latina victims of domestic violence, a project that emerged from discussions at the Annual Salute.[24]

In Iowa, Latinas also worked to improve employment practices and opportunities in industries beyond agriculture. Dolores Carrillo of Davenport understood that for many Mexican Americans, even a high school diploma did not guarantee union jobs with living wages such as those available to employees at the Oscar Mayer packinghouse in Davenport. A second-generation Mexican American, Carrillo had studied for the general equivalency diploma (GED) to encourage her daughters to stay in school. She became discouraged when, despite their educational accomplishment, her daughters were unsuccessful in gaining entry to better-paying blue-collar jobs. In 1970, the thirty-six-year-old Carrillo saw the issue in terms of race and gender-based discrimination.[25]

That year Carrillo organized a boycott of the Oscar Mayer plant to draw attention to the company's discriminatory hiring practices. She understood the power of public protest from her experience in the local grape boycott campaign. "That's what I learned from that—fight for your rights," she explained. "You have the same right as anybody else. Fight for it. If you don't get it . . . you can picket until you do." An experienced factory worker, Carrillo had expected to be hired on each of the numerous occasions she submitted her employment application. She suspected discrimination because, although the company stated that it was not hiring, Ernest Rodriguez—employed inside the plant at the time and also a member of the Davenport Human Relations Commission—confirmed that Anglos were being hired.[26]

Carrillo worked with Ernest Rodriguez and Mary Terronez to coordinate a protest. A welfare mother herself at the time, Carrillo gathered other Aid to Families with Dependent Children (AFDC, replaced in 1997 by TANF) mothers as well as African American women and men to picket the Oscar Mayer plant. Their signs proclaimed, "Brown is Beautiful," "Boycott Oscar Mayer: and "1970—Year of the Chicana." Their action received little attention from the Davenport media. However, an Iowa City feminist publication with national circulation, Ain't I a Woman?, covered the story. This front-page coverage by a feminist publication recognizes Latina labor feminism in Iowa, while the Oscar Mayer boycott illustrates the multifaceted and interracial approaches adopted by working-class Latinas as they confronted the dual oppression of race and gender discrimination.

Like Carrillo, Eva Savala applied for a nontraditional, blue-collar job, less as an expression of her feminist sensibilities than because it paid significantly more than the traditional women's jobs available in the region. The job involved manufacturing galvanized steel cabs for Mack semitrucks in East Moline, Illinois. In 1973, the McLaughlin Body Company hired Savala to fulfill its requirement to employ more women. She joined the union—UAW Local 1414—and entered a male-dominated workforce of hundreds with only three women working in the plant. Her job involved cleaning and hoisting truck parts after they came out of the press. The first few days were an unwelcome shock to Savala: "It was rough. I had never worked in a factory . . . and I almost walked out the first night—almost—because it was not very clean. The language! I was not happy. I would come home and be dirty from head to toe. I couldn't eat."[27]

Apart from the physically demanding work she did, Savala was routinely subjected to degrading sexual remarks from coworkers. As she pursued avenues for addressing her grievance, she read the union contract to consider her options. "[When] I went to my union steward," she recalled, "he laughed. I got upset." So she asked to see the contract. "After reading that book I said, 'I can do that.' So I went to the president of the union and complained and he said, 'Well if you don't like it, run against him.' So I did and I won." With just three months' seniority at the plant, Savala was elected to the position of union steward in UAW Local 1414, becoming the first woman and the first Latina to hold an office in that local. Savala attributed her victory to the availability of jobs and the high rate of employee turnover in the plant in the 1970s. Her male coworkers "didn't care. They thought it was a big joke and so I won."[28]

Eva Savala earned the respect of her coworkers, who continued to reelect her to represent them as their union steward for the next twelve years. She spearheaded local programs to uphold the voting rights of minority populations, gaining experience in community service and political action through the union. As she prepared to leave the plant and go on staff as the first Latina international representative for UAW Region 4, the personnel manager remarked to Savala, "if I was ever in a bargaining position, I would want you to represent me."[29]

Midwestern Latina activism around lesbian and gay rights emerged in the 1980s and 1990s. Carmen Murguia, a poet, writer, and LGBT activist in Milwaukee who is Mexican American, describes, in her oral history, how her parents' social justice work informed her own later development as an LGBT activist. Murguia describes her work as creating space for herself and for other gender-nonconforming Latinas. At the beginning of the twenty-first century, spurred by the tragic loss of a dear friend to antigay violence, Murguia helped to organize publicity and protests on the case.

> My friend Juana Vega was murdered in a hate crime. . . . I didn't want her to be just another poor, brown—she was dark-skinned—Mexican girl casualty on the South Side. . . . because there was more to this story . . . . I called LLEGÓ, a national Latino LGBT organization, and then I called the National Gay and Lesbian Task Force because I had been reporting for them in our local gay and lesbian paper the *Wisconsin Light*.[30]

Murguia's advocacy against antigay violence brought greater attention to gender and sexuality diversity among Latinas/os in Milwaukee, creating space for current and future queer generations to succeed—especially by creating a scholarship fund for queer youth—but her actions also rejected the cursory and superficial media attention given to violence against Latina/o youth generally.

Conclusion

The life stories of Latinas in this chapter underscore the importance of gender in collecting and recording history and of gender analysis in research on Latinas/os in the Midwest. Oral history provides a useful tool for beginning to fill significant gaps in our knowledge about the history of Latina experiences, but it should also prompt us to collect and preserve important documents in publicly accessible archival repositories. In other disciplines, we must remain attentive to gender in assessing, evaluating, and analyzing data and texts about Latinas/os in the Midwest. By conducting interviews with Latinas from many walks of life, we have presented a range of experiences—from agricultural and industrial laborers to professionals, and even women religious. In their own voices, Latinas from varied ethnic and class backgrounds describe the roles they and their foremothers played in shaping and leading their communities. These multiethnic and multiracial Latina/o communities, and their cross-class interactions, suggest important variations between Latinas in the Midwest and the better-studied urban metropolises of New York, Miami, Los Angeles, and San Antonio. In closing, we assert the need for further gender-based regional studies so that we can build a clearer picture of Latina history and experience in the United States.

Notes

Theresa Delgadillo thanks her students in fall 2015 Introduction to Latina/o Studies class for their comments and feedback on this research.

Except as otherwise noted, material in this chapter concerning Iowa Latinas is from Janet Weaver, "Barrio Women: Community and Coalition in the Heartland," in *Breaking the Wave: Women, Their Organizations, and Feminism, 1945–1985* (New York: Routledge, 2011), 173–88. Reproduced here by permission of Taylor and Francis Group, LLC, a division of Informa PLC. To see digitized documents from the Mujeres Latinas Project of the Iowa Women's Archives, see the *Migration Is Beautiful* website, migration.lib.uiowa.edu.

1. For further discussion of this research on Latinas in Wisconsin, see Theresa Delgadillo, *Latina Lives in Milwaukee* (Urbana: University of Illinois Press, 2015).

2. See also Kimberlé W. Crenshaw, "Mapping the Margins: Intersectionality, Identity Politics, and Violence Against Women of Color," *Stanford Law Review* 43, no. 6 (1991): 1241–99; Patricia Hill Collins, *Black Feminist Thought: Knowledge, Consciousness and the Politics of Empowerment*, 2nd ed. (New York: Routledge, 2008); Chela Sandoval, "U.S. Third World Feminism: The Theory and Method of Oppositional Consciousness in the Postmodern World," *Genders* 10 (spring 1991): 1–24.

3. Historian Marc Simon Rodriguez notes the interethnic character of Milwaukee Latina/o life in his work though his research does not explore its dimensions. See his "Defining the Space of Participation in a Northern City: Tejanos and the War on Poverty in Milwaukee," in *The War on Poverty: A New Grassroots History, 1964–1980*, ed. by Annelise Orleck and Lisa Gayle Hazirjian (Athens: University of Georgia Press, 2011),

110–30. See also *The Tejano Diaspora: Mexican Americanism and Ethnic Politics in Texas and Wisconsin* (Chapel Hill: University of North Carolina Press, 2011), 9.

4. Important research on Latinas/os in the Midwest includes Gabriela F. Arredondo, *Mexican Chicago: Race, Identity, and Nation, 1916–39*, Statue of Liberty–Ellis Island Centennial Series (Urbana: University of Illinois Press, 2008); Dionicio Nodín Valdés, *Barrios Norteños: St. Paul and Midwestern Mexican Communities in the Twentieth Century* (Austin: University of Texas Press, 2000); Zaragosa Vargas, *Proletarians of the North: A History of Mexican Industrial Workers in Detroit and the Midwest, 1917–1933* (Berkeley: University of California Press, 1993). Public histories include several volumes of photo collections focused on midwestern Latina/o communities and published by Arcadia Publishing of Charleston, S.C., in its Images of America Series. Historical research on Latinas, including Latinas in the Midwest includes Vicki L. Ruiz and John R. Chávez, eds., *Memories and Migrations: Mapping Boricua and Chicana Histories* (Urbana: University of Illinois Press, 2008); Vicki L. Ruiz and Virginia Sánchez Korrol, eds., *Latina Legacies: Identity, Biography, and Community*, Viewpoints on American Culture Series (New York: Oxford University Press, 2005); and Leonard G. Ramírez, *Chicanas of 18th Street: Narratives of a Movement from Latino Chicago*, Latinos in Chicago and the Midwest Series (Urbana: University of Illinois Press, 2011).

5. Latina Feminist Group, *Telling to Live: Latina Feminist Testimonios*, ed. Luis del Alba Acevedo et al., Latin America Otherwise Series (Durham, N.C.: Duke University Press, 2001), 6. The *Telling to Live* volume joins an important list of autobiographies, memoirs and multi-genre accounts of Latina experiences in higher education that has grown more extensive since the 1980s. See the bibliography of that volume.

6. Kären M. Mason and Tanya Zanish-Belcher, "Raising the Archival Consciousness: How Women's Archives Challenge Traditional Approaches to Collecting and Use, Or, What's in a Name?," *Library Trends* 56, no. 2 (fall 2008): 344–58.

7. Arredondo, *Mexican Chicago*, 109.

8. Martina Morado Vallejo, "The Labor of a Mother," 1956, Florence Vallejo Terronez Papers, Iowa Women's Archives, University of Iowa Libraries, Iowa City, hereafter IWA.

9. Maria Monreal-Cameron, interviews by Theresa Delgadillo, audio recording, Milwaukee, Wisc., Dec. 29, 2008, and Jan. 12, 2009.

10. Ramona Arisiniega, interview by Theresa Delgadillo, audio recording, Milwaukee, Wisc., Dec. 1, 2008.

11. Elvira Sandoval Denk, interview by Theresa Delgadillo, audio recording, Milwaukee, Wisc., July 2, 2010.

12. Daisy Cubias, interview by Theresa Delgadillo, audio recording, Milwaukee, Wisc., June 25, 2010.

13. Eva Savala, interview by Janet Weaver, tape recording, East Moline, Ill., Sept. 27, 2005, IWA.

14. Antonia Morales, interview by Theresa Delgadillo, audio recording, Milwaukee, Wisc., Aug. 21, 2008.

15. Quotation from LULAC Council 10 membership meeting, Davenport, Iowa, Feb. 26, 2012 (author's files).

16. Dorothy Sue Cobble, *The Other Women's Movement: Workplace Justice and Social Rights in Modern America* (Princeton, N.J.: Princeton University Press, 2004). For the role of rank-and-file women in legitimizing the demands of middle-class feminist organizations, see Dennis Deslippe, *Rights, Not Roses: Unions and the Rise of Working-Class Feminism, 1945–1980* (Urbana: University of Illinois Press, 2000).

17. On economic citizenship in general, see Alice Kessler-Harris, *In Pursuit of Equity: Women, Men and the Quest for Economic Citizenship in 20th-Century America* (New York: Oxford University Press, 2001).

18. Janet Weaver, "From Barrio to 'Boicoteo': The Emergence of Mexican American Activism in Davenport," *Annals of Iowa* 68, no. 3 (summer 2009): 215–55.

19. Irene Muñoz, interview by Janet Weaver and Iskra Nuñez, tape recording, Aug. 3, 2005, Ottumwa, Iowa, IWA.

20. Ibid.

21. United States. National Commission on the Observance of International Women's Year, *The Spirit of Houston, the First National Women's Conference: An Official Report to the President, the Congress and the People of the United States* (Washington, D.C.: National Commission on the Observance of International Women's Year, 1978), 280.

22. Olga Valcourt Schwartz, interview by Theresa Delgadillo, audio recording, Milwaukee, Wisc., June 21, 2010.

23. Ibid.

24. Maria Monreal-Cameron, interviews by Theresa Delgadillo, tape recording, Milwaukee, Wisc., Dec. 29, 2008, and Jan. 12, 2009.

25. *Ain't I a Woman? A Midwest Newspaper of Women's Liberation*, Aug. 21, 1970, IWA.

26. Dolores Carrillo Garcia interviews, interviewed by Janet Weaver, Sept. 22, 2005, and Sept. 26, 2006, IWA.

27. Savala interview.

28. Ibid.

29. Ibid.

30. Carmen A. Murguia, interview by Theresa Delgadillo, audio recording, Milwaukee, Wisc., July 5, 2010. LLEGÓ, the National Latino/a Lesbian and Gay Organization dedicated to organizing Latino LGBT communities through mobilization and networking, operated from 1987 to 2004 out of its Washington, D.C., headquarters.

Reconfiguring Documentation

Immigration, Activism, and Practices of Visibility

REBECCA M. SCHREIBER

Over the last decade, Chicago has become an increasingly significant and influential site of (im)migrant activism.[1] Amalia Pallares describes the importance of Chicago as a location of Latina/o activism in recent years by pointing not only to the 2006 Immigrant Rights March, but also to those of 2007 and 2008, which were larger in Chicago than in other cities. The participation of Latinas/os in these marches corresponds to the long history of Latina/o involvement in political activism in the city, with a focus on immigrant rights. According to Amalia Pallares, much of this activism has involved Mexicans and Mexican Americans and has concentrated specifically on the rights of undocumented (im)migrants.[2] Some scholars have also noted that the 2006 Immigrant Rights March, which involved (im)migrants protesting HR4437, the Border Protection, Antiterrorism, and Illegal Immigration Control Act, influenced the involvement of undocumented youth in forms of political activism during the years that followed.[3] Roberto G. Gonzales argues that this was related to their viewing other undocumented (im)migrants who were willing to publicly participate in an event to support (im)migrant rights.[4] This chapter focuses on how in recent years the strategies developed by undocumented youth activists in organizations such as the Immigration Youth Justice League (IYJL) in Chicago have circulated across regional (im)migrant activist networks in the United States. Tactics developed by IYJL have been employed within numerous campaigns, including No Papers, No Fear, which was organized by the National Day Labor Organizing Network (NDLON) and the Puente movement in Arizona.[5]

It was activists involved in the IYJL who developed the strategy of declaring their immigration status publicly as part of the Undocumented and Unafraid campaign in 2010 in order to speak out on behalf of the issues that concerned them.[6] This strategy is part of a broader approach in which activists take part in civil disobedience actions that they publicize through digital and social media. (Im)migrant activists in NDLON and the Puente movement drew on some of the same strategies in their organizing for the No Papers, No Fear campaign in Arizona.[7] Specifically, activists involved in the No Papers, No Fear campaign organized direct actions during which they publicly declared their immigration status in order to challenge state and federal laws that criminalize them.[8] In addition, I also examine a video that activists involved in the campaign produced from one of the actions that they uploaded onto activist websites, YouTube, and blogs. In exploring contemporary (im)migrant activists' use of media tactics, including video documentation of actions that they circulate on activist websites and on YouTube, this chapter investigates how these activists are using digital and social media as a means to organize against anti-(im)migrant state and federal laws. In analyzing the video *Si No Nos Invitan, Nos Invitamos Solos* [If you don't make space for us, we will make it ourselves]: *No Papers, No Fear Protest in Alabama* from a protest at a U.S. Commission on Civil Rights (USCCR) field briefing in Birmingham, Alabama, I focus attention not on (im)migrant activists' representation of their disruption of a USCCR field briefing in the form of a video, but rather on the way in which the activists made this action public by embedding the video in various online media platforms.[9] The circulation of the video exemplifies how (im)migrant activists are using digital and social media in order to publicize their political actions, and to connect with other undocumented (im)migrant activists across the United States.

In analyzing the tactics deployed by undocumented (im)migrant activists within the No Papers, No Fear campaign, I suggest that activists involved in the Ride for Justice Tour deliberately countered the policing and attempts at state surveillance of undocumented (im)migrants in the United States through forms of circulation, mobility and mobilization. Moreover, the tour worked in tandem with the activists' use of documentary footage of their actions, which they circulated through various media platforms. In examining the significance of publicity and visibility for (im)migrant activists who were involved in the campaign, I focus on the production of what I term counter-documents, including videos of their actions that are deliberately oppositional. Counter-documents are an image practice that references the sort of truth claims of traditional documentary in order to provide evidence that challenges official forms of documentation and the state's ability to determine the parameters of political inclusion. I contend that through the circulation of these counter-documents to other undocumented (im)migrants, allies, and supporters, (im)migrant activists adopt mobility as a political strategy, and as a means of mobilization, as opposed to seeking inclusion and citizenship. This emphasis on mobility and mobilization within the No

Papers, No Fear campaign is also part of a strategy to connect undocumented (im)migrant activists across different regions of the United States, which draws on elements of the Turning the Tides Summit and the tactics of some sectors of the undocumented youth movement.[10] Walter Nicholls has suggested that, while mainstream (im)migrant rights organizations have a centralized "top-down" structure, the undocumented youth movement developed a decentralized infrastructure, which as he argues "has drawn resources up and out from the grassroots . . . and circulated these resources horizontally to other DREAMers operating at local, statewide and national scales."[11] This strategy or structure involved networks in which undocumented youth activists located in states with more support for undocumented (im)migrants organized with activists in states with anti-(im)migrant laws, including Arizona, Alabama and Georgia, as well as in counties with 287(g) agreements.[12] For example, activists in Chicago, such as those involved in IYJL, were in communication with activists around the country. In the spring of 2011, undocumented youth activists involved in IYJL traveled from Chicago to join local activists to protest Alabama HB56: The Beason-Hammon Alabama Taxpayer and Citizen Protection Act and Georgia HB87, the Illegal Immigrant Reform and Enforcement Act of 2011. In Georgia, the activists collaborated with a local group on a civil disobedience action at the state capitol on June 28, 2011.[13] This action was streamed online, with supporters watching from all over the country. While the undocumented youth involved in actions that included civil disobedience risked being arrested, and possibly detained and deported, this did not stop them from participating.[14] These activists understood that publicizing their activism was a way to inspire other undocumented (im)migrants to act. Their protests in Alabama, which involved civil disobedience, also included the participation of an older generation of undocumented (im)migrant activists.

In the following section I examine the Immigration Youth Justice League's involvement in the development of the Undocumented and Unafraid campaign as an instance of these concerns and approaches to documentation and publicity. Then I investigate how some of the strategies developed by IYJL and other undocumented youth activists were deployed as part of the No Papers, No Fear campaign, focusing on a protest at a USCCR briefing in Birmingham, Alabama, in August 2012.

The IYJL Undocumented and Unafraid Campaign

The Immigration Youth Justice League (IYJL) was formed in 2009 by a group of undocumented students in Chicago, including Tania Unzueta Carrasco.[15] As Unzueta Carrasco and Hinda Seif describe, the formation of this organization signaled a break from undocumented youth activists solely focusing on getting the DREAM Act passed to their working on campaigns to prevent the deportation of undocumented youth who had been put into removal (deportation) proceedings.[16] They relate these changes within IYJL and the undocumented-youth movement to activists responses to the ways in which undocumented (im) migrants were being criminalized by the U.S. government.[17] Since its founding, IYJL has affiliated with national organizations, such as the National Immigrant Youth Alliance (NIYA), and local organizations, including the LGBTQ Immigrant Rights Coalition of Chicago. IYJL's involvement in the latter organization is related to its interest in "highlighting the intersections between the LGBTQ and immigrant communities."[18]

Undocumented youth activists in Chicago who founded the IYJL organized the first National Coming Out of the Shadows Day on March 10, 2010, exactly four years after the 2006 Immigrant Rights March in Chicago.[19] The campaign slogan for this event was "Undocumented and Unafraid." A press release, quoted Ireri Unzueta Carrasco: "We cannot wait anymore. Not while our parents are getting deported and our youth's dreams fall apart due to an obsolete immigration system that has failed us and the country."[20] In Chicago, this action included a march and then press conference at Federal Plaza, during which time seven young people announced their first names, stated that they were undocumented, and proclaimed their support for the DREAM Act.[21] By sharing their stories of how they learned that they were undocumented, these young people signaled that they were not afraid of letting the public know their immigration status.[22] Further, undocumented youth activists started to create videos as part of this campaign in which they stated their names and shared their stories of how they found out that they were undocumented, which they posted on activist websites and YouTube. Producing videos in which they declared their undocumented status was also a way for these activists to reach out to activists across the country.[23]

Even before undocumented youth activists started to lead their own organizations, they used digital media technologies as part of their approach to political mobilization. Scholars such as Seif have suggested that digital has been the medium of choice for undocumented young people who experience various limitations due to their immigration status.[24] Sasha Costanza-Chock argues that media production by undocumented youth has been "dispersed systematically across multiple media platforms, creating a distributed and participatory social movement 'world,'" which is characteristic of a process that he refers to as "transmedia mobilization."[25] As such, he contends that undocumented youth activists "engage in their own forms of 'transmedia mobilization,' by providing multiple entry points to a larger narrative that extends across platforms into face-to-face space and encourages participation."[26] Transmedia mobilization thus involves undocumented youth activists communicating with one another through forms of digital and social media in order to strategize and organize.

Following the first National Coming Out of the Shadows Day, undocumented youth activists in IYJL discussed the possibility of employing strategies such as civil disobedience in their attempt to influence immigration policy, and they spoke with immigration attorneys about the possible risks of their participation. Members of IYJL were involved in organizing the first civil disobedience action with other undocumented youth activists on May 17, 2010, the fifty-sixth anniversary of *Brown v. Board of Education*, when a group of five activists held a sit-in at Senator John McCain's office in Tucson, Arizona, calling on him to support the DREAM Act.[27] As a result of their participation in this action, four of the activists were arrested and sent to the Pima County jail. The next day, three of these activists were transferred to a processing facility run by Immigration and Customs Enforcement (ICE).[28] This action took place as an increasing number of undocumented (im)migrants around the United States were being placed in removal proceedings under ICE's Secure Communities program, which involved local law enforcement agencies in the policing and reporting of an individual's immigration status.[29] Participating in civil disobedience could thus have severe repercussions for these undocumented youth activists who could be detained or deported by ICE.[30] However, after eight hours in the ICE processing facility, the activists were issued a field-released supervision with no explanation from the Department of Homeland Security.[31] In this context, undocumented youth activists walked a fine line between bringing attention to their issues and becoming vulnerable to punitive state action.[32] Activist Mohammad Abdollahi realized around this time that "the more public we are with our stories, the safer we are." This statement by Abdollahi, a founder of DreamActivist.org and NIYA, suggests that declaring their undocumented status could instead serve as a form of protection for undocumented activists who want to participate in direct actions in order to publicize and draw support for undocumented (im)migrants.[33]

The focus on direct action and civil disobedience became part of a broader strategy developed by undocumented youth activists to protest anti-(im)migrant state and federal laws. Specifically, undocumented youth activists focused their activism on challenging U.S. immigration policies and programs, such as 287(g) and Secure Communities (S-COMM), which contributed to a significant rise in the number of undocumented migrants who were being arrested, detained, and deported. As such, undocumented youth activists acknowledged the disjuncture between the ways in which legislators had represented DREAM Act–eligible young people as "innocent," while viewing their parents as criminals. In 2011 undocumented youth activists in IYJL and other organizations started to plan actions that drew attention to the effects of federal immigration policies and programs. They also began to collaborate with activists in Alabama and Georgia to challenge the development of anti-(im)migrant state laws, including Arizona Senate Bill 1070 (SB1070) and copycat laws such as Alabama HB56 and Georgia HB87.[34]

The interest of undocumented youth activists in organizing against anti-(im) migrant state laws as well as U.S. immigration policies and programs such as 287(g) and S-COMM was in many ways a response to the localization of federal immigration policy. Monica Varsanyi and other scholars have written about the devolution of federal immigration powers to states, counties, and municipalities, beginning with the Illegal Immigration Reform and Immigrant Responsibility Act (IIRIRA, 1996).[35] While some states, countries, and municipalities have developed policies that are inclusive of undocumented (im)migrants, including sanctuary laws, or those that allow them to obtain drivers licenses or municipal ID cards, others have passed anti-(im)migrant laws that emphasize "attrition through enforcement," in addition to enforcing U.S. immigration policies and programs by participating in the 287(g) program and S-COMM. In response, undocumented youth and (im)migrant activists have developed political strategies to challenge local immigration policies as well as the participation of local law enforcement in federal immigration programs. Further, Walter Nicholls has suggested that the localization of federal immigration policy has contributed to the decentralized structure of some sectors of the undocumented youth movement, as mentioned earlier.[36]

No Papers, No Fear

In the summer of 2012, NDLON and the Puente Movement together with activists in the IYJL and other groups formed the No Papers, No Fear campaign. This included the No Papers, No Fear Ride for Justice tour, which involved a multigenerational group of forty activists, ranging in age from nineteen to sixty-five, traveling on a bus (referred to as the "undocuBus"), through eleven states from Phoenix, Arizona, to Charlotte, North Carolina, in order to publicly oppose and organize against the spread of SB1070 copycat laws and to protest against the federal government's immigration policies and programs, including S-COMM and 287(g), at the Democratic National Convention held in September 2012. No Papers, No Fear drew on initiatives developed at the Turning the Tide Summit in New Orleans in 2010, which emphasized what activists referred to as a trans-local approach to organizing.[37] This approach focused on organizing within specific locations, such as those that had introduced SB1070 copycat laws. The name of the campaign—No Papers, No Fear—was developed to challenge state laws such as Arizona SB1070, Alabama HB56, and Georgia HB87, which allowed police

to ask for the "papers" of those who they believed to be undocumented (im)
migrants. The No Papers, No Fear campaign continued the work already begun
by undocumented youth activists from IYJL and the San Gabriel Dream Team,
among others groups, who along with local activists in Alabama and Georgia
planned protests against these anti-(im)migrant state laws in 2011.

The strategies of (im)migrant activists who were part of the No Papers, No
Fear campaign emphasized mobility and mobilization through the undocuBus
tour, as well as through the circulation of videos of their actions, both of which
were also forms of publicity and visibility. As part of the campaign, activists
focused attention on anti-(im)migrant laws on the state and federal levels that
led to the arrest, detention, and deportation of undocumented (im)migrants.
Through their actions, activists on the undocuBus highlighted the cooperation
between local law enforcement and federal immigration officials in detaining
and deporting undocumented (im)migrants. They also emphasized the consequences of anti-(im)migrant state laws in Alabama, Georgia, and Arizona on (im)
migrant communities by co-organizing protests and workshops that addressed
issues such as how to contend with being in deportation proceedings.[38] During
their actions, some (im)migrant activists publicly declared their immigration
status while protesting the effects of state and federal immigration policies on
their communities.[39] However, (im)migrant activists also found that publicizing
their actions through the dissemination of videos that documented these actions
could protect them from being deported.[40] Thus, both the undocuBus tour and
the circulation of videos provided a form of visibility, a "counter-visibility," which
simultaneously disrupts state norms of inclusion and protects undocumented
(im)migrants against state violence. The ways in which undocumented (im)mi-
grant activists represent themselves in defiance to the machinations of the U.S.
government relates to Jonathan X. Inda's and Julie Dowling's notion of "migrant
counter-conducts" or "acts or forms of comportment that contest the criminalization and exclusion of undocumented migrants."[41] Their notion of "migrant
counter-conducts" is key to understanding undocumented (im)migrant activists'
strategies of counter-visibility and their production of counter-documents.

As part of an action at a USCCR field briefing in Birmingham, Alabama, held
on August 17, 2012, (im)migrant activists involved in the No Papers, No Fear Ride
for Justice tour produced a protest video, *Si No Nos Invitan, Nos Invitamos Solos:
No Papers, No Fear Protest in Alabama*. This field briefing focused on the civil
rights effects of state immigration laws following the U.S. Supreme Court *Arizona
v. United States* decision in 2012.[42] During these briefings, the USCCR, which
describes itself as an "independent, bipartisan agency charged with monitoring
federal civil rights enforcement," determines who will speak, which means that
those who are not on the agenda are not given an opportunity to publicly share

their perspectives with members of the commission.[43] While the speakers chosen to testify at this briefing varied from politicians to educators to individuals who ran organizations such as the Federation for American Immigration Reform (FAIR), the Center for Immigration Studies, and the Mexican American Legal Defense and Education Fund (MALDEF), not one undocumented (im)migrant was included on the agenda. This absence reflects the status of undocumented (im)migrants in the United States as permanently criminalized people and, as Lisa Marie Cacho argues, as members of groups who are "subjected to laws but refused the legal means to contest those laws as well as denied both the political legitimacy and moral credibility necessary to question them."[44] During the action at the USCCR field briefing, undocumented (im)migrant activists were involved in "unthinkable politics," sharing their undocumented status, and disrupting one of the speakers in order to testify themselves about the effects of anti-(im)migrant laws on undocumented (im)migrants. Thus, through their presence at the field briefing, these activists contributed their perspectives and experiences to a discussion that was initially based on their absence. This action, as well as the videotaping of the action, is an example of the activists' strategies of disruption, counter-visibility, and counter-documentation.

By August 2012, when this action took place, Alabama's anti-(im)migrant state law HB56 was considered to be the "toughest in the nation."[45] Members of the USCCR invited individuals, including Kansas Secretary of State Kris Kobach, the so-called "legal mind" behind SB1070 and HB56, to speak and answer questions at the hearing.[46] Considering that Kobach helped author SB1070 with Arizona State Senator Russell Pearce, it is not surprising that the action was timed to coincide with and thus disrupt Kobach's testimony. While Kobach was speaking, four participants in the Ride for Justice Tour, including Gerardo and MariCruz from the Puente movement, as well as Juan José from Teatro Jornalero Sin Frontera in Los Angeles and María from Mujeres Unidas y Activas in Northern California, disrupted the briefing by shouting in both English and Spanish about the effects of anti-(im)migrant laws, while holding signs indicating that they were undocumented (fig. 5.5.1).

During this USCCR hearing, these activists not only declared that they were undocumented but also spoke about the effects of these anti-(im)migrant state laws on their communities. The activists' emphasis on their undocumented status brought added significance to their physical presence at the briefing, focusing attention on the fact that they had overcome their fear in order to speak out against these laws. In their testimony, these activists indicated that they saw themselves as representing a broader community of people who had been affected by these laws. In her statement, María emphasized how immigration policies had violated her civil rights as well as those of her family members:

5.5.1   María in a still from *Si No Nos Invitan, Nos Invitamos Solos* [If you don't make space for us, we will make it for ourselves]: *No Papers, No Fear Protest in Alabama.*

Ya basta! Bola de corruptos! Mi nombre es María. . . . Soy madre de familia. He recibido mucha discriminación. Soy María Reyes. . . . Indocumentada y sin miedo! No tengo miedo! Aquí estoy! Deben respetar nuestros derechos! Son derechos civiles! Esto es una basura! Allí se las dejo, quédense con ella. No saben respetar el dolor humano. A mis hijos le han quitado la troca dos veces! Tienen que pagar dos mil dólares . . . para sacar aquel vehículo! Hace un año, perdimos nuestra casa. No hay derechos humanos!

[Enough! You are all corrupt. My name is María. . . . I am the mother of the family. I am facing powerful discrimination. I am María. . . . I am undocumented and unafraid. I do not have fear. I am here! You are supposed to respect my civil rights! They are civil rights! This paper [commission briefing] is trash. I will leave it here! You can keep it. You don't know how to respect human suffering. They have taken the truck from my sons, twice! They have to pay $2,000 to get this vehicle out! One year ago, we lost our house. There are no human rights!][47]

Within the context of the USCCR briefings, undocumented (im)migrants were "legally recognized as rightless" and as such were not viewed as having the "political legitimacy" to speak before the commission about the impact of laws like SB1070.[48] However, undocumented (im)migrant activists intervened in the USCCR field briefing in order to challenge the legitimacy of those involved, as well as to point to the ways in which it was devised to make their perspectives absent.[49] The activists' emphasis on their undocumented status brought added significance to their physical presence at the briefing, directing attention to the risks they faced in order to speak out against these laws. Further, the recording of the action and the circulation of the video on a range of media platforms brought attention and visibility to the ways in which these laws affect undocumented (im) migrants, as well as to the deliberate exclusion of those same people from the briefing.

What I would like to draw attention to is not just that (im)migrant activists recorded this action at a USCCR field briefing, but that the activists' circulation of the video accomplishes certain kinds of political work. The activists' decision to document the protest, and to post this video on the No Papers, No Fear website and on YouTube, was a means to publicize the action to other undocumented (im)migrants. This approach to documenting and publicity also demonstrates how those involved in this action have been influenced by strategies employed by undocumented youth activists, such as those in IYJL. Undocumented youth activists were some of the first to use digital and social media technologies, such as texting, Facebook, YouTube, and Twitter, to organize locally and nationally.[50] The use of media within the No Papers, No Fear campaign, including the internet and forms of social media, was a significant aspect of (im)migrant activists' political organizing. No Papers, No Fear has its own website, which describes the campaign and provides information on how to "engage," "endorse," and "converge" with the campaign. This robust site has a section featuring press coverage of the campaign; there are also a blog and a gallery of music, photographs, poetry, posters, videos, and instructions on how to submit work. Site visitors learn how to donate to the No Papers, No Fear campaign and how to receive information about the campaign through emails, Facebook, and Twitter. Further, the website is an archive of "counter-documents" that provide publicity and visibility for the campaign and that enable these activists to contribute to counter-networks comprised of (im)migrant activists and their supporters.[51]

In the context of the action in Alabama, the *No Papers, No Fear* website was a platform for political action, as the video served as a means to document the ways in which activists challenged state law, mobilized in support of the No Papers, No Fear campaign, and protected undocumented (im)migrants who took part in the action from being detained or deported. The media strategy involved in publicizing the action in Alabama was modeled on one that activists had developed after a civil disobedience action in Knoxville, Tennessee, during a stop on the No Papers, No Fear tour. As a result of this action, the (im)migrant activists who were involved had been arrested and thus faced deportation. However, activists from the No Papers, No Fear campaign posted videos of those arrested on the website, which included a message to call ICE to release them. Organizers of the No Papers, No Fear campaign who had built an email list, and a Facebook and Twitter following, were thus able to mobilize on behalf of those arrested. As a result, all of those arrested were released.[52] This approach was seen as a model for actions that followed, including the one in Alabama, as organizers believed that if these actions were publicized, the activists would not face arrest or deportation.

Conclusion

In examining the use of digital and social media by (im)migrant activists, it is important to attend both to the ways in which their videos circulate and how they address different publics and make possible forms of political action. For activists who were not involved in this action, as well as for allies and supporters, these videos may be their only access to these political actions by (im)migrant activists. As such, it is the broad circulation of these videos that is what makes these protests public. Thus, it is not just the interruption of the USCCR field briefing that can be viewed as a political act in this context, but also the ways in which representations of the protest circulate. By intervening in a USCCR field briefing on state-based anti-(im)migrant laws, and by circulating the video of their action on the *No Papers, No Fear* website, YouTube, and elsewhere, these (im)migrant activists were able to influence others to see what political acts were possible for undocumented (im)migrants.

As representations of their public activism, this video serves as a means for those within the (im)migrant movement to articulate the terms of their depiction and to make public political claims. What is significant about these activists' focus on visibility is the specific context of their enunciation. While the general liberal claim about "visibility" is frequently touted as necessary in order for certain marginalized groups to have a "voice" and be fully included in U.S. society, these activists' emphasis on the production and circulation of visual media is specific to the context of immigration policies that can render visibility a form of surveillance linked to detention and deportation. These activists deliberately and strategically publicize the actions of undocumented (im)migrants who engage in direct action, rather than reaffirm the norms of inclusion. These tactics are a response to the ways in which U.S. governmental agencies, including ICE, an arm of the Department of Homeland Security, have removed or threatened to remove undocumented (im)migrants through detention and deportation. As such, (im)migrant activists are not making general claims about the importance of being "visible" as an abstract form of empowerment and inclusion, but instead are publicizing their political actions as a means to draw attention to the effects of these laws on undocumented (im)migrants and to mobilize supporters while also inverting the visual terms of surveillance in order to shield themselves from possible detention and deportation.

While Chicago has been a center for undocumented (im)migrant activism, activists in Chicago have also supported local (im)migrant organizing in other parts of the United States, particularly the Southeast. This organizing across regional networks developed as part of a strategy within some sectors of the undocumented (im)migrant and youth movement to confront the localization of federal immigration policies, as well as the introduction of SB1070 copycat laws. The strategies developed by IYJL activists in Chicago—including undocumented youth declaring their immigration status during political actions, as well as other tactics utilized by undocumented youth activists, such as the distribution of videos of their actions through digital and social media—were taken up by undocumented (im)migrant activists as part of the No Papers, No Fear campaign. This form of immigration activism combines trans-local place-based events with an extension of the political to social media counter-documents.

Drawing from the strategies of undocumented youth activists involved in the IYJL, the No Papers, No Fear campaign invokes circulation, mobility, and mobilization as political strategies, rather than seeking inclusion or citizenship. Further, these activists reworked notions of visibility from an *abstract* form of empowerment to a more *specific* strategy, which involved publicizing their political actions that directly challenged anti-(im)migrant laws on the state and federal levels. The activists' decision to organize an action during a USCCR briefing on the impact of state-based laws, such as SB1070, was thus part of their strategy to publicize their perspectives regarding the effects of laws that advocate "attrition through enforcement" on undocumented (im)migrants. Further, circulating videos that represent their activism enabled those within the (im)migrant movement to provide an example of organizing that then served as a model for other undocumented (im)migrants.[53] In their rejection of liberal claims to the inherently transformative capacity of visibility, the strategies practiced by these activists challenge conventions of representation and documentation that demand inclusion as a normative imperative.

Notes

1. My use of "(im)migrant" as opposed to "immigrant" draws from the work of Mae Ngai and others who argue that scholars should not privilege permanent settlement over other kinds of migration. See Mae Ngai, *Impossible Subjects: Illegal Aliens and the Making of Modern America* (Princeton, N.J.: Princeton University Press, 2004).

2. Amalia Pallares, "The Chicago Context," in *¡Marcha!: Latino Chicago and the Immigrant Rights Movement*, ed. Amalia Pallares and Nilda Flores-González (Urbana: University of Illinois Press, 2010), 38.

3. I describe these individuals as undocumented "youth" activists to distinguish them from either DREAM activists or (im)migrant activists who are not DREAM Act eligible

due to their age. However, I am aware that it isn't entirely accurate to use the term "youths" to describe activists whose ages span from teenagers to young adults. I have intentionally withheld surnames of activists in this essay

4. See Roberto G. Gonzales, "Left Out but Not Shut Down: Political Activism and the Undocumented Student Movement," in *Governing Immigration through Crime: A Reader*, ed. Jonathan X. Inda and Julie A. Dowling (Stanford, Calif.: Stanford University Press, 2013), 269–84.

5. NDLON's self-described mission is to "improve the lives of day laborers in the United States." See www.ndlon.org/en/. According to their website, Puente "promotes justice, non-violence, interdependence and human dignity. Puente Arizona works to empower the community and build bridges by working collaboratively with various organizations and individuals." See www.puenteaz.org.

6. See the "Who We Are" webpage at the IYJL website, www.iyjl.org/whoweare/.

7. In addition to drawing on strategies from undocumented youth activists in IYJL and other groups, the No Papers No Fear campaign also developed some of its strategies from the previous work of NDLON and the Puente movement during the Alto Arizona campaign, as well as approaches that emerged out of the Turning the Tides Summit in New Orleans in September 2010. B. Loewe, NDLON staff member, phone interview with author, Sept. 26, 2012.

8. It should be noted that there are limits to these strategies for undocumented (im) migrants, since any evidence of a criminal record could lead to their arrest, detention and deportation. Nicholas De Genova and Natalie Peutz suggest that we "consider deportation as a disciplinary practice while also an instrument of state sovereignty that renders certain populations 'deportable,' regardless of their practical connections or affective ties to the 'host' society." Nicholas De Genova and Natalie Peutz, introduction, in *The Deportation Regime: Sovereignty, Space and the Freedom of Movement*, ed. Nicholas De Genova and Natalie Peutz (Durham, N.C.: Duke University Press, 2010), 5.

9. *Si No Nos Invitan, Nos Invitamos Solos: No Papers, No Fear Protest in Alabama*, video, dir. Barni Axmed Qaasim (Puente), posted Aug. 18, 2012, www.youtube.com/watch?v =Iaj95A8ac8U. Qaasim is a member of the Puente movement.

10. According to its website, "Turning the Tide seeks to create a coordinated network of community organizations to build power in our communities in order to turn the tide against criminalization." See http://altopolimigra.com/, accessed Dec. 18, 2016.

11. Walter Nicholls, *The DREAMers: How the Undocumented Youth Movement Transformed the Immigrant Rights Debate* (Stanford, Calif.: Stanford University Press, 2013), 116–17. Nicholls notes that the term *DREAMer* was developed by professional rights associations that attempted to get the DREAM Act passed. He also mentions that in creating the "DREAMer," these organizations specified that "these youths were exceptionally good immigrants and particularly deserving of legalization" (13).

12. These laws include Arizona's SB1070 and copycat laws in Alabama and Georgia. According to ICE, "the 287(g) program . . . allows a state and local law enforcement entity to enter into a partnership with ICE, under a joint Memorandum of Agreement (MOA). The state or local entity receives delegated authority for immigration enforcement within

their jurisdictions." U.S. Immigration and Customs Enforcement, "Delegation of Immigration Authority Section 287(g) Immigration and Nationality Act," U.S. Immigration and Customs Enforcement, Immigration Enforcement, www.ice.gov/287g/.

13. Hinda Seif, "Unapologetic and Unafraid: Immigrant Youth Come out from the Shadows," *New Directions for Child and Adolescent Development* 2011, no. 134 (winter 2011): 72. On their website *The Dream Is Coming*, these local activists articulated their motivation in protesting HB87: "We are compelled by our frustration and the fierce urgency of our dreams to act as agents of our destinies and be the catalyst for a future in which we are empowered, mobilized, and living with the dignity we deserve. We are group of undocumented youth who worked for years on a path to legalization. We are at a point in our movement where radical action has become necessary for ourselves and our communities." Quoted in Cindy Casares, "Watch 'Georgia 6' Undocumented Students Get Arrested While Protesting at State Capital," *Guanabee*, June 29, 2011, www.guanabee.com, accessed July 24, 2012.

14. Nataly Ibarra, a teenager who participated in the action, explained her motivation in joining the movement to a local journalist: "The message we're trying to send is that it's been too many times that we've waited for someone else to do something. This isn't a time to be scared anymore." She also believed that others would join them, suggesting that "other young people seeing that we are able to stand up will do the same." Nataly Ibarra quoted in Kiri Walton, "Undocumented Pebblebrook Student Speaks Out after Arrest," *South Cobb Patch*, June 29, 2011, accessed July 24, 2012.

15. Tania A. Unzueta Carrasco and Hinda Seif, "Disrupting the Dream: Undocumented Youth Reframe Citizenship and Deportability through Anti-Deportation Activism," *Latino Studies* 12, no. 2 (2014): 287–88.

16. Ibid, 288. Another group that focused on anti-deportation campaigns at this time was the undocumented-led online organization DreamActivist.org (ibid.). For further information, see DREAM Act in the glossary.

17. Part of the IYJL mission statement reflects this position: "[the group is] led by undocumented youth working towards full recognition of the rights and contributions of all immigrants through education, leadership development, policy advocacy, resource gathering and mobilization." Immigrant Youth Justice League, "Who We Are," Immigrant Youth Justice League, www.iyjl.org/whoweare/, accessed July 18, 2012.

18. IYJL, "Who We Are." IYJL also notes that "IYJL members have come out as 'undocuqueer' and used their stories for advocacy and creating community." Ibid. For a more in-depth analysis of the strategy of "coming out" as undocumented, see Karma R. Chávez, "Coming Out as Coalitional Gesture?," ch. 3 in *Queer Migration Politics: Activist Rhetoric and Coalitional Possibilities* (Urbana: University of Illinois Press, 2013).

19. This strategy reflected both the presence of gay and lesbian undocumented youth in positions of leadership, as well as a queer approach within the undocumented youth movement. According to Michael Warner, "'queer' rejects a minoritizing-logic of toleration or simple political-interest representation in favor of a more thorough resistance to regimes of the normal." Michael Warner, introduction, in *Fear of a Queer Planet: Queer Politics and Social Theory*, ed. Michael Warner (Minneapolis: University of Minnesota Press, 1993), xxvi.

20. They added "Unapologetic" to the slogan in 2011. Immigrant Youth Justice League, "National Come Out of the Shadows Day!," Immigrant Youth Justice League, Feb. 17, 2010, www.iyjl.org/national-coming-out-of-the-shadows-day/, accessed Dec. 18, 2016.

21. It should be noted that since 2010 undocumented youth activists in IYJL and other organizations have been critical of the ways in which they represented themselves as having certain "normative characteristics." Unzueta Carrasco and Seif, "Disrupting the Dream," 291.

22. Aswini Anburajan notes that both public rallies and social media have been a means for undocumented (im)migrant activists "to take away the stigma associated with being paperless." Aswini Anburajan, "Immigrant Youth 'Come Out' as Undocumented, Push for DREAM Act," *Feet in 2 Worlds: Telling the Stories of Today's Immigrants*, March 21, 2011, http://fi2w.org/2011/03/21/immigrant-youth-come-out-as-undocumented/.

23. Nadia Sol Ireri Unzueta Carrasco, untitled presentation at "Everyday Forms of Popular Power: Art, Media and Immigration" symposium, Nov. 9, 2012, University of New Mexico.

24. Specifically, Hinda Seif contends that "digital media allows them [undocumented students] to network nationally and internationally and express themselves with less peril." Seif, "Unapologetic and Unafraid," 71.

25. Costanza-Chock defines "transmedia mobilization" as "a critical emerging form for networked social movements to circulate their ideas across platforms; it involves consciousness building, beyond individual campaign messaging; it requires co-creation and collaboration by different actors across social movement formations; it provides roles and actions for movement participants to take on in their daily life; it is open to participation by the social base of the movement, and it is the key strategic media form for an era of network social movements." Sasha Costanza-Chock, "*Se Ve, Se Siente*: Transmedia Mobilization in the Los Angeles Immigrant Rights Movement" (PhD diss., University of Southern California, 2010), 115. See also Sasha Costanza-Chock, *Out of the Shadows, into the Streets! Transmedia Mobilization in the Immigrant Rights Movement* (Cambridge, Mass.: MIT Press, 2014).

26. Costanza-Chock, "*Se Ve, Se Siente*," 190.

27. Julia Preston, "Illegal Immigrant Students Protest at McCain Office," *New York Times*, May 17, 2010, www.nytimes.com.

28. See "Undocumented Youth Leaders Released, Still Facing Deportation," *Dream Act—Texas*, Breaking News, May 19, 2010, http://dreamacttexas.blogspot.com, accessed April 8, 2013.

29. ICE's Secure Communities initiative, a "comprehensive plan to identify and remove criminal aliens," involves the use of "biometric identification technologies," which provides state and local law enforcement agencies with the equipment to perform record checks of both the criminal history and immigration status for those in their custody. The results of these screenings are then disseminated to state and local law enforcement agencies and to ICE. U.S. Immigration and Customs Enforcement, "Secure Communities," www.ice.gov, accessed Sept. 15, 2010 (inactive). Since the Secure Communities program was first enacted, ICE has detained and deported hundreds of thousands of undocumented

migrants, including young undocumented migrants who came to the United States with their parents as young children.

30. In an interview with Sasha Costanza-Chock about this strategy, one activist stated that "some people think it's a perfect way of just giving ourselves up. However, more and more we're looking at these kinds of strategies." Costanza-Chock, "*Se Ve, Se Siente*," 195.

31. According to journalist Maggie Jones, "while the Obama administration is deporting a record number of immigrants convicted of crimes, the Department of Homeland Security has so far spared undocumented youth who have been arrested during DREAM Act protests." Maggie Jones, "Coming Out Illegal," *New York Times Magazine*, Oct. 21, 2010.

32. Anburajan, "Immigrant Youth 'Come Out' as Undocumented."

33. Mohammad Abdollahi quoted in Alan Gomez, "DREAMers Personalize Cases to Stall Deportation," *USA Today*, March 12, 2012, http://usatoday30.usatoday.com/news/nation/story/2012–03–12/dream-act-illegal-immigration/53502528/1, accessed Nov. 13, 2016.

34. For example, as Unzueta Carrasco and Seif note, a member of IYJL moved to Georgia in 2011 in order "to support the creation of a local undocumented-led advocacy group in the state, the Georgia Undocumented Youth Alliance." Unzueta Carrasco and Seif, "Disrupting the Dream," 291.

35. However, as Varsanyi contends, it wasn't until after 9/11 that state and local enforcement agencies signed 287(g) agreements. See Monica W. Varsanyi, "Immigration Policy Activism in U.S. Cities and States: Interdisciplinary Perspectives," in *Taking Local Control: Immigration Policy Activism in U.S. Cities and States*, ed. Monica Varsanyi (Stanford, Calif.: Stanford University Press, 2010).

36. Nicholls, *DREAMers*, 116–17.

37. Loewe interview.

38. Chris Garcia, executive director, Puente movement, interview by members of Generation Justice, KUNM, Albuquerque, N.M., broadcast, Sept. 16, 2012.

39. Legal scholars Rose Cuison Villazor and Elizabeth Glaser wrote about the decision of those on the Ride for Justice Tour to "come out" as undocumented, noting that the effects of this action would vary from person to person. For some, becoming public about their undocumented status might mean deportation, whereas for others, it might lead to "discretionary relief from removal (temporary or permanent) and the possibility of adjusting their status to permanent legal resident." Rose Cuison Villazor and Elizabeth Glaser, "A First Step," *New York Times*, Aug. 1, 2012, www.nytimes.com.

40. Sarah Lai Stirland, "Website Yes, Legal Status, No: 'No Papers, No Fear' Hopes to Build a Movement for Undocumented Immigrations," http://nopapersnofear.org, accessed Dec. 18, 2016.

41. Inda's and Dowling's concept of "migrant counter-conducts" draws on Michel Foucault's notion of "counter-conduct," which he describes as "the sense of struggle against the processes implemented for conducting others." Michel Foucault, *Security, Territory, Population: Lectures at the Collège de France, 1977–1978* (New York: Palgrave McMillan, 2007), 201. Expanding on Foucault's definition of counter-conduct, Inda and Dowling explain further that it indicates that there is a "strategic reversibility to power relations such that any governmental effort to shape the conduct of individuals and populations is

interwoven with dissenting counter-conducts." Jonathan X. Inda and Julie A. Dowling, "Introduction: Governing Migrant Illegality," in *Governing Immigration through Crime: A Reader*, ed. Julie A. Dowling and Jonathan Xavier Inda (Stanford, Calif.: Stanford University Press, 2013), 24.

42. See the press release: U.S. Commission on Civil Rights, "U.S. Commission on Civil Rights Announces Agenda for Alabama Field Briefing on Civil Rights Effects of State Immigration Laws," press release, Aug. 3, 2012, www.usccr.gov.

43. USCCR mission statement at www.usccr.gov/about/index.php. The press release indicates that "members of the public and interested organizations are invited to submit written statements for the record on the specific topic of the briefing by sending them to: immigration2012@USCCR.gov." U.S. Commission on Civil Rights, "U.S. Commission on Civil Rights Announces Agenda."

44. Lisa Marie Cacho, *Social Death: Racialized Rightlessness and the Criminalization of the Unprotected* (New York: New York University Press, 2012), 6.

45. Diane McWhorter, "The Strange Career of Juan Crow," *New York Times*, June 16, 2012, www.nytimes.com. Due to a federal lawsuit initiated by the National Immigration Law Center, the American Civil Liberties Union Foundation and ACLU Foundation of Alabama, the Mexican American Legal Defense and Education Fund and other organizations, specific key provisions of HB56 were blocked in October 2013: requiring schools to verify the immigration status of newly enrolled K–12 students; criminalizing the solicitation of work by unauthorized immigrants; a provision that made it a crime to provide a ride to undocumented immigrants or to rent to them; a provision that infringed on the ability of individuals to contract with someone who was undocumented and a provision that criminalized failing to register one's immigration status. (Lawsuits also led to the blocking of key provisions of laws in Arizona, South Carolina, and Georgia.) Southern Poverty Law Center, "SPLC Victorious against Alabama Anti-Immigrant Law," Southern Poverty Law Center, News, Oct. 28, 2013, www.splcenter.org., accessed Oct. 30, 2013. See also Julia Preston, "Alabama: Deal Reached over Immigration Crackdown," *New York Times*, Oct. 30, 2013, A17.

46. See U.S. Commission on Civil Rights, "U.S. Commission on Civil Rights Announces Agenda." In a blog post that Puente member Gerardo wrote for the IYJL website after the briefing, he describes his experience listening to Kobach's testimony regarding these anti-(im)migrant state laws, which differed from Gerardo's perceptions of how SB1070 had affected undocumented (im)migrants in Tucson: "I remember sitting there and listening to Kobach speak about the importance of SB1070, and how people who were not doing anything wrong should have nothing to fear. He said that the law did not lead to racial profiling, or to fear. Meanwhile, I remember thinking about the fear and anger that I have felt, and seeing my neighborhood change. Every day in Arizona, I see people leave their homes out of fear of the immigration laws in our state. There are abandoned homes, empty lots, closed stores, and people displaced. I see children with fear, mothers crying, and people without freedom to move around freely in their own neighborhoods." Gerardo, "Fearless and Speaking for Ourselves," *No Papers No Fears*, blog, Aug. 18, 2012, http://nopapersnofear.org.

47. This testimony is captured in *Si No Nos Invitan, Nos Invitamos Solos*.

48. Cacho, *Social Death*, 7.

49. While some of the statements articulated by these activists resemble the positions taken up by those involved in the mainstream (im)migrant rights movement, it is important to contextualize these comments in relation to Cacho's argument that "because undocumented immigrants are often refused recognition as people with the right to demand rights and just treatment, they must frame their demands outside the arbitrary and absolute confines of U.S. law by drawing on different moral rubrics that could confer the right to demand rights such as labor rights, human rights, or the 'natural' rights of nuclear families." Cacho, *Social Death*, 131. However, she also mentions that, by saying they are not criminals, but mothers, human beings, etc. they "unintentionally reify other legally vulnerable, legally constructed categories" (132).

50. As numerous scholars have noted, these activists' use of these forms of digital media increased the visibility, size, and impact of their movement. See for example, Costanza-Chock, "*Se Ve, Se Siente*," 188.

51. See *No Papers, No Fear: Ride for Justice* at http://nopapersnofear.org/.

52. Stirland, "Website Yes, Legal Status, No."

53. Ibid.

Afterword

Intimate (Trans)Nationals

FRANCES R. APARICIO

Nothing is like Chicago.
—Milagros

Intralatinas/os in Chicago

Milagros, a Chicago-born MexiRican, describes her city of birth as an exceptional cultural space where MexiRicans feel a sense of belonging. She juxtaposes the Windy City—where "you actually have both of us, both of our communities here"—to the East and West Coasts, where, during her travels there, "you do feel a little bit lonely."[1] In contrast to the traditional and deep-seated profiles of a Puerto Rican–dominated New York, a Mexican or Chicana/o Los Angeles, and a Cuban American Miami, Chicago has been historically characterized as the city of Latinidad, a sort of exceptionalist paradigm in which no national Latin American group supposedly dominates, although Mexicans constitute 79 percent of Latina/o Chicago.[2] Yet, despite the dominant presence of Mexicanos, this urban center includes nineteen Latin American nationalities in its population, clearly making it one of the most diverse Latina/o cities in the United States.[3] In addition, the long history of Mexican and Puerto Rican marriages and social interactions since the late 1930s has made Chicago a space of Latinidad.[4] Southern California has witnessed similar MexiRican marriages in the first half of the twentieth century, and in New York, Puerto Ricans and Cubans lived and worked together since the turn of the twentieth century. Thus, Milagros's characterizations of the East and West Coasts as geo-cultural regions where she could not find other MexiRicans is not historically accurate, although it is subjectively true.[5]

Milagros's reference to feeling "lonely" in a "different coast" points to a real, public invisibility and lack of acknowledgment nationwide about Intralatinas/

os in the United States, that is, subjects who are of two or more Latin American national heritages. Hailing Angie Chabram-Dernersesian's call in 1994 for "break[ing] out of the prisonhouse of nationalism" and for engaging the "social panorama" of "mixed racial and ethnic identities" in Los Angeles as a result of "global transnational identities . . . fashioning particular ethnic subjects," this research project addresses the dearth of scholarship and academic attention to Latinas/os of mixed national heritages as a sector of our population.[6] Famous Latinas/os—such as federal judge Pedro Castillo and Alderman Carlos Ramírez-Rosa in Chicago, civil rights activist Silvia Méndez in Southern California, broadcast journalist Natalie Morales in New York, actress Zoë Saldana in Hollywood, poet Emanuel Xavier in Brooklyn, and novelist Cristina García in Los Angeles—are all of mixed Latin American nationalities. Yet this national hybridity remains undocumented and unacknowledged publicly. In this chapter I share a select number of anecdotes from interviews with Chicago-based Intralatinas/os to illustrate how they negotiate between their two or more national identities and how they get racialized relationally by both national communities. Given the long history of social interactions between Mexicans and Puerto Ricans in Chicago, it is appropriate to situate our study of Intralatina/o subjects in Chicago as a model for future scholarship on these mixed identities.

Chicago as a Site of Latinidad

Latina/o Chicago demographics challenge the still-strong, national, segmented frameworks that inform our scholarship. The 2010 U.S. Census indicates that Latinas/os constitute 28.9 percent of the Chicago population and 15.8 percent of Illinois. In Chicago, Mexicans are by far the largest group, accounting for 21.4 percent of the total Chicago population, followed by Puerto Ricans at 3.8 percent and Guatemalans at 0.7 percent. Ecuadoreans are the fourth largest group of Latinos in Chicago at 0.6 percent, followed by Cubans and Colombians at 0.3 percent. Dominicans constitute 0.1 percent.[7] These figures clearly signal that the trinity of U.S. Latinas/os—the Mexican American, Puerto Rican, and Cuban—that has served as the central paradigm of national identities in Latina/o studies is not dismantled, but reconfigured. In fact, Chicago mirrors the national demographic shifts among Latinas/os, now that a Central American immigrant group (Salvadorans) has displaced Cubans as the third-largest Latina/o group.[8] We need much more knowledge about the local histories of these "other Latinas/os," and about the interactions and dynamics among the nineteen groups in order to identify the relational and historically shifting power dynamics among them.[9] Indeed, if so much scholarship about Chicago has characterized it as a city of Mexicano immigrants rather than of Latinidad, I would claim that this publicly emerging, yet not so new, Latinidad remains silenced and elided by most scholars of Latina/o studies.

Between 2008 and 2012, I interviewed twenty Intralatina/o subjects from Chicago. They are mostly between eighteen and twenty-five in age, all 1.5, second-, and third-generation Latinas/os raised in Chicago. All were college students in the Chicago area, and some had been exposed to Latina/o studies courses, a factor that may have influenced their pride in their mixed identities. There are six MexiRicans; five Mexican Guatemalans; two Mexican Colombians; one Chilean Colombian; one Guatemalan, Nicaraguan, and Puerto Rican; one Dominican, Chicano, and Puerto Rican; one Bolivian Cuban; one Puerto Rican Ecuadoran; one Salvadoran Puerto Rican; and one Mexican Peruvian. As Elena Padilla documented in her 1947 study of Puerto Rican identity formation in New York and Chicago, Yolanda Torres, a "dark, curly haired [Puerto Rican] woman" moved to Chicago following a Mexican family she had met in New York. In 1935 she married Pedro Vélez, a relative of the Mexican family with whom she lived who worked in the steel mills. This is, perhaps, the first documented MexiRican marriage in Chicago, which Padilla explains ended in divorce by 1938, and thus evinces the beginnings of shared living spaces and both tense and positive social dynamics between both groups.[10]

Chicago and the Midwest have served, historically, as sites of hemispheric encounters among Latin Americans of diverse nationalities. It is not arbitrary that other scholars in this anthology—Ramón Rivera-Servera, Theresa Delgadillo, Lilia Fernández, and Kim Potowski—highlight the pan-Latina/o social interactions or identities that characterize this region.[11] MexiRicans are much more numerous than other potential mixtures in Chicago because of the early migration of both groups to the area. Yet the fact that the second largest profile is that of Mexican Guatemalans reveals demographic changes. Guatemalans are now the third-largest Latin American group in the city, followed by Ecuadorians, while Cuban Americans are now the fifth-largest group. That a Bolivian married a Cuban in Chicago, and that a Guatemalan man fell in love with a woman who was half Nicaraguan and half Puerto Rican and who was born herself in the middle of the Atlantic Ocean, on a U.S. Navy ship between Panama and New York, serve as metaphors for the transnational movements and border crossings that constitute Latina/o local and personal histories in Chicago. Thus, I prefer to characterize Latina/o Chicago as an urban space informed by what Chabram-Dernersesian calls "local transnational plurality," that is, a domestic transnational community in which Latinas/os cross national borders within their everyday, local lives, within the same urban space, without necessarily having to travel outside of the United States.[12] In this chapter, I propose that Intralatina/o lives re-situate the transnational flows throughout the hemisphere from the exclusive political and sociological realms into individual family rooms and kitchens, from the macro to the micro, from the structural or social to the intimate realms. This concept adds a new layer to our multiple understandings of transnationalism, which has been celebrated, generalized, and diluted as any act of border crossing, and at times dangerously neutralized in terms of its power differentials. Yet transnationalism, as Nina Glick-Schiller argues, does not necessarily undermine or weaken national identities; at times it strengthens and reifies national boundaries.[13] These interviews reaffirm these contradictions and tensions within Latina/o Chicago.

As Mérida Rúa has written, "the city of Chicago is an ideal site to explore Latinidad via Inter-Latina/o relations because it is a space where Puerto Rican migrants and Mexican (im)migrants have had to strategically negotiate Latina/o identities both in the past and in contemporary times." Rúa argues that examining Latinidad in Chicago now is imperative for future studies in other Latina/o urban centers. Given the long history of encounters between Puerto Ricans and Mexicans in Chicago, which, according to Rúa, suggests that the Midwest is the site where the East meets the West Coast, these narratives and anecdotes about negotiating nationalities and relational racializations will reveal also the hidden ways in which national identities continue to erect boundaries as well as allow for new hybridities in our local everyday lives with family, friends, classmates and coworkers.[14]

These twenty interviews serve as narratives through which Intralatinas/os self-reflect on their own struggles for belonging and for carving a sense of place amid family and social tensions. While they exemplify a sort of hybridity of hybridity, or national "microdiversity," it is essential to acknowledge that hybridity is not parity and that new power and social differentials emerge in these mixed national social spaces.[15] Practices of self-narrating during the interviews produce stories and anecdotes from everyday life that allow Intralatinas/os "a means of examining the ways in which they [individuals] make sense of their lives within a changing sociohistorical context."[16] Narratives serve as a genre that offers "culturally developed ways of organizing experience and knowledge."[17] Telling stories and personal narratives allow us to transcend the national boundaries imposed by political histories and national imaginaries. In Michel de Certeau's words, "what the map cuts up, the story cuts across."[18]

Intralatinas/os and the Performance of Latinidad

While for years scholars have denounced the homogenizing impulses of the umbrella term "Latina/o," they simultaneously have added the term to their book titles in order to make them more palatable to the global market. These contradictory tensions between the specific national communities such as Chicana/o, U.S. Puerto Rican, and Cuban American, and the larger term of "Latina/o" continue to characterize our deployment of these labels. While we have used the terms as complementary and opposing identities—pan-ethnic versus national—the term "Latinidad" has been gradually redefined and rewritten by various scholars, thus undergoing semantic shifts that are ultimately integrating it into our theoretical frameworks.[19] More significantly, it has become a central site for theorizing our demographic shifts, our transcultural interactions and social dynamics, and our sense of collectivity and community. Rúa and García's proposal in "Processing Latinidad: Mapping Latino Urban Landscapes through Chicago Ethnic Festivals," has acknowledged that the pan-ethnic Latinidad and national identities should not be approached as an either/or proposition, but rather they coexist together in healthy and productive tensions.[20] According to the authors, one can find expressions of nationalism within spaces of Latinidad and a sense of Latinidad within national expressions. Their illustrations—from a young girl carrying a small Mexican flag during Fiesta Boricua or the Mexicanization of the Puerto Rican *plena* during the Mexican Independence Parade in Little Village—clearly reveal the ways in which nationalism still structures Latinidad and in which Latinidad embraces the performance of national identities. Rather than representing Latinidad either as a site of "cultural wars," as Seth Kugel does in the context of New York City, or as a homogenizing signifier that most Latina/o scholars have disavowed for decades, the personal narratives and everyday anecdotes of family life by Intralatinas/os in Chicago reveal the complicated and shifting meanings of their multiple nationalities, as well as the tensions they experience in reclaiming and reconceptualizing both.[21] While all Intralatinas/os embraced the term "Latina/o" as a label that truly indexes who they are, their voices remind us that national identities are still extremely powerful in the lives of these mixed subjects, as they themselves perform their fluidities, their partial dissolutions, and their simultaneous reifications in daily performances of culture, class, gender, and race. This project also proposes that Intralatinas/os embody Latinidad, not as a biological paradigm of identity, but rather as individuals whose very own, everyday lives as hybrid, social subjects engage transnational crossings and transculturations among Latin American identities and who perform Latinidad within their families, social networks, and public lives. Their stories illustrate both the pleasures and the profound pain that their hybrid national identities represent in their family and social lives. These experiences negotiating between national spaces and confronting relational racializations clearly unsettle the hegemonic discourses of homogeneous national imaginaries that reproduce discursive binaries between standard notions of purity as nation in contrast to hybridity as transnational.

Negotiating Nationalities

In "Colao Subjectivities," Mérida Rúa proposes the metaphor of *colando café* (brewing coffee; *colar*, lit. to strain), a vernacular household practice among Puerto Rican families, as a framework for understanding the negotiations between the Mexican and Puerto Rican identities among MexiRicans in Chicago. In addition to the metaphor of the *colao* subject as one who can pass, Rúa also defines "*colando*-ing" as processes through which MexiRicans in Chicago situated themselves, in relational and strategic ways, in both dominant and strong identities (*cargao*), and at other times, within diluted, weak, and undermined nationalities (*aguao*, lit. diluted). The *cargao* and *aguao* concepts help to unravel the processes of negotiating, compromising, and straddling two or more national cultures and legacies among Intralatinas/os.[22] These terms clearly reveal that two or more identities cannot be equally performed. At any particular moment in time, individuals choose to foreground or perform one national identity at the expense of the others. This definitely leads to a context of inequality among national groups, and particularly, to processes of "othering" each other. It also reveals the performative nature of identity. When I asked my interview subjects if they had experienced any sort of rejection or subordination by any of their family groups or friends for being mixed or Intralatina/o, most said they had not. Yet once they shared some of their experiences with me during the interview, examples emerged about the strong tensions and mutual othering among nationalities, thus revealing that domestic transnational flows are always embedded in power differentials and processes of relational subordination.

Mariana, whose mother is Cuban and whose father is Bolivian, was candid about the power inequalities between these two groups, as these are enacted within her family and social life.[23] When her parents met in Chicago in the 1970s, age differences—her mother was seventeen and her father twenty-eight—and Spanish-language differences were the central challenges they had to resolve. Mariana mentioned that her Cuban family members are prejudiced against Bolivians because they consider themselves superior, more elite, white and educated than most Bolivians—"everybody in Cuba is very educated and they think in Bolivia everybody's *indios*, you know, Indian people." Mariana commented that, given Bolivia's indigeneity, "there cannot be progress in Bolivia, it is not as good as Cuba." Mariana's father, although Bolivian, is light-skinned and is identified as of Spanish heritage, so there were no major racial anxieties over her parents' marriage. Mariana's Cuban relatives are Cuban exiles, and since the presidency of Evo Morales in Bolivia, the tensions over political ideologies and socialism continue to grow. Although Mariana's parents did not face any resistance to their marriage from either set of parents and relatives—they met in family events since a Cuban aunt was already married to a Bolivian—the racializing discourses against Bolivians has been a constant in Mariana's life. In addition, Bolivians in their own way also erected boundaries with Mariana in Chicago. While she grew up predominantly among her Cuban mother's family and relatives, her father eventually connected to a Bolivian civic group in the Chicago area and Mariana began to participate in their dancing group. Yet she confessed that the Bolivians never accepted her as one of them and always referred to her as "la cubana." These experiences within her family reveal the ways in which Latin American and Caribbean racial ideologies still inform these tensions in nationally hybrid families such as Mariana's. This transnational flow of racial politics in the diaspora, which is transforming Black/White racial binaries in the United States, is also articulated and enacted within the space of the family and home, otherwise considered private and personal.[24]

For Elena, her Mexican and Guatemalan families are constantly competing to be the dominant culture in her life.[25] Her performance of culture through language and accents, foods, favorite music, and travel are all evaluated by both sets of relatives. Elena has a Guatemalan boyfriend who makes fun of her Mexican Spanish. Yet her Mexican grandfather has stopped talking to her because she is not dating a Mexican. Her Mexican relatives hate her Guatemalan side, and she has had to accommodate to each national group. One could say that in being Mexican for her Mexican relatives and being Guatemalan for her Guatemalteco family implies "sacrificing [her] personal freedom of racial/cultural expression for the increased cohesion of one group identity."[26] Overall, most MexiGuatemalans shared with me that their Guatemalan identity was systematically overshadowed by their Mexican side, a power differential that, as Arturo Arias has suggested, may be informed by the political and historical relations between Mexico and Guatemala.[27]

Additionally, Intralatinas/os with more than two national identities may experience the dilution or silencing of one of their national heritages. For Vivian, whose mother is half Puerto Rican and half Irish, her Puerto Rican side was silenced for many years, since her mother never interacted with her own Puerto Rican father, who left his wife and child a long time ago.[28] Thus, Vivian's own mother was never able to perform and reaffirm her Puerto Rican side. This *aguao* identity, however, has shifted. Vivian's mother grew up in an Irish environment and later became Mexicanized as she lived with the family of her Mexican partner—Vivian's father—when she was seventeen and pregnant with Vivian. Yet many of her Mexican friends in the neighborhood and in high school have called Vivian "pork chops," alluding to the association of Puerto Ricans with *chuletas*, pork chops. Vivian herself has reclaimed and recovered some of her Puerto Rican identity through her Puerto Rican friends in high school, some of whom introduced her to *jibaritos* (plantain sandwiches), Puerto Rican music and rhythms, and other signifiers and icons of Puerto Rican cultural identity, thus illustrating how *aguao* identities can reemerge and surface again, how they can be reclaimed by performances, rituals, and practices that reenact them in everyday life. In fact, Vivian's Irish side and identity have been gradually undermined and silenced, as she has grown up with a strong sense of Mexicanness from her father and a growing sense of Puerto Ricanness through her friends. She states that she considers herself more Mexican than Puerto Rican "because I know a lot more about like Mexican heritage than I do Puerto Rican." Her family history, her trip to Mexico to visit with relatives and cousins, and her summer work in the Mexican family business all have contributed to her cementing her Mexicanness over the "repressed" Puerto Ricanness.[29] At the time of our interview, Vivian was planning to participate in the Puerto Rican pageant in Aurora, so she was engaging in research to find out more about her Puerto Rican family history. Since her mother never met her own Puerto Rican father, "that's something—like, it's really hard to get in touch with the Puerto Rican side." Her participation in this pageant not only will lead her to continue reclaiming her *aguao* identity, but it will also serve as a path for her to recover part of her history as a Boricua in Chicago.

Diana, whose father is Mexican and mother is Guatemalan, associated her extended family with her dominant, *cargao* identity.[30] She talked about how her Mexican dad's family lives in Chicago and in a Mexican-dominant suburb southwest of downtown Chicago, so she has had more contact with them. While she mentioned that she has visited Mexico only once, she feels much more closely bonded with her Mexican relatives than with her Guatemalan mother's family: "with Guatemala I have to make more of an effort than with Mexico, because in Chicago there are more Mexicans, and I do have more of my Mexican family around." For Diana, then, her Mexican identity is reaffirmed not only by her relatives and extended family but also by the larger demographics of Mexicanos, Mexican Americans, and Mexican immigrants in the city. In many ways, the Mexican community represents *familia*. However, Diana also shared with me her strong motivations to retain her Guatemalan identity, particularly after her mother's death from leukemia. This is her way of memorializing her mother's influence in her life. Her mother was the "main link" between herself, her siblings, and her Guatemalan relatives. She was a "proud Guatemalan," but not in the sense of "'oh, I am Guatemalan so it's better,' but she did show us the culture and she loved it and she loved going back and everything." The family was planning to travel to Guatemala that summer and would take some of her mother's ashes to her home country. Diana's personal narrative exemplifies the possibility of performing two *cargao* identities simultaneously. The strong Mexican presence in her family has not undermined her affective bonding with her Guatemalan identity, even after her mother's death and absence in their everyday lives.

José, on the other hand, spoke about his *cargao* identity in a very different context.[31] For him, his sense of belonging to the Colombian side of his mother's family, or to his father's Mexican relatives, has been informed by social class, economics, and age. As he was growing up, José preferred to play with his Colombian cousins because they would drive to festivals and play video games, while with his Mexican cousins "we'd have to watch TV. I guess it was financial . . . there would be less things to do." The class difference between his mother's and father's families is clearly articulated in the phrase "we'd have to," which emphasizes the lack of choices they had as young cousins living under financial constraints. José also attributed these different social activities to the differences in age, for the Colombian cousins were older, could drive, and thus had mobility, whereas the Mexican cousins were younger and could not leave the house.

More than age, José's stronger identification with his Colombian family is clearly informed by social class differences. He struggled with this gap between the Mexican working-class lifestyle, fashion, and rituals associated with his father, and his mother's apparent need to differentiate herself from her husband's class identity. She persistently dressed up in high fashion in order to differentiate herself from working-class and working-poor Mexicans. José shared with me how his mother's higher expectations for him were usually associated with his Colombian identity. Relationally, the need he felt to better himself and to meet high standards was a way of shedding his "Mexicanness." These ideologies, played out within his nuclear family, reveal that the reaffirmation of certain nationalities among Intralatinas/os can be clearly informed by social class. The fact that his Colombian mother disavows her husband's working-class identity speaks volumes about the internalized ideologies and social hierarchies that do not always disappear through marriage. José, as the offspring, has borne the burden of these class disparities. As he put it, "my mom has always had higher standards for me and I feel like when I meet them I feel good. When other people look at me and say, 'oh, I would have never thought that you had done something like that,' maybe because they think I am Mexican and that I am probably going to end up doing nothing and be like some dead end job or something." José's painful struggle to disidentify from the negative and racialized associations around his Mexican identity reveal the national hierarchies in the United States that rank Mexicanidad lower than Colombianidad and the affective consequences of internalizing them. The public discourses in the United States against Mexican immigrants, coupled with the racialization of Mexicanos in terms of labor and education, are strong influences in José's sense of self as a Mexicano.

Yet José's life story and processes of negotiating nationalities do not stop there. During the interview, he acknowledged that he has made a conscientious effort to become closer to his Mexican side of the family. He noticed that he was "shunning them and I [he] just started to attend more things in the Mexican family." Ironically, he attributes this shift also to his mother, for she has "become more interested because she made friends with my dad's family more now." According to José, his mother is now more bonded with her husband's family through "gossip," an instance of the relationship between gender and Latinidad that merits further study.

Relational Racializations

Marisa, Enrique, and Marco are dark-skinned and have faced forms of racialization from the national sets of both sides of their families. This is most prevalent among MexiRicans. However, central to this experience is the process of subordinating the national identity that is associated with darker skin, such as the Puerto Rican for Marisa and Enrique, who are MexiRicans, or the Colombian for Marcos, who is Chilean and Colombian. This analysis of race and skin color is central to understanding the ways in which national identities cannot be separated from racial paradigms both in the United States and in Latin America. Again, these examples of relational racializations, experienced both in the home countries of the parents as well as in Chicago neighborhoods, reveal the ways in which these individuals struggle with both racial systems simultaneously.

Marisa, with a Puerto Rican, dark-skinned father and a Mexican mother, shared with me during the interview that her maternal grandmother did not attend her parents' wedding.[32] "My dad and mom went back to Mexico and they got married there in the little town where my mom is from. But my grandma, my mother's mom, did not go to the wedding because she did not agree with the marriage." I asked Marisa if this was because her father was Puerto Rican. Marisa responded: "It was partly that my father was *not* Mexican." And, as she continued narrating her parent's experience getting married, and her grandmother's negative attitude toward Marisa's father, race and skin color surfaced as a central factor in the grandmother's resistance to the marriage. Marisa described her dad as "looking black, and he is very dark skinned—he has African blood in him." The erasure of blackness from the major national imaginary in Mexico informs individual Mexicano attitudes toward other Latinas/os of African descent. If racial attitudes trickle down from one generation to another, Marisa's family exemplifies this racializing heritage. Her cousins from Mexico would call her and her brother "los prietos." In Chicago, "los prietos" refers to African Americans, so Marisa was confused: "why are you calling me this, even though I had cousins who were darker than me and they were indigenous"? Marisa reflected throughout her interview on this racial dilemma in her life and with her Mexican family. She said that her mother is light-skinned, sometimes confused for Polish in Chicago. Marisa's black friends in grammar school used to tell her that she "had good hair," an inverse discourse of what her Mexican cousins would say. Thus, Marisa's racial positioning as a MexiRican, in that in-betweenness of hemispheric racial systems, reveals that this form of racialization is relational, dependent on the social and racial group with which she is interacting. While Marisa was indexed as nonblack by her black friends because of her hair, her cousins in Mexico racialized her as black. "Being *prieta*" for Marisa is not an objective reality but a construction produced to differentiate her as the Other and to maintain her outside the national boundaries, as someone who does not belong in and to Mexico.

These forms of relational racializations are also evident in Chicago. Enrique, who is dark-skinned like his Puerto Rican father, was raised by his mother in a largely Mexican neighborhood in the city after his parents' divorce when he was three years old.[33] As a dark-skinned boy, he always felt "like an outsider, sort of looking-in kind of thing." He commented that he "looked too Puerto Rican to be Mexican." Like Marisa, his Mexican mother's family also expressed racial anxieties at her marriage to a dark-skinned Puerto Rican man. In Enrique's words, "it was just as bad as marrying a black person." For Enrique and Marisa, the Mexican community's racializations of them as "black" individuals has had a tremendous impact on the way they see themselves and on their sense of non-belonging to the Mexican nation.

Marco, on the other hand, whose mother is Chilean and whose father is from Cartagena, Colombia, feels much more strongly identified with his Colombian, *costeño* (from the Caribbean coastal region of Colombia) culture rather than with his Chilean side.[34] While he is close to his mother, particularly after the divorce of his parents, he speaks of Colombian *costeño* culture in an idealizing language and discourse that reveals a strong connection to his father's family. He was born in Colombia but came to the United States as a baby, then was taken back to Colombia once as a child; he plans to return to Colombia to visit. He told me that he does not feel accepted by the Chileans he has met, because he is racially mixed and because his looks reveal that he is not 100 percent Chilean, thus suggesting how racial identity and skin color are embedded in these national negotiations.

Rewriting Labels and Refusing to Choose

Ignacio made a comment that resonates with most of the Intralatina/o subjects interviewed for this project: "My real identity was me. At the end of the day, it all comes down to who you want to be, which I think is more important."[35] They reiterated the ways in which they resist the dominant forces that push them to choose one national group over the other. Elena, for instance, who has experienced a habitual competition between her Mexican and Guatemalan relatives, commented that she tries to accommodate to each as they make demands on how she performs her dual identity, yet she reflected that "there's not like you can choose—I mean at times you can choose which one you prefer or what to be at that time, but depending on what group of people you are with, I don't think you can really choose what side you want to be." Or, as Mariana said: "I don't identify myself as either. I identify myself as both because I cannot be totally Cuban I cannot be totally Bolivian because neither of them they are so different, their cultures are so different that I cannot be one and not the other, like I am a mix. I see myself as Cuban Bolivian." Diana, who is Mexican and Guatemalan, told me that having to choose one identity over the other is like "abandoning myself."

Others reaffirmed the uniqueness and originality of their own cultural and national mixtures, creating and coining new labels and terms that reflect their personal identities and transforming traditional terms of identity, particularly the hegemonic Anglo imperialist connotations of the term "American." Mariana said that she is an ABC, an American Bolivian Cuban. Diana told me that she was "made in America with Mexican and Guatemalan parts." Marco, who does not identify as a U.S. Latino, however, confessed to embracing the term Latino "as a mediated way of being American."

Many of my interviewees also imbued terms with new meanings. Daniel, whose mother is Dominican and whose father is both Puerto Rican and Chicano, said that the term "Hispanic" for him means that he is from the island of Hispaniola, thus rewriting the more conservative ideologies that have historically informed the term and re-rooting it to the island, back to the Caribbean.[36] Many Intralatina/o individuals embrace the term "Latina/o" as a true reflection of who they are. As Nilda Flores-González has written, the term "resolves the dilemmas of not being able to claim complete membership in one national group, or of having to choose one side over the other."[37] These examples not only illustrate the resistance to choosing one identity over another, but also the creative ways in which they are reimagining hybridity beyond the racial and cultural and rewriting the concept of "American."

For Elena, being mixed is a condition that she associates with "being modern" and with Chicago ("you see it a lot here"). Diana "loves" being mixed. Mariana said that being mixed has implications for everything you do in life. These subjects constantly negotiate crossing Latin American national boundaries within the United States, and in the context of their everyday lives they are creating new paradigms of identity as articulations of the ways in which identity is the product of their self-imagination and the result of a dialogue with existing, traditional discourses of nation.

These personal narratives serve as a central discourse from which to begin to theorize about Intralatina/o subjects. Writings by and about mixed race individuals have helped me to reflect on these experiences of in-betweenness. If mixed-race people are deemed as "unclassifiable," given what some have called the "compulsory monoraciality" of U.S. racial politics and discourses as well as our investment in reaffirming "racial difference," a possible analogy can be drawn between mixed-race subjects and Intralatina/o subjects.[38] As SanSan Kwan and Kenneth Speirs write, "the personal is the best avenue to understanding that which is necessarily unclassifiable. It is only through the individual lived experience of mixed-race people that we can understand the plural nature of multiracialities."[39] These individual narratives are each very rich, complicated, and unique in terms of their particularities. However, each story also remits us to the larger, historical, social, political, cultural, gender, and structural factors that constitute a sort of domestic transnationalism that does not cross geographical borders. These Intralatina/o individuals perform Latinidad in their everyday lives, giving flesh, a history, and multiple intimate and social meanings to this long-contested term.

Notes

1. The epigraph and quotations are from Milagros, interview by the author, Chicago, Nov. 12, 2008; subsequent quotations are from this interview. All names are pseudonyms.

2. Juan Flores's earlier analysis about the pan-Latinization of New York, in "Pan-Latino/Trans-Latino: Puerto Ricans in the 'New Nueva York,'" *From Bomba to Hip Hop* (New York: Columbia University Press, 2000) describes Chicago as "the first example to come to mind" of cities with "more or less equally sizable Latino groups" (142). Although when Flores was writing, Chicago was indeed still balanced in terms of both populations, later, the Mexican population increased significantly.

3. Timothy Ready and Allert Brown-Gort, *This Is Home Now: The State of Latino Chicago* (University of Notre Dame Latino Research Institute, 2004).

4. Gabriela Arredondo, in *Mexican Chicago: Race, Identity, and Nation: 1916–1939* (Statue of Liberty–Ellis Island Centennial Series, Urbana: University of Illinois Press, 2008), has documented that by 1930 the U.S. Census had already indicated a Latin American presence in Chicago that contributed to a social pan-Latina/o identity beyond the dominant Mexican presence (153–57). While Mexicans were the largest group, the other nationalities who shared the rubric of Latin American immigrants with them were not significantly smaller in number. See also Elena Padilla, "Puerto Rican Immigrants in New York and Chicago: A Study in Comparative Assimilation" (master's thesis, University of Chicago, 1947).

5. Due to significant demographic changes since the 1980s, Chicago is not necessarily exceptional as an urban space where Latinas/os hailing from different nationalities meet, fall in love, and eventually marry. Even much earlier, examples emerge of MexiRican families. For instance, Silvia Méndez, who received the Presidential Medal of Freedom from President Obama in 2011, is the daughter of a Mexican father, Gregorio Méndez, and a

Puerto Rican mother, Felícitas Méndez, who met in Southern California in the late 1930s. The married couple sued the Westminster school district in California for segregation and for excluding Mexican American children. The 1947 *Méndez v. Westminster* decision preceded *Brown v. Board of Education* (1954), thus highlighting the ways in which Latina/o agency gets erased within the black/white racial binaries that inform U.S. history. Now in her seventies, Silvia declined to be interviewed for this project. Her mother, whose family migrated to Arizona to find agricultural work, moved to Southern California after a brief stint in the former state, a migration history that reminds us of the intercultural hidden movements among U.S. Latinas/os yet to be unveiled.

6. See Angie Chabram-Dernersesian, "Chicana! Rican? No, Chicana-Riqueña!": Refashioning the Transnational Connection," in *Multiculturalism: A Critical Reader*, ed. David Theo Goldberg (Cambridge, Mass.: Blackwell, 1994), 274. Among the small number of articles and scholarship devoted to MexiRicans, please also see: Angie Chabram-Dernersesian, "Growing Up Mexi-Rican: Remembered Snapshots of Life in La Puente," *Latino Studies* 7, no. 3 (2009): 378–92. Mérida Rúa, "Colao Subjectivities: PortoMex and MexiRican Perspectives on Language and Identity," *Centro: Journal of the Center for Puerto Rican Studies* 13, no. 2 (fall 2001): 116–33. Kim Potowski, "'I Was Raised Talking Like My Mom': The Influence of Mothers in the Development of Mexiricans' Phonological and Lexical Features," in *Linguistic Identity and Bilingualism in Different Hispanic Contexts*, ed. Jason Rothman and Mercedes Niño-Murcia (New York: John Benjamins, 2008), 201–220.

7. See the American Community Survey 2010 through the U.S. Census Bureau American FactFinder Finder website, American Community Survey, U.S. 2010 Census, Chicago population, https://factfinder.census.gov.

8. See Mark Hugo Lopez, Ana Gonzalez-Barrera, and Danielle Cuddington, "Diverse Origins: The Nation's 14 Largest Hispanic-Origin Groups," Pew Research Center, Hispanic Trends, June 19, 2013, www.pewhispanic.org.

9. See José Luis Falconi and José Antonio Mazzotti, ed., *The Other Latinos: Central and South Americans in the United States* (Cambridge, Mass.: Harvard University Press and the David Rockefeller Center Series on Latin American in Latino Studies, Harvard University, 2007). See also Suzanne Oboler, "Introduction: *Los Que Llegaron*: South American Migration (1950–2000)—An Overview," *Latino Studies* 3, no. 1 (April 2005): 42–52, and Arturo Arias and Claudia Milián, eds., "US Central Americans: Representations, Agency and Communities," special issue, *Latino Studies* 11, no. 2 (summer 2013).

10. Elena Padilla, who completed her master's in anthropology at the University of Chicago in 1947, was a pioneering scholar in the study of Puerto Ricans in Chicago and in New York as well as for anticipating the social interactions between Mexicans and Puerto Ricans in the Windy City. Her master's thesis (see note 4) already points to the potential Mexicanization of Puerto Ricans. See also Mérida Rúa, ed., *Latino Urban Ethnography and the Work of Elena Padilla* (Urbana: University of Illinois Press, 2010); Michael Innis-Jiménez, *Steel Barrio: The Great Mexican Migration to South Chicago, 1915–1940* (New York: NYU Press, 2013); and Lilia Fernández, *Brown in the Windy City: Mexicans and Puerto Ricans in Postwar Chicago* (Chicago: University of Chicago Press, 2012), for detailed chronologies of these two community formations. In addition, Delia Fernández, in "Becoming Latino: Mexicans and Puerto Ricans in Grand Rapids, Michigan," *Michi-*

gan Historical Review 39, no. 1 (spring 2013): 71–100, shows that "in the 1950s and 1960s Mexicans and Puerto Ricans in Grand Rapids began building personal relationships and alliances that enriched their experiences in Michigan" (74).

11. Rivera-Servera introduces readers to the life and work of Latina drag queen Ketty Teanga, who grew up as Ecuadorian and Puerto Rican. Although not born there, she made Chicago her home. Delgadillo highlights how Elvira, who is Mexican American in Milwaukee, works with both Mexican American and Puerto Rican communities. Elvira's words suggest practices of "passing" as Puerto Rican in order to work with that community. In her historical narrative of Chicago, Lilia Fernández comments about inter-ethnic marriages and marriages between Puerto Ricans and Mexicans in Chicago, thus evincing the Midwest's historical and personal experiences of Latinidad, while Kim Potowski highlights the presence of MexiRican students in Chicago's public schools.

12. Chabram-Dernersesian, "Chicana! Rican? No, Chicana-Riqueña!," 273.

13. Nina Glick-Schiller, "Terrains of Blood and Nation: Haitian Transnational Social Fields," *Ethnic and Racial Studies* 22, no. 2 (1999): 340–67.

14. Rúa, "Colao Subjectivities," 120.

15. Naomi Zachs, in her introduction to *American Mixed Race: The Culture of Microdiversity* (Lanham, Md.: Rowman and Littlefield, 1995), proposes the term "microdiversity" to refer to mixed racial identities that challenge the hegemonic force of imaginaries of racial purity in the United States (xv–xxv). Coco Fusco, "Who's Doin' the Twist? Notes toward a Politics of Appropriation," in *English Is Broken Here: Notes on Cultural Fusion in the Americas* (New York: New Press, 1995), critiques the ideologies of cultural appropriations embedded in postcolonial celebrations of hybridity and reminds readers that we should not "conflate hybridity with parity" (76).

16. J. S. Phinney, "Identity Formation across Cultures: The Interaction of Personal, Societal, and Historical Change," *Human Development* 43 (2000): 27–28.

17. Colette Daiute and Cynthia Lightfoot, "Editors' Introduction: Theory and Craft in Narrative Inquiry," in *Narrative Analysis: Studying the Development of Individuals in Society*, ed. Colette Daiute and Cynthia Lightfoot (Thousand Oaks, Calif.: Sage Press, 2004), x.

18. Michel de Certeau, *The Practice of Everyday Life*, 129, quoted in E. Patrick Johnson, *Sweet Tea: Black Gay Men in the South: An Oral History* (Raleigh: University of North Carolina Press, 2008), 11.

19. See the scholarly interventions by Nicholas De Genova and Ana Yolanda Ramos Zayas, *Latino Crossings: Mexicans, Puerto Ricans and the Politics of Race and Citizenship* (New York: Routledge, 2003); Marta Caminero, *On Latinidad: U.S. Latino Literature and the Construction of Ethnicity* (Gainesville: University of Florida Press, 2007); Cristina Beltrán, *The Trouble with Unity: Latino Politics and the Creation of Identity* (New York: Oxford University Press, 2010); and Ramón Rivera-Servera, *Performing Queer Latinidad: Dance, Sexuality, Politics* (Ann Arbor: University of Michigan Press, 2012) for a sample of the diverse meanings of "Latinidad" in Latina/o studies.

20. Lorena García and Mérida Rúa, "Processing Latinidad: Mapping Latino Urban Landscapes through Chicago Ethnic Festivals," *Latino Studies* 5, no. 3 (2007): 317–39.

21. Seth Kugel, in "The Latino Culture Wars" (*New York Times*, Feb. 24, 2002, www .nytimes.com), discovers the pan-Latina/o New York that Juan Flores had already announced

in 2000. He highlights the competition for power and dominant identities among Latina/o national groups and tends to elide the alliances, negotiations, and solidarities that all groups engage strategically and politically. However, Kugel does observe the "passing" practices among Latinas/os, a topic that merits further detailed analysis.

22. Rúa, "Colao Subjectivities," 123.

23. Mariana, interview by the author, Chicago, Sept. 12, 2008; subsequent quotations are from this interview.

24. See Eduardo Bonilla-Silva, "From Bi-racial to Tri-racial: Towards a New System of Racial Stratification in the USA," *Ethnic and Racial Studies* 27, no. 6 (2004): 931–50.

25. Elena, interview by the author, Chicago, April 25, 2008; subsequent quotations are from this interview.

26. Carole DeSouza, "Against Erasure: The Multiracial Voice in Cherríe Moraga's *Loving in the War Years*," in *Mixing It Up: Multiracial Subjects*, ed. SanSan Kwan and Kenneth Speirs, Louann Atkins Temple Women and Culture Series (Austin: University of Texas Press, 2004), 183.

27. Arturo Arias has proposed the "politics of invisibility" as a trope that explains the Guatemalan social dynamics in the United States. He argues that, given the long history of Mexico's domination over its neighbor to the south, Guatemala, the Guatemalan diaspora continues to reproduce these power dynamics in the United States. Arturo Arias, "Central American–Americans: Invisibility, Power and Representation in the US Latino World," *Latino Studies* 1 (13 March 2003): 168–87.

28. Vivian, interview by the author, Chicago, March 16, 2009; subsequent quotations are from this interview.

29. On repressed identity, see Chabram-Dernersesian, "Chicana! Rican? No, Chicana-Riqueña!," 284.

30. Diana, interview by the author, Chicago, Oct. 26, 2009; subsequent quotations are from this interview.

31. José, interview by the author, Chicago, July 15, 2010; subsequent quotations are from this interview.

32. Marisa, interview by the author, Chicago, June 24, 2008; subsequent quotations are from this interview.

33. Enrique, interview by the author, Chicago, June 26, 2008; subsequent quotations are from this interview.

34. Marco, interview by the author, Chicago, March 11, 2008; subsequent quotations are from this interview.

35. Ignacio, interview by the author, Chicago, Oct. 29, 2010; subsequent quotations are from this interview.

36. Daniel, interview by the author, Chicago, March 7, 2008; subsequent quotations are from this interview.

37. Nilda Flores-González, "The Racialization of Latinos: The Meaning of Latino Identity for the Second Generation," *Latino Studies Journal* 10, no. 3 (1999): 25.

38. DeSouza, "Against Erasure," 182–83.

39. SanSan Kwan and Kenneth Speirs, introduction, in Kwan and Speirs, *Mixing It Up*, 4.

Glossary

287(g): This refers to a section of the Immigration and Nationality Act, which was added through the Illegal Immigration Reform and Immigrant Responsibility Act of 1996. Section 287(g) authorizes the federal government to enter into agreements with state and local law enforcement agencies so that state and local law enforcement officers could assume immigration law enforcement functions.

agentic identity: Moje and Lewis (2007) define agency in a sociocultural sense as "the strategic making and re-making" of oneself or one's identity within structures of power (4). Identity is the conception of self that is constructed by a person with agency who has control over his or her own behavior in moments when power or powerful others are present. A person with an agentic identity is motivated to take action even in the presence of powerful others.

Americanization: Assimilation to U.S. customs and character.

Arizona SB1070: Arizona State Bill 1070, the Support Our Law Enforcement and Safe Neighborhoods Act, was signed into law in 2010. Among the bill's far-ranging and strict immigration enforcement provisions was allowing police to ask for the "papers" of those whom they believed to be undocumented (im)migrants. Arizona SB1070 is part of a wave of twenty-first-century anti-immigrant legal initiatives advocating "attrition through enforcement," along with federal immigration policies including so-called Secure Communities, which have contributed to the deportations of millions of undocumented (im)migrants in the United States. Arizona SB1070 inspired copycat laws across the U.S. South, such as Alabama's HB56, the Beason-Hammon Alabama Taxpayer and Citizen Protection Act (in 2011); and Georgia's HB87, the Illegal Immigrant Reform and Enforcement Act of 2011. Arizona SB1070 and related initiatives served as a catalyst to mobilize immigrants' rights movements across the United States. At the time of publication, legal challenges to the provisions of SB1070 are pending, while some provisions of SB1070 have been upheld by the U.S. Supreme Court.

critical regionalism: a concept identified with architect and critic Kenneth Frampton (1983) who argues for a place- or context-based approach to architecture, which is informed by local geography and culture as well as global movements. Critical regionalism has been adapted by scholars in literary and cultural studies, including Cheryl Herr (1996) and Douglas Powell (2007), to explore the potential for locations to generate resistive practices to capitalist modernity, sometimes out of selected forms of modernity itself. Herr further develops the concept toward comparative regionalist studies; this permits her to explore "twinned" locations, such as Ireland and the Midwest, which share a similar migratory history.

cultural citizenship: a concept developed in the work of Latina/o Studies social scientists and humanists (Rosaldo 1997; Rosaldo and Flores 1997; Flores and Benmayor 1997), which describes the strategies utilized by Latinas/os and for claiming rightful membership in a place or nation, while also maintaining collective cultural practices and identifications. The concept has been widely adapted by scholars working on other social groups and contexts.

DREAM Act: A number of Development, Relief and Education for Alien Minors Act (DREAM Act) versions were proposed in the 2000s. The original DREAM Act (Student Adjustment Act) introduced in 2001 had an emphasis on developing a path to citizenship for undocumented youths who had arrived in the United States as children (U.S. Senate, Development, Relief, and Education for Alien Minors Act, S. 1291, 107th Cong., 2d Session, June 20, 2002, www.govtrack.us/congress/bills/107/s1291/text). When proposed, this version of the DREAM Act had supporters in both houses of Congress. However, in response to concerns that it applied to too many people, Senator Richard Durbin (D-IL) and others changed the language of the act to include more restrictive eligibility criteria (Nicholls, *DREAMers*, 34–35). This revised DREAM Act proposed that migrant youths of "good moral character" who had lived in the United States for at least five years and graduated from U.S. high schools or the equivalent would become eligible to apply for a six-year conditional resident status. ("Bill Text—112th Congress (2011–2012)—THOMAS (Library of Congress)—S.952.IS," Library of Congress, http://thomas.loc.gov). This second version of the DREAM Act was more problematic than the original in that it required undocumented youth to consent to a normative rhetoric, in which they would have to present themselves as having "good moral character," implying that others (such as those with criminal records) did not. However, even with these added restrictions, the DREAM Act did not become a law (American Immigration Council, "The Dream Act: Creating Opportunities for Immigrant Students and Supporting the U.S. Economy," American Immigration Council, Fact Sheet, 13 July 2010, www.immigrationpolicy.org/just-facts/dream-act#congress). Advocates then pushed for the DREAM Act to be included as part of the Comprehensive Immigration Reform Act (CIR) because many supporters believed that this would aid in getting this piece of legislation passed in Congress. However, when the CIR Act failed to pass in 2007, Senator Durbin of Illinois put forward the idea that the DREAM Act be disentangled from CIR and presented on its own (Nicholls, *DREAMers*, 43).

ELL (English language learner): "An active learner of the English language who may benefit from various types of language support programs. This term is used mainly in the United States to describe K–12 students." There are other terms (limited English proficient student) that educators may use to describe this population of students, but the more commonly used term is ELL. For more, see www.ncte.org/library/NCTEFiles/Resources/PolicyResearch/ELLResearchBrief.pdf.

ethnic nationalist movements: These are movements that during the 1960s and 1970s promoted the racial pride, self-determination, and anti-imperialist sentiments of historically oppressed groups including African Americans, Mexican Americans, Puerto Ricans, Indigenous groups, and Asian Americans. Ethnic nationalist movements were often led by charismatic leaders who carried a strong sense of community consciousness and unity as they organized against the historic marginalization of their own group in the United States. However, these movements varied in their approaches to community engagement and activism. Some groups remained loyal to the mantra of "My people first!," while other groups embraced a radical ethnic nationalism that extended beyond the needs of one particular racial or ethnic group. Examples of this include Latinas/os and Asian Americans who joined the Black Panther Party and Mexican Americans in Chicago who were part of the Young Lords, a Puerto Rican ethnic nationalist movement.

ethno-racial identity: An individual or group's social classification based on either race, ethnicity, or a combination of both.

ethno-religious: Groups whose religious and ethnic traditions are historically linked. For example, in the Midwest, groups like the Dutch Reformed and Mennonites, many of whom immigrated to the region in the nineteenth century, both constitute ethno-religious groups. Traditionally these are groups whose religious identifications are inseparable from their ethnic identities, whether they be Swiss, German, or Russian.

evangélicos: Latinas/os who identify as "born-again" Christians and belong to a number of mainline Protestant and Pentecostal groups in the United States and throughout Latin America. Nearly 25 percent of the overall Latina/o population in the United States adheres to some form of evangelical faith tradition.

Greater México: A phrase associated with the writings of Chicano writer and intellectual Américo Paredes. Paredes's early usage of this phrase stresses local and regional Mexican and Mexican-U.S. cultural formations in the U.S.-Mexican borderlands, in contrast to national or geopolitical categories. Later in his career, Paredes (and many scholars after him), broadened the inflection of Greater México to encompass those areas within the United States inhabited by Mexicans and Mexican Americans and marked by Mexican cultural formations (Paredes 1966, 1976; Limón 1998; Calderón 2004).

im/migration, im/migrant, (im)migrant, (im)migration: the use of "im/migrant" [or (im)migrant] as opposed to "immigrant" draws from the work of Mae Ngai (2004) and others who demand that scholars not privilege permanent settlement over other kinds of migration.

Intralatina/o: U.S. Latinas/os who are of two or more Latin American national heritages. Usually second or third generation, these individuals embody the history of Latin

American hemispheric encounters in U.S. urban centers. MexiRicans are the most well-known given the longer presence of Mexicans and Puerto Ricans in the United States. Marriages between Mexicans and Puerto Ricans have dated back as early as 1935. Other combinations—such as MexiGuatemalans, Cuban Bolivian, Ecuadoran Puerto Rican, and Mexican Colombian, reveal the diverse national and ethnic crossings that constitute Latinidad. One may find different national profiles in the various Latina/o urban centers in the United States that reflect local migrations and social interactions. Most Intralatinas/os embrace the term "Latina/o" as a true reflection of their mixed identities.

Lao: Refers both to the official language of Laos, a country in Southeast Asia, and its people. Individuals from Laos often self-identify as Lao (an abbreviation of Laotian).

the Midwest, the heartland: According to the U.S. Census Bureau, the Midwest includes twelve states in the north central United States: Illinois, Indiana, Iowa, Kansas, Michigan, Minnesota, Missouri, Nebraska, North Dakota, Ohio, South Dakota, and Wisconsin. The Midwest is often referred to as the heartland, a phrase that in its most basic sense refers to the region's landlocked status but that also carries a host of affectionate and derogatory connotations, including normalcy, simplicity, core values, conservatism, and niceness.

mutualistas **(mutual aid societies):** Organizations formed to provide mutual aid, insurance, and ethnic solidarity and community.

nativists: People who advocate for maintaining what they perceive to be the "original" culture and language of the nation-state's "founding fathers." The philosophy of nativism they adhere to is often an intensified and reactionary form of "official" nationalism. It is narrowly construed to include only those considered to be "authentic" citizens (i.e., "America" is for WASPs) or founders of the nation. This form of nationalism excludes indigenous and conquered peoples because they are perceived as "outside" the history of the nation's existence. Because nativists see immigrants from any homeland different from their own as outsiders, they therefore support polices that favor the dominant group over perceived newcomers.

national imaginary: A set of ideas people have about the nation that are shaped discursively by social institutions such as the media (in all its forms), educational institutions, and the government. This powerful understanding of what and who constitute the nation is often built in contradistinction to those perceived as different or as outsiders. *The national imaginary is not an ideology, but a popular or widely held understanding of what is true about a nation.*

placemaking, worldmaking, homemaking: the collective, everyday forms of communication and community formation practiced by Latinas/os that are enacted through diverse self-representational strategies, including performance, storytelling, art and visual culture, bilingualism, and soundscapes, as well as through physical presence in churches, workplaces, schools, nightclubs, community centers, and museums.

pro patria organizations: Organizations created by Mexican immigrants or Mexican consular officials to organize patriotic celebrations, Mexican cultural events, and other events aimed and boosting Mexican patriotism.

queer gesture: a performance studies concept developed in the work of José Esteban Muñoz (1999, 2009), which stresses the capacity for embodied performative gestures, such as dance moves and poses, to encapsulate and transmit dense historical and cultural formations. Muñoz, moreover, identifies performative gestures with desire and the ephemeral. Thus, they open a window not only to utopian futurity but also to dimensions of queer histories and world making that are often elided in positivist historiography.

racial ascription: The assigning of a racial identity to an individual or group. While racial classifications are socially constructed, they are generally based on human biological characteristics such as skin color or hair texture, and can include social and cultural characteristics as well.

racialization: The process of giving a person a racial distinction or giving racial character to someone (in this case Mexicans) to serve racist ends.

racialized geography: Acknowledges that place is neither neutral nor passive in marking racial inequalities and determining segregationist patterns across communities that tend to privilege white and middle-class status. The interplay between race and place also reveals how society perceives these social spaces as inherently racialized. For example, historically "inner cities" and "suburbs" have each been marked along lines of race and class status and thus are deemed as dangerous or safe places.

self-deportation: This approach to reducing the number of undocumented residents in the United States creates legal structures (at both the state and the local level) that make life in the United States untenable for people without documents. The idea is that people without documents will choose to return to their home countries rather than endure the hardships created by such laws. Typically, laws that require proof of citizenship for daily activities (like accessing health services, renting homes, and attending school) and that encourage law enforcement to stop individuals who look like they might be undocumented are associated with the legal strategy of "self-deportation." Arizona's SB1070, passed in 2010, is perhaps the most widely known example of an immigration bill that is meant to encourage self-deportation.

Sensenbrenner Bill: In 2005, House Resolution 4377, the Border Protection, Antiterrorism, and Illegal Immigration Control Act (also known as the Sensenbrenner Bill) was passed by the U.S. House of Representatives. Among its other proposed changes to immigration policy, HR4377 called for increased security on both the U.S.-Mexican border and the U.S.-Canadian border, made it a federal offense to house a known undocumented immigrant (punishable by a minimum of three years in jail), and instituted much stiffer penalties for knowingly employing an undocumented worker. While HR4377 failed to garner enough votes in the U.S. Senate to become law, it was part of a broader national strategy to reduce immigration and encourage self-deportation through the passage of highly punitive laws at both the state and local level. There was strong resistance to the Sensenbrenner Bill among immigrant communities and their allies, most notably the massive "Day without Immigrants" marches that took place across the country on May 1, 2006. In Los Angeles, at least 600,000 people participated, while in Chicago the numbers were almost as high, at 400,000.

spatial ontologies: Social spaces, be they urban or rural communities, home or work life, or participation in social institutions, are composed of people in relationship to one another, and relationships are fraught with power. Spatial ontologies refers to the way in which community relations and individual and community identities are dynamic, reciprocal, and nuanced as they are impacted by regional cultural mores and political dynamics among residents. With respect to Latina/o (im)migration, communities are reshaped by new residents in ways that are often at odds with older residents' view of their communities. New (im)migrants bring to their receiving communities new cultural practices, sometimes a different language, different lifestyles that become part of, if not integrated with, the preexisting community.

tienditas: Little neighborhood stores, often operated as a family business. In Latina/o neighborhoods, these stores often have an edge over corporate-owned franchise stores because they stock ethnic specific spices, food, breads, fruits, and vegetables, and the proprietors speak Spanish, the native language of their customers.

translocal, transregional: The connection of two or more places or regions as created and experienced by migrants (Hoerder 2013). Translocalism and transregionalism impact diverse phenomena from the local to the international levels, including land use and the built environment, dialects, economies, and cultural practices.

transnational: Refers to the interconnectedness of people and social, economic, or cultural processes that transcend national boundaries. As a scholarly method, a transnational framework acknowledges that our understanding of people and societies is enriched if we connect the continuity of people's lives across borders, and understand that the significance of boundaries among nation states is receding as economic processes are globalized.

Bibliography

Aaron, Jesse, and José Esteban Hernández. (2007). "Quantitative Evidence for Contact-Induced Accommodation: Shifts in /s/ Reduction Patterns in Salvadoran Spanish in Houston." In *Spanish in Contact: Policy, Social, and Linguistic Inquiries*, edited by K. Potowski and R. Cameron, 329–44. Amsterdam: John Benjamins, 2007.

Adichie, Chimamanda. "The Danger of a Single Story." Filmed July 2009. TEDGlobal video, 18:49. Posted 2009. www.TED.com.

Alba, Richard, John Logan, Amy Lutz, and Brian Stults. "Only English by the Third Generation? Loss and Preservation of the Mother Tongue among the Grandchildren of Contemporary Immigrants." *Demography* 39, no. 3 (2002): 467–84.

Alcoff, Linda Martin. "Latinos beyond the Binary." *Southern Journal of Philosophy* 47, no. 2 (2009): 112–28.

Allatson, Paul. *Latino Dreams: Transcultural Traffic and the U.S. National Imaginary*. New York: Rodopi, 2002.

Allegro, Linda, and Drew Wood, eds. *Latino Migrations to the U.S. Heartland: Redrawing Boundaries, Forging Communities and Shaping Geographies*. Urbana: University of Illinois Press, 2012.

American Immigration Council. "The Dream Act: Creating Opportunities for Immigrant Students and Supporting the U.S. Economy." American Immigration Council, Fact Sheet. July 13, 2010. www.immigrationpolicy.org/just-facts/dream-act#congress.

Anaya, Rodolfo, Denise Chávez, and Juan Estevan Arellano. *Descansos: An Interrupted Journey*. Albuquerque, N.M.: El Norte Publications, 1995.

Anburajan, Aswini. "Immigrant Youth 'Come Out' as Undocumented, Push for DREAM Act." *Feet in 2 Worlds: Telling the Stories of Today's Immigrants*. March 21, 2011. http://fi2w.org/2011/03/21/immigrant-youth-come-out-as-undocumented/.

Año Nuevo Kerr, Louise. "The Chicano Experience in Chicago, 1920–1970." PhD diss., University of Illinois, Chicago, 1976.

Anzaldúa, Gloria. *Borderlands/La Frontera: The New Mestiza*. 3rd ed. San Francisco: Aunt Lute Books, 2007.

Aranda, Elizabeth, and Guillermo Rebollo-Gil. "Ethnoracism and the Sandwiched Minorities." *American Behavioral Scientist* 47, no. 7 (March 2004): 910–27.

Arias, Arturo. "Central American–Americans: Invisibility, Power and Representation in the US Latino World." *Latino Studies* 1 (March 13, 2003): 168–87.

———, and Claudia Milián, eds. "US Central Americans: Representations, Agency and Communities." Special issue, *Latino Studies* 11, no. 2 (summer 2013).

Arredondo, Gabriela F. *Mexican Chicago: Race, Identity, and Nation: 1916–1939*. Statue of Liberty–Ellis Island Centennial Series. Urbana: University of Illinois Press, 2008.

Atkins, Annette. *Creating Minnesota: A History from the Inside Out*. St. Paul: Minnesota Historical Society Press, 2007.

Attinasi, John. "Hispanic Attitudes in Northwestern Indiana and New York." In Elías-Olivares et al., *Spanish Language Use and Public Life*, 27–58.

Auerbach, Susan. "From Moral Supporters to Struggling Advocates: Reconceptualizing Parent Roles in Education through the Experience of Working-Class Families of Color." *Urban Education* 42 (2007).

Bacon, David. "How US Policies Fueled Mexico's Great Migration." *Nation*, Jan. 4, 2012. www.thenation.com.

———. *Illegal People: How Globalization Creates Migration and Criminalizes Immigrants*. Boston: Beacon Press, 2008.

Badillo, David A. *Latinos in Michigan*. East Lansing: Michigan State University Press, 2003.

Baker, Colin. *Foundations of Bilingual Education and Bilingualism*. Clevedon, U.K.: Multilingual Matters, 2011.

Balibar, Étienne. *We, the People of Europe? Reflections on Transnational Citizenship*. Princeton, N.J.: Princeton University Press, 2004.

Banton, Michael. *Racial and Ethnic Competition*. New York: Cambridge University Press, 1983.

Barton, Paul "*Ya Basta!* Latino/a Protestant Activism in the Chicano/a and Farm Worker Movements." In *Latino Religions and Civic Activism in the United States*, edited by Gastón Espinosa, Virgilio Elizondo, and Jesse Miranda, 127–43. New York: Oxford University Press, 2005.

Beaudrie, Sara. "Research on University-Based Spanish Heritage Language Programs in the United States." In *Spanish as a Heritage Language in the United States: The State of the Field*, edited by Sara Beaudrie and Marta Fairclough, 203–21. Washington, D.C.: Georgetown University Press, 2011.

Beirich, Heidi. "The Anti-Immigrant Movement." Southern Poverty Law Center, Intelligence Files, 2011. http://dialogic.blogspot.com.

Beltrán, Christina. *The Trouble with Unity: Latino Politics and the Creation of Identity*. New York: Oxford University Press, 2010.

Bennett, Brian. "High Deportation Figures Are Misleading." *Los Angeles Times*, April 1, 2014. www.latimes.com.

Berne, J., A. Clark, A. Hammerand, and K. Potowski. "Spanish for K–8 Heritage Speakers: A Standards-Based Curriculum Project." *Hispania* 91, no. 1 (2008): 25–41.

Bhabha, Homi. *The Location of Culture*. London: Routledge, 1994.

Blocker, Jane. *Where Is Ana Mendieta? Identity, Performativity, and Exile*. Durham, N.C.: Duke University Press, 1999.

Boer, J. Tom, et al. "Is There Environmental Racism? The Demographics of Hazardous Waste in Los Angeles County." *Social Science Quarterly* 78, no. 4 (1997): 793–810.

Boland, Philip. "Sonic Geography, Place and Race in the Formation of Local Identity: Liverpool and Scousers." *Geografiska Annaler*, series B, *Human Geography* 92, no. 1 (2010): 1–22.

Bonilla-Silva, Eduardo. "From Bi-racial to Tri-racial: Towards a New System of Racial Stratification in the USA." *Ethnic and Racial Studies* 27, no. 6 (2004): 931–50.

Breckinridge, Sophonisba P., and Edith Abbott. "Housing Conditions in Chicago, V: South Chicago and the Gates of the Mill." *American Journal of Sociology* 17, no. 2 (January 1911).

Brimelow, Peter. *Alien Nation: Common Sense about America's Immigration Disaster*. New York: Harper Perennial, 1996.

Brooks, Charlotte. "In the Twilight Zone between Black and White: Japanese American Resettlement and Community in Chicago, 1942–1945." *Journal of American History* 86, no. 4 (March 2000): 1655–87.

Brown, Anna, and Mark Hugo Lopez. "Mapping the Latino Population, by State, County, and City." Pew Research Center, Hispanic Trends, Aug. 29, 2013. www.pewhispanic.org.

Buchanan, Patrick. *The Death of the West: How Dying Populations and Immigrant Invasions Imperil Our Country and Civilization*. New York: St. Martin's Press, 2002.

Burnett, Christina Duffy, and Burke Marshall, eds. *Foreign in a Domestic Sense: Puerto Rico, American Expansion, and the Constitution*. Durham, N.C.: Duke University Press, 2001.

Cacho, Lisa Marie. *Social Death: Racialized Rightlessness and the Criminalization of the Unprotected*. New York: New York University Press, 2012.

Calafell, Bernadette Marie. "Disrupting the Dichotomy: 'Yo Soy Chicana/o?' in the New Latina/o South." *Communication Review* 7, no. 2 (April 2004): 175–204.

Calderón, Héctor. *Narratives of Greater Mexico: Essays on Chicano Literary History, Genre, and Borders*. Austin: University of Texas Press, 2004.

Caminero-Santangelo, Marta. *On Latinidad: U.S. Latino Literature and the Construction of Ethnicity*. Gainesville: University of Florida Press, 2007.

Cantú, Lionel. "The Peripheralization of Rural America: A Case Study of Latino Migrants in America's Heartland." *Sociological Perspectives* 38, no. 3 (1995): 399–414.

Cantú, Norma. "Se me enchina el cuerpo al oír tu cuento . . ." In *Latino Boom: An Anthology of U.S. Latino Literature*, edited by John S. Christie and José B. Gonzalez, 125. New York: Longman, 2006.

Cárdenas, Gilberto. *La Causa: Civil Rights, Social Justice and the Struggle for Equality in the Midwest*. Houston: Arte Público, 2004.

Carr, Patrick J., and Maria J. Kefalas. *Hollowing out the Middle: The Rural Brain Drain and What It Means for America*. Boston: Beacon Press, 2009.

Caruth, Cathy. *Unclaimed Experience: Trauma, Narrative, and History*. Baltimore, Md.: Johns Hopkins University Press, 1996.

Casares, Cindy. "Watch 'Georgia 6' Undocumented Students Get Arrested while Protesting at State Capital." *Guanabee*, June 29, 2011. www.guanabee.com (inactive).

Casillas, Dolores Inés. "Sounds of Surveillance: U.S. Spanish-Language Radio Patrols La Migra." *American Quarterly* 63, no. 3 (2011): 808–29.

Center for Applied Linguistics. *Directory of Two-Way Bilingual Immersion Programs in the U.S.* 2007. http://webapp.cal.org/Immersion/.

Certeau, Michel de. *The Practice of Everyday Life*. Translated by Steven F. Rendall. Berkeley: University of California Press, 1984.

Chabram-Dernersesian, Angie. "'Chicana! Rican? No, Chicana-Riqueña!': Refashioning the Transnational Connection." In *Multiculturalism: A Critical Reader*, edited by David Theo Goldberg, 269–95. Cambridge, Mass.: Blackwell, 1994.

———. "Growing up Mexi-Rican: Remembered Snapshots of Life in La Puente." *Latino Studies* 7, no. 3 (2009): 378–92.

Chávez, Ernesto. *"¡Mi Raza Primero!": Nationalism, Identity, and Insurgency in the Chicano Movement in Los Angeles, 1966–1978*. Berkeley: University of California Press, 2002.

Chávez, Karma R. "Coming Out as Coalitional Gesture?" Chap. 3 in *Queer Migration Politics: Activist Rhetoric and Coalitional Possibilities*. Urbana: University of Illinois Press, 2013.

Chavez, Leo R. *The Latino Threat: Constructing Immigrants, Citizens and the Nation*. Stanford, Calif.: Stanford University Press, 2008.

Chavira, Alicia. "'Tienes Que Ser Valiente' Mexicana Migrants in a Midwestern Farm Labor Camp." In *Mexicanas at Work in the United States*, edited by M. Melville. Houston: University of Houston, 1988. 64–74.

Chicago History Museum. Global Communities Collection. Jesse Escalante Oral Histories.

Clayton, Andrew R. L. "The Anti-Region: Place and Identity in the History of the American Midwest." In *The American Midwest: Essays on Regional History*, edited by Andrew R. L. Clayton and Susan E. Gray. Bloomington: Indiana University Press, 2001.

Clear Lake Chamber of Commerce. "Plane Crash Site—The Day the Music Died." http://members.clearlakeiowa.com/list/member/plane-crash-site-of-buddy-holly-ritchie-valens-jp-the-big-bopper-richard-7383, accessed June 5, 2014.

Cobble, Dorothy Sue. *The Other Women's Movement: Workplace Justice and Social Rights in Modern America*. Princeton, N.J.: Princeton University Press, 2004.

Cohen, Adam, and Elizabeth Taylor. *American Pharaoh: Mayor Richard J. Daley: His Battle for Chicago and the Nation*. Boston: Little Brown, 2000.

Cohen, Lizabeth. *Making a New Deal: Industrial Workers in Chicago, 1919–1939*. New York: Cambridge University Press, 1990.

Coleman, Matthew. "Immigration Geopolitics beyond the Mexico-US Border." *Antipode* 39, no. 1 (2007): 54–76.

Colomer, Soria Elizabeth, and Linda Harklau. "Spanish Teachers as Impromptu Translators and Liaisons in New Latino Communities." *Foreign Language Annals* 23, no. 4 (2009): 658–72.

Conde, Yvonne M. *Operation Pedro Pan: The Untold Exodus of 14,048 Cuban Children*. New York: Routledge, 1999.

Conner, Janis, and Joel Rosenkranz. "Josef Mario Korbel." In *Rediscoveries in American Sculpture, Studio Works, 1893–1939*, 95–103. Austin: University of Texas Press, 1989.

Costanza-Chock, Sasha. *Out of the Shadows, into the Streets! Transmedia Mobilization in the Immigrant Rights Movement*. Cambridge, Mass.: MIT Press, 2014.

———. "*Se Ve, Se Siente*: Transmedia Mobilization in the Los Angeles Immigrant Rights Movement." PhD diss., University of Southern California, 2010.

Cotera, María Eugenia. "Epilogue: 'What's Love Got to Do with It?' Toward a Passionate Praxis." In *Native Speakers: Ella Cara Deloria, Zora Neale Hurston, Jovita González, and the Poetics of Culture*, 225–32. Austin: University of Texas Press, 2008.

Cowie, Jefferson. *Capital Moves: RCA's Seventy-Year Quest for Cheap Labor*. Ithaca, N.Y.: Cornell University Press, 1999.

Craig, Richard B. *The Bracero Program: Interest Groups and Foreign Policy*. Austin: University of Texas Press, 1971.

Crenshaw, Kimberlé W. "Mapping the Margins: Intersectionality, Identity Politics, and Violence Against Women of Color." *Stanford Law Review* 43, no. 6 (1991): 1241–99.

Cressey, Paul Frederick. "The Succession of Cultural Groups in the City of Chicago." PhD diss., University of Chicago, 1930.

Cruz, Miriam, Carmen Rivera, Pastora Cafferty, and Arthur Velasques. "Chicago's Spanish Speaking Population: Selected Statistics." Chicago: City of Chicago, Department of Development and Planning, 1973.

Cuison Villazor, Rose, and Elizabeth Glaser. "A First Step." *New York Times*, Aug. 1, 2012. www.nytimes.com.

Daiute, Colette, and Cynthia Lightfoot. "Editors' Introduction: Theory and Craft in Narrative Inquiry." In *Narrative Analysis: Studying the Development of Individuals in Society*, edited by Colette Daiute and Cynthia Lightfoot, vii–xviii. Thousand Oaks, Calif.: Sage Publications, 2004.

Daniels, Rogers. *Coming to America: A History of Immigration and Ethnicity in American Life*. New York: HarperCollins, 1990.

Danielson, Marivel T. *Homecoming Queers: Desire and Difference in Chicana Latina Cultural Production*. New Brunswick, N.J.: Rutgers University Press, 2009.

Davidson, Osha Gray. *Broken Heartland: The Rise of America's Rural Ghetto*. New York: Free Press, 1990.

Davila, Arlene. "Talking Back: Hispanic Media and U.S. Latinidad." *CENTRO Journal* 12, no. 1 (2000): 37–47.

De Genova, Nicholas. "Migrant 'Illegality' and Deportability in Everyday Life." *Annual Review of Anthropology* 31 (2002): 419–47.

———. *Working the Boundaries: Race, Space, and "Illegality" in Mexican Chicago*. Durham, N.C.: Duke University Press, 2005.

———, and Ana Yolanda Ramos-Zayas. *Latino Crossings: Mexicans, Puerto Ricans and the Politics of Race and Citizenship*. New York: Routledge, 2003.

———, and Natalie Peutz. Introduction. In *The Deportation Regime: Sovereignty, Space and the Freedom of Movement*, edited by Nicholas De Genova and Natalie Peutz, 1–32. Durham, N.C.: Duke University Press, 2010.

Del Castillo, Gustavo. "NAFTA and the Struggle for Neoliberalism: Mexico's Elusive Quest for First World Status." In *Neoliberalism Revisited: Economic Restructuring and Mexico's Political Future*, edited by G. Otero, 27–42. Boulder, Colo.: Westview Press, 1996.

Delgadillo, Theresa. "Exiles, Migrants, Settlers, and Natives: Literary Representations of Chicano/as and Mexicans in the Midwest." Julian Samora Research Institute, Occasional Paper No. 64, Latino Studies Series, Michigan State University, August 1999.

———. *Latina Lives in Milwaukee.* (Urbana: University of Illinois Press, 2015.

DePaul University. Young Lords Newspaper Collection. DePaul University Library, Digital Collections. http://digicol.lib.depaul.edu/cdm/landingpage/collection/younglords.

DeSena, Judith. *Protecting One's Turf: Social Strategies for Maintaining Urban Neighborhoods.* Lanham, Md.: University Press of America, 1990.

Deslippe, Dennis. *Rights, Not Roses: Unions and the Rise of Working-Class Feminism, 1945–1980.* Urbana: University of Illinois Press, 2000.

DeSouza, Carole. "Against Erasure: The Multiracial Voice in Cherríe Moraga's *Loving in the War Years.*" In *Mixing It Up: Multiracial Subjects,* edited by SanSan Kwan and Kenneth Speirs, 181–206. Louann Atkins Temple Women and Culture Series, Austin: University of Texas Press, 2004.

Dewan, Shaila. "Immigration and Social Security." *New York Times,* July 2, 2013. http://economix.blogs.nytimes.com.

Diaz McConnell, Eileen. "Latinos in the Rural Midwest: The Twentieth-Century Historical Context Leading to Contemporary Challenges." In *Apple Pie and Enchiladas: Latino Newcomers to the Rural Midwest,* edited by Ann V. Millard and Jorge Chapa, 26–40. Austin: University of Texas Press, 2004.

———, and Faranak Miraftab. "Sundown Town to 'Little Mexico': Old-timers and Newcomers in an American Small Town." *Rural Sociology* 74, no. 4 (2009): 605–29.

Dinshaw, Carolyn. *How Soon Is Now? Medieval Texts, Amateur Readers, and the Queerness of Time.* Durham, N.C.: Duke University Press, 2012.

Dobrowolsky, Alexandra. "Interrogating 'Invisibilization' and 'Instrumentalization': Women and Current Citizenship Trends in Canada." *Citizenship Studies* 12, no. 5 (2008): 465–79.

Dolan, Jill. *Utopia in Performance: Finding Hope at the Theater.* Ann Arbor: University of Michigan Press, 2005.

Dominguez Barajas, Elias. *The Function of Proverbs in Discourse: The Case of a Mexican Transnational Social Network.* New York: De Gruyter Mouton, 2010.

Doss, Erika. *Memorial Mania: Public Feeling in America.* Chicago: University of Chicago Press, 2010.

DREAM Act—Texas. "Undocumented Youth Leaders Released, Still Facing Deportation." *Dream Act—Texas,* Breaking News, May 19, 2010. http://dreamacttexas.blogspot.com.

Driscoll, Barbara A. *The Tracks North: The Railroad Bracero Program of World War II.* Austin, Tex.: Center for Mexican American Studies, 1999.

Duggan, Lisa. *The Twilight of Equality? Neoliberalism, Cultural Politics, and the Attack on Democracy.* Boston: Beacon Press, 2003.

Durand, Jorge, Douglas S. Massey, and Chiara Capoferro. "The New Geography of Mexican Immigration." In Zúñiga and Hernández-León, *New Destinations,* 1–20.

———, Douglas S. Massey, and Emilio A. Parrado, "The New Era of Mexican Migration to the United States." *Journal of American History* 86, no. 2 (September 1999): 518–36.

Elías-Olivares, Lucía, Elizabeth Leone, René Cisneros, and John Gutiérrez, eds. *Spanish Language Use and Public Life in the United States*. New York: Mouton, 1985.

Epstein, Joyce L. *School, Family and Community Partnerships: Preparing Educators and Improving Schools*. Boulder, Colo.: Westview Press, 2011.

——. "School/Family/Community Partnerships: Caring for the Children We Share." *Phi Delta Kappan* 76, no. 9 (2001): 701–12.

Erman, Sam. "Meanings of Citizenship in the U.S. Empire: Puerto Rico, Isabel Gonzalez, and the Supreme Court, 1898 to 1905." *Journal of American Ethnic History* 27, no. 4 (summer 2008): 5–33.

Falcón, Rafael. *The Hispanic Mennonite Church in North America*. Translated by Ronald Collins. Scottdale, Pa.: Herald Press, 1986.

——. "La Iglesia Meno-Latina en Norte América: una interpretación." *Ecos Menonitas* 9, no. 3 (July 1983): 5–7.

Falconi, José Luis and José Antonio Mazzotti, eds. *The Other Latinos: Central and South Americans in the United States*. Cambridge, Mass.: Harvard University Press and the David Rockefeller Center Series on Latin American in Latino Studies, Harvard University, 2007.

Farr, Marcia, ed. *Latino Language and Literacy in Ethnolinguistic Chicago*. Mahwah, N.J.: Lawrence Erlbaum, 2005.

——. *Rancheros in Chicagoacán: Language and Identity in a Transnational Community*. Austin: University of Texas Press, 2006.

Fennelly, Katherine. "Immigration in the Midwest." Scholars Strategy Network, Basic Facts. April 2012. www.scholarsstrategynetwork.org.

——. "Prejudice Towards Immigrants in the Midwest." In Massey, *New Faces in New Places*, 206–43.

——, and Anne Huart. "The Economic Impact of Immigrants in Minnesota." St. Paul: Minnesota Business Immigrant Coalition, 2010.

——, and Helga Leitner. *How the Food Processing Industry Is Diversifying Rural Minnesota*. Working Paper 59, Julian Samora Research Institute, Michigan State University, East Lansing, 2002.

Fernández, Delia. "Becoming Latino: Mexicans and Puerto Ricans in Grand Rapids, Michigan." *Michigan Historical Review* 39, no. 1 (spring 2013): 71–100.

Fernández, Johanna. "The Young Lords and the Postwar City: Notes on the Geographical and Structural Reconfigurations of Contemporary Urban Life." In *African American Urban History since World War II*, ed. Kenneth L. Kusmer and Joe W. Trotter. Chicago: University of Chicago Press, 2009.

Fernández, Lilia. *Brown in the Windy City: Mexicans and Puerto Ricans in Postwar Chicago*. Chicago: University of Chicago Press, 2012.

——. "Of Migrants and Immigrants: Mexican and Puerto Rican Labor Migration in Comparative Perspective, 1942–1964." *Journal of American Ethnic History* 29, no. 3 (spring 2010): 6–39.

Fernández-Kelly, M. Patricia, and Richard Schauffler. "Divided Fates: Immigrant Children and the New Assimilation." In *The New Second Generation*, edited by Alejandro Portes, 30–53. New York: Russell Sage Foundation, 1996.

Fink, Deborah. *Cutting into the Meatpacking Line: Workers and Change in the Rural Midwest.* Chapel Hill: University of North Carolina Press, 1998.

Fishman, Joshua. *Language and Ethnicity in Minority Sociolinguistic Perspective.* Clevedon, U.K.: Multilingual Matters, 1989.

Fitzgerald, David. "Inside the Sending State: The Politics of Mexican Emigration Control." *International Migration Review* 40 (2006): 259–93.

Flores, Juan. "Pan-Latino/Trans-Latino: Puerto Ricans in the 'New' Nueva York." In *From Bomba to Hip-Hop*, 141–66. New York: Columbia University Press, 2000.

Flores, William V., and Rina Benmayor. *Latino Cultural Citizenship: Claiming Identity, Space, and Rights.* Boston: Beacon Press, 1997.

Flores-González, Nilda. "The Racialization of Latinos: The Meaning of Latino Identity for the Second Generation." *Latino Studies Journal* 10, no. 3 (1999): 3–31.

———. *School Kids/Street Kids: Identity Development in Latino Students.* New York: Teachers College, 2002.

Floyd, MaryBeth. "Spanish in the Southwest: Language Maintenance or Shift?" In Elías-Olivares et al., *Spanish Language Use and Public Life*, 13–25.

Foucault, Michel. *Security, Territory, Population: Lectures at the Collège de France, 1977–1978.* New York: Palgrave McMillan, 2007.

Frampton, Kenneth. "Towards a Critical Regionalism: Six Points for an Architecture of Resistance." In *The Anti-Aesthetic: Essays on Postmodern Culture*, edited by Hal Foster, 16–30. Seattle: Bay Press, 1983.

Freeman, Elizabeth. *Time Binds: Queer Temporalities, Queer Histories.* Durham, N.C.: Duke University Press, 2010.

Freier, Luisa Feline. "Religion, Ethnicity, and Immigrant Integration: Latino Lutherans versus Mexican Catholics in a Midwestern City." *Studies in Ethnicity and Nationalism* 8, no. 2 (2008): 267–89.

Fry, Richard, and Mark Hugo Lopez. "Hispanic Student Enrollments Reach New Highs in 2011." Pew Research Center, Pew Hispanic Center, Aug. 20, 2012. www.pewhispanic.org.

Fung, Richard. *My Mother's Place.* Documentary film. Chicago: Video Data Bank, 1990. Videocassette (VHS), 49 min.

Fusco, Coco. "Who's Doin' the Twist? Notes toward a Politics of Appropriation." In *English Is Broken Here: Notes on Cultural Fusion in the Americas*, 65–77. New York: New Press, 1995.

Gamboa, Erasmo. *Mexican Labor and World War II: Braceros in the Pacific Northwest, 1941–1947.* Austin: University of Texas Press, 1990.

Gamio, Manuel. *Mexican Immigration into the United States: A Study of Human Migration and Adjustment.* New York: Dover Publications, Inc., 1971 [1930].

Garcia, Chris. Interview by members of Generation Justice, Albuquerque, N.M. KUNM broadcast, Sept. 16, 2012.

García, Juan R. *Mexicans in the Midwest, 1900–1932.* Tucson: University of Arizona Press, 1996.

———. *Operation Wetback: The Mass Deportation of Mexican Undocumented Workers in 1954.* Westport, Conn.: Greenwood Press, 1980.

García, Lorena, and Mérida Rúa. "Processing Latinidad: Mapping Latino Urban Landscapes through Chicago Ethnic Festivals." *Latino Studies* 5, no. 3 (2007): 317–39.

García, Ofelia. "Racializing the Language Practices of U.S. Latinos: Impact on Their Education." In *How the United States Racializes Latinos: White Hegemony and Its Consequences*, edited by Jose A. Cobas, Jorge Duany, and Joe R. Feagin, 101–15. Boulder, Colo.: Paradigm Publishers, 2009.

———, and Ricardo Otheguy. "The Language Situation of Cuban Americans." In *Language Diversity: Problem or Resource?*, edited by Sandra Lee McKay and Sau-Ling Cynthia Wong, 166–92. New York: Newbury House, 1988.

García, Ricardo, and Carlos F. Díaz. "The Status and Use of Spanish and English among Hispanic Youth in Dade County (Miami) Florida: A Sociolinguistic Study." *Language and Education* 6 (1992): 13–32.

Garcia, Tadeo, dir. *On the Downlow*. Movie, 90 min. Chicago: Iconoclast Films, 2004.

García, Teresa A. "Mexican Room: Public Schooling and the Children of Mexican Railroad Workers in Fort Madison, Iowa, 1923–1930." PhD diss., University of Iowa, 2008.

García Bedolla, Lisa. "The Identity Paradox: Latino Language, Politics, and Selective Dissociation." *Latino Studies* 1, no. 2 (2003): 264–83.

García-Ferraz, Nereida, Kate Horsfield, and Branda Miller. *Ana Mendieta: Fuego de Tierra*. Videocassette (VHS). New York: Women Make Movies, 1987.

García y Griego, Manuel. "The Importation of Mexican Contract Laborers to the United States, 1942–1964." In *Between Two Worlds: Mexican Immigrants in the United States*, edited by David G. Gutiérrez, 45–85. Wilmington, Del.: Scholarly Resources, 1996.

Garcilazo, Jeffrey Marcos. *Traqueros: Mexican Railroad Workers in the United States, 1870–1930*. Denton: University of North Texas Press, 2012.

Gard, Wayne. *The Chisholm Trail*. Norman: University of Oklahoma Press, 1979.

Genthe, Arnold. "The Work of Mario Korbel and Walter D. Goldbeck." *Studio International* 57, nos. 225–28 (November/December 1915 and January/February 1916): xix.

Ghosh Johnson, E. "Mexiqueño? A Case Study of Dialect Contact." Penn Working Papers in Linguistics, vol. 11, no. 2, *Selected Papers from NWAV 33* (2005): 91–104.

Gilbertson, Greta, Joseph P. Fitzpatrick, and Lijun Yang. "Hispanic Intermarriage in New York City: New Evidence from 1991." *International Migration Review* 30, no. 2 (1996): 445–59.

Glazer, Nathan, and Daniel Patrick Moynihan. *Beyond the Melting Pot: The Negroes, Puerto Ricans, Jews, Italians, and Irish of New York City*. Cambridge, Mass.: MIT Press, 1963.

Glick-Schiller, Nina. "Terrains of Blood and Nation: Haitian Transnational Social Fields." *Ethnic and Racial Studies* 22, no. 2 (1999): 340–67.

Golash-Boza, Tanya. "Dropping the Hyphen: Becoming Latino(a)-American through Racialized Assimilation." *Social Forces* 85, no. 1 (2006): 27–55.

Gomez, Alan. "DREAMers Personalize Cases to Stall Deportation." *USA Today*, March 12, 2012. http://usatoday30.usatoday.com/news/nation/story/2012-03-12/dream-act-illegal-immigration/53502528/1.

Gonzales, Alfonso. "The 2006 Mega Marchas in Greater Los Angeles: Counter-Hegemonic Moment and the Future of El Migrante Struggle." *Latina/Latino Studies Journal* 7, no. 1 (2009): 30–59.

Gonzales, Manuel G. *Mexicanos: A History of Mexicans in the United States*. Bloomington: Indiana University Press, 1995.

González, Nora, and Irene Wheritt. "Spanish Language Use in West Liberty, Iowa." In *Spanish in the United States: Sociolinguistic Issues*, edited by John J. Bergen, 67–78. Washington, D.C.: Georgetown University Press, 1990.

Gonzales, Roberto G. "Left Out but Not Shut Down: Political Activism and the Undocumented Student Movement." In *Governing Immigration Through Crime: A Reader*, edited by Jonathan X. Inda and Julie A. Dowling, 269–84. Stanford, Calif.: Stanford University Press, 2013.

Gorman, Lillian, and Kim Potowski. "Spanish 'Recontact' between U.S. Born and Recent Arrival Latinos in Chicago." Paper presented at the 22nd Conference on Spanish in the United States, Coral Gables, Fla., 2009.

Gorski, Paul. "The Myth of the Culture of Poverty." *Poverty and Learning* 65, no. 7 (2008): 32–36.

Gouveia, Lourdes, and Donald Stull. "Dances with Cows: Beefpacking's Impact on Garden City, Kansas, and Lexington, Nebraska." In *Any Way You Cut It: Meat Processing and Small-Town America*, edited by Donald D. Stull, Michael J. Broadway, and David Griffith, 85–107. Lawrence: Kansas University Press, 1995.

———, Miguel A. Carranza, and Jasney Cogua. "The Great Plains Migration: Mexicans and Latinos in Nebraska." In Zúñiga and Hernández-León, *New Destinations*, 23–49.

Grey, Mark, and Anne Woodrick. "'Latinos Have Revitalized Our Community': Mexican Migration and Anglo Responses in Marshalltown, Iowa." In Zúñiga and Hernández-León, *New Destinations*, 133–54.

Griffith, James. *Beliefs and Holy Places: A Spiritual Geography of the Pimería Alta*. Tucson: University of Arizona Press, 1992.

Guerra, Juan. *Close to Home: Oral and Literate Practices in a Transnational Mexicano Community*. New York: Teachers College, 1998.

Guglielmo, Thomas. *White on Arrival: Italians, Race, Color and Power in Chicago, 1890–1945*. New York: Oxford University Press, 2003.

Gutiérrez, David G. "Migration, Emergent Ethnicity, and the 'Third Space': The Shifting Politics of Nationalism in Greater Mexico." *Journal of American History* 86, no. 2 (1999): 481–517.

Gutiérrez, Kris D., Patricia Baquedano-López, and Héctor H. Alvarez. "Literacy as Hybridity: Moving beyond Bilingualism in Urban Classrooms." In *The Best for Our Children: Critical Perspectives on Literacy for Latino Students*, edited by Marìa de la Luz Reyes et al., 122–41. Language and Literacy Series. New York: Teachers College Press, 2001.

Gutiérrez y Muhs, Gabriella, Yolanda Flores Niemann, Carmen G. González, and Angela P. Harris. *Presumed Incompetent: The Intersections of Race and Class for Women in Academia*. Boulder: University Press of Colorado, 2012.

Halberstam, Judith [J. Jack]. *In a Queer Time and Place: Transgender Bodies, Subcultural Lives*. New York: New York University Press, 2005.

Harnish, David. "Tejano Music in the Urbanizing Midwest: The Musical Story of *Conjunto* Master Jesse Ponce." *Journal of the Society for American Music* 3 (2009): 195–219.

Harvey, David. *A Brief History of Neoliberalism*. New York: Oxford University Press, 2005.

Henderson, Anne T., and Karen L. Mapp. *A New Wave of Evidence. The Impact of School, Family, and Community Connections on Student Achievement*. Annual Synthesis 2002.

Austin, Tex.: National Center for Family and Community Connections with Schools, and Southwest Educational Development Laboratory (SEDL), 2002.

"Henry B. Gonzalez, Early Life and Entry into Politics." Briscoe Center for American History, University of Texas at Austin. www.cah.utexas.edu/feature/0611/bio_three.php.

Hernández Alvarez, José. "A Demographic Profile of the Mexican Immigration to the United States." *Journal of Inter-American Studies* 8, no. 3 (July 1966): 471–96.

———. "The Movement and Settlement of Puerto Rican Migrants within the United States, 1950–1960." In *Latinos in the United States: Historical Themes and Identity*, edited by Antoinette Sedillo-López, 372–84. New York: Garland Publishing, 1995.

Hernandez-Fujigaki, Jorge. "Mexican Steelworkers and the United Steelworkers of America in the Midwest: The Inland Steel Experience (1936–1976)." PhD diss., University of Chicago, 1991.

Hernández-León, Rubén, and Víctor Zúñiga. "Making Carpet by the Mile: The Emergence of a Mexican Immigrant Community in an Industrial Region of the U.S. Historic South." *Social Science Quarterly* 81, no. 1 (2000): 49–66.

Herr, Cheryl Temple. *Critical Regionalism and Cultural Studies: From Ireland to the American Midwest.* Gainesville: University Press of Florida, 1996.

Hershberger, Paul. "Housing Project Proposed." *Goshen (Ind.) News*, Dec. 17, 1971.

———. "Miller May Close Housing." *Goshen (Ind.) News*, December 1971.

Herzberg, Julia A. "Ana Mendieta's Iowa Years, 1970–1980." In *Ana Mendieta: Earth Body; Sculpture and Performance, 1972–1985*, edited by Olga Viso, 137–80. Washington, D.C.: Hirshhorn Museum and Sculpture Garden, Smithsonian Institution; Ostfildern-Ruit, Germany: Hatje Cantz Verlag, 2004.

———. "Ana Mendieta, The Iowa Years: A Critical Study, 1969 through 1977." PhD diss., City University of New York, 1998.

Hill, Jane H. "English-Language Spanish in the United States as a Site of Symbolic Violence." In *How the United States Racializes Latinos: White Hegemony and Its Consequences*, edited by Jose A. Cobas, Jorge Duany, and Joe R. Feagin, 116–33. Boulder, Colo.: Paradigm, 2009.

Hill Collins, Patricia. *Black Feminist Thought: Knowledge, Consciousness and the Politics of Empowerment.* 2nd ed. New York: Routledge, 2008.

Hinojosa, Felipe. *Latino Mennonites: Civil Rights, Faith, and Evangelical Culture.* Baltimore, Md.: Johns Hopkins University Press, 2014.

Hinojosa, Rolando. *The Valley.* Tempe, Ariz.: Bilingual Press, 1983.

Hirsch, Arnold. *Making the Second Ghetto: Race and Housing in Chicago, 1940–1960.* Cambridge: Cambridge University Press, 1983.

Hirschman, C., and Douglas S. Massey. "Places and People: The New American Mosaic." In Massey, *New Faces in New Places*, 1–32.

History Task Force Centro de Estudios Puertorriqueños. *Labor Migration under Capitalism: The Puerto Rican Experience.* New York: Research Foundation of the City University of New York, 1979.

Hoerder, Dirk. "Translocalism." *Encyclopedia of Global Human Migration*, edited by Emmanuel Ness. Hoboken, N.J.: Wiley-Blackwell, 2013. http://dx.doi.org/10.1002/9781444351071.wbeghm540.

hooks, bell. *Teaching to Transgress: Education as the Practice of Freedom*. New York: Routledge, 1994.

Horsley, Scott. "5 Things to Know about Obama's Enforcement of Immigration Laws." *National Public Radio*, Aug. 31, 2016. www.npr.org.

"How Alabama's Immigration Law Is Crippling Its Farms." *Washington Post*, editorial, Nov. 3, 2011. www.washingtonpost.com.

Huerta, Francisco. "Las Organizaciones Méxicanas." *Correo Méxicano*, Chicago, Sept. 6, 1926.

Hughes, Elizabeth Ann. *Living Conditions for Small Wage Earners in Chicago*. Chicago: City of Chicago Department of Public Welfare, 1925.

Immigrant Youth Justice League. "National Come Out of the Shadows Day!" Immigrant Youth Justice League. Posted Feb. 17, 2010. www.iyjl.org/national-coming-out-of-the-shadows-day/.

———. "Who We Are." Immigrant Youth Justice League, www.iyjl.org/?page_id=405.

Inda, Jonathan X., and Julie A. Dowling. "Introduction: Governing Migrant Illegality." In *Governing Immigration through Crime: A Reader*, edited by Jonathan X. Inda and Julie A. Dowling, 1–36. Stanford, Calif.: Stanford University Press, 2013.

Innis-Jiménez, Michael. *Steel Barrio: The Great Mexican Migration to South Chicago, 1915–1940*. New York: NYU Press, 2013.

Iowa Department of Education. *A Report on Prekindergarten, Elementary, and Secondary Education in Iowa*. Des Moines: Iowa Department of Education, 2006.

Jeffries, Judson. "From Gang-Bangers to Urban Revolutionaries: The Young Lords of Chicago." *Journal of the Illinois State Historical Society* 96, no. 3 (2003): 288–304.

Jensen, Leif. *New Immigrant Settlements in Rural America: Problems, Prospects, and Policies*. Reports on Rural America, vol. 1, no. 3. Durham: University of New Hampshire / Carsey Institute, 2006.

Jiménez, José. *Tierra y Libertad: Two Interviews with Corky Gonzales and Cha Cha Jimenez*. Detroit: Radical Education Project, 1970. Accessed at http://alexanderstreet.com.

———, and Ángel G. Flores-Rodríguez. "The Young Lords, Puerto Rican Liberation, and the Black Freedom Struggle: Interview with José 'Cha Cha' Jiménez." *OAH Magazine of History* 26, no. 1 (2012): 61–64. doi:10.1093/oahmag/oar058.

Johnson, E. Patrick. *Sweet Tea: Gay Black Men of the South—An Oral History*. Raleigh: University of North Carolina Press, 2008.

Jones, Maggie. "Coming Out Illegal." *New York Times Magazine*, Oct. 21, 2010.

Juffer, Jane. "Hybrid Faiths: Latino Protestants Find a Home among the Dutch Reformed in Iowa." *Latino Studies* 6, no. 3 (2008): 290–312.

Juhnke, James C. *Vision, Doctrine, War: Mennonite Identity and Organization in America, 1890–1930*. Scottdale, Pa.: Herald Press, 1989.

Kahn, Dorothea. "Mexicans Bring Romance to Drab Part of Chicago in Their Box-Car Villages: 30,000 Now Make City." *Christian Science Monitor*, May 23, 1931.

Kandel, William, and Emilio Parrado. "Restructuring of the US Meat Processing Industry and New Hispanic Migrant Destinations." *Population and Development Review* 31, no. 3 (2005): 447–71.

Kaufmann, Karen M. "Cracks in the Rainbow: Group Commonality as a Basis for Latino and African-American Political Coalitions." *Political Research Quarterly* 56, no. 2 (June 2003): 199–210.

Kearney, Michael. "Transnationalism in California and Mexico at the End of Empire." In *Border Identities: Nation and State at International Frontiers*, edited by Thomas M. Wilson and Hastings Donnan, 117–41. Cambridge: Cambridge University Press, 1998.

Kessler-Harris, Alice. *In Pursuit of Equity: Women, Men and the Quest for Economic Citizenship in 20th-Century America.* New York: Oxford University Press, 2001.

Kirstein, Peter N. *Anglo over Bracero: A History of the Mexican Worker in the United States from Roosevelt to Nixon.* San Francisco: R and E Research Associates, 1977.

Klassen, Don. "Plea for Migrants." *Goshen (Ind.) News*, Nov. 14, 1969.

Kollmann de Curutchet, Marta Isabel. "Localization of the Mexican and Cuban Population." Master's thesis, University of Chicago, 1967.

Krogstad, Jens Manuel, and Mark Hugo Lopez. "Hispanic Nativity Shift: U.S. Births Drive Population Growth as Immigration Stalls." Pew Research Center, Hispanic Trends, April 29, 2014. www.pewhispanic.org.

Kugel, Seth. "The Latino Culture Wars." *New York Times*, Feb. 24, 2002. www.nytimes.com.

Kuspit, Donald. "Ana Mendieta, Autonomous Body." In Moure, *Ana Mendieta*, 35–63.

Kwan, SanSan, and Kenneth Speirs, eds. Introduction. In *Mixing It Up: Multiracial Subjects*, 1–10. Louann Atkins Temple Women and Culture Series. Austin: University of Texas Press, 2004.

La Fountain-Stokes, Lawrence, Lourdes Torres, and Ramón H. Rivera-Servera. "Toward an Archive of Latina/o Queer Chicago: Art, Politics, and Social Performance." In *Out in Chicago: LGBT History at the Crossroads*, edited by Jill Austin and Jennifer Brier, 127–53. Chicago: Chicago History Museum, 2011.

Lai Stirland, Sarah. "Website Yes, Legal Status, No: 'No Papers, No Fear' Hopes to Build a Movement for Undocumented Immigrations." http://nopapersnofear.org.

Lane, James B. and Edward J. Escobar, eds. *Forging a Community: The Latino Experience in Northwest Indiana, 1919–1975.* Chicago: Cattails Press, 1987.

Latina Feminist Group. *Telling to Live: Latina Feminist Testimonios.* Ed. Luz del Alba Acevedo et al. Latin America Otherwise Series. Durham, N.C.: Duke University Press, 2001.

Latino Writers Collective. *Cuentos del Centro: Stories from the Latino Heartland.* Kansas City: Scapegoat Press, 2009.

Leacock, Eleanor Burke, ed. *The Culture of Poverty: A Critique.* New York: Simon and Shuster, 1971.

Lee, Sara. "Love Sees No Color or Boundaries? Interethnic Dating and Marriage Patterns of Dominican and CEP (Colombian, Ecuadorian, Peruvian) Americans." *Journal of Latino/Latin American Studies* 2 (2006): 84–102.

Leonard, Karen I., Alex Stepick, Manuel E. Vasquez, and Jennifer Holdaway, eds. *Immigrant Faiths: Transforming Religious Life in America.* Walnut Creek, Calif.: AltaMira Press, 2005.

Leone, Rene, and Elizabeth Cisneros. "Mexican-American Language Communities in the Twin Cities: An Example of Contact and Recontact." In *Spanish in the U.S. Setting:*

Beyond the Southwest, edited by Lucía Elías-Olivares, 181–209. Rosslyn, Va.: National Clearinghouse for Bilingual Education, 1983.

Lepecki, André. *Exhausting Dance: Performance and the Politics of Movement*. New York: Routledge, 2006.

Lewis, Earl. "Connecting Memory, Self, and the Power of Place in African American Urban History." *Journal of Urban History* 21, no. 3 (1995): 347–71.

Lewis, Oscar. *La Vida: A Puerto Rican Family in the Culture of Poverty—San Juan and New York*. New York: Random House, 1966.

Licona, Adela C., and Marta María Maldonado. "The Social Production of Latino/a Visibilities and Invisibilities: Geographies of Power in Small Town America." *Antipode*, Sept. 9, 2013. doi:10.1111/anti.12049.

Lieberson, Stanley, Guy Dalto, and Mary Ellen Johnston. "The Course of Mother-Tongue Diversity in Nations." *American Journal of Sociology* 81 (1975): 34–61.

Limón, José E. *American Encounters: Greater Mexico, the United States, and the Erotics of Culture*. Boston: Beacon, 1998.

———. *Américo Paredes: Culture and Critique*. Austin: University of Texas Press, 2012.

Lindholm, Kathryn. *Dual Language Education*. Clevedon, U.K.: Multilingual Matters, 2001.

Loewen, Harry, and Steve M. Nolt. *Through Fire and Water: An Overview of Mennonite History*. 2nd ed. Scottdale, Pa.: Herald Press, 2010.

Loewen, James W. *Sundown Towns: A Hidden Dimension of American Racism*. New York: New Press, 2005.

Lopez, Mark Hugo, Ana Gonzalez-Barrera, and Danielle Cuddington. "Diverse Origins: The Nation's 14 Largest Hispanic-Origin Groups." Pew Research Center, Hispanic Trends, June 19, 2013. www.pewhispanic.org.

López-Morín, José R. *The Legacy of Américo Paredes*. College Station: Texas A&M University Press, 2006.

Lukkas, Lynn, and Howard Oransky, cur. *Covered in Time and History: The Films of Ana Mendieta*. Minneapolis: Katherine E. Nash Gallery at the University of Minnesota, in association with University of California Press, 2015.

Lyndersen, Kay. "La Cueva: The Oldest Latino Drag Club in the Country Has Done Much to Change Attitudes in Chicago's Mexican Community." *Colorlines Magazine*, July 1, 2006.

Lyons, Stephen J. "Nuevos Americanos: Is the Current Influx of Latinos so Different from Past Immigrations?" *LAS News* (University of Illinois, Urbana-Champaign), fall/winter 2005–6. www.las.illinois.edu/alumni.

Magaña, Gilberto. "On the Downlow." Plot summary. IMDb.com. www.imdb.com.

Maharidge, Dale. *Denison, Iowa: The Search for the Soul of America through the Secrets of a Midwestern Town*. New York: Free Press, 2005.

Maldonado, Edwin. "Contract Labor and the Origins of Puerto Rican Communities in the United States." *International Migration Review* 13, no. 1 (1979): 103–21.

Marsden, George M. *Fundamentalism and American Culture*. 2nd ed. New York: Oxford University Press, 2006.

Martínez, Richard. *PADRES: The National Chicano Priest Movement*. Austin: University of Texas Press, 2005.

Martínez, Rubén O. *Crossing Over: A Mexican Family on the Migrant Trail.* New York: Metropolitan Books, 2001.

———. *Latinos in the Midwest.* East Lansing: Michigan State University, 2011.

Mason, Kären M., and Tanya Zanish-Belcher. "Raising the Archival Consciousness: How Women's Archives Challenge Traditional Approaches to Collecting and Use, Or, What's in a Name?" *Library Trends* 56, no. 2 (fall 2008): 344–58.

Massey, Douglas S., ed. *New Faces in New Places: The Changing Geography of American Immigration.* New York: Russell Sage Foundation, 2008.

Matless, David. "Sonic Geography in a Nature Region." *Social and Cultural Geography* 6, no. 5 (2005): 745–66.

McCarthy, Malachy Richard. "Which Christ Came to Chicago: Catholic and Protestant Programs to Evangelize, Socialize, and Americanize the Mexican Immigrant, 1900–1940." PhD diss., Loyola University of Chicago, 2002.

McEnaney, Laura. "Nightmares on Elm Street: Demobilizing in Chicago, 1945–1953." *Journal of American History* 92, no. 4 (2006): 1265–91.

McWhorter, Diane. "The Strange Career of Juan Crow." *New York Times,* June 16, 2012. www.nytimes.com.

Medina, Lara. *Las Hermanas: Chicana/Latina Religious-Political Activism in the Catholic Church.* Philadelphia: Temple University Press, 2005.

Medrano, Manuel F. *Américo Paredes: In His Own Words, an Authorized Biography.* Denton: University of North Texas Press, 2010.

Mendieta, Ana. "Personal Writings." In Moure, *Ana Mendieta,* 167–222.

Mendieta, Raquel. "Childhood Memories: Religion, Politics, Art." In Moure, *Ana Mendieta,* 223–28.

Mendoza, Louis. *Conversations across Our America: Talking about Immigration and the Latinoization of the United States.* Austin: University of Texas Press, 2012.

———. *A Journey around Our America: Memoir on Cycling, Immigration, and the Latinoization of the U.S.* Austin: University of Texas Press, 2012.

Mendoza-Denton, Norma. "Sociolinguistics and Linguistic Anthropology of U.S. Latinos." *Annual Review of Anthropology* 28 (1999): 375–95.

Millard, Ann V., and Jorge Chapa, eds. *Apple Pie and Enchiladas: Latino Newcomers in the Rural Midwest.* Austin: University of Texas Press, 2004.

Miller, Char. "Streetscape Environmentalism: Floods, Social Justice, and Political Power in San Antonio, 1921–1974." *Southwestern Historical Quarterly* 118, no. 2 (2014): 158–77.

"The Minorities Ministries Council: Mexicanos, Puerto Ricans, Blacks, and American Indians Working Together." *La Luz* (Denver) 2, no. 1 (April 1973): 20–23.

Moje, Elizabeth Birr, and Tisha Lewis Ellison. "Extended—and Extending—Literacies." *Journal of Education* 196, no. 3 (September 2016): 27–34. Psychology and Behavioral Sciences Collection, EBSCOhost.

Montejano, David. *Anglos and Mexicans in the Making of Texas, 1836–1986.* Austin: University of Texas Press, 1987.

Montrul, Silvina, and Kim Potowski. "Command of Gender Agreement in School-Age Spanish-English Bilingual Children." *International Journal of Bilingualism* 11, no. 3 (2007): 301–28.

Mora, Pat. *Tomás and the Library Lady.* Edmond, Okla.: Dragonfly, 2000.

Morales, Adam. *American Baptists with a Spanish Accent.* Valley Forge, Pa.: Judson Press, 1964.

Morris, Willie. *North toward Home.* New York: Houghton-Mifflin, 1967.

Moure, Gloria, ed. *Ana Mendieta.* Barcelona: Fundación Antoni Tàpies; Santiago de Compostela: Centro Galego de Arte Contemporánea, 1997.

Muñoz, José Esteban. *Cruising Utopia: The Then and There of Queer Futurity.* New York: New York University Press, 2009.

———. *Disidentifications: Queers of Color and the Performance of Politics.* Minneapolis: University of Minnesota Press, 1999.

———. "Gesture, Ephemera, and Queer Feeling: Approaching Kevin Aviance." In *Cruising Utopia: The Then and There of Queer Futurity,* 65–82.

Nagel, Joane, and Susanne Olzak. "Ethnic Mobilization in New and Old States: An Extension of the Competition Model." *Social Problems* 30, no. 2 (December 1982): 127–43.

Naples, Nancy. *Economic Restructuring and Racialization: Incorporation of Mexicans and Mexican-Americans in the rural Midwest.* Working Paper 7, Center for Comparative Immigration Studies at UC San Diego, 2000.

Nelson, Lise, and Nancy Hiemstra. "Latino Immigrants and the Renegotiation of Place and Belonging in Small Town America." *Social and Cultural Geography* 9 (2008): 319–42.

Ngai, Mae. *Impossible Subjects: Illegal Aliens and the Making of Modern America.* Princeton, N.J.: Princeton University Press, 2004.

Nicholls, Walter. *The DREAMers: How the Undocumented Movement Transformed the Immigrant Rights Debate.* Stanford, Calif.: Stanford University Press, 2013.

Nieto, Leo D. "The Chicano Movement and the Gospel." In *Hidden Stories: Unveiling the History of the Latino Church,* edited by David Cortés-Fuentes and Daniel R. Rodríguez-Díaz, 143–57. Decatur, Ga.: Asociación para la Educación Teológica, 1994.

Núñez, Guillermina Gina. "The Political Ecology of Colonias in the Hatch Valley: Towards an Applied Social Science of the U.S.-Mexico Border." PhD diss., University of California, Riverside, 2006.

Obejas, Achy. "Juanga Forever." *TriQuarterly Online,* July 5, 2010, http://triquarterly.org.

Oboler, Suzanne. *Ethnic Labels, Latino Lives: Identity and the Politics of (Re)Presentation in the United States.* Minneapolis: University of Minnesota Press, 1995.

———. "Introduction: *Los Que Llegaron:* South American Migration (1950–2000)—An Overview." *Latino Studies* 3, no. 1 (April 2005): 42–52.

Ogbar, Jeffrey. "Puerto Rico en mi corazón: The Young Lords, Black Power, and Puerto Rican Nationalism in the U.S., 1966–1972." *Centro Journal* (fall 2006): 149–69.

Okamoto, Dina G. "Toward a Theory of Panethnicity: Explaining Asian American Collective Action." *American Sociological Review* 68, no. 6 (December 2003): 811–42.

O'Leary, Josh. "Family Made Whole Again." *Iowa City Press-Citizen,* March 1, 2103.

Olivos, Edward M., Oscar Jiménez-Castellanos, and Alberto M. Ochoa, eds. *Bicultural Parent Engagement: Advocacy and Empowerment.* New York: Teachers College Press, 2011.

Orellana, Marjorie Faulstich. *Translating Childhoods: Immigrant Youth, Language, and Culture.* New Brunswick, N.J.: Rutgers University Press, 2009.

O'Rourke, Erim, and Kim Potowski. "Phonetic Accommodation in a Situation of Spanish Dialect Contact: /s/ and /r/ in Chicago." *Journal of Hispanic and Lusopone Linguistics* 2, no. 9 (2016): 1–44.

Owens, Greg, Jessica Meyerson, and Christa Otteson. *A New Age of Immigrants: Making Immigration Work for Minnesota.* St. Paul, Minn.: Wilder Foundation, 2010.

Paciotto, Carla, and Gloria Delany-Barmann. "Planning Micro-Level Language Education Reform in New Diaspora Sites: Two-Way Immersion Education in the Rural Midwest." *Language Policy* 10, no. 3 (2011): 221–43.

Padilla, Elena. "Puerto Rican Immigrants in New York and Chicago: A Study of Comparative Assimilation." Master's thesis, University of Chicago, 1947.

Padilla, Felix M. *Latino Ethnic Consciousness: The Case of Mexican Americans and Puerto Ricans in Chicago.* Notre Dame, Ind.: University of Notre Dame Press, 1985.

———. *Puerto Rican Chicago.* Notre Dame, Ind.: University of Notre Dame Press, 1987.

Pallares, Amalia. "The Chicago Context." In *¡Marcha!: Latino Chicago and the Immigrant Rights Movement,* edited by Amalia Pallares and Nilda Flores-González, 37–61. Urbana: University of Illinois Press, 2010.

Paratore, Jeanne R., Alisa Hindin, Barbara Krol-Sinclair, and Pilar Durán. "Discourse between Teachers and Latino Parents during Conferences Based on Home Literacy Portfolios." *Education and Urban Society* 31, no. 1 (1999): 58–82.

Paredes, Américo. "El folklore de los grupos de origen mexicano en los Estados Unidos." *Folklore Americano* 14 (1966): 146–63.

———. *A Texas-Mexican Cancionero: Folksongs of the Lower Border.* Urbana: University of Illinois Press, 1976.

———. *"With His Pistol in His Hand": A Border Ballad and Its Hero.* Austin: University of Texas Press, 1958.

Parrado, Emilio, and William Kandel. "The Transformation of the U.S. Food Processing Industry and the Emergence of New Immigrant Destinations." In Massey, *New Faces in New Places,* 132–65.

Parrott, Timothy C. *The Enigma of Theresa Dolezal Feldwert and the "Black Angel."* Iowa City, Iowa: self-published, 2007.

Passel, Jeffrey S., D'Vera Cohn, and Mark Hugo Lopez. "Hispanics Account for More than Half of Nation's Growth in Past Decade." Pew Research Center, Hispanic Trends, March 24, 2011. www.pewhispanic.org.

Pedraza, Pedro. "Language Maintenance among New York Puerto Ricans." In Elías-Olivares et al., *Spanish Language and Public Life,* 59–71.

Peña, Elaine A. *Performing Piety: Making Space Sacred with the Virgin of Guadalupe.* Berkeley: University of California Press, 2011.

Peña, Manuel. *Música Tejana: The Cultural Economy of Artistic Transformation.* College Station: Texas A&M University Press, 1999.

———. *The Texas-Mexican Conjunto: History of a Working-Class Music.* Austin: University of Texas Press, 1985.

Pérez, Gina M. *The Near Northwest Side Story: Migration, Displacement, and Puerto Rican Families.* Berkeley: University of California Press, 2004.

———. "Puertorriqueñas rencorosas y mejicanas sufridas: Gendered Ethnic Identity Formation in Chicago's Latino Communities." *Journal of Latin American Anthropology* 8, no. 2 (2003): 96–125.

———. "An Upbeat West Side Story: Puerto Ricans and Postwar Racial Politics in Chicago." *Centro Journal* 13, no. 2 (2001): 47–71.

Philpott, Thomas. *The Slum and the Ghetto: Neighborhood Deterioration and Middle-Class Reform, Chicago, 1880–1930.* New York: Oxford University Press, 1978.

Phinney, Jean S. "Identity Formation across Cultures: The Interaction of Personal, Societal, and Historical Change." *Human Development* 43 (2000): 27–31.

Portes, Alejandro, and Richard Schauffler. "Language and the Second Generation: Bilingualism Yesterday and Today." In *The New Second Generation*, edited by Alejandro Portes, 8–29. New York: Russell Sage, 1996.

Potowski, Kim. "'I Was Raised Talking Like My Mom': The Influence of Mothers in the Development of Mexiricans' Phonological and Lexical Features." *Linguistic Identity and Bilingualism in Different Hispanic Contexts*, edited by Jason Rothman and Mercedes Niño-Murcia, 201–20. New York: John Benjamins, 2008.

———. *Intra-latino Language and Identity: MexiRicans.* Amsterdam: John Benjamins, 2008.

———. *Language Diversity in the USA.* New York: Cambridge University Press, 2010.

———. "Spanish Language Shift in Chicago." *Southwest Journal of Linguistics* 23, no. 1 (2004): 87–116.

———, Jorge Berne, Amy Clark, and Amy Hammerand. "Spanish for K–8 Heritage Speakers: A Standards-Based Curriculum Project." *Hispania* 91, no. 1 (2008): 25–41.

———, and Janine Matts. "Interethnic Language and Identity: MexiRicans in Chicago." *Journal of Language, Identity and Education* 6, no. 3 (2008): 137–160.

———, and Lillian Gorman. "*Quinceañeras*: Hybridized Tradition, Language Use, and Identity in the U.S." In *Bilingual Youth: Spanish in English-Speaking Societies*, edited by Kim Potowski and Jason Rothman, 57–58. Amsterdam: John Benjamins, 2011.

———, and Lourdes Torres. *Spanish in Chicago.* Oxford University Press, forthcoming.

———, MaryAnn Parada, and Kara Morgan-Short. "Developing an Online Placement Exam for Spanish Heritage Speakers and L2 Students." *Heritage Language Journal* 9, no. 1 (2012): 51–76.

———, and María Carreira. "Towards Teacher Development and National Standards for Spanish as a Heritage Language." *Foreign Language Annals* 37, no. 3 (2004): 421–31.

Powell, Douglas Reichert. *Critical Regionalism: Connecting Politics and Culture in the American Landscape.* Chapel Hill: University of North Carolina Press, 2007.

Preston, Julia. "Alabama: Deal Reached over Immigration Crackdown." *New York Times*, Oct. 30, 2013, A17.

———. "Illegal Immigrant Students Protest at McCain Office." *New York Times*, May 17, 2010. www.nytimes.

———. "Report Finds Deportations Focus on Criminal Records." *New York Times*, April 29, 2014. www.nytimes.com.

Pucci, Sandra. "Spanish Print Environments Implications for Heritage Language Development." In *Mi Lengua: Spanish as a Heritage Language in the United States, Research and Practice*, edited by Ana Roca and M. Cecilia Colombi, 269–90. Washington, D.C.: Georgetown University Press, 2003.

Puente, Silvia, and Sara McElmurry. "Chicago's Next Education Crisis Isn't Limited to Chicago—Here's Why." *Huffington Post*, Sept. 4, 2013. www.huffingtonpost.com.

Pulido, Alberto López, Barbara Driscoll Alvarado, and Carmen Samora. *Moving beyond Borders: Julian Samora and the Establishment of Latino Studies*. Chicago: University of Illinois Press, 2009.

Question Mark and the Mysterians. "96 Tears." *YouTube*, uploaded Nov. 8, 2006. www .youtube.com/watch?v=XeoIH-kzx4c.

"Question Mark and the Mysterians Biography." Sing365: More than Lyrics, updated Aug. 12, 2014. www.sing365.com.

Quinones, Sam. *Antonio's Gun and Delfino's Dream: True Tales of Mexican Migration*. Albuquerque: University of New Mexico Press, 2008.

Ramírez, Leonard G., ed. *Chicanas of 18th Street: Narratives of a Movement from Latino Chicago*. Latinos in Chicago and the Midwest Series. Urbana: University of Illinois Press, 2011.

Ramos-Pellicia, Michelle. "Language Contact and Dialect Contact: Cross-Generational Phonological Variation in a Puerto Rican Community in the Midwest of the United States." PhD diss., Ohio State University, 2004.

Ramos-Zayas, Ana Yolanda. *National Performances: The Politics of Class, Race, and Space in Puerto Rican Chicago*. Chicago: University of Chicago Press, 2003.

Ready, Timothy, and Allert Brown-Gort. *This Is Home Now: The State of Latino Chicago*. Notre Dame, Ind.: University of Notre Dame Latino Research Institute, 2004.

Reisler, Mark. *By the Sweat of Their Brow: Mexican Immigrant Labor in the United States, 1900–1940*. Westport, Conn.: Greenwood Press, 1976.

Rhodes, Nancy C., and Ingrid Pufahl. *Foreign Language Teaching in U.S. Schools: Results of a National Survey*. Washington, D.C.: Center for Applied Linguistics, 2010.

Rivera, Angelica. "Re-inserting Mexican-American Women's Voices into 1950s Chicago Educational History." PhD diss., University of Illinois at Urbana-Champaign, 2008.

Rivera, Tomás. "The Great Plains as Refuge in Chicano Literature." In *Tomás Rivera*, 319–32.

———. "Las salamandras"/"The Salamanders." In *Tomás Rivera*, 127–30 and 159–61.

———. *Tomás Rivera: The Complete Works*. Edited by Julián Olivares. Houston: Arte Público Press, 2008 [1971].

———. *Y no se lo tragó la tierra/And the Earth Did Not Devour Him*. In *Tomás Rivera*, 1–124.

Rivera-Mills, Susana. "Acculturation and Communicative Need: Language Shift in an Ethnically Diverse Hispanic Community." *Southwest Journal of Linguistics* 20 (2001): 211–23.

———. "Intraethnic Attitudes among Hispanics in a Northern California Community." In *Research on Spanish in the United States: Linguistic Issues and Challenges*, edited by Ana Roca, 377–89. Somerville, Mass.: Cascadilla Press, 2000.

Rivera-Servera, Ramón H. "Choreographies of Resistance: Latina/o Queer Dance and the Utopian Performative." *Modern Drama* 47, no. 2 (2004): 269–89.

———. "José E. Muñoz's Queer Gestures." *QED: A Journal of GLBTQ Worldmaking* 1, no. 3 (2014): 146–49.

———. *Performing Queer Latinidad: Dance, Sexuality, Politics*. Ann Arbor: University of Michigan Press, 2012.

Roach, Jack, and Orville Gursslin. "An Evaluation of the Concept 'Culture of Poverty.'" *Social Forces* 45, no. 3 (1965): 383–92.

Rodriguez, Marc Simon. "Defining the Space of Participation in a Northern City: Tejanos and the War on Poverty in Milwaukee." In *The War on Poverty: A New Grassroots History, 1964–1980*, edited by Annelise Orleck and Lisa Gayle Hazirjian, 110–30. Athens: University of Georgia Press, 2011.

———. *The Tejano Diaspora: Mexican Americanism and Ethnic Politics in Texas and Wisconsin*. Chapel Hill: University of North Carolina Press, 2011.

Román, David. *Performance in America: Contemporary U.S. Culture and the Performing Arts*. Durham, N.C.: Duke University Press, 2005.

Romano, Octavio V. "Charismatic Medicine, Folk-Healing, and Folk-Sainthood." *American Anthropologist* 67 (1965): 1151–73.

Rosaldo, Renato. "Cultural Citizenship, Inequality, and Multiculturalism." In Flores and Benmayor, *Latino Cultural Citizenship*, 27–38.

———. "Cultural Ethnicity and Educational Democracy." *Cultural Anthropology* 9, no. 3 (1994): 402–11.

———, and William V. Flores. "Identity, Conflict, and Evolving Latino Communities: Cultural Citizenship in San José, California." In Flores and Benmayor, *Latino Cultural Citizenship*, 57–96.

Rosenblum, Marc R., and Doris Meissner. "The Deportation Dilemma: Reconciling Tough and Humane Enforcement." Migration Policy Institute, April 2014. www.migrationpolicy.org/research/deportation-dilemma-reconciling-tough-humane-enforcement.

Rúa, Mérida. "Colao Subjectivities: PortoMex and MexiRican Perspectives on Language and Identity." *Centro Journal* 13, no. 2 (fall 2001): 117–33.

———. *A Grounded Identidad: Making New Lives in Chicago's Puerto Rican Neighborhoods*. New York: Oxford University Press, 2012.

———, ed. *Latino Urban Ethnography and the Work of Elena Padilla*. Urbana: University of Illinois Press, 2010.

Ruiz, Vicki L. *From Out of the Shadows: Mexican Women in Twentieth-Century America*. New York City: Oxford University Press, 2008.

———, and John R. Chávez, ed. *Memories and Migrations: Mapping Boricua and Chicana Histories*. Urbana: University of Illinois Press, 2008.

———, and Virginia Sánchez Korrol, ed. *Latina Legacies: Identity, Biography, and Community*. Viewpoints on American Culture Series. New York: Oxford University Press, 2005.

Sáenz, Andrés. *Early Tejano Ranching: Daily Life at Ranchos San José and El Fresnillo*. College Station: Texas A&M University Press, 1999.

Sáenz, Rogelio. "The Changing Demography of Latinos in the Midwest." In *Latinos in the Midwest*, edited by R. Martinez, 33–56. East Lansing: Michigan State University, 2011.

———. "Engine of U.S. Population Growth: Latinos and the Changing of America." Paper presented at the University of Minnesota, Jan. 27, 2012.

———. "Latinos in America 2010." *Population Bulletin Update*, December 2010.

Saldívar, Ramón. *The Borderlands of Culture: Américo Paredes and the Transnational Imaginary*. Durham, N.C.: Duke University Press, 2006.

Sánchez, George J. *Becoming Mexican American: Ethnicity, Culture, and Identity in Chicano Los Angeles*. New York: Oxford University Press, 1995.

Sánchez-Korrol, Virginia. "The Historical Narrative." Part 1 of *The Story of U.S. Puerto Ricans*. Centro: Center for Puerto Rican Studies. https://centropr.hunter.cuny.edu/research-education.

Sandoval, Chela. "U.S. Third World Feminism: The Theory and Method of Oppositional Consciousness in the Postmodern World." *Genders* 10 (spring 1991): 1–24.

Santa Ana, Otto. *Brown Tide Rising: Metaphors of Latinos in Contemporary American Public Discourse*. Austin: University of Texas Press, 2002.

Schwei, Tamara Downs, and Katherine Fennelly. "Diversity Coalitions in Rural Minnesota Communities." *Cura Reporter* 37, no. 4 (winter 2007): 13–22. www.cura.umn.edu.

Seif, Hinda. "Unapologetic and Unafraid: Immigrant Youth Come Out of the Shadows." *New Directions for Child and Adolescent Development* 2011, no. 134 (winter 2011): 59–75.

Shenk, Dan. "Minorities Seek Closer Ties with Total Mennonite Church." *Happenings* (Mennonite Church USA) 2, no. 2 (Dec. 5, 1972).

Shenk, Elaine. "Choosing Spanish: Dual Language Immersion and Familial Ideologies." In *Bilingualism and Identity: Spanish at the Crossroads with Other Languages*, edited by Jason Rothman and Mercedes Niño-Murcia, 221–56. Amsterdam: John Benjamins, 2008.

Silva-Corvalán, Carmen. *Language Contact and Change: Spanish in Los Angeles*. New York: Oxford University Press, 1994.

Si No Nos Invitan, Nos Invitamos Solos: No Papers, No Fear Protest in Alabama. Video. Directed by Barni Axmed Qaasim (Puente). Posted Aug. 18, 2012. www.youtube.com/watch?v=Iaj95A8ac8U.

Southern Poverty Law Center. "SPLC Victorious against Alabama Anti-Immigrant Law." Southern Poverty Law Center, News, Oct. 28, 2013. www.splcenter.org.

Spickard, Paul. *Almost All Aliens: Immigration, Race, and Colonialism in American History and Identity*. New York: Routledge, 2007.

Suárez-Orozco, Carola, and Marcelo M. Suárez-Orozco. *Children of Immigration*. The Developing Child. Cambridge, Mass.: Harvard University Press, 2001.

———, Marcelo M. Suárez-Orozco, and Irina Todorova. *Learning a New Land: Immigrant Students in American Society*. Cambridge, Mass.: Belknap Press of Harvard University Press, 2008.

Suttles, Gerald. *Social Order of the Slum: Ethnicity and Territory in the Inner City*. Chicago: University of Chicago Press, 1968.

Taylor, Diana. *The Archive and the Repertoire: Performing Cultural Memory in the Americas*. Durham, N.C.: Duke University Press, 2003.

Taylor, Paul S. *Mexican Labor in the United States*. New York: Arno Press, 1975 [1932].

———. *Mexican Labor in the United States: Chicago and the Calumet Region*. University of California Publications in Economics, vol. 7, no. 2. Berkeley: University of California Press, 1932.

Taylor, Paul, Mark Hugo Lopez, Jessica Martínez, and Gabriel Velasco. *When Labels Don't Fit: Hispanics and Their Views of Identity*. Washington, DC: Pew Hispanic Center Report, April 4, 2012.

Thomas, Lorrin. *Puerto Rican Citizen: History and Political Identity in Twentieth-Century New York.* Chicago: University of Chicago Press, 2010.

Thomas, Wayne P., and Virginia P. Collier. "The Multiple Benefits of Dual Language." *Educational Leadership* 61, no. 2 (2003): 61–64.

Torres, Edén E. *Chicana without Apology: The New Chicana Cultural Studies.* New York: Routledge, 2003.

Torres, Gerardo. "Fearless and Speaking for Ourselves." *No Papers No Fears*, blog, Aug. 18, 2012. http://nopapersnofear.org/blog.

Trabalzi, Ferro, and Gerardo Sandoval. "The Exotic Other: Latinos and the Remaking of Community Identity in Perry, Iowa." *Community Development* 41, no. 1 (2010): 76–91.

Trollinger, William. *God's Empire: William Bell Riley and Midwestern Fundamentalism.* Madison: University of Wisconsin Press, 1991.

"Turning the Tide." http://altopolimigra.com/.

Tweed, Thomas. *Crossing and Dwelling: A Theory of Religion.* Cambridge, Mass.: Harvard University Press, 2006.

United Press International. "Iowa Passes English-Only Measure." UPI, Feb. 26, 2002. www.upi.com.

United States. National Commission on the Observance of International Women's Year. *The Spirit of Houston, the First National Women's Conference: An Official Report to the President, the Congress and the People of the United States.* Washington D.C.: National Commission on the Observance of International Women's Year, , 1978.

U.S. Census Bureau. "FFF: Hispanic Heritage Month 2016." Newsroom, Facts for Features, release CB16-FF.16, Oct. 12, 2016. www.census.gov/newsroom/facts-for-features/2016/cb16-ff16.html.

U.S. Commission on Civil Rights. "U.S. Commission on Civil Rights Announces Agenda for Alabama Field Briefing on Civil Rights Effects of State Immigration Laws." Press release, Aug. 3, 2012. www.usccr.gov.

———. Mission statement. www.usccr.gov/about/index.php.

U.S. Immigration and Customs Enforcement. "Delegation of Immigration Authority Section 287(g) Immigration and Nationality Act." U.S. Immigration and Customs Enforcement, Immigration Enforcement. www.ice.gov/287g/.

———. "Secure Communities." U.S. Immigration and Customs Enforcement, www.ice.gov/pi/news/factsheets/secure_communities.htm (inactive).

Unzueta Carrasco, Nadia Sol Ireri. Untitled presentation at "Everyday Forms of Popular Power: Art, Media and Immigration" symposium, Nov. 9, 2012, University of New Mexico.

Unzueta Carrasco, Tania A., and Hinda Seif. "Disrupting the Dream: Undocumented Youth Reframe Citizenship and Deportability through Anti-Deportation Activism." *Latino Studies* 12, no. 2 (2014): 287–88.

Valdés, Dennis Nodín. *Al Norte: Agricultural Workers in the Great Lakes Region, 1917–1970.* Austin: University of Texas Press, 1991.

———. "Settlers, Sojourners, and Proletarians: Social Formation in the Great Plains Sugar Beet Industry, 1890–1940." *Great Plains Quarterly* 10 (spring 1990): 110–23.

Valdés, Dionicio Nodín. *Barrios Norteños: St. Paul and Midwestern Mexican Communities in the Twentieth Century.* Austin: University of Texas Press, 2000.

Valdés, Guadalupe. *Con Respeto: Bridging the Distances between Culturally Diverse Families and Schools: An Ethnographic Portrait.* New York: Teachers College Press, 1996.

———. "Ethnolinguistic Identity: The Challenge of Maintaining Spanish-English Bilingualism in American Schools." In *Bilingual Youth: Spanish in English-Speaking Societies,* edited by Kim Potowski and Jason Rothman, 113–48. Amsterdam: Benjamins, 2011.

Valerio-Jiménez, Omar S. *River of Hope: Forging Identity and Nation in the Rio Grande Borderlands.* Durham, N.C.: Duke University Press, 2013.

———. "The United States–Mexico Border as Material and Cultural Barrier." In *Migrants and Migration in Modern North America: Cross-Border Lives, Labor Markets, and Politics in Canada, the Caribbean, Mexico, and the United States,* edited by Dirk Hoerder and Nora Faires, 228–50. Durham, N.C.: Duke University Press, 2011.

Vargas, Zaragosa. "Armies in the Fields: The Mexican Working Classes in the Midwest in the 1920s." *Mexican Studies/Estudios Mexicanos* 7, no. 1 (winter 1999): 47–71.

———. *Crucible of Struggle: A History of Mexican Americans from the Colonial Period to the Present Era.* New York: Oxford University Press, 2011.

———. *Labor Rights Are Civil Rights: Mexican American Workers in Twentieth-Century America.* Princeton, N.J.: Princeton University Press, 2005.

———. *Proletarians of the North: A History of Mexican Industrial Workers in Detroit and the Midwest, 1917–1933.* Berkeley: University of California Press, 1993.

Varsanyi, Monica W. "Immigration Policy Activism in U.S. Cities and States: Interdisciplinary Perspectives." In *Taking Local Control: Immigration Policy Activism in U.S. Cities and States,* edited by Monica Varsanyi, 1–27. Stanford, Calif.: Stanford University Press, 2010.

Vásquez, Manuel A., Chad E. Seales, and Marie Friedmann Marquardt. "New Latino Destinations." In *Latinas/os in the United States: Changing the Face of America,* edited by Havidán Rodríguez, Rogelio Sáenz, and Cecilia Menjívar, 19–35. New York: Springer, 2008.

Vásquez Ignatin, Hilda. "Young Lords Serve and Protect." *Movement,* May 1969, 4–5.

Vatter, Harold G. *The U.S. Economy in the 1950s: An Economic History.* New York: Norton, 1963.

Vélez-Ibáñez, Carlos. "Regions of Refuge in the United States: Issues, Problems and Concerns for the Future of Mexican-Origin Populations in the United States." Malinowski Award Lectures, *Human Organization* 63, no. 1 (2004): 1–20.

Veltman, Calvin. "The American Linguistic Mosaic: Understanding language Shift in the United States." In *New Immigrants in the United States: Readings for Second Language Educators,* edited by Sandra Lee McKay and Sau-ling Cynthia Wong, 58–93. New York: Cambridge University Press, 2000.

Viso, Olga. *Unseen Mendieta: The Unpublished Works of Ana Mendieta.* Munich: Prestel, 2008.

Walker, Randi Jones. *Religion and the Public Conscience: Ecumenical Civil Rights Work in Seattle 1940–1960.* Winchester, U.K.: Circle Books, 2012.

Walsh, Bryan O. "Cuban Refugee Children." *Journal of Inter-American Studies and World Affairs* 13, nos. 3–4 (July–October 1971): 378–415.

Walton, Kiri. "Undocumented Student Speaks Out after Arrest." *South Cobb Patch*, June 29, 2011. www.patch.com/georgia/southcobb/.

Ward, Jon. "Jason Richwine Dissertation on Low Hispanic IQ Puts Heritage on Defensive." *Huffington Post*, May 8, 2013.

Warner, Michael. Introduction. *Fear of a Queer Planet: Queer Politics and Social Theory*, edited by Michael Warner, vii–xxxi. Minneapolis: University of Minnesota Press, 1993.

Washington, Kenn. "Protesters to Boycott Pine Manor Products." *Goshen (Ind.) News*, Nov. 19, 1971.

Washington, Sylvia Hood. *Packing Them In: An Archaeology of Environmental Racism in Chicago, 1865–1954*. Lanham, Md.: Lexington Books, 2005.

Weaver, Janet. "Barrio Women: Community and Coalition in the Heartland." In *Breaking the Wave: Women, Their Organizations, and Feminism, 1945–1985*, edited by Kathleen A. Laughlin and Jacqueline L. Castledine, 173–88. New York: Routledge, 2010.

———."From Barrio to ¡Boicoteo!: The Emergence of Mexican American Activism in Davenport, 1917–1970." *Annals of Iowa* 68, no. 3 (summer 2009): 215–54.

Whalen, Carmen Teresa. *From Puerto Rico to Philadelphia: Puerto Rican Workers and Postwar Economies*. Philadelphia: Temple University Press, 2001.

Wortham, Jenna, "A Bold Struggle for Acceptance." *New York Times* (New York edition), May 6, 2016, C1.

Young, Michelle, and Carolyn Colvin. "Diversity and Open Enrollment in a Rural Midwestern School Community." Paper presented at the annual meeting of the American Educational Research Association, Seattle, Wash., April 2002.

Yuen, Laura. "Newcomers Say It's 'Nice,' but Not Warm." Minnesota Public Radio, March 12, 2012. http://minnesota.publicradio.org.

Zachs, Naomi, ed. *American Mixed Race: The Culture of Microdiversity*. Lanham, Md.: Rowman and Littlefield, 1995.

———. "Lexical Leveling in Four New York City Spanish Dialects: Linguistic and Social Factors." *Hispania* 73 (1990): 1094–105.

Zúñiga, Víctor, and Rubén Hernández-León, eds. *New Destinations: Mexican Immigration in the United States*. New York: Russell Sage, 2005.

Zurer Pearson, Barbara, and Arlene McGee. "Language Choice in Hispanic-Background Junior High School Students in Miami: A 1988 Update." In *Spanish in the United States: Linguistic Contact and Diversity*, edited by Ana Roca and John Lipski, 91–102. New York: Mouton de Gruyter, 2000.

Contributors

AIDÉ ACOSTA is the DREAMer supports manager for the Noble Network in Chicago, Illinois. Her research and teaching areas include Latina/o migration and diaspora; labor, race, and citizenship; social movements; immigrant rights; Latina/o cultural production; and gender and Chicana feminism. She is working on a book about Latino diasporic settlement and cultural practices in the rural heartland.

FRANCES R. APARICIO is a professor of Spanish and Portuguese and director of the Latina and Latino Studies Program at Northwestern University. A founding editor of the *Latinos in Chicago and the Midwest* book series at the University of Illinois Press, she has facilitated and fostered book publications and new research on Latinas/os in the Midwest. She is coeditor of the forthcoming *Routledge Companion to Latina/o Literatures* (with Suzanne Bost) and is also writing on Intralatinas/os.

JAY ARDUSER teaches English and is a Model United Nations Adviser at a language and special-needs high school in Doha, Qatar. He is also a master of education student with Augustana University. He specializes in English-language learning while having created highly scaffolded writing programs for students with special needs and gaps in education; his programs have been selected for presentation at the Near East South Asia Teacher Conference in Bangkok, Thailand, and the Teaching and Learning Forum in Doha. Arduser completed his undergraduate degree in elementary education at the University of Iowa, where he worked with Carolyn Colvin and Liz Willmore-Brown in a tutoring program, which lead to collaborative work on a parent-teacher communication research project.

JANE BLOCKER is a professor of art history at the University of Minnesota. She is author of *Seeing Witness: Visuality and the Ethics of Testimony* (2009), *What the Body Cost: Desire, History, and Performance* (2004) and *Where Is Ana Mendieta? Identity, Performativity, and Exile* (1999). She has published articles in *Performance Research, Grey Room, Art Journal, Camera Obscura, Cultural Studies, Visual Resources,* and *Performing Arts Journal.* She has also contributed chapters to *Perform, Repeat, Record: Live Art in History* (Jones and Heathfield, eds., 2012), *The Aesthetics of Risk* (Welchman, ed., 2008), *After Criticism: New Responses to Art and Performance* (Butt, ed., 2004), *An Introduction to Women's Studies: Gender in a Transnational World* (Grewal and Kaplan, eds., 2002), and *The Ends of Performance* (Phelan and Lane, eds., 1998).

CAROLYN COLVIN is an associate professor in the Language, Literacy, and Culture (LLC) Program in the University of Iowa College of Education Department of Teaching and Learning. Since January 1993, she has been involved in a community-based research project where the focus is a literacy tutoring program for immigrant adults. A second strand of this work involves children of the immigrant adults who have attended the literacy program. Her community partner in these endeavors is the West Liberty, Iowa, community school district, where high school faculty members serve as collaborative partners to support and education of local immigrant families. Current themes in her scholarship include literacy for immigrant adults, parent teacher communication, literacy and the U.S. citizenship test, and exploring the connections between local rural economies and the arts. Her work has appeared in prominent educational journals, including *Journal of Adolescent and Adult Literacy, Journal of Educational Psychology, Journal of Multicultural Education,* and various conference proceedings.

MARÍA EUGENIA COTERA is an associate professor of American culture and women's studies and former director of the Latina/o Studies Program at the University of Michigan. Her *Native Speakers: Ella Deloria, Zora Neale Hurston, Jovita González and the Poetics of Culture* (2010) examines the ethnographic fiction of three authors. Her research now centers on recovering the theoretical writing and cultural productions of Chicana feminists from 1965 to 1985.

THERESA DELGADILLO is a professor in the Department of Comparative Studies at the Ohio State University. She is the author of *Spiritual Mestizaje: Religion, Gender, Race, and Nation in Contemporary Chicana Narrative* (2011) and *Latina Lives in Milwaukee* (2015). Delgadillo works on spirituality and religion, African diaspora and Latinidad, and Latinas/os in the Midwest. Her objects of study include novels, autobiographies, memoirs, photography, cinema, poetry, and music.

LILIA FERNÁNDEZ holds the Henry Rutgers Term Chair and is an associate professor in the History and Latino and Caribbean Studies Departments at Rutgers University. She teaches courses on modern U.S. history, immigration and migration in the United States, Latina/o history, and other topics. She specializes in twentieth-century Latina/o history in Chicago and has published articles, book chapters, and essays on Mexican American community formation, Mexican and Puerto Rican labor migration, and nativism and xenophobia throughout the world. Her *Brown in the Windy City: Mexicans and Puerto Ricans in Postwar Chicago* (2012) is the first comparative historical study of distinct Latina/o ethnic groups in the United States. It explores how, in post–World War II Chicago, Mexican and Puerto Rican migrants made a place for themselves in the city's local racial order and dramatically shifting geography.

CLAIRE F. FOX is a professor in the departments of English and Spanish and Portuguese at the University of Iowa. Her teaching and research areas include the literatures and cultures of the Americas, U.S.-Mexican border arts and culture, visual culture studies, and cultural policy studies. She is the author of *The Fence and the River: Cultural and Politics at the U.S.-Mexico Border* (1999) and *Making Art Panamerican: Cultural Policy and the Cold War* (2013).

FELIPE HINOJOSA is an associate professor of history at Texas A&M University. His teaching and research interests include Latina/o-Chicana/o studies, U.S. religion, social movements, gender, and comparative race and ethnicity. A native of Brownsville, Texas, Hinojosa is the recipient of numerous fellowships and is the author of "*¡Medicina Sí, Muerte No!* Race, Public Health, and the 'Long War on Poverty' in Mathis, Texas, 1948–1971" (2013) and of *Latino Mennonites: Civil Rights, Faith, and Evangelical Culture* (2014).

MICHAEL INNIS-JIMÉNEZ is an associate professor and the director of graduate studies in the Department of American Studies at the University of Alabama. He also consults for the Latino New South Project, a public-history project sponsored by a consortium of the Levine Museum of the New South (Charlotte, N.C.), the Atlanta History Museum, and the Birmingham Civil Rights Institute. Educated at the University of Iowa with a PhD in history, his research has focused on Mexican immigrant and Mexican American communities in the U.S. Midwest and South. He is the author of *Steel Barrio: The Great Mexican Migration to South Chicago, 1915–1945* (2013). His current book project focuses on the role of Mexican food in maintaining community in interwar Mexican Chicago and examines the impact of cultural tourism and "gawking" on Mexicans in the area adjacent to Hull House.

JOSÉ E. LIMÓN is a professor emeritus of English at the University of Notre Dame, where he also held the Julian Samora Chair in Latino studies and was the director of the Institute for Latino Studies. He has published in major scholarly journals and authored four books: *Mexican Ballads and Chicano Poems: History and Influence in Mexican-American Social Poetry* (1992); *Dancing with the Devil: Society and Cultural Poetics in Mexican-American South Texas* (1994); *American Encounters: Greater Mexico, the United States, and the Erotics of Culture* (1998); and, *Américo Paredes: Culture and Critique* (2012). His new book project compares Mexican American and Anglo-American writers in the literary making of Texas.

MARTA MARÍA MALDONADO is an associate professor of ethnic studies in the School of Language, Culture and Society at Oregon State University. Her research explores the sociospatial politics of immigration, incorporation, and integration; ethnoracial relations in communities and institutional contexts; and the racialized, gendered, and classed experiences of Latin@s in the United States.

LOUIS MENDOZA is a professor and the director of the School of Humanities, Arts, and Cultural Studies at Arizona State University. He has authored numerous books and articles on Latina/o literature and culture, including *Conversations across Our America: Talking about Immigration and the Latinoization of the United States* (2012), and *A Journey around Our America: A Memoir on Cycling, Immigration, and the Latinoization of the U.S.* (2012).

AMELIA MARÍA DE LA LUZ MONTES is an associate professor of English and ethnic studies and the director of the Institute of Ethnic Studies at the University of Nebraska, Lincoln. She works on North American and Latin American narratives that complicate and contradict national, social, and personal identities. She has published articles on the nineteenth-century Mexican American author, María Amparo Ruiz de Burton, and edited and introduced a new edition of Ruiz de Burton's first novel, *Who Would Have Thought It?* (2009). Her new book project, *Corazón y Tierra: Latinas Writing from the Midwest*, examines the writing of Latinas in the Great Plains and Midwest.

KIM POTOWSKI is a professor of Spanish linguistics in the Department of Hispanic and Italian Studies at the University of Illinois at Chicago. She works on bilingualism in educational settings and the teaching of Spanish to heritage speakers, and is the author of *Language and Identity in a Dual Immersion School* (2005), as well as other books and numerous articles. She has received numerous fellowships, including a Fulbright grant to study the educational experiences of U.S.-raised students whose families return to Mexico.

RAMÓN H. RIVERA-SERVERA is an associate professor, chair, and the director of graduate studies in the Department of Performance Studies at Northwestern University. He is author of *Performing Queer Latinidad: Dance, Sexuality, Politics* (2012). He is coeditor of *Performance in the Borderlands* (with Harvey Young, 2011), *Solo/Black/Woman: Scripts, Interview, and Essays* (with E. Patrick Johnson, 2013), *The Goodman Theatre's Festival Latino: Six Plays* (with Henry Godinez, 2013), and *Blacktino Queer Performance* (with E. Patrick Johnson, 2016). His next book project considers how race and museum cultures interact in live events.

REBECCA M. SCHREIBER is an associate professor in the American Studies Department at University of New Mexico. She is the author of *Cold War Exiles in Mexico: U.S. Dissidents and the Culture of Critical Resistance* (2008). Her current book project examines contemporary immigration issues in the United States through forms of visual representation, particularly how Mexican and Central American migrants have depicted themselves and their communities through documentary photography, film, and video since 9/11.

OMAR VALERIO-JIMÉNEZ is an associate professor in the Department of History at the University of Texas at San Antonio, where he teaches courses on the history of immigration, comparative borderlands, ethnic relations, the U.S. West, and Latinas/os. His *River of Hope: Forging Identity and Nation in the Rio Grande Borderlands* (2013), explores state formation and cultural change along the Mexico–United States border during the eighteenth and nineteenth centuries. He is also coeditor of *Major Problems in Latina/o History* (with Carmen Teresa Whalen, 2014). His next book project is a study of history and memory of the U.S.-Mexican War, focusing on the ways Mexican Americans' memories of the 1848 U.S. conquest have shaped their writing, oral discourse, public rituals, and explicitly politicized activism.

SANTIAGO VAQUERA-VÁSQUEZ is an associate professor of Hispanic Southwest studies in the Department of Spanish and Portuguese at the University of New Mexico. He teaches courses on Chicana/o movement literature and popular culture, the U.S.-Mexican borderlands, contemporary Latin American literature, and creative writing in Spanish. His books include one chapbook, *Algún día te cuento las cosas que he visto* (2012), and three collections of short stories *Luego el silencio* (2014); *One Day I'll Tell You the Things I've Seen: Stories* (2015); and *En el Lost 'n' Found* (2016).

DARREL WANZER-SERRANO is an associate professor of communication studies at the University of Iowa. His research and teaching interests relate generally to questions of discourse, race-ethnicity, and the coloniality of knowledge-power-being, especially in Puerto Rican and other U.S. Latin@ contexts. Darrel is author of *The New York Young Lords and the Struggle for Liberation* (2015) and editor of *The Young Lords: A Reader* (2010). He has also written numerous journal articles in the *Quarterly Journal of Speech*, *Communication Theory*, *Rhetoric and Public Affairs*, and elsewhere.

JANET WEAVER is an assistant curator at the Iowa Women's Archives in the University of Iowa Libraries. Her interests encompass public history and twentieth-century U.S. labor and Latina/o history with current research focusing on industrial unionism in the Progressive Era. She is the author of "Barrio Women: Community and Coalition in the Heartland" in *Breaking the Wave: Women, Their Organizations, and Feminism*, edited by Kathleen Laughlin and Jacqueline Castledine (2011).

ELIZABETH WILLMORE is an employee in the Division of Student Life at the University of Iowa. She is a former international school teacher with an interest in working with English language learners and immigrant families. Elizabeth has a master's degree in elementary education from the University of Iowa, and a bachelor of arts from UC Berkeley. She worked with Carolyn Colvin and Jay Arduser in tutoring program for adults in East Town.

Index

LATINOS IN CHICAGO AND THE MIDWEST

The University of Illinois Press
is a founding member of the
Association of American University Presses.

Composed in 10.5/13 Minion Pro
with Frutiger LT Std display
by Lisa Connery
at the University of Illinois Press
Cover designed by Dustin J. Hubbart
Cover illustration: Ambar Aragón, West Liberty, Iowa,
March 8, 2015. Photo by Patricia León.
Manufactured by Sheridan Books, Inc.

University of Illinois Press
1325 South Oak Street
Champaign, IL 61820-6903
www.press.uillinois.edu